Intellectual Property in the Global Trading System

Wei Shi

Intellectual Property in the Global Trading System

EU-China Perspective

 Springer

Dr. Wei Shi
Lecturer in Law
School of Law
Bangor University
Bangor, Gwynedd LL57 2DG
United Kingdom
w.shi@bangor.ac.uk

ISBN: 978-3-540-77736-6   e-ISBN: 978-3-540-77737-3

Library of Congress Control Number: 2008930797

Cover design: WMX Design, Heidelberg

9 8 7 6 5 4 3 2 1

springer.com

Preface

This book is an expanded and revised version of my thesis, submitted for the Ph.D degree in October 2006 at the University of Cambridge. It has been an honour and joy to work with many individuals, both inside and outside the university town, who made this book possible.

First and foremost, my most sincere appreciation goes to my PhD supervisor, mentor and friend Nick Sinclair-Brown for his careful, insightful and efficient supervision during my doctoral studies in Cambridge. Without his generous and indispensable help neither the conduct of the Ph.D. study nor the accomplishment of the book would have been possible. The design and plan of the doctoral work were wholly due to him. I still remembered the day when he met me at the Finlay Library of the Lauterpacht Centre, for there I received first encouragement to study this challenging topic, an encouragement provided by generous interest and support of Nick. Over the following years, his outlook and confidence in my work gave me much inspiration, and his penetrating comments contributed enormously to the production of my thesis. I appreciate his wisdom, vigilance and sense of humour, without which I would have been either flattered or perplexed on numerous occasions. I have been deeply grateful that, during his heavy cancer treatment in Brussels, he still managed to read through my thesis and offered me detailed feedback and comments. Unfortunately, Nick passed away after fighting the illness with his bravery and morality without seeing the completion of my dissertation and my book in which he had invested much time and energy.

I must also express my particular thanks to my supervisor, mentor and friend Dr. Robert Weatherley for his timely and effective guidance at the late stage of my work. Dr. Weatherley had been fully supportive of my work from the moment we had the first meeting and encouraged me to develop the thesis further into a book. As a leading China expert, his discussions with me concerning the role of China in its transitional period and its impact on global trade helped expand my perspectives. I have learned much from him, particularly in understanding the inherent complexities at the interface of law, politics and history.

I would also express my heartfelt thanks to my Ph.D. examiner Dr. Nick Foster, who graciously offered me his stimulating comments and thought-provoking observations on various portions of my thesis. His insightful perspectives, particularly on comparative law and legal transplants, offered me a constant source of inspiration, reflection and affirmation.

Special thanks also belong to my fellow mentors at the Centre of International Studies and the Lauterpacht Centre for International Law, University of Cambridge, where students are nourished not only by theory but also by spirit. I would like to express my gratitude to Professor Christopher Hill, Professor James Crawford, Dr. Charles Jones, Dr. Philip Towle, Dr. Brendan Simms, Mr. John Forsyth and Dr. Shogo Suzuki for their different forms of support.

My deepest thanks are also given to my College – St John's, which provides me a cosy home and favourable guidance. Living and working for more than five years at St John's, a "so pretty and picturesque" College that the Queen Victoria admired, has been an inspirational and unforgettable experience. I owe a special debt of gratitude to my College Tutors Dr. Sue Colwell, Dr. Maire Ni Mhaonaigh and Dr. Victoria Best for their care and a sense of proportion. I should also thank the College library and its helpful staff. It was in the library that I spent most of my stressful but enjoyable working time during my doctorate study in Cambridge.

I would also like to mention Professor Pierre Klein of Centre de Droit International, ULB, Brussels, for his generous help during my field trip to Brussels. I would also like to thank Mr. Christopher De Vroey at DG Trade, European Commission, for offering me firsthand knowledge of EU-China Trade Relations and Intellectual Property and his comments on my project. Thanks should also be given to Dr. Amanda Perry for her fascinating ideas on the survey infrastructure. I would also like to express my gratitude to Mr. Yong Zhu at the Chinese Ministry of Foreign Affairs and Mr. Wuwei Jin at the Legislative Affair Office of the State Council, for providing me helpful research materials.

A special debt of gratitude is owed to Professor Robert Gordon and his family who have committed their time, passion and love over the past years during my time in Cambridge. Without their sustaining support, I would certainly have stagnated at some point.

Mention should also be made to my friends Boping Yuan, Jianbo Lou, Kyuseok Moon, Alex Broadbent, Beth Bower, and Wengang Weng who lent emotional support and shared their knowledge with me over the years, particularly during my times of struggle.

I thank Bangor University Law School for a world of hope, encouragement and wisdom. I am grateful for Thomas Watkin, Howard Johnson, Dermot Cahill, Aled Griffiths and other distinguished colleagues who placed much confidence in me and offered me much support in finalising this book.

I would also like to express my deep appreciation to Ms Brigitte Reschke and Ms Manuela Ebert of Springer for their high degree of confidence and patience, and their continuous support during various stages of the publication process. Their consideration, determination and great expertise have helped me improve the manuscript of this book considerably.

My very special appreciation goes to my parents Shengyun Shi and Xinru Liang, my wife Aihua, my son Xiaotian, as well as my brothers and sisters who have given me endless love and tireless support. My parents, who had taught in different schools for over thirty years before their retirement, have given me as much as they can. I have been thankful to my parents for inheriting some of my father's faith and some of my mother's scepticism and I have tried to reconcile and integrated the two in my lifelong experiences. I owe a particular debt to my elderly parents for not being able to look after them in a time when they did need caring. I am grateful for the sacrifice of my wife who quitted her government position in China and endeavoured to manage the home in Cambridge; I have to thank my fabulous son for tolerating me to tap into his innocence of his young life, despite his consecutive good grades in his schools.

Finally, and by no means last, the financial contributions from St John's College, Cambridge Overseas Trust, and the China Scholarship Council are gratefully acknowledged.

February 2008   Wei Shi

Table of Contents

List of Abbreviations

AICs	Administration of Industry and Commerce
BSA	Business Software Alliance
CCPIT	China Council for the Promotion of International Trade
CEC	Commission of the European Communities
CL	Compulsory Licensing
CSA	China Software Alliance
DMC	Doha Ministerial Conference
DSB	Dispute Settlement Body
DSU	Dispute Settlement Understanding
DTPH	Doha Declaration of TRIPs and Public Health
ECJ	European Court of Justice
EPC	European Patent Convention
EU	European Union
EUCCC	EU Chamber of Commerce in China
EUCIPD	EU-China Intellectual Property Rights Dialogue
EUCJC	EC-China Joint Committee
GATT	General Agreement on Tariffs and Trade
IIPA	International Intellectual Property Alliance
IP	Intellectual Property
IPEC	Intellectual Property Executive Conference
IPHC	Intellectual Property High Court
IPR	Intellectual Property Rights
IPSR	Intellectual Property Special Regions
MES	Market Economy Status
MNE	Multinational Enterprise
MOFCOM	Ministry of Commerce
MOU	Memorandum of Understanding
NCA	National Copyright Administration

NGO	Non-governmental organisation
NIEO	New International Economic Order
NIPS	National Intellectual Property Strategy
NPC	National People's Congress
NWGIPR	National Working Group for IPR Protection
PRC	People Republic of China
R&D	Research and Development
SAIC	State Administration of Industry and Commerce
SEZ	Special Economic Zone
SIPO	State Intellectual Property Office
TPR	Trade Policy Review
TRAB	Trademark Review and Adjudication Board
TRIPs	Trade-Related Aspects on Intellectual Property Rights
UN	United Nations
UNCTAD	UN Conference on Trade and Development
UNESCO	UN Educational Scientific and Cultural Organisations
USTR	United States Trade Representatives
WIPO	World Intellectual property Organisation
WTO	World Trade Organisation

Abstract

The main purpose of this book is to address intellectual property rights (IPR) enforcement in world trading system from EU-China perspective. It examines special features of EU-China IPR debate compared to Sino-U.S. IPR conflicts, and summarises that the enormous challenge for the EU and China is to set up a harmonious relationship in an effort to avoid the unsuccessful outcome of the experience which has reflected the Sino-American sentimental tie amid strains over IPR enforcement.

This book explores the multifaceted issues of IPR enforcement in China. Having examined the paradox of Confucian determinism, this book argues that IPR enforcement problem is not an actual outcome of Confucian philosophy and "to steal a book" is not an "elegant offence." Rather, the Confucian ethics act as a unique moral foundation for IPR protection. It compares China with Japan and Korea, which share similar Confucian values. By tracing and comparing development trajectories of different economies, this book demonstrates that counterfeiting and piracy are not problems caused by Confucian ethics, as the mainstream view states, but rather common inevitable consequences of inadequate economic development, and a by-product of a unique set of socioeconomic crises deriving from the development of a dysfunctional institutional regime.

It is the author's belief that China's IPR enforcement problem lies in its unique political-culture, institutional impediments and insufficient economic development. During China's critical transitional period, a lack of flexibility may exacerbate its socio-economic problems and, accordingly, deteriorate its hard-earned economic development, making IPR enforcement even worse.

Although much has been written about IPR enforcement in China, the existing literature focuses predominantly on Sino-U.S. issues. Very little scholarship, however, has been devoted to the significance of IPR concerning EU-China issues. By examining areas of compatibilities between European and Chinese cultures and analysing painful lessons from the Sino-U.S. negotiations over IPR protection, this book uses the prism of Sino-EU trade relations to suggest ways to reconcile the minimum standards imposed by international standards and the specific conditions of particular states, and provide insight into the unresolved issues as to how and when China's WTO commitments will be implemented.

1 Introduction

1.1 The Context within which this Book is Located

1.1.1 Areas of Generic Tension

In the twelfth annual edition of the *Global Economic Prospects*,[1] the World Bank provides an in-depth examination of the global trading architecture and its impact on developing countries over the next decade. It ends with the following comment:

"The TRIPs Agreement[2] significantly increased the requirements for protecting intellectual property incumbent upon nations that wish to be part of the global trading system. While promising some eventual benefits, the new regime is asymmetric in its likely effects across countries. Low-income economies may expect to incur net costs for some time, suggesting that patience and assistance are needed... ..."

As this comment illustrates, developing countries attempted to achieve a variety of goals in addition to participating in the global trading system. However, they have found the promise of long-term benefits elusive and the administrative costs and policy problems a significant burden. This has led to a view that the need for, and benefits of, stronger IPR protection varies with economic strength and technological sophistication, and as such TRIPs requirements should be adjusted to the specific conditions of particular states. [3] Accordingly, it is no surprise that the relationship between developing and developed nations concerning the protection of IPR is delicate nor that it is also at the cutting edge of the debates as to the constituent components of sustainable development.

---

[1] *See* "Global Economic Prospects and the Developing Countries 20002," World Bank (2001), at 148-149. *Available at* the website: <http://siteresources.worldbank.org/INT-GEP2002/Resources/gep2002complete.pdf>, last accessed September 12, 2006.

[2] *See* "Agreement on Trade-Related Aspects of Intellectual Property Rights," Article 1, April 15, 1994, Marrakesh Agreement Establishing the World Trade Organisation, Annex 1C, 33 I.L.M. 1197, TRIPs thereinafter.

[3] *See* Sanjaya Lall, "Indicators of the Relative Importance of IPRs in Developing Countries," UNCTAD/ICTSD Capacity Building Project on Intellectual Property Rights and Sustainable Development, November 2001, at 1.

Within the controversies, a common tension can be observed between developed and developing countries, notwithstanding reasons to believe that enforcement of IPR has, overall, a positive impact on economic growth.[4] As some commentators have demonstrated, a tolerant IPR policy fuels economic development until the country reaches the stage where IPR protection becomes economically advantageous to a sufficiently strong set of domestic vested interests.[5] Within the global trading system, if a country is not economically ready to change its economic behaviour, the risky strategy for stronger demands will only turn into a tragic legal failure.[6] In this context, it is important for developed countries to formulate long-term strategies and extend as much cooperation and assistance as possible in order to bridge the economic divide and help developing countries reach the "development stage" and change their "economic behaviour."

It is important to note that, this claim is consistent with the core mission of the WTO, such as sustainable development. According to the principles of the WTO, the trading system "should be more accommodating for less-developed countries, giving them more time to adjust, greater flexibility, and more privileges."[7]

1.1.2 Legal Transplants in a Multicultural World

In order to avoid being marginalised in a fast changing global economy, developing nations have made a dramatic turn towards their foreign policies and shown unpredictable enthusiasms in upgrading their national legal systems. As a result, upon the establishment of the TRIPs Agreement, the international intellectual property protection has been managed in an accelerated standardisation process across the world with developing nations being active participators. The transplantation of intellectual property law via the WTO has posed as a unique model of legal reform imposed by industrialised nations in the context of neoliberal globalisation.

Substantial emphasis has been placed on the concept of legal transplants in the context of comparative law. While divergence between the optimists and sceptics of the theory remains, more scholars tend to believe the transferability

---

[4] *See infra* § 2.1.1.

[5] *See, e.g.,* Stefan Kirchanski, "Protection of U.S. Patent Rights in Developing Countries: US Efforts To Enforce Pharmaceutical Patents in Thailand," 16 (2) *L.A. Int'l & Comp. L. Rev.* 598 (1994); Frederick M. Abbott, "The WTO TRIPs Agreement and Global Economic Development," in *Public Policy and Global Technological Integration* 3, 4-12 (1997).

[6] *See* Robert E. Hudec, *Enforcing Intellectual Property Law: The Evolution of the Modern GATT Legal System* 364 (1993).

[7] Principles of the trading system, Understanding the WTO, Basics, *available at* <http://www.wto.org/English/thewto_e/whatis_e/tif_e/fact2_e.htm>, last visited September 26, 2006.

of foreign laws provided that a "fitting-in" process in a different socioeconomic environment is guaranteed. This "fitting-in" process is a key step to ensure a foreign law taking roots in indigenous soil and, to this end, requires necessary flexibility for countries with varied social, economic, and cultural conditions. However, TRIPs adopts a 'universal' standard of harmonisation of intellectual property norms and does not define standards and procedures to be followed on an *ad hoc* basis. Under such circumstances, developing countries may hesitate to achieve the international standard before domestic adaptation takes place. It is therefore not surprising that, while the transplant of TRIPs has ostensibly been embraced by almost all the countries, there still remain unresolved tensions as to the legal reform in light of law and development. This is the issue that we will discuss in greater detail in the following chapter.

1.1.3 A Nexus of World Trade and Intellectual Property

Intellectual property (IP) had been traditionally regarded as a cultural concept until 1994, when IPR was formally elevated as a trade issue in the TRIPs Agreement. Concluded at the Uruguay Round of GATT in 1994,[8] TRIPs has been seen as a logical consequence of efforts of developed countries to harmonise the standards for international IPR protection.[9] As one of the most significant features of the TRIPs agreement, TRIPs links IPR to trade for the first time in a multilateral agreement and requires members to implement and enforce minimum standards [10] for protecting IPR.[11] Nations are obliged to accept the prevailing view on the "proper" role of IPR as a bid to participate in the "world trading club."[12]

---

[8] "Uruguay Round" negotiation is a multilateral trade negotiation which was considered the largest trade negotiation ever, and most probably the largest negotiation of any kind in history. It covered almost all trade, from banking to telecommunications and from the genes of wild rice to AIDS treatments. For a detailed introduction, *see* "Understanding the WTO: Basics, The Uruguay Round," *available at* <http://www.wto.org/english/ thewto_e/whatis_e/tif_e/fact5_e.htm>.

[9] *See* Terence P. Stewart, *The GATT Uruguay Round: A Negotiating History (1986-1992)*, 2249 (1993).

[10] The TRIPs Agreement seeks to resolve enforcement problems by requiring a standard set of minimum enforcement measures "so as to permit effective action against any act of infringement of intellectual property rights covered by this Agreement, including expeditious remedies to prevent infringements and remedies which constitute a deterrent to further infringement." *See* TRIPs 41(1), *supra* note 2.

[11] Wei Shi, "The Impact of TRIPs on the Protection of Intellectual Property Rights in China," *Chinese Yearbook of Private International Law and Comparative Law*, Law Press 54-55 (1998).

[12] *See* Matt Jackson, "Harmony or Discord? The Pressure toward Conformity in International Copyright," 43 *IDEA: J. L. & Tech.* 635 (2003).

The main purpose of this reallocation is to create, through the dispute settlement mechanism of the WTO, an enforceable standard for global trade. By linking intellectual property to trade, intellectual property exporting members can take advantage of the WTO's dispute settlement mechanism against other members which are found in violation of the WTO obligations.

Furthermore, as Harris pointed out, through the platform of WTO, TRIPs Agreement "transforms intellectual property issues from a domestic matter to a matter for international governance." [13] By providing criteria for universal minimum standards of domestic law,[14] TRIPs exerts a powerful harmonising effect, thus providing a point of leverage for developed states to enhance standards under bilateral negotiations.[15] As a consequent, from a technical point of view, IPR enforcement in developing countries becomes a trade issue. In this context, the IPR related issues at the international arena reflect tensions between the developed and the developing worlds. This will be discussed in length in the following chapter.

1.2 Location of Topic within this Context

1.2.1 Focus on China

The position of People's Republic of China[16] in the controversies concerning TRIPs is significant. Claiming approximately twenty per cent of the world's population, China provides the biggest potential marketplace for both trade and investment.[17] In November 2001, after fifteen years of hard bargaining and tough negotiations, China entered into the WTO, and was thus enabled to involve itself fully in the global trade community. China is now in a position to boost its credibility as a rising world trade giant. In 2001, China became the second largest importer in the world, sharing 9.41 percent of the total imports.[18] China has gained a leading position in a number of global markets – it is the worldwide leader in the textile sector and produces seventy percent of all mobile phones, sixty percent of all digital cameras and fifty percent of all

---

[13] Donald P. Harris, "TRIPs Rebound: An Historical Analysis of How the TRIPs Agreement Can Ricochet Back Against the United States," *Nw J. Int'l L. and Bus.* 116 (2004).

[14] *See* TRIPs, *supra* note 2, Article 41-50.

[15] Harris, *supra* note 12, at 100.

[16] "China" thereinafter. This book focuses on mainland China, meaning that discussions thereof exclude Taiwan, Hong Kong and Macau, excepting the points which shed light on the relevant issues.

[17] Ramona L. Taylor, "Tearing Down the Great Wall: China's Road to WTO Accession," 41 *IDEA: J. L. Tech.* 151 (2001).

[18] *UN Comtrade Database, available at* <http://unstats.un.org/unsd/comtrade/>, last visited August 28, 2006.

computers.[19] It is now the world's largest market for refrigeration and air conditioning systems, the second largest energy market and the third largest electronics market.[20] However, although China has come out publicly and unequivocally in favour of a new round of multilateral trade negotiations, expectations that it would assume a positive role on issues arising out of TRIPs have yet to be realised,[21] and IPR protection in China seems to be constantly in controversy.

1.2.2 Focus on Enforcement

When it comes to the protection of IPR in China, there is mounting concern among the developed countries about the willingness and genuineness of China to provide adequate protection of IPR, which has, over time, evolved into one of the most sensitive issues in the ongoing trade debates with Western nations. China's accession to the WTO in 2001 has directed foreign attention towards the issue of IPR and, in particular, on whether improvements in Chinese intellectual property laws and WTO commitments to enforcing these laws will lead to these concerns being addressed; and if so, in which way and within what period of time.

The effectiveness of an IPR regime depends not only on legal structures but also on political ecology, cultural diversity, economic infrastructure, and technical capacity. Although formal compliance with TRIPs obligations has been reasonably good, related enforcement has been poor.[22] A United States Section 301 Report shows that Chinese copyright law, for instance, is compliant with the requirements of the TRIPs Agreement both in terms of scope and period; however, copyright piracy remains a major problem, which is getting worse in

---

[19] Ian McCartney MP, "Trade Unions and Globalisation, Unions 21 Fringe Event at the TUC Conference," September 11, 2006, *available at* <http://www.dti.gov.uk/about/dti-ministerial-team/page34009.html>, last visited on October 16, 2006.

[20] *See* "European Business in China Position Paper 2005," European Union Chamber of Commerce in China.

[21] *See* Kautilya: Jairam Ramesh, "The Dragon Strikes Again," *India Today*, July 30, 2001.

[22] *See e.g.*, Warren Newberry, "Copyright Reform in China: A "Trips" Much Shorter and Less Strange Than Imagined?," 35 Conn. L. Rev.(2003), at 1425, 1447 (mentioning that China's accession to the WTO has not accordingly reduce the level of counterfeiting and piracy as expected). *See also*, Wei Shi, "Cultural Perplexity in Intellectual Property: Is Stealing a Book an Elegant Offense?" 32 *N.C.J. Int'l L. & Com. Reg.* 31 (2006) (demonstrating that the IPR infringement will remain persistent or even become aggravated during the adaptive phase before China's WTO accession will eventually result in the removal of the various impediments to an effective IPR enforcement regime).

such areas as sound recordings,[23] and is colouring the perception of developed states despite China's accession to the WTO.

Theoretically, the TRIPs Agreement covers both substantive and enforcement aspects; however, the latter is essential to ensure the effective protection of IPR and thus this book will focus on the enforcement of IPR. Therefore, resolving the enforcement problem is essential to the resolution of a broader range of issues arising out of WTO membership – if it is resolved, these other issues of trade dispute can be re-framed as technical matters for negotiation.

1.2.3 What is at Stake

The reasons for IPR enforcement problem in China are manifold and are interdependent. The reasons behind this deficiency entail China's culture uniqueness, institutional impediments and economic insufficiency. Here, this book will address the following issues which have been little explored.

The Paradox of Confucian Determinism

It is apparent that the predominant commentary on Confucian philosophy serves to obscure rather than illuminate China's enforcement insufficiency. This is true because it is difficult to comprehend the prevalent theft of intellectual property in China as an inevitable outcome of an ethic that advocates "honesty," unless of course the ethical concepts derived from Confucius have somehow been subverted. China's IPR enforcement insufficiency is not a traditional cultural phenomenon reflected by Confucian ethics, and the IPR enforcement problem is not an actual outcome of Confucian philosophy; rather, the Confucian ethics can act as moral foundation for IPR protection. "To steal a book" is not an "elegant offence." Rather, it is, from a Confucian viewpoint, an act that is against the "natural order."[24]

Stage Theory and Intellectual Property

In developing countries, the package of IPR under the confines of TRIPs is perceived as a coercive demand imposed by the interest of the West, and as a restriction on the ability of developing states to obtain technologies necessary for its economic development.[25] However, TRIPs also provides a standard of protection for domestic innovators that might not ordinarily have applied until a later stage in a country's development. Within the global trading system, if a

---

[23] For example, the IIPA report claims that China accounted for some 202 million dollars worth of pirated motion picture videos and recorded music in 2004, 204 million dollars in 2005, and 206 in 2006. *See* IIPA Report at <www.iipa.com/countryreports.html>.

[24] The paradox of Confucian determinism is fully discussed in *infra* Chapter 4.

[25] *See, infra* § 2.2 & § 2.3.

country is not economically prepared to change their economic policies, any radical strategy for stronger demands can only lead to failure by giving up halfway.[26] However, once development reaches a more mature and diversified phase, IPR protection will eventually become an indispensable factor of commercial success. This stage theory provides an interesting challenge to developing states as to when and how they should engage with international IPR norms whilst ensuring legislation is appropriately balanced between the interests of local innovators and the needs of the societies of which they are a part.[27] China remains a consumer of intellectual property and is therefore unlikely to see gains from the vigorous protection of IPR;[28] instead profits will result from the imitation of existing products.

By-products of Imperfect Political Reform

Apart from the common reason of insufficient economic development, the intellectual enforcement problem in China is a unique political phenomenon resulting from the systemic dystrophy fundamental to Chinese institutional development and, in a broader sense, it may be the source for recasting and strengthening legal enforcement in China as a whole. China is experiencing critical transition – the prospect of a splendid economic landscape marred by lagging political reform. Although China has committed itself to a socialist "rule of law" state, without spirit of the liberal democracy, rule of law in China will unsurprisingly remain symbolic and problematic. As a consequence, economic reform has not only brought about greater prosperity, but also created grievous crises. The cascading problems have, in many circumstances, frustrated the efforts of ordinary Chinese citizens to earn their living in normal ways. As a result, utilitarianism seems to dominate many people's minds throughout the country. In addition, the restriction of religious beliefs and the tough control over freedom of speech have contributed to the growing of utilitarian impulse. In this context, there is no exaggeration that counterfeiting and piracy are by-products of imperfect political reform.[29]

Confucianism and EU-China Relations

Moreover, the harmonious philosophy of Confucius provides a positive cultural background for cooperative approaches to resolving trade disputes.[30] Here. EU and China share common values. Unlike U.S.-China relations, over-

---

[26] *Infra* § 4.1.3.

[27] *Infra* § 4.3.3.

[28] Michael Yeh, "Up against a Great Wall: The Fight against Intellectual Property Piracy in China," 5 *Minn. J. Global Trade* 516 (1996).

[29] For a comprehensive discussion towards IPR enforcement problems as by-products of imperfect institutional system in Chapter 4.

[30] *See infra* § 5.1 & § 5.5.

all, EU and China have optimistic prospect in maintaining a harmonious bilateral relations because of the cultural compatibilities, which have made for an excellent ethical foundation for a constructive bilateral relationship. [31]

1.3 Objectives

Achieving effective IPR implementation and enforcement in a way acceptable and beneficial to both developed and developing countries may establish the future basis of competition and cooperation in a global context reflected in the Uruguay Round. The objective of the book is thus to study the IPR enforcement in the world trading system in EU-China perspective, with particular focus on the domestic enforcement of IPR in China.

1.3.1 EU-China Interaction in Normative Integration

Notwithstanding that the EU and China share common values and enjoy cooperative relations, there are still institutional obstacles between the two. These concerns need to be addressed as this will provide an essential context within which future bilateral negotiations can proceed.

Chinese Problems with EU Law & Policy

Of key significance will be the developing relationship between the EU and China. This will require each party to be clear as to the capacity of the other. From the Chinese side, the boundaries between the powers of the EC and the powers of the member states remain far from clear.[32] The unique dual regime characterised by the lack of policy cohesiveness at the EU level has been cumbrous with regard to IPR protection, resulting in unnecessary and sometimes counterproductive effects.

Despite national fragmentation of attitudes within the EU, the decision-making in the trade policy process between these states and China is becoming increasingly "Europeanised," in the sense that the EU itself as an institution, as distinct from its Member States, is assuming an augmented role in both political and economic spheres. This process stems not only from the dynamic impetus of the internal market of the EC as one of the policy pillars of the EU,[33] but also as a result of the strengthening of economic organisation and

---

[31] For a detailed analysis of cultural compatibilities between EU and China and the feasible approaches to settling EU-China IPR disputes, *see infra* § 6.3.

[32] *See infra* § 5.2.1.

[33] *See* "Pillars of the European Union", *Europa Glossaries*, *available at* <http://europa.eu/scadplus/glossary/eu_pillars_en.htm>.

legal discipline at international level, by the WTO.[34] The steady progress of the integration across the continent thus provides the institutional foundation for the EU-China cooperation.

EU Problems with Chinese Law and Policy

Correspondingly, from the EU's perspective there are two problematic aspects of Chinese law and policy. The main area of concern, and one that is colouring broader reservations, relates to the counterfeiting and piracy at the unacceptable level. Companies based in the EU have found their exports to established foreign markets significantly undermined by counterfeit products originating from China, often with packaging almost indistinguishable from the original.[35] As depicted by the Business Software Alliance (BSA) when appealing to the European Commission, this amounts to "draining billions of Euros and hundreds of thousands of jobs from the European economies."[36] This in turn is driving the EU's broader concern to make effective enforcement of IPR a key agenda in their negotiations with China.

In the context of EU-China relations, the mutual concerns combine to create a complex negotiating environment. Accordingly they provide a natural focus of this book which will aim to contribute to the fostering of constructive cooperation between the two parties. The asymmetrical nature of concerns will entail not simply delineating a *via media* but the more delicate task of manoeuvring seemingly intractable issues, within the setting of volatile negotiations, in a way that is congruent with the progressive development of international trade.

1.3.2 The Creation of the Six-Step Approach

This book seeks to capture the significance and dilemmas associated with IPR protection from EU-China perspective and to demystify the mysteries of the enforcement problems. Departing from conventional interpretations of WTO accession, this book looks beyond terminological commitments and devotes attention to the practical reality. It assesses shortcomings of the IPR enforcement and sheds new light on enforcement problems by exploring and explicating various obstacles associated with IPR enforcement. The author argues that China's unique political-culture, institutional impediments and economic in-

---

[34] The institutional duality with regard to the responsibilities for foreign trade is of strategic significance, since the status of the EU has developed into a dual structure entity on one hand, and a unique contact point within the WTO on the other. *See infra* Chapter 5.

[35] *See* "the Final Report on the European Commission Green Paper on Counterfeiting and Piracy" (June 1999).

[36] *Ibid.*

sufficiency formed knotty points of the enforcement deficiency.[37] This book summarises a six-step approach to mitigating the counterfeiting menace and undoing the Gordian Knot.[38] The six-step approach suggests that the EU should try to foster and facilitate six shifts of China to initiate a virtuous circle of improved IPR protection. Collaboration as a strategy is the best solution to help China find its way forward in IPR protection. By this logic, the EU should apply a strategy to "cast a long line to catch a big fish" rather than "killing the goose that lays golden eggs." By facilitating conversion of China from an "IP imitation" to an "IP creation" nation and promoting the transformation of China from perceived infringer to unfortunate victim, we will eventually find the key to undoing the "Gordian Knot."

1.3.3 Significance of this Book

To Knowledge

An extensive literature has attempted to examine the stubborn enforcement problems. However, there is little of significance addressing the multifaceted issues related to IPR enforcement with a more incentive explanation than merely applying a cultural approach. An early and most influential analysis is from Professor William Alford and his renowned book, "*To Steal a Book Is an Elegant Offense: Intellectual Property Law in Chinese Civilization,*" published in the mid 1990s.[39] In this book, Alford explained that Confucian culture militated against copyright protection and did not allow intellectual property protection to take root.[40] The 1990s witnessed drastic debates between the United States and China over intellectual property protection during which two Memorandums of Understanding (MOU) were signed, and the repercussion of this book was significant. Jill Chiaing Fung made an argument that the modern Chinese laws have incorporated the pure Confucian ideas inherent in traditional Chinese legal thinking, which has especially influenced the development of China's intellectual property laws.[41] Alexander Chen further claimed that Confucianism provided strong barriers to the perception of intellectual property.[42] Eric Griffin argued that the more important than the lack of

---

[37] *See infra* § 3.3 & § 3.4.

[38] *See infra* § 6.5.

[39] William P. Alford, *To Steal a Book is an Elegant Offense: Intellectual Property Law in Chinese Civilisation*, Stanford University Press (1995).

[40] *See ibid*, at 8, 19-22.

[41] *See* Jill Chiang Fung, "Can Mickey Mouse Prevail in the Court of the Monkey King? Enforcing Foreign Intellectual Property Rights in the People's Republic of China," 18 *L.A. Int'l & Comp. L.J.* 616-624 (1996).

[42] Alexander C. Chen, "Climbing the Great Wall: A Guide to Intellectual Property Enforcement in the People's Republic of China," 25 *AIPLA Quarterly* 10 (1997).

protective influence by the government is the influence of Confucianism.[43] Peter Yu contained that "the culprit behind the Chinese piracy problem is the Confucian beliefs ingrained in the Chinese culture," which contradicts intellectual property rights."[44] Andrew Evans gave a similar interpretation, suggesting that Confucian ethics has been a philosophical and cultural disorder to combating Chinese counterfeiting and piracy.[45] One cynical commentator has even asserted that "until it abandons its twisted Confucianism, the [Asian] region will trail the West,"[46] and alleged that "it is time to deconstruct Confucius." [47] The prevailing point of view is that traditional Chinese philosophy – Confucianism in particular – provides a pervasive and unconscious influence on the comprehension of, and commitment to, intellectual property laws.

Confucianism has become the concept most frequently cited by commentators, while the literature criticising Confucian philosophy as the root of China's IPR enforcement problems is plenteous. However, most involves addressing cultural gaps or supporting or challenging specific premises on which international norms are based. Few scholars, if any, have shed any light on exploring cultural underpinnings from a prismatic lens, and establishing a mechanism whereby IPR can be implemented in a way which addresses current and foreseeable circumstances of underdevelopment whilst facilitating its alleviation.

This book considers the enforcement problem through a discussion of the evolving cultural phenomena associated with the fundamental systemic weakness of China's institutional problems. It argues that current mainstream legal epistemology incorrectly links China's enforcement problem to Confucian values which is misleading. It challenges the mainstream viewpoint by providing clues to the genuine Chinese cultural underpinnings and further creates a new cultural perspective.

Moreover, although much has been written about the protection of international IPR in China, the existing literature focuses predominantly on Sino-U.S. issues.[48] While some attention has been paid to the general field of EU-China trade and economic relations, there is little of significance concerning EU-

---

[43] Eric M. Griffin, "Stop Relying on Uncle Sam! – A Proactive Approach to Copyright Protection in the People's Republic of China," 6 *Tex. Intell. Prop. L.J.*182 (1998).

[44] Peter K. Yu, "The Second Coming of Intellectual Property Rights in China," 11 *Benjamin N. Cardozo School of Law Occasional Papers in Intellectual Property*, 44 (2002).

[45] Andrew Evans, "Taming the Counterfeit Dragon: The WTO, TRIPs and Chinese Intellectual Property Laws," 31 *Ga. J. Int'l & Comp. L.* 588-590 (2003).

[46] Sin-ming Shaw, "It's True. Asians Can't Think," *Time International*, May 31, 1999, at 23.

[47] *Ibid.*

[48] Almost all the articles concerning China's IPR protection were published with American law reviews and periodicals. *See, e.g.*, Fung, "Can Mickey Mouse Prevail in the Court of the Monkey King"; *supra* note 41; Chen, "Climbing the Great Wall," *supra* note 42; Griffin, "Stop Relying on Uncle Sam," *supra* note 36; Yu, "The Second Coming of Intellectual Property Rights in China," *supra* note 44.

China IPR debates.[49] By examining the special features of the EU-China IPR debate compared with the Sino-U.S. IPR discord, the book aims not only to fill this gap but also to use the prism of EU-China trade relations to suggest ways to reconcile the minimum standards demanded by developed countries with the necessity other states have for development. Through examining the characteristics of EU-China trade relations and exploring feasible solutions to the IPR debates, we can see that cultural compatibility and adaptability play a large role in maintaining a constructive bilateral relationship. Sensitivity to this together with sensitivity to unique Chinese culture may well provide a common basis for collaboration and thus a key element in an EU strategy for a settlement of bilateral commercial relations. In closing down counterfeiters, an emphasis on incentives such as the establishment of an enhanced cooperation mechanism in terms of IPR enforcement is likely to be more productive than the exclusive focus of the trade sanctions. With this strategy the EU is more likely to obtain strong commitments to enforcing IPR and to ensure that politicians remain focused on the necessity to implement them.

To Practice

EU-China bilateral relations have blossomed into multifaceted interactions with China's emergence in the global economy. The EU and China are two of the biggest markets in the world and they thus face common challenges in relation to globalisation,[50] as well as share the opportunity to deepen their commercial ties,[51] which have the potential to surpass their respective relations with the U.S. and Japan. As expected, China in 2002 overtook Japan to be-

---

[49] *See, e.g.*, Roger Strange, *Trade and Investment in China: the European Experience* (Routledge, 1998)(Strange demonstrates the bilateral economic relationship between China and Europe, with emphasis being paid to the flow of trade and direct investment, involving no effort on intellectual property protection); Christopher Dent, *The European Union and East Asia: An Economic Relationship* (London: Routledge, 1999)(the author takes a broader view of European's bilateral trade relationship with the East Asian regions. While it shed some light on EU-China bilateral relations, there is no specification for intellectual property issues. However, Dent's work accounts for EU-China relations in one of the nine chapters. *See* Chapter 5, at 118-151); Kenneth Pomeranz, *The Great Divergence: China, Europe, and the Making of the Modern World Economy* (Princeton University Press Revised edition 2001)(the author brings new insight to origins of capitalism and the rise of the West and the fall of the East from a historical perspective, but it does not involve in trade issues, let alone international intellectual property protection).

[50] Globalisation is used here to represents economic globalisation and does not extend to the possibility that this in turn can facilitate cultural globalisation by discouraging diversity.

[51] "A Maturing Partnership - Shared Interests and Challenges in EU-China Relations," Commission Policy Paper for Transmission to the Council and the European Parliament, Commission of the European Communities, Brussels, 10/09/03, COM (2003) 533 fin.

come the EU's second-largest trading partner outside Europe.[52] Trade between the EU and China has more than doubled since 1999,[53] and was worth 210 billion euros in 2005.[54] In 2005 China remained the EU's second biggest trading partner after the U.S.,[55] albeit with a substantial surplus in China's favour.[56] Similarly, the EU has, since 2005, surpassed Japan and the U.S. to become China's largest trade partner.[57] The EU is also China's largest technology supplier, second largest source of foreign direct investment (FDI)[58] and a major direct investor.[59] Accordingly, competing effectively against the U.S. and Japan is of significant importance to the EU whilst Chinese concerns are to ensure upgrading of technological capabilities of enterprises.[60] There is potential for massive mutual benefits if the interests of each can be addressed in a way which furthers the interests of the other.

FACILITATING CHINA'S CREDIBILITY WITHIN INTERNATIONAL ECONOMIC STRUCTURE

Managing and facilitating China's further integration into the world economy by bringing it more fully into the world trading system and by supporting the process of economic and social reform underway in the country is not only a great challenge to the EU but also an important contribution it can make especially in terms of capacity building.[61] Clearly, appropriate IPR protection is a key expectation on the part of developed nations in relation to the process of economic integration. Although China's accession to the WTO is a strong symbol of its integration into the global economic order, China will still need

---

[52] *See ibid.*

[53] *See* Peter Gumbel, "Pack Your Bags for the Orient Express," *Time Magazine*, 10 October 2004, *available at* <http://www.time.com/time/europe/html/041018/business.html>, last visited 17 October 2006.

[54] *EU-China Bilateral Relations, available at* <http://ec.europa.eu/comm/trade/issues/bilateral/countries/china/index_en.htm>, last visited August 17, 2006.

[55] *Ibid.*

[56] The EU has gone from a trade surplus at the beginning of the 1980s to a deficit of 78 billion euros in 2004. *See* Economic and Trade Relations, Trade with China, *available at* <http://europa.eu.int/comm/external_relations/china/intro/index.htm>.

[57] Chinese Customs statistics show that bilateral trade in 2004 hit 177.3 billion dollars (Chinese export 95.9/import 63.4), up 35 percent from the prior year. *See* China MOFCOM Information Release, *available at* <http://boxilai2.mofcom.gov.cn/aarticle/activity/200505/20050500086060.html>.

[58] By the end of October, 2004, EU companies had set up 19193 businesses in the fast growing economy. Contractual foreign capital from EU was worth 73.46 billion dollars while the actual inflow totalled 41.74 billion dollars, leaving large spheres to develop. *See* "150 Billion USD Trade Makes EU the largest Trade Partner of China," *People's Daily*, January 7, 2005.

[59] Statistics: MOFCOM, at <http://www.mofcom.gov.cn/>.

[60] "A Maturing Partnership," *supra* note 51.

[61] *Ibid.*

to restructure its prosecutorial, administrative and border control systems to gain credibility in the West. The EU has gained valuable experience in this regard, stemming from its strategic position in promoting Eastern Europe's integration into the Community.[62]

A MODEL FOR DEVELOPING STATES

Protection of IPR presents a significant unresolved tension in the relations between developed and developing countries.[63] Here the way in which EU-China problems are resolved will provide a precedent which can either assist or impede a resolution of the broader tension.

POLICY SUGGESTIONS

This book touches upon two areas of key public interests. On one hand, IPR enforcement has constantly been in flux and contentious and has been acknowledged as an arena characterised by complexity and uncertainty; on the other hand, China and its ongoing economic reform and institutional transition have attracted dramatic attention in a wide variety of spheres. This book offers suggestions on legal reforms to facilitate interests among policymakers, think tanks and private foundations. There is no significant literature at present and this book will also be of interest to lawyers, scholars and law students in general. Further, it is hoped that this book will attract attention of the European Commission, Chinese Government and TRIPs Council of the WTO.

1.4 Research Methodology

1.4.1 Research Strategy

Contextual Analysis

This book provides an interdisciplinary survey of justification of IPR protection. In addition to surveying the procedures implemented by China in response to its obligations under TRIPs, this book explores reasons and solutions of the enforcement problems. In light of the current international IPR regime, this book reviews EU-China trade relations and demonstrates bilateral concerns over IPR issues. Within this context, a two-fold analysis provides points of reference in identifying elements of cooperative design and the limits of coercive trade policy. The first will be an analysis of the TRIPs Agreement, and the short-term strategic options open to the EU and China in negotiating compliance. The second analysis will seek to identify and evaluate ways in

---

[62] *Ibid.*

[63] In this book, a "developed country" refers to a country that has a high income per capita; a "developing country" is a country with a relatively low income per capita.

which the standards applicable under TRIPs may be ameliorated to the benefit of longer-term IPR strategies.

EU-CHINA TRADE RELATIONS AND IPR ISSUES

This book examines the depth and breadth of EU-China IPR issues and illustrates characteristics of these issues compared to the U.S.-China IPR debate. This book explores how China's government should interact with the EU and take constructive steps to strengthen its IPR mechanism, and how policymakers of the EU should tailor its IPR protection to local practice, and thus provide an analytical framework on which EU-China cooperation is based.

EU and China have established consensus towards building a constructive strategic partnership. Within EU-China relations, the enormous challenge for both sides is to ensure that what has been agreed on paper, apparently beneficial in theory, is applied in practice without having to repeat the unsuccessful outcome of experience, which reflects Sino-American sentimental tie amid strains over IPR protections. It is possible for the EU and China to set an example for the world regarding the enforcement of IPR with an approach that recognises that there are bound to be short-term frustration but that seeks to build confidence in the system. [64]

Current signs are encouraging but it will be a difficult task to find ways to isolate and resolve specific difficulties without merely displacing them elsewhere. The *EU-China Intellectual Property Rights Cooperation Programme* [65] is contributing to the progress of both reform and implementation of IPR protection. This is being reinforced by the institutional arrangements deriving from the establishment of the European Chamber of Commerce in China[66] (EUCCC), the EU-China Business Dialogue (ECBD)[67], and the EU-China Intellectual Property Dialogue (EUIPD).[68] These constitute the processes within which my research will aim to make a contribution.

---

[64] *See* Speech by Pascal Lamy, European Commissioner for Trade, to the China Europe International Business School, Shanghai, China, December 3, 2001, *available at* <http://www.delchn.cec.eu.int/en/eu_china_wto/wto1.htm>.

[65] The EU-China Intellectual Property Rights Cooperation Programme, managed by the European Patent Office and overseen from a Beijing-based office, was established in 1996. Activities include training programmes, roadshows and seminars throughout China for judges, lawyers, customs officials and others in IPR enforcement and prosecution. For a more detailed introduction, *see infra* § 6.3.2.

[66] The European Union Chamber of Commerce in China is a corporate and autonomous private sector body representing the views of the business community of the Member States of the European Union in China and endeavouring to improve access of European business to the Chinese market. *See infra* § 6.3.2 for a comprehensive introduction.

[67] *See infra* § 6.3.2.

[68] On October 30, 2003, just ahead of the first EU-China Summit in Beijing, the EU and China agreed to launch a structured dialogue on IPR to discuss bilateral and multilateral issues related to the enforcement of IPR. *See infra* § 6.3.2.

SUBJECTIVE PERCEPTIONS

The analysis of this book will not only be empirical but will also address perceptions concerning EU-China trade disputes involving IPR enforcement. In establishing their relations *inter se* an important factor has been each party's perception of the legal reforms undertaken by the other and which, in turn, influence its willingness to amend the content and use of its own law. Changes in law, legal processes, and legal culture regarding IPR thus provide both a mirror and a stimulant to the evolving economic relations between the trading partners. Accordingly, this book will provide an analysis of each party's IPR legislation not only objectively, but also as perceived by the other. This will facilitate a better understanding of the complex interaction of perceptions on which continuing negotiations will be premised.

COMPARATIVE ANALYSIS: JAPAN, KOREA AND THE UNITED STATES

Apart from focusing on EU-China trade relations, this book also draws on the experience of other states in developing and managing their domestic standards of IPR protection. The response of Japan and South Korea[69] to TRIPs compliance will be examined to assess the extent to which Chinese Confucian values influence the notion of IPR, and the correlation between the initiatives of IPR protection and economic development environment. Their experience will be considered as examples of states that had followed a strategy of avoiding IPR protection so as to encourage local industries and undergone a similar transformation in their IPR policies.[70]

In addition, as a counterpoint to EU policy on IPR protection in China, this book will compare the U.S. approach and Chinese response to the unresolved issues of how and when China's WTO commitments will be implemented. Before its accession to the WTO, China's response to Section 301[71] pressure was invariably prompt. However, whilst seeming to confirm the success of U.S. policy, China's implementation of ameliorating policies is more or less perfunctory. The cat-and-mouse game has continued and the American policy has proved to be misconceived.[72] Not only was its constant use of trade threats enabling China to improve its ability to resist, but by cultivating habitual an-

---

[69] Korea thereinafter.

[70] *See infra* § 4.2 & § 4.3.

[71] Section 301 of the Trade Act of 1974, as amended (19 U.S.C. § 2411), is the principal statutory authority, aiming to eliminate unfair trade practices and open foreign markets. Section 301 permits the President of the United States to investigate and impose sanctions on countries engaging in unfair trade practices that threaten the U.S.'s economic interests. In 1988, U.S. Congress introduced the Omnibus Trade and Competitiveness Act of 1988, which amended section 301 by including two new provisions-Super 301 and Special 301. *See* Jean Heilman Grier, "Section 301 of the 1974 Trade Act," *available at* <http://www.osec.doc.gov/ogc/occic/301.html>.

[72] For a more comprehensive discussion of US-China intellectual property debate, *see infra* § 6.2.

tagonism among the Chinese people, the government was encountering obstacles in implementing necessary reforms.[73] Since the accession of China to the WTO, the U.S. has substituted recourse to the dispute settlement mechanism. However, it remains to be seen whether this will provide a more successful approach.

MULTIDISCIPLINARY APPROACH

IPR issue is increasingly contentious in a globalising society because it exists at the intersection of economic growth, social development, and cultural values. This book adopts a multidisciplinary approach taking into account economic, political and philosophical considerations that have influenced the making and implementation of international IPR norms and also surveys business practice to monitor the effectiveness of the IPR enforcement. To debate the role, or merely the existence, of IPR in such a diversified environment will serve as a litmus test in assessing the broader debate on development.

HISTORICAL APPROACH

An innate assumption underpinning the EU-China trade relationship is that although Chinese and Western views of IPR are traditionally different,[74] they are not inherently irreconcilable and that such differences as exist can be bridged.

This excursion with historical approach is crucial to understanding some aspects of Chinese intellectual property law *per se*, as well as China's commitments. Whilst technically China has a good legislative structure and the legal tools to enforce IPR and eliminate infringements, these have seldom been used effectively and willingly. To some extent this is a problem of value orientation rather than legislation. For this reason, the analysis of legislation will be supplemented by a historical analysis to identify the extent to which friction between the West and China stems from inherent difficulties of reconciling the different cultural perception and value orientation of the parties.

Chinese culture provides a pervasive and unconscious influence on comprehension of, and commitment to, intellectual property laws. Indeed, historically speaking, China indigenously lacks a modern notion of IPR. Most importantly, Chinese ideology over the past decades has stifled private rights and deterred Chinese inventors, authors, or entrepreneurs who might otherwise lobby for stronger IPR protection and the new utilitarian philosophy derived from China's defective political institution has detracted from a clear conception of the IPR. As a result, gains from imitation of others IPR are still regarded by many people as *de facto* legitimate and the unique political-culture deriving from dysfunctional institutional regime development is likely to have

---

[73] *See* Peter Yu, "From Pirates to Partners, Protecting Intellectual Property in China in the Twenty-First Century," 50 Am. U. L. Rev. (2000), at 133-4.

[74] *See infra* § 3.3.1 and § 6.4.1.

a continuous influence on attitudes to IPR protection.[75] This throws some doubt as to whether Chinese understanding has reached the level necessary to meet the EU expectations and indicates a need for phase-in periods to allow time for a strong domestic constituency to develop in China.

Limitations

The limitations of a project and the need for a definable scope of enquiry impose certain constraints, particularly in addressing material that although relevant may not be essential. There are two main exclusions. The first concerns the IPR to be explored. In general, IPR can be defined as the monopoly rights conferred upon creation and innovation over a period of time. TRIPs requirement for observance of minimum standards covers a variety of rights each one of which is conceptualised on a different view of how related interests can be defined and balanced.[76] The book will shed light on copyright, trademarks and patents as those are the IPR most likely to give rise to disputes. While focusing the enforcement issues of these aspects, this book does not address other equally relevant issues, such as the proliferation of TRIPs-plus[77] bilateral and regional agreements, which have been discussed elsewhere, nor issues still subject to negotiation in WTO, such as biological diversity and geographical indications.

The second concerns investment. IPR is a significant factor in both trade and investment. Whilst on the focus of the book will be restricted to "trade-related" aspects of the TRIPs Agreement, this will necessarily touch upon the role of TRIPs in stimulating foreign investment especially technology transfer.

1.4.2 Research Sources

Existing Scholarship

Although there is a dearth of literature directly applicable to EU-China negotiations, an extensive contextual bibliography concerning international trade and IPR has been identified. The book will shed new light on IPR enforcement in the world trading system from EU-China perspective.

---

[75] *See infra* § 4.1.2.

[76] For a substantive introduction, *see infra* Chapter 2.

[77] "TRIPS-Plus" means bilateral agreements which contained intellectual property protection standards that exceeded those found in TRIPs or required developing countries to implement their treaty obligations before the end of TRIPs transition periods. *See, e.g.,* Margo A. Bagley, "The Nexus Symposium: An Interdisciplinary Forum on the Impact of International Patent and Trade Agreement in the Fight against HIV and AIDS," *Emory Int'l L. Rev.* 781(2003).

Primary Materials

The book will also draw upon available statistical evidence collected in Europe and China. Here, a major problem will be the quality of China's legal databases where, even in the case of Chinese Customs and the Ministry of Commerce (MOFCOM), information is unreliable and often out of date. This will necessitate original empirical work by way of surveys that are conducted in various government departments, companies and non-governmental organisations (NGOs).

The Survey Backed by the Interviews

This book is supported by a survey informed by a series of interviews, conducted in both Europe and China. The survey not only focuses upon high level trade officials on both sides, but also domestic Chinese companies and their foreign trading partners who are in commercial ties in China and have reason to have particular concerns on IPR protection.

The interviews also concentrate on those who have passed through the EU-China Intellectual Property Rights Cooperation Programme, managed by the Beijing office of the European Patent Office.[78] In the proposed period, semi-structured interviews were conducted with Chinese and foreign businessmen, non-legal advisers, lawyers, NGOs staff, diplomats and government officials.

PURPOSE OF THE INTERVIEWS

The interviews were designed to be between 30 minutes and 40 minutes long, and took place at the working place of interviewees in selected cities such as Brussels, London, Beijing and Shanghai. The material gained through the interviews was used to provide background information on issues raised throughout the book.

The generalisation of secondary sources including legislation, government, professional, and media reports as well as academic work was also made, both in Europe and China, to help identify interviewees and develop the questions around which interviews should be based.

STRUCTURE OF THE INTERVIEWS

Detailed questions were prepared to test the research hypotheses by obtaining empirical evidence. The questions were designed for trade officials and companies in both Europe and China which have foreign investments in China involving IPR. The questions focused on EU companies involving business in China, but simultaneously threw light on some domestic Chinese companies in order to learn the response of Chinese companies concerning IPR protection at different levels.

---

[78] *Infra* § 6.3.2.

First, the interview questions aimed to test respondents' perceptions by asking them to complete a series of statements about the international IPR regime, by answering a number of questions or, where the semi-structured questions were appropriate, by placing a tick next to one of the response option selections "never, rarely, sometimes, frequently, mostly, always, don't know or don't understand" and "completely predictable, highly predictable, fairly predictable, frequently unpredictable, mostly unpredictable, completely unpredictable, don't know or don't understand."

Second, these questions aimed at testing how participants would evaluate the Chinese IPR regime and the potential impact on their business. The domestic participants were asked whether domestic companies have the internal initiative to call for high standard IPR protection at the national level, and if not, for what reason; Foreign participants were asked whether they had assessed the effect of Chinese IPR protection system before entering into Chinese market, and if yes, by what method.

Third, the questions during the interviews aimed to ask the participants for comments on the shortfall of current IPR enforcement in China, and whether these had been communicated to any organisation for further action; if so to whom, if not why.

Finally, the questions measured the participants' perceptions as to implementation and enforcement of IPR. These substantive questions aimed to test participants' responses on the business losses due to counterfeiting and piracy, and what their preferred strategy was for countering or improving the level of implementation and enforcement of IPR. These were indicated along a range of designated options including, for example, bringing the case to court judicial support, accepting traditional business practices, or tolerating a certain degree of infringement.

ACCURACY OF THE SURVEY

Since the sample of the survey would be to some extent self-selecting, participants would tend to be predisposed towards taking potential risks. Thus, it is essential to determine whether they reflect an accurate picture of the need for and the benefit of strong IPR protection, and genuine responses to the international norms. In so doing, the author took advantage of professional affiliations, such as being a Director of the Chinese Society of Private International Law, which enabled him to have both personal contacts with relevant authorities and access to databases on regulations and policies via related organisations such as MOFCOM and State Intellectual Property Office (SIPO). Meanwhile, the author made use of personal relations to be sure that the interviewees were the representatives who had been involved in the initial decision-making process in the companies concerned. Due to technical and constitutional reasons, it was necessary, and more useful, for some sources to remain unidentified.

1.4.3 Chapter Outline

The introduction has tried to capture the significance and dilemmas associated with IPR enforcement in EU-China perspective. Key concepts have been introduced and fundamental tensions and assumptions stated. However, all of these merely provide a starting point for analysis. Following the introduction chapter, in Chapter 2 the book will explore the justifications for protecting IPR from a multidisciplinary approach. This will lay a theoretical ground for Chapter 3 for assessing the Chinese response to the TRIPs Agreement and the shortcomings of the IPR enforcement, which in turn will provide a context for Chapter 4 to examine the rooted reason relating to the enforcement problems, supplemented by a comparison of similar analysis of Japan and Korea. Having identified issues of implementation and enforcement difficulty, Chapter 5 will consider the legislation of China and the EU in more detail to identify the quality of response. It uses a matrix, showing on one axis current and potential problem areas of the EU and the Chinese concerns on the other. It draws on the experiences and reactions of each side in negotiating trade issues and coordinating domestic standards of IPR protection. Having illustrated a matrix of mutual concerns within integrations, Chapter 6 will look at the more specific issues arising out of negotiations between EU and China and offer feasible solutions. It summarises a six-step approach to mitigating the counterfeiting menace and undoing the Gordian Knot.

The questions, such as design by which IPR is properly and efficiently protected between the EU and China, have already been mentioned and gone to the heart of the debate. By way of conclusion in Chapter 7, the book will summarise those points from the intervening chapters that have been found to have most bearing on the problems faced by the EU and China in developing a consensus on IPR and offer some insights as to how such problems may be best addressed.

2 The Justification for IPR Protection

"Intellectual property (IP)" refers to inventions, devices, new varieties of designs and other properties that are produced through "mental or creative labour" by human beings, and the law regulating intellectual property is "highly politicised."[1] "Intellectual property rights (IPR)" is a catch-all term used to describe the legal status and protection that allows people to own intellectual properties – the intangible products of their creativity and innovation imbedded in physical objects – in the form that they own physical properties.[2] According to the official interpretation of World Intellectual Property Organisation (WIPO), IPR comprises those legal rights, by which the products of intellectual activity over a range of endeavours are defined.[3] For the purposes of the TRIPs Agreement, IPR refers to copyright and related rights, trademarks, geographical indications, industrial designs, patents, integrated circuit layout-designs, protection of undisclosed information and anti-competitive practices in contractual licenses.[4]

The reasons for which protection is afforded to such rights are twofold. One is to give expression to the moral sentiment that a creator, such as a craftsman, should enjoy the fruits of their creativity; the second is to encourage the investment of skills, time, finance, and other resources into innovation in a way that is beneficial to society.[5] This is usually achieved by granting creators certain time-limited rights to control the use made of those products.[6]

However, the tension between stimulating creation and disseminating its benefits to society at large is delicate.[7] IPR as a concept has been discussed

---

[1]   *See* L. Bently and B. Sherman, *Intellectual Property Law*, OUP (2001), at 1-2.

[2]   *Ibid*, at 2-3 (noting that intellectual properties "share a similar image of what means to 'create' (or produce)," for example a book, a design for a car, or a new type of pharmaceutical).

[3]   *See* "About Intellectual Property," WIPO Online Information and Introduction, *available at* <http://www.wipo.int/about-ip/en/>.

[4]   *See* TRIPs Agreement Article 1(2).

[5]   *See* "WIPO Intellectual Property Handbook: Policy, Law and Use," WIPO Publication No. 489, *available at*: <http://www.wipo.org/about-ip/en/ iprm/pdf/ch1.pdf>.

[6]   *Ibid.*

[7]   *See, e.g.*, Thomas Cottier, *Intellectual Property: Trade, Competition, and Sustainable Development*, University of Michigan Press (2003). *See* also, Philippe Cullet, *Intellectual Property and Sustainable Development*, New Delhi: Lexis/Nexis Butterworths (2005).

and debated throughout history and, with a global economy, this debate has become increasingly controversial and confrontational.[8] This contention leads to a necessary justification regarding the international framework of IPR protection.

The way in which IPR is comprehended in any society is shaped by its legal, economic, political and cultural dimensions. Scholars from different backgrounds have often debated the validity and legitimacy of IPR from different perspectives.[9] In this chapter, the author attempts to review IPR from its economic, legal and political perspective and justify the correlation between IPR and economic growth and transfer of technology, identify legal flexibility to implement international IPR standards, and examine the political implications of the existing IPR regime, particularly under TRIP Agreement.

2.1 Intellectual Property and Economic Growth – An Economic Analysis

In the context of economic analysis of law, a logic starting point of the justification for IPR protection seems to be to compare and contrast the components of such fundamental issues as intellectual property and economic growth.

Economic growth, in the sense attributed to this concept in contemporary macroeconomics, is a natural phenomenon of industrialisation.[10] Economic growth depends, to large part, on technological change (*e.g.* innovation) and reflects the increase and accumulation of technological and other knowledge of commercial value.[11] From its early days, economic analysis has focus on issues concerning economic growth and its correlation with technological change, since these issues concern the human welfare in the long run.[12] As one

---

[8]   *See* Brigitte Binkert, "Why the Current Global Intellectual Property Framework under TRIPs is Not Working," *Intellectual Property Law Bulletin* 143 (Spring 2006).

[9]   *See* Bently and Sherman, *supra* note 1, at 3.

[10]   The contemporary concept of economic growth has distant origins, since it stems back from the early days of the Industrial Revolution and is constantly evolving. In 1950s, following the publication of papers by Robert Solow and Nicholas Kaldor, growth theory became dominating topics until the early 1970s. The emerged "new growth theory" (also known as endogenous growth theory) asserts that new ideas are the root source of economic growth since they promote technological innovation and hence stimulate productivity improvements. For a substantive introduction, *see, e.g.,* Neri Salvadori, "Introduction", 54 (2-3) Metroeconomica, 125–128 (2003); Michael Borrus and Jay Stowsky, "Technology Policy and Economic Growth", Berkeley Roundtable on the International Economy, Paper BRIEWP97, at 3; *see* also, Charles I. Jones, *Introduction to Economic Growth* (2nd ed.), W. W. Norton and Company, New York·London (2002).

[11]   *See* Gene M. Grossman and Elhanan Helpman, "Endogenous Innovation in the Theory of Growth," 8 (1) *The Journal of Economic Perspectives* 25-7 (1994).

[12]   *See* Jones, *supra* note 10, at 3-16.

of the most popular fields in contemporary macroeconomics, economic growth is not only essential to theorists but also valuable to policy makers.[13] In order to maintain economic growth, countries have endeavoured to establish varied mechanisms to foster innovation and facilitate the transfer of technology. The creation and protection of IPR exemplify a central part of this strategy.

While many scholars and policy-makers tend to allege that a strengthened IPR regime act as an important catalyst of economic growth,[14] over the past years since the establishment of the global trading system, it still remains undecided as to whether and how the imposition of the Western-style IPR regime and its infrastructure would generate significant economic growth and progress as expected in the developing world. To identify and evaluate the real linkage of the two aspects in a global context is a rather difficult task. In this section, the author seeks to re-examine the correlation between IPR protection and economic growth as means to justify the validity and legitimacy of the existing international IPR system.

2.1.1 An Outlook on Theory of Economics and Law

The law does not exist in isolation. It is well recognised that problems with both a legal and economic dimensions often benefit from an understanding of both subjects. As Professor Posner has pointed out, economists have developed models which seem to provide an analytical framework for studying law, and although these are often based on "unrealistic" assumptions, these are a necessary component of the theory, since "[t]he true test of a theory is its utility in predicting or explaining reality and, judged by this criterion, economic theory, despite the unrealistic nature of its assumptions, may be judged a success."[15]

Indeed, the two disciplines, law and economics, are interrelated. The purpose of law, according to the economic theory, is to alleviate market failures and thereby increase the efficiency of markets and produce a multitude of economic benefits to the society.[16] The market failure paradigm has become the dominant terminology of policy analysts in their decision-making process, whereby an understanding of economics can highlight how laws may be applied to alter economic behaviour, and assess the effect they have had or may have on economic efficiency.[17] Laws are expected to attain this purpose by

---

[13] *Ibid.*

[14] Steven P. Reynolds, "Antitrust and Patent Licensing: Cycles of Enforcement and Current Policy," 37 *Jurimetrics J.* 138 (1997).

[15] *See* Richard Posner, *Economic Analysis of Law* (1977).

[16] Sidney A Shapiro, "Keeping the Baby and Throwing out the Bathwater: Justice Breyer's Critique of Regulation," 8 *Admin. L.J. Am. U.* 725 (1995).

[17] *Ibid.*

forbidding certain actions or by altering the balance of incentives so that people act in one way instead of another.[18] Laws can also be used, intentionally or not, to facilitate or hamper participation of transactions.[19]

The law and economics movement began in the 1960s with economists such as Ronald Coase and Guido Calabresi,[20] and later Richard Posner.[21] Ronald Coase and Guido Calabresi are generally identified as the starting point for the modern school of law and economics.[22] In 1973, Posner published his landmark work, *Economic Analysis of Law*,[23] and brought this groundbreaking topic to the attention of the general legal academy.[24] Posner's book received wide acclaim amongst legal academia and was considered to be the "bible of the law and economics movement."[25]

2.1.2 IPR: Incentive for Innovation?

In an information age, few people would deny the significance of creativity, inventions and innovation to economic growth and technological development. Over the past two centuries or so, the acceleration of technological advancement has radically changed the life of mankind and demonstrated values of innovation in creating our everyday reality. The perpetual exponential advance of technology has rendered increasingly visible the intellectual content to innovation at a time when the globalisation of world markets creates global opportunities for the products of innovation. In a knowledge-driven economy, the effective protection of IPR is emerging as a critical element of commercial success.[26] With increasing levels of international trade, the amount of trade involving IPR also increases, causing significant resources to be devoted to effective protection.

---

[18]   *See* Posner, *Economic Analysis of Law*, at 10-13.

[19]   *Ibid.*

[20]   In 1961, Coase and Calabresi, independently from each other, published their groundbreaking articles in the interacting area of law and economics, which has had significant impact towards legal thinking. *See* Ronald Coase, "The Problem of Social Cost," 3 *J. L. Econ.* No.1 (1960); *see* also Guido Calabresi, "Some Thoughts on Risk Distribution and the Law of Torts," 70 *Yale L. J.* (1961).

[21]   *Ibid.*

[22]   *See* Posner, *the Economics of Justice* 4 (1983).

[23]   *See* Posner, *Economic Analysis of Law, supra* note 15.

[24]   *See* Lewis Kornhauser, "The Economic Analysis of Law," *The Stanford Encyclopedia of Philosophy*, Edward N. Zalta (ed.)(2007), *available at* <http://plato.stanford.edu/archives/fall2007/entries/legal-econanalysis/>.

[25]   Nan Aron, *et al*, "Economics, Academia, and Corporate Money in America: The 'Law and Economics Movement,'" 24 *Antitrust Law and Economics Review* (1994).

[26]   Grossman and Helpman, *supra* note 11, at 25-7.

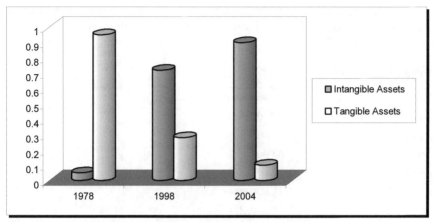

Source from Value Based Management, at <http://www.valuebasedmanagement.net/ faq_importance_intangible_assets.html>, chart designed by the author

Figure 1 Relative Significant of Intangible Assets Compared to Tangible Peers in Business

As a consequence of significant economic growth and explosive technological development, world trade now has more knowledgeable and technological content than ever before. The importance of IPR for trade has gained more significance as the share of knowledge-based or high-tech products in total world trade has doubled between 1980 and 1994 from twelve percent to twenty-four percent.[27] As shown in the Figure 1 above, the percentage of intangible assets was increased from five percent in 1978 to seventy-two percent in 1998. Another eighteen percent was gained in the following six years. The intellectual assets have become major value drivers in our modern economic world.

A case to point is the United States. According to Professor Juan Enriquez, the leading authority on the economic and political impacts of the life sciences, the United States generates the most patents per capita.[28] As shown in Table 1 below, it takes about 3,000 Americans to generate one U.S. patent, compared to 4,000 Japanese, 6,000 Taiwanese, 1.8 million Brazilians, 10 million Chinese and 21 million Indonesians.[29] IPR has been carefully refined over many years to meet the challenges of countries as it developed an industrial base and post-industrial service economies. With ever increasing levels of international trade, the question arises as to whether IPR as it has evolved will

---

[27] *See* UN Comtrade Database, *available at* <https://unp.un.org/special_comtrade.aspx>.
[28] Bruce P. Mehlman, "The Changing Wealth of Nations: Intellectual Property in the Age of Innovation," Licensing Executives Society Spring Meeting, United States Department of Commerce, May 3, 2002, Washington, DC, *available at* <www.technology.gov/ Speeches/p_BPM_020503_Wealth.htm>, last visited October 16, 2006.
[29] *Ibid.*

be up to the challenge of levelling the per capita levels of innovation between the developed and developing world or whether they will merely reinforce the existing levels of difference.

Table 1 Patents Per Capita/U.S.

Nations	Population/per patent
The United State	3,000
Japan	4,000
Taiwan	6,000
Brazil	1,800,000
China	10,000,000
Indonesia	21,000,000

Sources from Professor Juan Enriquez, available at <http://www.technology.gov/Speeches/ p_BPM_020503_Wealth.htm>

The illustration and interpretation of the economic rationale and function of IPR as a necessary policy-making instrument that stimulates innovations might seem abstruse and obscure. As a matter of conceptual design, IPR legislation confers on the holder of the right an exclusive "monopoly" for a limited period of time. [30] This will enable them to control the commercial exploitation by setting the level of revenue arising from their use and safeguarding it by excluding others from making, selling, or using it.[31] Ensuring that social benefit derived from knowledge-based innovation outweighs the social cost is at the core of balancing the factors to be considered. However, in high technology sectors such as pharmaceuticals, the risk of failure of expensive research to bear fruit is high and entrepreneurs must have good reason to expect that the cost of failure can be recaptured from the profits of future success. Otherwise there is little incentive to undertake innovative activities.

Another aspect is whether an IPR regime is the appropriate vehicle for stimulating enabling, rather than applied, technologies, or whether industry-funded Research & Development (R&D), government-funded awards, or the public sector are more effective vectors.[32] IPR is important to us since the de-

---

[30]   *See* W. R. *Cornish, Intellectual Property: Patents, Copyright, Trade Marks and Allied Rights,* London, Sweet and Maxwell 38 (1999).

[31]   *Ibid.*

[32]   Randall Kroszner, "Economic Organization and Competition Policy," 19 *Yale Journal on Regulation,* 541-97 (2002)(arguing that, "on the one hand, it is impossible for IPR regime to provide profound protection without exception. On the other hand, some innovation may be too difficult to imitate that, even without IPR protection, the innovator can enjoy a substantial cost or quality advantage over its competitors for some period. In either case, other characteristics of some dynamically competitive industries are important in making it likely that a successful innovation will yield a firm the leading position in a market, and profits that are essential to encourage such innovation").

cision to grant property rights in intangibles impinges on both competitors and the public.[33] As noted by Nancy Gallini and Suzanne Scotchmer, "if the balance between private gain and public good slips too far beyond what is necessary to spur innovation, it will instead become a drag on innovation and impede creating further innovations."[34]

How the right balance is achieved and whether the same balance is capable of universal adoption has engaged much academic debate. Ishac Diwan and Dani Rodrik, on one hand, conclude that developing nations may embark on protecting IPR of developed nations to facilitate the invention of technologies that are indigenously appropriate to the developing world.[35] Josh Lerner has taken a different approach to the analysis of the impact of patent reform by "examining the impact of major patent policy shifts in 60 nations over the last 150 years that enhanced the amount of patent protection provided," using a "differences-in-differences analysis."[36]

On the other hand, recent economic analysis offers somewhat a different interpretation from the traditional views. Judith Chin and Gene Grossman analysed a 'static' model of symmetric duopoly whereby all innovation takes place in developed nations and all imitation takes place in developing nations and discovered that developing nations have little incentive to agree to positive IPR protection because their competitive position in the output market would be weakened after paying a higher wage.[37] Similarly, Alan Deardorff designs another static model and indicates that the welfare effect of worldwide patent coverage could have an "offsetting effect," in the event that "all innovation originates in one part of the world," since "on one hand, permitting inventors to earn monopoly profits on their inventions and thus stimulating inventive activity and, on the other hand, distorting consumer choice by monopoly

---

[33] Bently and Sherman, *supra* note 1, at 4.

[34] *See* Nancy Gallini and Suzanne Scotchmer, "Intellectual Property: When Is It the Best Incentive System?" *UC Berkeley Department of Economics Working Paper* (2001).

[35] *See* Ishac Diwan and Dani Rodrik, "Patents, Appropriate Technology, and North-South Trade," 30 *J. Int'l Econ.*, at 27-47 (1991).

[36] *See* Josh Lerner, "Patent Protection and Innovation Over 150 Years," *NBER Working Papers* 8977, National Bureau of Economic Research, Inc (2002).

[37] Judith Chin and Gene Grossman, "Intellectual Property Rights and North-South Trade," 1988 *NBER Working Paper*, No.2769, *available at*: <http://www.nber.org>, last visited March 29, 2006 (the authors show in their model that there are certain circumstances where a less-developed country may be better off with weak IPR protection. In their model, a Northern firm and a Southern firm have divergent access to patent protection and produce a same good in a same market. In the first instance, the Southern firm can benefit from weak protection of IPR; however, after achieving a high global share of production output and gaining adequate technological advance, the protection of IPR becomes authentic).

pricing."[38] He subsequently suggests that there may be geographical limitation on the coverage of patents as to how far IPR should be extended internationally.[39]

Elhanan Helpman applies a more intrinsic approach to examining the benefits and costs of stronger IPR enforcement in a general equilibrium model where innovation originates in the developed world while the developing world relies upon the imitation of the innovation produced by the former.[40] Helpman advocates incremental improvement of IPR standards and demonstrates in his model that it is feasible for the innovation of developed nations to slow down the speed of the unification process of the IPR protection in the developing world lest the stricter IPR protection may ultimately hurt both developed and developing nations.[41] He concludes that, in general, the developing world has little to gain from higher IPR protection due to the terms of trade deterioration from an initial position of equilibrium.[42] Similarly, Stephen Richardson and James Gaisford also argue that in a country where knowledge gap is significant and domestic invention is scarce, a heightened protection of IPR could impair the overall welfare of that country and result in the reduced world welfare.[43]

In a similar vein, Gene Grossman and Edwin Lai show in their findings that the impact of strengthened IPR abroad does not necessarily have a strong positive impact on global innovation.[44] Edwin Lai and Larry Qiu established a model with two regions in the world – the developed and developing world, "which trade two types of goods, new products and traditional products."[45] They find that developed and developing nations have differentiated capability to innovate.[46] These studies find that the strengthening of IPR yields no proportional stimulating effects on endogenous innovation.

---

[38]   A. V. Deardorff, "Welfare Effects of Global Patent Protection," 59 (233) *Economica* 49(1992)(demonstrating the "offsetting effects" of the patent protection and their implications for the less-advanced countries).

[39]   *Ibid*, at 35-6.

[40]   Elhanan Helpman, "Innovation, Imitation, and Intellectual Property Rights," 61(6) *Econometrica* 1247-1280 (1993), also *available at* <www.nber.org/papers/w4081.pdf>.

[41]   *Ibid*.

[42]   *Ibid*.

[43]   *See, e.g.*, Stephen Richardson and James Gaisford, "North-South Disputes over the Protection of Intellectual Property," 29 *Canadian J. Econ.* (Special Issue, April) 376-381 (1996). *See* also James Gaisford and Stephen Richardson, "The Trips Disagreement: Should GATT Traditions Have Been Abandoned," 1 (2) *Estey Centre Journal of International Law and Trade Policy* 137-69 (2000).

[44]   *See* Gene Grossman and Edwin Lai, "International Protection of Intellectual Property," *NBER Working Papers* 8704 (2002), National Bureau of Economic Research, Inc. *Available at* <http://www.nber.org/papers/w8704.pdf>, last visited 19 March 2003.

[45]   *See* Edwin Lai and Larry Qiu, "the North's Intellectual Property Rights Standard for the South?" 59(1) *J. Int'l Econ.* 183-209 (2003).

[46]   *Ibid*.

Some scholars go even further. In a paper concerning technological change, Michele Boldrin and David Levine argue that "while awarding a monopoly to an innovator increases the payoff to the original innovator, by giving her control over subsequent uses of the innovation, it reduces the incentive for future innovation."[47] They stress that "[f]rom the perspective of the functioning of markets, [...]what is ordinarily referred to as 'intellectual property' protects not the ownership of copies of ideas, but rather a monopoly over how other people make use of their copies of an idea."[48] As noted by Boldrin and Levine, "economic theory shows that perfectly competitive markets are entirely capable of rewarding (and thereby stimulating) innovation, making copyrights and patents superfluous and wasteful."[49] The paper concludes that, in light of social welfare, current legislation on intellectual property plays a thoroughly pernicious role in the innovation process.[50] Apparently, this paper has attempted to challenge the conventional wisdom and evoked an enormous response.[51]

The most recent contribution in this area is the book *the Economic Structure of Intellectual Property Law* contributed by William Landes and Richard Posner.[52] By identifying and testing the interaction patterns of intellectual property law and economics, Landes and Posner argue that "expanding IPR can actually reduce the amount of new IPR that is created by raising the creators input costs, since a major input into new intellectual property is existing such property."[53] The key insight of their economic approach is to demon-

---

[47] *See* Michele Boldrin and David K. Levine, "Perfectly Competitive Innovation," Working Paper Archive from *UCLA Department of Economics* (2003), SSCNET, UCLA, *available at* <http://levine.sscnet.ucla.edu/papers/pci23.pdf>, at 4.

[48] *See* Lewis Kornhauser, "The Economics of Ideas and Intellectual property," *available at* <http://levine.sscnet.ucla.edu/papers/pnas18.pdf>, at 1.

[49] Douglas Clement, "Creation Myths: Does Innovation Require Intellectual Property Rights?" Reason Online, March 2003, *available at* <http://www.reason.com/news/show/28703.html> (quoting Boldrin and Levine, "Perfectly Competitive Innovation", *ibid*).

[50] Boldrin and Levine, "Perfectly Competitive Innovation," *supra* note 47, at 1.

[51] Commentators have given this paper a mixed reception. Robert Solow, the 1987 Nobel Prize laureate for his work on growth theory, highly praised this paper as "an eye-opener"; in a working paper entitled "24/7 Competitive Innovation", Danny Quah of the London School of Economics calls the Boldrin-Levine analysis "an important and profound development" that "seeks to overturn nearly half a century of formal economic thinking on intellectual property." By contrast, the negative responses include Benjamin Klein, a UCLA economist, who criticises their analysis "unrealistic" and Paul Romer, a Stanford economist, who considers their logic flawed and their assumptions implausible. *See* Douglas Clement, "Creation Myths", *supra* note 49; *see also* David Warsh, "The Case against Intellectual Property," *Economic Principals*, July 21, 2002, *available at* <www.economicprincipals.com/issues/02.07.21.html>.

[52] William Landes and Richard Posner, *The Economic Structure of Intellectual Property Law*, Belknap Press of Harvard University Press (2003).

[53] *Ibid*, at 422.

strate that overprotection of IPR undermines the traditional balance between right proprietors and society. Paradoxically, over-extended protection of IPR may have a counteraction effect to the innovation.[54]

Apparently, while IPR plays an important role in knowledge-oriented world economies and acts as an irreplaceable factor behind the incentives as a burst in innovation, like many things that cannot make the best of both worlds, IPR has merits and faults. Apart from the virtue to stimulate the innovation, the obvious defect is the "deadweight loss due to monopoly pricing."[55] IPR can either trigger or thwart innovation; it can either promote or hinder economic growth, depending on how it is oriented in the application. As noted by Nancy Gallini and Suzanne Scotchmer, in terms of the protection duration, if the sole concern is to encourage innovation, the IPR should not be terminated; if the sole concern is to avoid deadweight loss that occurs through proprietary prices, the IPR should not exist at all from its inception.[56] The main regulator is the duration of protection balancing these two concerns.

2.1.3 IPR: Stimulator of Trade Flow?

Apart from encouraging the innovation required for economic growth, IPR is also designed to contribute to the public benefit by ensuring effective short-term dissemination and long-term assimilation of technology.[57] Whilst this may be conventional wisdom in a domestic setting, the worldwide impact of IPR has so far been largely unexamined in spite of what is at stake in terms of trade, investment and transfer of technology. Recent studies have been somewhat inconclusive and acrimonious. In the area of bilateral trade, Keith Maskus and Mohan Penubarti attempted to set up a linkage between IPR protection and imports, and reiterated that stronger patent rights in developing countries would significantly increase imports from developed countries and, in some circumstances, some other developing countries as well.[58] Primo Braga and Carsten Fink in 2000[59] and Pamela Smith in 2001 carried on this project,

---

[54] *See* Daniel Levine, *'05, Profiles: The Economic Structure of Intellectual Property Law*, *available at* <http://www.law.uchicago.edu/alumni/record/landes-posner-book.html>.

[55] Nancy Gallini and Suzanne Scotchmer, "Intellectual Property: When Is It the Best Incentive System?" Institute of Business and Economic Research, Department of Economics, *UCB*, Paper E01-303 (2001).

[56] *Ibid.*

[57] According to Article 7 of TRIPs Agreement, protection and enforcement of IPR "should contribute to the transfer and dissemination of technology". *See* TRIPs Agreement, Article 7.

[58] K. Maskus & M. Penubarti, "How Trade-Related Are Intellectual Property Rights?" 39 *J. Int'l Econ.*, 227-48 (1997).

[59] *See* Primo Braga and Carsten Fink, "Intellectual Property Rights and Economic Development," *World Bank Background Paper*, *available at* <http://www1.worldbank.org/wbiep/trade/papers_2000/bpipr.pdf>.

devoting their research effort to the interaction of market size and the strength of the IPR regime and yielded similar results that are convergent and coherent with conventional theories.[60]

Nevertheless, as Maskus has clarified, some imports are attributed to technology transfer; however, strengthening IPR tends to increase imports of low technology consumer items, leading to the decline of indigenous industries based on imitation.[61] This implies that countries with limited technological capacity may experience reduced imports since intellectual property laws have the effect of increasing overall import prices and thus restricting import capacity.[62]

The main argument is that, whether or not there is full interaction between stronger IPR protection and higher lever technology transfer remains untested. More and more evidence shows that there is no strong positive correlation between IPR protection and foreign trade. A case in point is China. China, with weak IPR protection, has continued to enjoy rapid trade growth for many years and has still maintained a strong momentum of growth.[63] According to the International Trade Statistics 2003 released by the WTO, China was the fourth-largest merchandise trader in 2002, if the European Union is counted as a single unit.[64] In the 1990s, China's trade growth was three times that of global trade and, between 2000 and 2002, the value of exports and imports rose by thirty percent while world trade stagnated.[65]

Another case in point is Microsoft. Microsoft is undoubtedly the biggest victim of the weak copyright protection in its Chinese market. However, as Bill Gates revealed, Microsoft needs piracy to occupy the market and consolidate its position.[66] Clearly, Microsoft understands the two significant features of software. One is its zero marginal cost, thus using piracy to open up the market does not cause much loss; the other is its "locking effect," by which users of pirated software are easy to get "addicted." As Bill Gates noted with foresight, "[a]lthough about 3 million computers get sold every year in China,

---

[60] Pamela Smith, "How Do Foreign Patent Rights Affect U.S. Exports, Affiliate Sales, and Licenses?" 55 (2) *J. of Int'l Econ.* 411-439 (2001).

[61] K. Maskus, "Intellectual Property Rights in the Global Economy," *Institute for International Economics* 113 (2001).

[62] "Integrating Intellectual Property Rights and Development Policy," Report of the Commission on Intellectual Property Rights (CIPR, UK), September 2002, *available at* <www.iprcommission.org/graphic/documents/final_report.htm>, last accessed February 18, 2008.

[63] China's foreign trade grew 15 percent in 2005, and China has set a foreign trade growth target of 10 percent from 2006 to 2010. *See,* "China Sets Foreign Trade Growth Target for Next Five Years," *People's Daily Online,* October 11, 2006, *available at* <http://english.people.com.cn/200610/11/eng20061011_310896.html>.

[64] *See* "International Trade Statistics 2003," WTO, *available at* <www.wto.org/english/res_e/statis_e/its2003_ e/its2003_e.pdf>, last visited March 23, 2005.

[65] *Ibid.*

[66] Gao Xing, "Microsoft is Taking Action," *China Youth Daily,* May 31, 1999 (14).

but people don't pay for the software [...]. Someday they will, though. As long as they are going to steal it, we want them to steal ours. They'll get sort of addicted, and then we'll somehow figure out how to collect sometime in the next decade."[67] Gates's forethoughtful perspective on Microsoft's willingness to bear millions of dollars of losses to Chinese piracy implied of his firm confidence that Microsoft will eventually receive huge returns despite today's lax protection.[68]

2.1.4 IPR: Engine of Technology Transfer?

There remains a divergence of opinion on IPR and transfer of technology between developed and developing countries. This controversy is characterised by the premise that developing countries go for the TRIPs standards in order to attract Foreign Direct Investment (FDI) necessary for development.[69] However, the huge administrative costs and policy burden in implementing TRIPs provisions serve to counterbalance the motivations and endeavours of developing countries.[70]

Normatively, TRIPs supporters, usually the policy-makers from the developed countries, assert that a uniform set of relatively high standards of protection facilitates the security required by FDI, and thereby encourages a more rapid and effective transfer of technology.[71] From this viewpoint, strong domestic IPR rules are essential to the technological development.[72] By contrast, developing nations consider their acceptance of TRIPs conditional on economic rewards including acquisition of advanced technology. As noted by Laurence Helfer, developing countries see the TRIPs as part of a WTO "package deal" in which they are privileged to receive freer access to the markets of industrialised nations in exchange for their willingness to afford protection to foreign countries. [73] However, "with implementation proving increasingly slow, costly, and a source of domestic opposition, TRIPs had begun to look increasingly problematic for many developing countries."[74]

---

[67] Corey Grice & Sandeep Junnarkar, "Gates, Buffett A Bit Bearish", *CNET*, July 2. 1998.
[68] *See* Yahong Li, "The Wolf Has Come: Are China's Intellectual Property Industries Prepared for the WTO?" 20 *UCLA Pacific Basin L. J.* (2002), at 80.
[69] Warren Newberry, "Copyright Reform in China: A 'TRIPs' Much Shorter and Less Strange Than Imagined?" 35 *Conn. L. Rev.* 1448, 1449 (2003)(contesting that "[t]his controversy [about the technology transfer and IPR protection] goes to the heart of the TRIPs Agreement").
[70] *Ibid.*
[71] Laurence R. Helfer, "Regime Shifting: The TRIPs Agreement and New Dynamic of International Intellectual property Lawmaking," 29 *Yale J. Int'l L.* (2004), at 2.
[72] *Ibid.*
[73] *Ibid.*
[74] *Ibid*, at 70.

Scholarly literature to date concerning the transfer of technology and IPR is also controversial. One epistemological stance insists that stronger IPR protection gradually but surely benefits developing countries by stimulating more FDI and transfers of technology, "ensuring a relatively equal distribution of gains."[75]

Another influential research finding can be found from a series of discussion papers of the International Finance Corporation (IFC).[76] As an affiliate of the World Bank, the IFC aims to promote the economic development of its member countries through investment in the private sector.[77] An IFC discussion paper entitled "IPR Protection, Foreign Direct Investment, and Technology Transfer" (IFC Discussion Paper Number 19) was released in 1994.[78] As a continuation of the above analyses, one year later, another discussion paper, entitled "Intellectual Property Protection, Direct Investment, and Technology Transfer: Germany, Japan, and the United States" (IFC Discussion Paper Number 27) was released.[79] By analysing a survey of major global corporations in Germany, Japan, and the United States on the importance they attach to IPR protection in making FDI and IPR decisions, this report concludes that, "in certain relatively high-technology industries like chemicals, pharmaceuticals, machinery, and electrical equipment, a country's system of IPR protection often has a significant effect on the amount and kinds of technology transfer and direct investment [...]. Also, when a variety of relevant factors are held constant in an econometric model, the effects of such protection on U.S. direct foreign investment are substantial and statistically significant."[80]

Edwin Mansfield, the author of the IFC Discussion Papers, used an econometric approach in its empirical analysis. Firms of Japanese, German and United States domicile were asked whether the protection of IPR in selected countries was too weak to risk licensing its newest or most effective technology to unrelated firms in that country.[81] As shown in Table 3 below, in the chemical and pharmaceutical industries, over forty percent of the firms felt that protection in India, Thailand, and Argentina was too weak to consider li-

---

[75] Lee G. Branstetter *et al*, "Do Stronger Intellectual Property Rights Increase International Technology Transfer?" Empirical Evidence from U.S. Firm-Level Panel Data, *NBER Working Paper*, July 2005, *available at* <www.people.hbs.edu/ffoley/IPRReform.pdf>.

[76] *See e.g.*, Edwin Mansfield, "Intellectual Property Protection, Foreign Direct Investment, and Technology Transfer," *IFC Discussion Papers*, No 19, *available at* <http://www.ifc.org>, last visited August 29, 2006; *see* also Michael W Nicholson, "Intellectual Property Rights, Internalization and Technology Transfer," *available at* <http://www.ftc.gov/be/ workpapers/wp250.pdf>, last visited August 29, 2006.

[77] *See* "Mission of IFC," *available at* <www.ifc.org/ifcext/about.nsf/Cotent/Mission>.

[78] *See* Edwin Mansfield, *supra* note 76.

[79] Edwin Mansfield, "Intellectual Property Protection, Foreign Direct Investment, and Technology Transfer," *IFC Discussion Paper* No. 27.

[80] *Ibid.*

[81] *Ibid.*

censing; by comparison, Singapore and Hong Kong received the highest grading (the numbers varying from 0 to 100 illustrate their attitudes towards risks in the transfer of technology in these countries).[82] In the chemical and pharmaceutical industries, U.S. firms seem to have a heightened sense of risk compared with Japanese firms, a fact that may reflect the U.S. being a leader, and having a strong comparative advantage in the chemical and pharmaceutical industries. The result of the model shows that strength or weakness of IPR protection has an important effect on some, but not all, kinds of transfer of technology.[83]

Table 2 Percentage of Selected Firms & Their Attitude towards IPR (Chemicals & Drugs)

Host Country	Germany	Japan	U.S.
Argentina	57	44	62
Brazil	43	36	69
Chile	33	55	47
Hong Kong	14	7	33
India	100	85	81
Philippines	43	38	47
Singapore	0	0	25
Korea	33	7	38
Taiwan	33	21	44
Thailand	57	50	73

Sources: Edwin Mansfield, "Intellectual Property Protection, Foreign Direct Investment and Technology Transfer," IFC Discussion Papers No. 19 & 27.

In 2000, Guifang Yang and Keith Maskus worked jointly to examine the correlation between the strength of the IPR protection and the effect of the extent of the high-quality licensing.[84] In 2003, Yang and Maskus continued their research and released their new findings in the form of the World Bank Policy Research Working Paper.[85] Their research findings show that stronger IPR in the developing world would increase the extent of high-quality licensing from the developed world to the developing world under a particular condition.[86] As Yang and Maskus explain, "[i]t is more optimistic about the impact of the TRIPs agreement than were the findings of prior literature" that "stronger

---

[82] *Ibid.*

[83] *Ibid.*

[84] *See* Guifang Yang and Keith Maskus, "Intellectual Property Rights, Licensing, and Innovation in an Endogenous Product Cycle Model," 53 *J. Int'l Econ.* 169-187 (2000).

[85] *See* Guifang Yang and Keith Maskus, "Intellectual Property Rights, Licensing, and Innovation," World Bank Policy Research Working Paper 2973, February 2003, *available at* <www.worldbank.org/research/trade/archive.html>.

[86] Guifang Yang and Keith Maskus, "Intellectual Property Rights, Licensing, and Innovation," *ibid*, at 37.

global protection of the fruits of R&D should encourage innovation" and facilitate transfer of technology.[87]

An NBER Working Paper co-authored by Lee Branstetter, Raymond Fisman, and Fritz Foley identified evidence that the existing international IPR regime seemed to increase the flow of royalty payments from affiliates to their parents.[88] This is more to do with transfer pricing and using royalties as a tax deductible form of dividend – this is particularly so in states where there are requirements for corporations to have local participation in ownership.[89] "An increase in the magnitude of licensing payments reflects either an increase in the price of ongoing technology flows or the importation of advanced technologies in the post-reform period."[90] Branstetter and Fisman's analytical examination of international patent filings confirms that "some component of the increased licensing revenue flows represents the introduction of advanced technology" and supports the belief that "improvements in IPR result in real increases in technology transfer within multinational enterprises."[91]

On the other side, however, opponents such as Abbott and Cottler, maintain that stronger IPR protection counteract the public interest by transferring royalties to multinational corporations headquartered in a few super economies and thus of benefit only to those in which such corporations are domiciled notably the United States, the EU and Japan.[92]

The Report of the Commission on IPR also presents a different point of view.[93] It suggests that "the determinants of effective technology transfer are many and various," and the "[a]bility of countries to absorb knowledge from elsewhere and then adapt it for their own purposes is of crucial importance."[94] For this a country requires the enhancement of local capacity building through promoting efficient educational programmes, facilitating active R&D strategies, and developing appropriate institutions "without which even technology transfer on the most advantageous terms is unlikely to succeed."[95]

---

[87]   *Ibid*, at 5.
[88]   Lee G. Branstetter *et al*, "Do Stronger Intellectual Property Rights Increase International Technology Transfer?" Empirical Evidence from U.S. Firm-Level Panel Data, *NBER Working Paper*, November 2002.
[89]   *Ibid*, at 2.
[90]   *Ibid*.
[91]   *Ibid*; *see* also Lee G. Branstetter *et al*, "Do Stronger Intellectual Property Rights Increase International Technology Transfer?" Empirical Evidence from U.S. Firm-Level Panel Data, *NBER Working Paper*, July 2005, at 4.
[92]   F. Abbott, T. Cottler and Francis Gurry, *The International Intellectual Property System*, The Hague: Kluwer (1999) at 909, 913 (stating that intellectual property is a crucial factor of wealth since the entire evolution of modern technologies has been framed by intellectual property laws).
[93]   "Integrating Intellectual Property Rights and Development Policy," *supra* note 62.
[94]   *Ibid*, at 28.
[95]   *Ibid*.

As concluded by the Intellectual Property Report, "for those developing countries that have acquired significant technological and innovative capabilities, there has generally been an association with 'weak' rather than 'strong' forms of IPR protection in the formative period of their economic development."[96] The analysis above suggests that IPR protection has no direct influence on the promotion of technology transfer during formative stages of development, where IPR reform met with resistance due to its high economic cost.[97]

Growing evidence tends to prove that there is no causality between IPR and FDI.[98] The case in point is China which has one of the highest piracy rates in the world, yet is still attracting substantial FDI and the transfer of technology.[99] According to a survey conducted among foreign businessmen in China, the size and potential of the market act as the determining factors that induce FDI and the transfer of technology.[100]

The understandings and interpretation of the role of IPR concerning the transfer of technology not only differ among commentators and scholars, but also differ over time. Indeed, theoretically, it is still the predominant discourse that IPR is the necessary appurtenants to the commercialisation of innovative products and that this is the necessary engine of growth in most high technology industries. It is also true that the effective protection of IPR tends to be a fundamental requirement in the ability of domestic industries contributing to economic growth, and an improved IPR protection acts as a potential catalyst for further economic development in a long run. However, in a global context, the fundamental questions as to how IPR stimulate creation and commercialisation of new knowledge, and how it can make the best contribution to the innovation required by varied domestic socio-economic environments remains unclear and calls for further studies.

2.1.5 The Optimal Level of Protection

The design of IPR has evolved quietly during the past centuries in a manner that has emphasised the value of ideas and knowledge. It is indeed inconceiv-

---

[96] *Ibid*, at 25.

[97] *Ibid*.

[98] Yahong Li, *supra* note 68, at 79.

[99] *For example*, in 1983 when China was still in its initial stage of reform and opening-up, China's real use of FDI only stood at 636 million U.S. dollars. In 2002, the figure soared to 52.743 billion dollars, an increase of 82 times as against that in 1983, outstripping that of the United States in the world. *See* "FDI fueling China's Economic Boom," *People's Daily*, December 13, 2003.

[100] Yahong Li, *supra* note 68, at 80 (quoting Paul Tackaberry, "Intellectual Property Risks in China: Their Effect on Foreign Investment and Technology Transfer," *J. Asian Bus.* (1998), at 34, 45).

able that the dazzling technologically innovative products, such as frequently upgraded computer software or biotechnology, could have been created without IPR protecting inventions from unauthorised copying so that investment in R&D can be captured and capitalised upon. In a modern society, an increasing number of companies have found their specialist knowledge one of their most valuable assets as it determines their future capacity to generate profit.

However, as the above passage has demonstrated, IPR is based on the notion of balance in that it must optimise benefit for both innovators and society at large. [101] In many developing nations which are only "beginning to exploit intellectual property of their own," [102] complaints have been raised as to the unsymmetrical and high contingent benefits they can expect from the existing IPR system, which tends to benefit foreign proprietors and discourage domestic inventors.[103] From the point of view of developing countries, stronger IPR protection may be argued as increasing the incentives for innovation and encouraging international technology transfer; however, "it also could raise the costs of acquiring new technology and products," entrenching the global terms of trade to the disadvantage of technology consumers and shifting the world trading system in favour of technology producers. [104]

In this respect, as Maskus has noted, the policy problems as extended consequences of the TRIPs regime have aroused diametrical points of view from both advocates and opponents of IPR, and the gaps are especially palpable in relation to sensitive issues such as consumer interest in affordable products, in particular patent protection of pharmaceuticals and biotechnological inventions,[105] which have been the focus of much attentions in the Doha round negotiation.[106]

The question addressed in this section is whether there is a universal optimal design of IPR or whether the design needs to vary to reflect domestic characteristics and if so what characteristics need to be taken into account.

Overprotection – Cultural Appropriation?

Faced with the dilemma of the current global IPR system, more and more scholars and political elites have discerned a tendency towards overprotection of IPR leading to anti-competitive effects that are pernicious to both develop-

---

[101] Cornish, *supra* note 30, at 11-2.

[102] *Ibid*, at 31.

[103] *See* Keith Maskus, *Intellectual Property Rights in the Global Economy* 175 (2000)(noting that "[o]wners of patents in developing countries are overwhelmingly foreign; there is little likelihood of that changing for a considerable period of time").

[104] *Ibid.*

[105] *Ibid.*

[106] *See infra* § 5.4.2

ing and developed countries by diluting important liberties and freedoms.[107] Taking copyright as an example, implementing a stronger IPR system in the short-run should be judged not only by its ability to protect the interests of owners of copyrights and related rights, but also by its commitment to avoid pitfalls caused by overprotection that may lead to cultural appropriation and hinder the pace of global civilisation. This is apparently inconsistent with the long-term goal set out by the TRIPs Agreement.

As Professor Lessig states, "[w]hile it is clear that patents spur innovation in many important fields, it is also clear that for some fields of innovation, patents do more harm than good," particularly in light of the cultural and technological divide that is hard to transcend in the foreseeable future.[108] It seems that the hypothesis linking high standards of IPR protection to trade flows and technology transfer for developing countries has not by any means been proven. On the contrary, overprotection on an improper development stage may hinder rather than stimulate the trade by which technology transfer is achieved and in the long run act to the detriment of global development.

Counterfeiting and Piracy – A Statistical Illustration

Counterfeiting, piracy,[109] and infringements of IPR in general, are reaching epidemic proportions and have become an international phenomenon in emerging economies, taking on an international dimension with dramatic repercussions on world trade.[110] Weak protection of IPR is, or used to be, part of economic planning in some developing and less-developed counties in a cer-

---

[107] Donald P. Harris, "TRIPs Rebound: An Historical Analysis of How the TRIPs Agreement Can Ricochet Back Against the United States," *Nw J. Int'l L. and Bus.* 116 (2004), at 101 (arguing that "TRIPs' focus on private interests will not only harm developing countries, but also will rebound back against the United States, thereby inflicting significant harm").

[108] Taken an empirical approach, Professor Lessig demonstrates a number of harms caused by high-level patent protection. As Lessig sees it, the global IPR regime, a system originally designed as a stimulator for innovation, has paradoxically become a weapon for safeguarding the multinational corporations, attacking cutting-edge creativity and ultimately harming public interests. *See* Lawrence Lessig, *the Future of Ideas*, Random House 259 (2001).

[109] There has been significant divergence among scholarly opinions concerning the exact definitions of counterfeiting and piracy. Nevertheless, in this book, counterfeiting refers to the production of fake products without the authority of the owner of a patent or trademark in respect of protected goods. Piracy refers to the use of the creative property of others without their permission. In general terms, counterfeiting means an infringement of an industrial property right while piracy means an infringement of copyright and related rights.

[110] *See* "Counterfeiting and Piracy: the Commission Proposes European Criminal-law Provisions to Combat Infringements of Intellectual Property Rights," Europa Press Release: IP/05/906, July 12, 2005.

tain stage of their economic development.[111] In order to expedite the process of economic development, developing countries are apt to apply for a tolerant IPR policy,[112] which allows their citizens to "steal" IPR without paying or paying less royalties.[113]

Patented pharmaceuticals have been seen as an appealing target for imitation through the production of pirated generic versions, either by applying methods disclosed in the patent itself or by accomplishing chemical analysis of the final product and the expiration of alternative synthetic routes.[114] The negative impact of the patented pharmaceuticals is not limited to developing countries; developed countries are also exposed to significant health risks associated with the untested generic drugs.[115] One official statistic shows that counterfeit drug sales are estimated to reach seventy-five billion dollars in 2010, a ninety-two percent increase from 2005.[116]

The software industry has been targeted as another vulnerable domain for piracy. A survey carried out by the International Data Corporation (IDC) research firm for the Business Software Alliance (BSA) suggests that, while fifty-one billion Pounds was spent globally in 2003 on software applications, another twenty-nine billion Pounds worth was illegitimately installed, representing fifty-eight percent equivalent of the legitimate market.[117] According to BSA, one out of every three copies of personal computing software installed in 2005 was pirated.[118] The piracy rate for commercial software was thirty-six percent, but that percentage has risen dramatically in parts of Asia and Eastern Europe.[119]

In Europe, counterfeiting and piracy affects "the proper functioning of the internal market,"[120] resulting in the loss of an estimated one hundred thousand jobs per annum in the EU.[121] The European Commission (EC) statistics show

---

[111] For a detailed explanation of stage theory of economic development, *see, infra* § 4.1.3.

[112] Fred Warshofsky, *The Patent Wars: the Battle to Own the World's Technology*, New York: John Wiley and Sons 10 (1994).

[113] *Ibid*, at 15.

[114] *See* Ronald J.C. Corbett, "Protecting and Enforcing Intellectual Property Rights in developing Countries," 35 *Int'l Lawyer* 1085 (2001).

[115] *Ibid*.

[116] *See* "Counterfeit Medicines: the Silent Epidemic," WHO News Releases 2006, *available at* <http://www.who.int/mediacentre/news/releases/2006/pr09/en/index.html>, last visited January 3, 2007.

[117] *See* "Enabling Tomorrow's Innovation," *IDC White Paper and BSA Opinion Poll*, October 2003, *available at* <http://www.globaltechsummit.net/press/IDC-CEOSurvey-2003.pdf>, last visited August 3, 2006.

[118] *See* "Study: Software Piracy Costs $34 Billion," *ZDNet News*, May 23, 2006.

[119] *Ibid*.

[120] "Counterfeiting and Piracy: Commission Proposes Criminal Law Provisions to Combat Intellectual Property Offences," IP/06/532, March 26, 2007.

[121] *See* "Memorandum to the Representatives of Community Trade Marks Registered with the Office on the Possibility of Defending the Rights of the Proprietors of Community

an increase of eight hundred percent in counterfeiting and pirated goods inter-cepted by EU Customs from 1998 to 2002.[122] In 2005, twenty-six thousand cases were dealt with, which is an increase of twenty percent over the 2004 figure.[123] In response, the EC implemented a Green Paper[124] in late 2000 aimed at combating counterfeiting and piracy within the internal market.[125]

The Green Paper shows that counterfeiting and piracy is estimated to ac-count for five to seven percent of world trade, representing two hundred to three hundred billion euros a year in lost revenue and the loss of an estimated two hundred thousand jobs worldwide.[126] It is estimated in the Green Paper that European businesses that operate internationally are losing between four hundred and eight hundred million euros in the single market and two thou-sand million euros in non-member countries.[127]

Optimal Protection – "Just Right"?

As discussed above, it may be uncontroversial to argue that countries ought to be able to have IPR standards that line up with their economic strengths and comparative advantages. Developing countries have over the last decades per-sistently called for flexibility of international rules, taking into account differ-ent economic stages of development.[128] In such developing countries, techno-logical competitiveness has not yet been established. While human capital plays the key role in promoting economic growth in the developing world, it has been insufficient to produce desirable inventions.[129] The argument is that

---

Trade Marks," OHIM, *available at* <http://oami.eu.int/EN/aspects/piracy/note.htm>, last visited October 19, 2007.

[122] *See* "EU Strategy to Enforce Intellectual Property Rights in Third Countries - Facts and Figures," Brussels, November 10, 2004.

[123] *Ibid.*

[124] From a European perspective, a Green Paper is a document published by the European Commission that is intended to stimulate discussion of chosen controversial issues at the European level. A Green Paper is usually meant to invite interested bodies or indi-viduals to participate in a consultation process and debate on the basis of the proposals they put forward. A Green Paper may also give rise to legislative developments that are then outlined in a White Paper which contains an official set of proposals in specific policy areas that are used as a vehicle for their development. *See* "Green Paper" at *Eu-ropa Glossary, available at* <http://europa.eu/scadplus/glossary/green_paper_en.htm>.

[125] The purpose of the EC Green Paper is to "assess the economic impact of combating counterfeiting and piracy in the Single Market, evaluate the effectiveness of the legisla-tion in this sphere and decide whether new initiatives are called for at Community level." For full text of the Green Paper, *see* "Green Paper on Combating Counterfeiting and Piracy in the Internal Market (1998)."

[126] *See* Green Paper, *ibid.*

[127] *Ibid.*

[128] Cornish, *supra* note 30, at 31.

[129] Mikhaelle Schiappacasse, "Intellectual Property Rights in China: Technology Transfers and Economic Development," 2 *Buff. Intell. Pro. L.J.* 166 (2003-2004)(stating that the

IPR protection in developing nations should not be as strong as that of developed nations in the early stage of their development. Overprotection of IPR is as, if not more, harmful as underprotection. To ensure the optimal level of IPR protection is advantageous not only for developing countries but also for developed countries as well. To this end, some scholars, particularly scholars from economics, have attempted to identify an optimal degree of IPR protection.[130] In reality, however, the choice for the IPR protection may be far more complex than designing a model, because the questions as to whether the optimal level of protection does exist, and whether both the overprotection and underprotection can be avoided are attributed to a number of interrelated factors. In the following sections, IPR protection will be examined from both legal and political perspectives.

2.2 IPR and WTO Agreement – A Legal Analysis

2.2.1 The Legal Concepts of IPR

In a legal context, the phrase "intellectual property" is a metaphor for a fashionable description of ideas in the form of inventions, artistic works, trade symbols and other aspirants. [131] The traditional legal classification of IPR defines the creative output protected by the law, for example, of patents, copyright and trademarks.[132] Significant social, political and technological developments over the past decades have exerted a considerable influence on how IPR is created, exploited and traded and, as a result, legal protection of IPR has become a subject of paramount importance and universal interest in not only the research but also the development and commercialisation of emerging technologies.

---

long-term beneficial effect from strengthened IPR protection in developing countries is dependent on various factors, such as increasing human capital).

[130] *See e.g.*, Yum K. Kwan & Edwin L.-C. Lai, "Intellectual Property Rights Protection and Endogenous Economic Growth," 27 *Journal of Economic Dynamics and Control* 853-873 (2003)(asserting that underprotection of IPR is much more likely than overprotection in their model).

[131] Cornish, *supra* note 30, at 3, 6-9 (noting that intellectual property "is a branch of the law which protects some of the finer manifestations of human achievement").

[132] *See* Cornish, *ibid*, at 6-11. *See also* Bently and Sherman, *supra* note 1, at 1-3.

2.2.2 The International Architecture of Protection

The protection of IPR has been an international issue since the second half of the nineteenth century.[133] The variety of international business transactions in which IPR forms a part is significant and the design of global strategies to manage intangible assets has become increasingly fashionable to the extent that the interests of international trade are safeguarded by a stable IPR system.[134] However, as developed economies have become increasingly knowledge-based and thus have far more comparative advantages than developing countries, the position of the latter is considerably marginalised. In this context, IPR protection has become a key issue involving substantially in both international law and development policy.

The strengthening of the global marketplace with the WTO Agreement and the compelling trend of the intensified globalisation have generated increasing pressure on the WTO members from developing world to liberalise their trading regimes by providing foreign nationals with national treatment. Whilst for the most part this means dismantling the protection afforded to domestic industry, in the case of IPR, the TRIPs Agreement operates to increase standards of domestic protection.

One of the significant characteristics of national law on IPR is territoriality.[135] If the IPR proprietors wish to extend recognition of their rights to other countries, they will have to make an application to the countries concerned. In this context, the "universal protection" of IPR is granted by individual countries. The lengthy and costly application process, as well as the considerable risks of procedural differences made it essential to find ways to ensure that protection obtained in one country could be extended to another. [136]

Attempts towards eliminating this obstacles was subsequently initiated in the last quarter of the nineteenth century with the main three pillars being the Paris Convention for the Protection of Industrial Property signed in 1883, the

---

[133] The first conventions concerning international protection of intellectual property are the Paris Convention for the Protection of Industrial Property (1883) and Berne Convention for the Protection of Literary and Artistic Works (1886). As a result of these two conventions, the IPR issues were converted from a national forum to an international arena. For a detailed account of this conversion, *see generally*, Vincenzo Vinciguerra, "A Brief Essay on the Importance of Time in International Conventions on Intellectual Property Rights", 39 *Akron L. Rev.* 635 (2006).

[134] *See* Adam I. Hasson, "Domestic Implementation of International Obligations: The Quest for World Patent Law Harmonization," 25 *B.C. Int'l & Comp. L. Rev.* 374 (2002).

[135] *See* Cornish, *supra* note 30, at 26 (stating that one way of expressing the close association of national policy and legal right lies in the principle of "territoriality," and this characteristic is often attributed to the major form of intellectual property).

[136] *Ibid*, at 747 (mentioning that intellectual property "forms a central barrier along the boundary between the fair and unfair competition, and ideas where the boundary should be drawn undoubtedly vary").

Berne Convention for the Protection of Literary and Artistic Work in 1886, and the Madrid Agreement Concerning the International Registration of Marks in 1891.[137] However it was not until 1967 that the World Intellectual Property Organisation (WIPO) was established to coordinate and oversee the protection of IPR generally within the member states.[138] WIPO, a United Nations specialised agency, has been particularly in promoting worldwide protection of various forms of intellectual property and assisting its members to meet their obligations for the protection of IPR.[139]

However, neither the Conventions nor the WIPO prescribed specific levels of IPR protection only the processes by which such protection can be accessed. To enable this change, the issues of IPR had to find a place on the agenda of international trade talks where it could be part of a negotiated package. The justification was that "weak protection of IPR distorts natural trading patterns and acts as an impediment to free trade."[140]

More to the point, the particular voting system of WIPO fell short of the interests of developed nations and impeded the efforts of developed countries to seek harmonised standards.[141] Accordingly, IPR protection was added to the agenda of the Uruguay Round of GATT negotiations at the request of developed countries in 1986. Since then, developed countries have started to "pull the debate away from WIPO," trying to integrate the issue of IPR with that of free trade.[142] In practical terms, this meant that negotiations over IPR were integrated into the GATT/WTO based on multilateral negotiations coupling free trade with IPR, leading to the TRIPs Agreement in Marrakesh in 1994.[143] By then, the United States and other developed countries had at last "achieved

---

[137] For full text of these two conventions, *see* Andrew Christie & Stephen Gare, *Statutes on Intellectual Property*, Blackstone's 354-8, 490-8 (2003).

[138] *See* Robert J. Pechman, "Seeking Multilateral Protection for Intellectual Property: The United States "TRIPs" Over Special 301," 7 *Minn. J. Global Trade* 179, 181 (1998) (stating that the Paris Convention left the enforcement of IPR up to each member state).

[139] While WIPO administers most of the international Conventions concerning IPR, some other agencies are also playing specific roles. For example, the UN Educational Scientific and Cultural Organisations (UNESCO), which is administering Universal Copyright Convention, is a UN institution, which has been playing an essential part in the broad areas concerning cultural diversity and pluralism.

[140] *See* Jacques Olivier and Aiting Goh, "Free Trade and Protection of Intellectual Property Rights: Can We Have One without the Other?" *Available at* <http://www.hec.fr/ hec/fr/professeur_recherche/cahier/finance/CR730.pdf>.

[141] Van Wijk and G. Junne, "Intellectual Property Protection of Advanced Technology-Changes in the Global Technology System: Implications and Options for Developing Countries," United Nations University, Institute for New Technologies, Maastricht, Working Paper No10 (1993).

[142] Joshua J Simons, "Cooperation and Coercion: The Protection of Intellectual Property in Developing Countries," 11 *Bond L.Rev.* 60 (1999).

[143] *Ibid.*

their objective of incorporating internationally enforceable IPR norms into the world trading system."[144]

Upon its establishment, the TRIPs Agreement has been hailed as the "milestone" in the development of international IPR regime at the end of the twentieth century,[145] and "the most far-reaching and comprehensive legal system ever concluded at the multinational level in the area of IPR,"[146] which "revolutionised international intellectual property law."[147]

Although the TRIPs Agreement does not impose substantial provisions and create a unitary framework for the IPR protection,[148] it does impose minimum international standards for the protection of IPR by which WTO members are obliged to demonstrate full compliance with the substantive obligations of the primary international intellectual property conventions, including the Berne Convention and the Paris Convention.[149] In its preamble, TRIPs specified as one of its objectives "to reduce impediments to international trade, to promote effective protection of IPR, and to ensure that measures to enforce IPR do not become barriers to legitimate trade."[150] In other words, although TRIPs does not introduce a uniform set of substantial rules, by explicitly underlining the obligation of each member to take measures to eliminate abuses of IPR, it potentially and indirectly establishes leverage against different member states.

The establishment of TRIPs within the WTO framework of the multilateral agreement is perhaps the most ambitious and adventurous attempt to harmonise IPR on a worldwide scale,[151] not least because TRIPs enables enforcement by private parties at the national level,[152] and where this fails to provide an effective remedy, it enables enforcement by states at an international level,[153] using "WTO's comparatively hard-edged dispute settlement mechanism in

---

[144] Helfer, "Regime Shifting," *supra* note 71, at 23.

[145] *See* Vincent Chiappetta, "The Desirability of Agreeing to Disagree: The WTO, TRIPs, International IPR Exhaustion and a Few Other Things," *21 Mich. J. Int'l L.* 333, 335-336, 368 (2000).

[146] *See e.g.*, Carlos M. Correa and Abdulqawi A.Yusuf, *Intellectual Property and International Trade: The TRIPs Agreement,* London: Kluwer Law International 17 (1998); Charles McManis, "Intellectual Property and International Mergers and Acquisitions," *66 Univ. Cincinnati L. Rev.* 1283, 1286 (1998).

[147] Helfer, *supra* note 71, at 23.

[148] Eric Allen Engle, "When is Fair Use Fair?: A Comparison of E.U. and U.S. Intellectual Property Law," 15 *Transnat'l L.* 187 (2002).

[149] Article 1 of TRIPs Agreement, *supra* note 2.

[150] *See* preface of Agreement on Trade Related Aspects of Intellectual Property Right, ANNEX 1C of The Uruguay Round Final Act.

[151] Paul Demaret, "The metamorphoses of the GATT: from the Havana Charter to the World Trade Organization, 34 *Colum. J. Transnat'l L.*162 (1995).

[152] Article 41-60 of TRIPs provides civil and administrative procedures and remedies, as well as provisional measures to prevent IPR infringement. Article 61 provides criminal procedure. *See* TRIPs Article 61.

[153] Donald P. Harris, *supra* note 107, at 116.

which treaty bargains are enforced through mandatory adjudication backed up by the threat of retaliatory sanctions."[154] For these reasons it exercises a profound influence on domestic legislation and trade policy and in this regard has increasingly marginalised the international IPR agreements negotiated under the auspices of the WIPO.

Indeed, the harmonising effect of TRIPs is significant. The United States has, for example, instituted WTO dispute settlement proceedings against Sweden, Ireland, Denmark, Greece, and the European Union.[155] In 1998, the United States announced the initiation of WTO dispute settlement proceedings against Greece concerning rampant television piracy in Greece and their failure to comply with the enforcement provisions of the TRIPs Agreement.[156] To address such concerns, Greece swiftly enacted legislation that provided additional administrative measures and procedures to strengthen its IPR enforcement system.[157] Similarly, in responding to external pressure, in late 1999, Sweden amended its intellectual property laws to provide prompt and effective provisional relief in civil enforcement proceedings.[158] In February 1998, Ireland committed to enact comprehensive copyright reform legislation and, in June 1998, passed expedited legislation increasing criminal penalties for copyright infringement and addressing other enforcement issues.[159] Denmark has duly established a Special Legislative Committee to consider the issues addressed by the United States and proposed options for amending its law to strengthen provisional remedies available to IPR holders.[160]

---

[154] Laurence R. Helfer, "Regime Shifting," *supra* note 71, at 2.

[155] To date, a number of cases have ever been brought to the WTO dispute settlement procedure. Among the early WTO complaints, the cases involving Sweden and Denmark were brought for failure to provide *ex parte* civil remedies, in violation of Article 50 of TRIPs, while the cases against Ireland and Greece (the latter for television piracy) were brought for violations of Articles 41 and 61. *See* "IIPA Paper on Copyright Enforcement under the TRIPs Agreement October 2004," IIPA, *available at* <http://www.iipa.com/rbi/2004_Oct19_ TRIPS.pdf>. The WTO complaint against China in April 2007 was a recent case which will be discussed in the following chapters.

[156] *See* "2000 Special 301 Report," Consulate General of the United States in Hong Kong & Macau, *available at* <http://hongkong.usconsulate.gov/uploads/images/J6EH6KGM-c0kwdU0CSnXhA/usinfo_301_00-special.pdf>.

[157] *Ibid.*

[158] *See* "USTU Announces Results of Special 301 Annual Review," USTR Press Releases, May 1, 1998, at 22, *available at* <http://hongkong.usconsulate.gov/uploads/images/Q8iJECEI_jcMpryiznqVkw/usinfo_301_1998050101.pdf >.

[159] "2000 Special 301 Report," *supra* note 155.

[160] "USTU Announces Results of Special 301 Annual Review," *supra* note 158, at 7, 23.

2.2.3 The "Transplant" of TRIPs: A Comparative Law Perspective

Developing nations have made a dramatic turn towards market-orientated policies over the past decades.[161] As Susan Sell observes, some years ago, developing nations were engaged in pressing for a New International Economic Order (NIEO)[162] based on economic nationalism, import substitution, and the rejection of comparative advantage and global liberalism.[163] Today, democratisation and globalisation have had a significant impact on "increase[ing] the number of legal transplants" and, as a consequence, "most major legislation [in developing countries] now has a foreign component."[164] As a notable instance, the establishment of the TRIPs regime has changed the scene of the IPR of the developing world beyond recognition, and aroused energetic legislative zeal that makes it rather difficult to keep pace with.[165] What has occasioned these changes?

Transplantation and Participation: A Reluctant Deal?

The energetic legislative zeal in the developing world reflects the fact that developing countries have adjusted their foreign policy as a strategy to avoid being marginalised in the global trading system. As Gunther Teubner describes, the invisible social networks, invisible professional communities, and invisible transborder markets have transcended territorial boundaries, making the global law of business transactions visible.[166] In such an increasingly open global

---

[161] Susan K. Sell, "Intellectual Property Protection and Antitrust in the Developing World: Crisis, Coercion, and Choice," in *Power and Ideas: North-South Politics of Intellectual Property and Antitrust*, State University of New York Press 175 (1995).

[162] The New International Economic Order, a broad model for restructuring the world economy, first put forward at a summit meeting of the non-aligned movement in early 1970s where developing nations voiced their opinions on enhanced economic opportunities. The NIEO has historically defined itself in opposition to the workings of the conventional international political agenda in which developing countries have been marginalised. For a further discussion, *see* Michael Hudson, *Global Fracture: The New International Economic Order*, Pluto Press (2005); Robert Gilpin, *Global Political Economy: Understanding the International Economic Order*, Princeton University Press (2001).

[163] Sell, *supra note* 161, at 175.

[164] *See* Jonathan M. Miller, "A Typology of Legal Transplants: Using Sociology, Legal History and Argentine Examples to Explain the Transplant Process," 51 *Am. J. Comp. L.* 839 (2003).

[165] Christopher Heath, "Intellectual Property Rights in Asia – Projects, Programmes and Developments," Online Publication of Max Planck Institute for Intellectual Property, Competition and Tax Law, *available at* <http://www.intellecprop.mpg.de/Online-Publikationen/Heath-Ipeaover.htm>.

[166] Gunther Teubner, "'Global Bukowina': Legal Pluralism in the World Society," at *Global Law without a State* (Gunther Teubner ed.), Dartmouth Publishing Group 3-7 (1997).

economy, it is inevitable for developing nations to respond to multinational treaties and to harmonise the participating countries' laws.[167] In addition, these countries are fully aware that there would be no way of claiming good records in areas such as international human rights and protection of the environment without importing some foreign or international models; similarly, there would be no way of engaging in global market or expecting foreign investment without moving their legal regimes towards international commercial standards.[168] As a result, upon the establishment of the WTO, the obligations to impose a series of international legal standards extended rapidly to the entire WTO members.

Earlier legal transplants, including the reception of Roman law in Europe, the enactment of the Chinese codes in Eastern and Southeastern Asia, and the introduction of Spanish and Portuguese laws to Latin America, have been carried on as ubiquitous practice for centuries.[169] Substantial literature has been generated on the concept of legal transplants in the context of comparative law. However, research to date leads to substantial divergence mainly embedded in bifurcated propositions of optimists and sceptics of the theory. As noted by Richard Small, in essence, the debate over this point "revolves around the question of whether and to what extent law is transferable between nations under different cultural environment."[170] While scholars such as Legrand link the fundamental differences between legal systems and cultural values in a strict sense, casting doubt over the possibility of legal transplant,[171] Alan Watson emphasises the autonomous nature of law, maintaining that there is no inherent relationship between law and the society in which it operates.[172] The theory put forward by Watson characterises the proposition that legal trans-

---

[167] See Miller, "A Typology of Legal Transplants," *supra* note 162, at 840. *See* also Vernon Valentine Palmer (ed.), *Louisiana: Microcosm of a Mixed Jurisdiction*, Carolina Academic Press 4 (1999)(asserting that "there doesn't exist in the modern world a pure judicial system formed without exterior influence"). Similar analysis can also be found in William Twining, *Globalisation and Legal Theory* (2000)(exploring globalisation and its implications for legal theory).

[168] *Ibid.*

[169] Daniel Berkowitz, *et al,* "The Transplant Effect," 51 *Am. J. Comp. L.* 172 (2003).

[170] *See* Richard G. Small, "Towards a Theory of Contextual Transplants," 19 *Emory Int'l L. Rev.* 1431 (2005).

[171] Pierre Legrand, "The Impossibility of 'Legal Transplants,'" 4 *Maastricht J. Eur. & Comp. L.* 114 (1997).

[172] Alan Watson, "Comparative Law and Legal Change", 37 *Cambridge L. J.* 313-4 (1978) (mentioning that "[t]here is no exact, fixed, close, complete, or necessary correlation between social, economic, or political circumstances and a system of rules of private law"); Watson, *The Evolution of Law*, 119 (1985) stating that "[l]aw is treated as existing in its own right [and...] has to be justified in its own terms[...]. This two features make law inherently conservative." For a detailed introduction of Watson's work and his theories, *see* William Ewald, "Comparative Jurisprudence (II): The Logic of Legal Transplants," 43 *Am. J. Comp. L.*, 489 (1995).

plants are socially feasible,[173] nevertheless, many commentators have empha-sised that a successful legal change through transplantation requires some level of domestic adaptation in an economic, political and cultural context.[174] During the transplanting process, legality can only be determined by the abil-ity of a receiving country "to give meaning to the transplanted formal legal or-der and to apply it within the context of its own socioeconomic conditions."[175] It may be true that, while the transferability is compelling, a "fitting-in" proc-ess is necessary to ensure effectiveness of a transplant in a unique socioeco-nomic environment. As Francis Cardinal George describes, neglecting the cul-tural reception process in legal transplantation under different social and ethi-cal environment amounts to "viewing law as the engine driving the cultural train," and is destined to fail.[176] Legal transplants are feasible, but the cultural adaptation is essential.

In this context, the enthusiastic and energetic legal transplants that take place in developing countries are often, if not always, outcomes of political expediency – developing countries accept these laws as part of a process of participation in international affairs. As a result, as noted by Miller, in many circumstances, developing countries initiate "transplants whose acceptance is motivated by a desire to please foreign states, individuals or entities," and to "facilitate international commerce."[177] It is unsurprising that developing coun-tries may have transplanted a whole set of Western styled legal regimes with-out the adaptation process.

TRIPs Norms: A "Hijacked Issue"?

Intellectual property law has posed as a radically new form of legal transplant in developing countries since it usually has no counterpart in the indigenous legal traditions of the participating states. However, upon the establishment of the TRIPs Agreement, the harmonised IPR global network, which had been owned exclusively by developed countries, extended to the developing world, including many developing countries whose previous commitment to IPR pro-tection was "nonexistent or at best equivocal."[178] The transplantation of intel-

---

[173] Alan Watson, *Legal Transplants: An Approach to Comparative Law* 7 (1993).

[174] *See* Kahn-Freund, "On Uses and Misuses of Comparative Law," 37 *Mod. L. Rev.* (1974), at 12-13; Ugo Mattei, "Efficiency in Legal Transplants: An Essay in Compara-tive Law and Economics," 14 *Int'l Rev. L. & Econ.*16, 19 (1994). *See* also William Ewald, "Comparative Jurisprudence (II): The Logic of Legal Transplants," 43 *Am. J. Comp. L.* 489 (1995) (emphasising the causal link between law and society). *See* also, Nicholas H. D. Foster, "Transmigration and Transferability of Commercial Law in a Globalized World," in Andrew Harding & Esin Orucu (eds.), *Comparative Law in the 21st Century*, Kluwer Law International 55, 58-9 (2002).

[175] Daniel Berkowitz, *et al,* "The Transplant Effect," 51 *Am. J. Comp. L.* 179 (2003).

[176] Francis Cardinal George, "Law and Culture," 1 *Ave Maria L. Rev.* 6 (2003).

[177] *See* Miller, *supra* note 164, at 847.

[178] Helfer, *supra* note 71, at 23.

lectual property law via the WTO has become one of the most visible fields of legal reform imposed by industrialised nations in the context of neoliberal globalisation advocated as the "Washington Consensus,"[179] and it is of practical significance to analyse the transplantation of TRIPs as an important international treaty from perspective of comparative law.

However, in the arena of TRIPs, any transplanted intellectual property structure only works properly after recasting the indigenous tradition of that imported law in the image of its original model. An overriding concern here is that, this "fitting-in" process in launching a substantial set of intellectual property protection system is usually lengthy and sometimes costly, but developed countries have a tendency to be geared towards pragmatism and a desire for prompt returns. As Assafa Endeshaw claimed, the "universal templates" created in the international lawmaking process are modelled after laws in developed countries and fail to take into consideration the socio-economic circumstances of developing and less-developed countries.[180] It should not be unexpected that in their implementation of TRIPs, developing countries may be reluctant to exceed the minimum necessary to achieve compliance and gain protection against possible retaliation from their trading partners. In this connection implementation will inevitably require domestic legislation. It is therefore not surprising that, while the transplant of TRIPs has ostensibly been embraced by almost all the countries, there remain unresolved tensions and debates as to the legal reform in light of law and development.

As Nick Foster has demonstrated, the manner of a recipient may affect, if not determine, the effectiveness of an importing law – if, for instance, a law is received passively through "imposition by a colonial power," this law may lack natural affinity, and the attitude towards enforcing it may be contrastingly different from law adopted actively and willingly.[181] Legal reform, in this context, has been depicted as "externally-dictated transplants" for developing countries.[182] In the area of world trade and intellectual property, many developing countries adopted high level standards of IPR due to the coercive demand of developed countries.[183]

---

[179] The phrase "Washington Consensus" is a concept synonymous with "neoliberalism" or "neoliberal globalisation" in the context of trade and development. It was initially expressed in late 1980s by John Williamson who coined the ideology for globalisation. For a comprehensive account of the phrase, see Tamara Lothian, "The Democratized Market Economy in Latin America (and Elsewhere): An Exercise in Institutional Thinking within Law and Political Economy," 28 *Cornell Int'l L.J.* 175-9 (1995).

[180] Assafa Endeshaw, "The Paradox of Intellectual Property Lawmaking in the New Millennium: Universal Templates as Terms of Surrender for Non-industrial Nations; Piracy as an Offshoot," 10 *Cardozo J. Int'l & Comp. L.* 47 (2002).

[181] Nicholas H. D. Foster, "Company Law Theory in Comparative Perspective: England and France," 48 *Am. J. Comp. L.* 612 (2000).

[182] *See* Miller, *supra* note 164, at 847.

[183] *Ibid*, at 848; for a comparative analysis of legal transplants, *see infra* § 6.2.3 & § 6.5.1.

While the degree of external pressure may affect acceptance of a transplanting law, the real success of a transplant depends on the extent of the participation of the recipient in the transplanting process and the genuine interests of the state to strengthen its protection mechanism. An externally-dictated transplant during its initial phase is apt to fail if the domestic incentives or external coercions disappear;[184] however, as has been demonstrated, "one clear motivation for a legal transplant is the presence in the receiving country of individuals interested in investing in the transplanted legal system so that they can obtain political or economic benefits from their investment."[185] Otherwise, the advocates are doing little more than breed disrespect for laws that are perceived by the recipients as "out of touch" with reality, making the laws colourful but unenforceable.[186] At the point where the new concept of IPR is slowly filtering into people's minds, and sufficient individuals such as inventors, authors and other IPR appropriators are tempted in an improved IPR standards, the legal transplant may take root during the process of local adaptations and become domestically assimilated and gradually indigenised.

In this context, from an objective perspective, TRIPs may well deserve criticism for its potentially asymmetric effects across countries despite the praise it has enjoyed as a milestone in world IPR harmonisation.[187] As Profes-

---

[184] *Ibid*, at 868.

[185] This theory creates legal base for what has been described as "entrepreneurial transplants." *See ibid*, at 850.

[186] Francis Cardinal George, *supra* note 238.

[187] *The Political Economy of International Trade Law*, Essays in Honour of Robert E. Hudec, Edited by Daniel L. M. Kennedy and James D. Southwick, Cambridge University Press 296-327 (2002) (where the authors argues that "[t]he relationship to trade is minimal and, indeed, often negative, so the term 'Trade-Related-Intellectual-Property' is close to being an oxymoron;" John F. Duffy, "Harmony and Diversity in Global Patent Law," 17 *Berkeley Tech. J.* 685 (2002) (the author, while acknowledging the value of certain harmonisation at national level, argues that "uniformity […] makes the law unresponsive to local variations, eliminates interjurisdictional competition and decreases the possibilities for legal experimentation"). Marci A. Hamilton, "The TRIPs Agreement: Imperialistic, Outdated, and Overprotective," Adam D. Moore (ed.), *Intellectual Property: Moral, Legal, and International Dilemmas* (1997)(arguing that TRIPs Agreement imposes a western-styled intellectual property legal regime, which is not necessarily the Ideal Paradigm for the developing world; Jerome H. Reichman, "Intellectual Property in International Trade: Opportunities and Risks of a GATT Connection," 22 *Vanderbilt J. Trans'l L.* 747-891 (1989)(discussing the violation of principle of economic sovereignty and deriving a set of analytical propositions to guide a TRIPs negotiation conducted in the spirit of cooperation and good faith); *see* also T. N. Srinivasan, *the TRIPS Agreement: A Comment Inspired by Frederick Abbott's Presentation* (1998)(arguing that "it was a colossal mistake to have included TRIPs in the WTO, as one of the agreements that was part of the single-undertaking framework of the Uruguay Round agreement, for at least two reasons: First, whatever be the merits of strengthening IPR protection around the world, incorporating IPR in the WTO framework by merely asserting that such protection is trade-related, seems primarily for the purpose of legitimizing the use of trade policy instruments to enforce IPR protection").

sor Vincent Chiappetta pointed out, the current harmonisation effort is "ill-conceived and unsupportable."[188] By attracting or forcing countries to adopt "universal' standards," the achievement of harmonisation could "mark 'progress' along an ill-defined path prematurely taken, or indeed the wrong path entirely."[189] Not only is there no international consensus regarding the inherent superiority of a market economics approach to IPR, "much work remains to be done regarding the related distributional inequities" it generates to ensure developing countries genuinely benefit from refocusing and implementing the core mission of the world trading system.[190] For these reasons, the TRIPs transplantation process did not generate the consensus in favour of higher IPR protection standards that some observers had predicted. Instead, as noted by Helfer, it fostered a growing belief, at least in the developing world, that "TRIPs was a hijacked provision" that should be resisted rather than embraced.[191]

TRIPs Standard: A One-Size-Fits-All Approach?

As Martin Khor points out, while TRIPs has established a new international IPR arena based on the minimum standards in contrast to previous flexibility to afford differentiated protection, no distinction has ever been made to accommodate the varied circumstances of the countries, except for the length of transition periods.[192] Without a natural consistency between IPR and the level of domestic adaptation, enforcement is likely to be sporadic.[193] It is only when IPR is consistent with social realities that enforcement becomes reliable. Applying a "one-size-fits-all" approach to counties of widely differing stages of development and innovation capacities was not likely to yield the best result.[194] Against this background, critical issues involving creating a new international standard of IPR protection are being discussed.[195] However, before a

---

[188] Vincent Chiappetta, "TRIP-ping Over Business Method Patents," 37 *Vanderbilt J. Trans'l L,* 181-2 (2004).

[189] *Ibid.*

[190] *Ibid.*

[191] Helfer, *supra* note 71, at 24.

[192] *See* Martin Khor, "How Intellectual Property Rights Could Work Better for Developing Countries and Poor People," A Remark at the Conference of the Commission on Intellectual Property Rights, February 21-22, 2002.

[193] Stefan Kirchanski, "Protection of US Patent Rights in Developing Countries: US Efforts to Enforce Pharmaceutical Patents in Thailand," 16 *Loy. L.A. Int'l & Comp. L. Rev.* 569, 598 (1994).

[194] *The Political Economy of International Trade Law, supra* note 185, 296-327 (where the authors suggest that "there is a death of empirical research" on this area because it is probably too early for an assessment; however, "[t]he evidence that does exist suggests that payoffs thus far have been limited at bet").

[195] For example, in February 2003, the United Nations Development Programme (UNDP) released a report entitled "Making Global Trade Work for People." It provides a critical

new international standard is created in the unpredictable future, it is worthwhile to consider the possibility of choice between different options as a temporary arrangement.

Among developing countries, two groups may be differentiated. The first comprises countries that have legislation which conforms to a considerable degree with international norms. [196] This may be due to the coercive effect of external pressures or the emergence and mobilisation of internal vested interests. In these countries, the level of substantive adjustment required may not be very significant, and may just need updating to reflect new rights such as layout designs of integrated circuits [197] or to tighten enforcement of IPR.[198]

A second group comprises those countries where the implementation of TRIPs falls far short of that required, and whose IPR, if they exist, fail to respond to the interests protected by TRIPs. Here there may be increasing structural problems preventing implementation that requires to be resolved. The IPR conceived for these types of countries fail to respond to the kind of questions that were raised and dealt with in developed countries way back through the centuries of their evolutions.[199] Here again how best to proceed may vary considerably in accordance with the level of economic and technological development of the country concerned. [200]

---

and valuable counterpoint to the exiting global trade mechanism, stating that the "relevance of TRIPs Agreement is highly questionable for large parts of the developing world." The report thus concluded that developing nations need to "begin dialogues to replace TRIPs" with "alternate intellectual property paradigms" and, in the interim, to "modify" in any way the agreement is interpreted and implemented. *See,* Kamal Malhotra, *Making Global Trade Work for People,* UN Development Programme (2003). Another empirical study, "Integrating Intellectual Property Rights and Development Policy – Report of CIPR," was published in September 2002. This report challenges the dominant principles of TRIPs, asserting that expansion of the IPR may lead to policy failure if differentiated circumstances of developed and developing countries are not taken into account. *See* "Integrating Intellectual Property Rights and Development Policy," *supra* note 62, at 13-30.

[196] *The TRIPs Agreement: A Guide for the South, The Uruguay Round Agreement on Trade-Related Intellectual Property Rights*, South Centre, Geneva (1997), at 33.

[197] *Ibid.*

[198] What can be characterised is enforcement procedures mandated by Part III of TRIPs, comprising no less than 20 Articles (Arts 41-61) on the enforcement of IPR.

[199] *See, generally,* Assafa Endenshaw, *Intellectual Property Policy for Non-Industrial Countries*, Dartmouth (1996), at 98.

[200] *The TRIPs Agreement: A Guide for the South, supra* note 196, at 34.

2.3 IPR and Development Policy – A Political Analysis

As many scholars and commentators suggest, the history of IPR is best not left to lawyers alone,[201] but left for a systematic analysis involving an interdisciplinary approach. Up to this point, it is necessary to examine the link between IPR protection and development issues in a political perspective.

2.3.1 Ideology of IPR Protection

In the context of political economy, the international protection of IPR refers, in large part, to the protection between developed and developing countries. As analysed previously, developed countries normally bear the brunt of IPR-related policies, while developing countries are exposed as far more passive, vulnerable and sentimental. Indeed, developing nations are sensitive to the standard of IPR protection set by TRIPs and the tendency to extend this bilaterally. Therefore, these countries maintain that different economic sophistication calls for different level of IPR protection.[202] These countries claim that, under the new norms set by TRIPs, something should be done to enable marginalised developing countries to lessen the heavy social cost imposed by the TRIPs standards,[203] and increase the gains accruing from higher international IPR protection.

Different commentators present different ideological and epistemological stances. David Demiray points out that a key motivation behind the introduction of TRIPs was a desire of developed states to protect their accrued competitive technological advantage in the face of the threats and opportunities of globalisation.[204] Harmonised IPR regime serves as a powerful political tool enabling trans-national corporations to internationalise the different phases of production without jeopardising IPR protection.[205] As noted by Jerome Reichman, the actual objective of TRIPs is merely to establish a global regime

---

[201] *See, e.g.*, Christopher May, *A Global Political Economy of Intellectual Property Rights: The New Enclosures?* 11-3 The Routledge (2000) (maintaining that intellectual property is a global political issue).

[202] *See, e.g.*, Marci Hamilton, "The TRIPs Agreement: Imperialistic, Outdated, and Over-protective, 29 *Vanderbilt J. of Trans'l L.* 613 (1996); A. Samuel Oddi, "TRIPs - Natural Rights and a 'Polite Form of Economic Imperialism,'" 29 *Vanderbilt J. of Trans'l L.* 415 (1996).

[203] These social costs, in developing nation's point of view, include costs towards attainment of necessary technologies, pursuit of fulfillment of the provision of social measures, and the access to health care and essencial medicines. *See, e.g.*, "Integrating Intellectual Property Rights and Development Policy," *supra* note 62.

[204] A. David Demiray, "Intellectual Property and the External Power of the European Community: The New Extension," 16 *Mich. J. of Int'l L.* (1995), at 187, 200.

[205] Kim Nayyer, "Globalisation of Information: Intellectual Property Law Implications," 7(1) *First Monday* (2002).

for proprietary rights regardless of the "anti-competitive effects under this hybrid regime of exclusive property rights proliferating in the developed countries."[206] In this sense, the functional outcome of TRIPs is, to some extent, to consolidate the global hegemony of a few developed nations.[207] By challenging the political limits of national sovereignty, TRIPs provisions require that member states provide higher protection for IPR thus providing a point of leverage for developed states to enhance standards under bilateral negotiations which has been viewed "as a drive to overcome pre-existing territorial limitations on intellectual property rights." [208]

A case in point is the United States. The percentage value of U.S. intellectual property exports skyrocketed in the second half of the twentieth century, and thus the U.S. was increasingly concerned about the erosion of its competitiveness caused by the widespread "piracy" occurring in developing countries.[209] By reducing piracy, the U.S. would "recapture the revenue involved diverting it to enhance profit taking."[210]

As Kim Nayer points out, assessment of the impact of the international harmonisation of IPR is "a value-laden exercise, partly driven by ideology." [211] For the bulk of developing countries, adopting a Western-style regime for IPR as an ideal paradigm is not necessarily the most predictable way of bringing visible and tangible benefits to developing countries as promised.

2.3.2 Development-related Aspects for IPR (DRIPs)

While there have long been controversies in the field of international IPR between developing and developed countries, it is perhaps true that the emerging global IPR system, like the "two-edged sword," comes with dual effect of stimulation and suppression to the society. [212] As suggested in the Report of the Commission on Intellectual Property Rights (CIPR, UK),[213] the crucial issue here is not whether it promotes trade or encourages transfer of technology, as we discussed in the previous sections, but how it fosters or hinders developing

---

[206] Jerome H. Reichman, "From Free Riders to Fair Followers: Global Competition under the TRIPs Agreement," 29 *N.Y.U. J. Int'l L. & Pol.* 16, 27 (1996).

[207] Engle, *supra* note 148, at 215.

[208] *See* Anthony D'Amato and Doris Estelle Long (eds.), *International Intellectual Property Law* 237 (1998).

[209] Donald P. Harris, *supra* note 107, at 138.

[210] *Ibid.*

[211] Nayyer, *supra* note 205.

[212] Shi, "The Impact of TRIPs on the Protection of Intellectual Property Rights in China," *supra* note 9, at 58-59.

[213] CIPR, *supra* note 62; for a detailed introduction of CIPR, *see* the official website of the Commission, *available at* <http://www.iprcommission.org/>.

countries in gaining access to technological and cultural resources that they require for their development needs. [214]

IPR rules are fundamentally associated with the attainment of sustainable development. They can influence the technology dissemination between the developed and developing world, impact the control that communities have over their traditional knowledge, and affect the access to medicines.[215] The TRIPs Agreement is also seen as an attempt to develop a new frontier for patent protection towards life forms and biological materials that has given rise to concerns over the impact of genetically modified organisms on the environment, basic food and public health, traditional knowledge, and biodiversity management. In this connection, IPR internationalisation will inevitably require domestic adaptation. Thus developing countries may implement the TRIPs Agreement in accordance with their own legal system, taking into account public interests as well as the overall community development.

While the role of the TRIPs Agreement in the global trading system is controversial, we are by no means pessimists towards the future of the WTO. It is our expectation, however, that the WTO is to be refocused on its long-term mission to tackle poverty and difference, and sustainable development reflects a prominent element of that mission. For example, according to the principles of the WTO, the trading system "should be more accommodating for less developed countries, giving them more time to adjust, greater flexibility, and more privileges."[216]

Sustainable Development

Sustainable development is "a two-word phrase with a thousand meanings."[217] It focuses on whole systems, long range planning, and front-end solutions, and seeks out partnerships between government, business as well as community and private sectors. [218] In doing so it encompasses, and opens to debate other vital issues such as human development, social justice, and promotion of democracy. [219]

The principle components of sustainable development emerged at the 1972 United Nations Conference on the Human Environment in Stockholm, Swe-

---

[214] *See* "Integrating Intellectual Property Rights and Development Policy," *supra* note 62, Chapter 1.

[215] "Addendum to Accreditation of Non-governmental Organisation," Standing Committee on the Law of Patents, Tenth Session, Geneva, May 10 to 14, 2004, World Intellectual Property Organisation, Geneva, *available at* <http://www.wipo.int/edocs/mdocs/scp/en/scp10/scp_10_7_add-annex1.pdf>.

[216] Principles of the trading system, Understanding the WTO, *supra* note 7, Chapter 1.

[217] Douglas R. Porter, *et al, The Practice of Sustainable Development*, Urban Land Institute 1-3 (2000).

[218] *Ibid.*

[219] *Ibid.*

den.[220] The central themes of the conference included the interdependence of human beings and the natural environment, the interactions between economic grown and social, environmental protection development.[221]

The most extensive examination of the relationship between sustainable development and IPR has been the Report of CIPR entitled "Integrating Intellectual Property Rights and Development Policy."[222] The Commission concluded that "development objectives needed to be integrated into the making of policy on IPR, both nationally and internationally and the report details both how national IPR regimes could best be designed to benefit developing countries within the context of international agreements, including TRIPs and also how the international regime itself might be beneficially developed."[223] In particular, it suggested broadening the contextual framework within which IPR is normally considered so as to include complementary regulation such as controlling anti-competitive practices through competition policy and law.[224]

In light of sustainable development, the implementation of TRIPs without adequate flexibility may limit the freedom of the developing members to shape their IPR strategies in accordance with their socio-economic conditions and ultimately impedes development.[225] From this perspective, sustainable development and intellectual property are intimately connected, particularly in the context of the Doha Development Agenda,[226] which highlights the expected contribution of trade towards achieving sustainable development.

Economic, Environmental and Social Development

Both economic development and economic growth have close linage with sustainable development. Growth refers to getting *bigger* – a quantitative increase, and development refers to getting *better* – a qualitative change.[227] In an effort to facilitate economic development, a community should have to pursue growth at some point in the development. However it also has to allocate the benefits of growth to the ends of development rather than enriching domestic vested interests. In this regard, free trade undermines the grip of local monopolies operating on government license, but does the TRIPs agreement

---

[220] Shanna L. Halpern, "The United Nations, Conference on Environment and Development: Process and Documentation," *available at* <www.ciesin.org/docs/008-585/unced-intro.html>.

[221] Porter, *et al*, *supra* note 216, at 1-3.

[222] "Integrating Intellectual Property Rights and Development Policy," *supra* note 62.

[223] *Ibid.*

[224] *Ibid*, preface, at iii-iv.

[225] *See, A Guide for the South, supra* note 196, at 33.

[226] *See infra* Chapter § 5.4.2.

[227] Ralph Nader and Jerry Brown, *The Case Against Free Trade: GATT, NAFTA, and the Globalization of Corporate Power*, North Atlantic 132 (1993)(illustrating that grown is "quantitative increase in physical size" whereas development is "qualitative change, realisation of potentialities, transition to a fuller or better state").

merely replace internal monopolies with external ones? Economic development requires not only an increase in wealth, but increased diversity in its allocation and attention to the quality of the consequences.

Need for Basic Food and Public Health

As noted by some commentators, the universal protection of IPR under the TRIPs Agreement "presents a paradox in that it runs against the basic tenets of liberalisation and favours monopoly restriction."[228] Within the global IPR regime, abuse of the monopoly power may lead to undesirable or even disastrous social consequences if such essential matters as human health or access to food were "held hostage."[229] Here the problem is ensuring that the monopoly protection afforded by IPR facilitate rather than impede the progressive realisation of the rights to food, health, and access to information that contribute to human welfare. There is a growing concern that the strength of industry influence over developed state policy positions on IPR, undermines the safeguarding of other rights, which have less prominence in the domestic politics of developed states, but are crucial to the policy priorities of developing states.

Traditional Knowledge

Traditional knowledge, also known as indigenous knowledge, generally refers to the matured long-standing traditions and practices of regional, indigenous, or local communities passed down through generations.[230] The fact that the current global IPR regime was set by developed countries has also led to gaps in the range of rights protected. Some of these omissions, most notably traditional knowledge, have emerged into the Doha Development Agenda as examples of abuse. For instance, traditional knowledge as to the medicinal use of particular plants is vulnerable to misappropriation by being decontextualised and refined into basic fundamental processes, which can then be patented notwithstanding generations of indigenous use.[231] This has led to the current regime being criticised as it allows "arrogant, cash-rich, resources-poor northern nations to solidify their economic position at the expenses of naïve, cash-

---

228 J. Oloka-Onyango & D. Udagama, "Health Intellectual Property & Human Right," in *WTO Needs Re-orientation*, South Centre Publication, South Bulletin - 19, August 30, 2001, at 3-4 (asserting that "the protection of IPR under TRIPs presents a paradox for international economic law").

229 Chakravarthi Raghavan, "Ensure More Definitive Rendering of TRIPs Exceptions, Say Jurists," *TWN Third World Network*, *available at* <http://www.twnside.org.sg/title/jrists.htm>, last accessed September 29, 2006.

230 *See* Graham Dutfield, *Intellectual Property, Biogenetic Resources and Traditional Knowledge*, Earthscan Publications 91-9 (2004).

231 *Ibid*, at 3, 185-6.

poor, resource-rich southern states." [232] Various initiatives have been undertaken to provide greater protection to traditional knowledge and cultural continuity, although there remains a tension as to whether traditional knowledge should be developed into a protected right itself.[233] Some countries require patent applications to acknowledging any reliance on traditional knowledge.[234] Alternatively schemes to codify and publish traditional knowledge to ensure they are recognised as forming part of the public domain, thereby denying novelty to any related application still leaves traditional knowledge open to commercial exploitation. Though still controversial, there seems little doubt that a sovereign state can "fashion a valuable bargaining chip" by prioritising specialised local traditional knowledge about the identity and preservation of various plant genetic resources.[235]

Biodiversity Management

"Biodiversity"[236] is also an important concern in two respects. First, certain developing countries may have comparative advantage in the quality of particular strains of crops that they need to protect from genetic piracy.[237] Second, the marketing of highly effective strains of crops, under strong IPR, can lead to intensive agriculture based on monocultures thereby causing a worldwide decrease in biodiversity, and also a pricing out of low income access to traditional crop species. This is of significant importance because biodiversity management has traditionally provided the options to maintain habitats and sustain ecosystems.

2.3.3 Diplomacy in the IPR Protection

Deal from "Overdraw" - Coerced Concessions

Notwithstanding the numerous international conventions, and related specialised organisations to which reference has already been made, the TRIPs Agreement is enforceable within the framework of the WTO, "a forum lacking

---

[232] Scott Holwick, "Developing Nations and the Agreement on Trade-Related Aspects of Intellectual. Property Rights," 49 *Colo. J. Int'l Envtl. L. & Pol'y* 53 (1999).

[233] Dutfield, *supra* note 230, at 127-136.

[234] *See* "Article 27.3b, Traditional Knowledge, Biodiversity, WTO Members' Documents," *available at* <www.wto.org/English/tratop_e/trips_e/art27_3b_e.htm>.

[235] Jerome H. Reichman, "The TRIPs Agreement Comes of Age: Conflict or Cooperation with the Developing Countries?" 32 *Case W. Res. J. Int'l L.* (2000), at 441-446.

[236] "Biodiversity" is usually described as an umbrella term for the diversity in ecosystems, species and genes. It represents, literally, all living plants and animals including humankinds. For a comprehensive account, *see* Kevin Gaston, John Spicer, *Biodiversity: An Introduction*, Blackwell Science (2003), at 4.

[237] Dutfield, *supra* note 230, at 52-6.

a tradition of work in the field of IPR." [238] As Carlos Correa has pointed out, the "TRIPs Agreement was not merely conceived as a mechanism to combat counterfeiting and piracy, an objective that most developing countries would have shared," [239] but "as a balance of different interests representing different groups." [240] As commonly argued by developing countries, "the process of drafting the TRIPs Agreement can hardly be considered to have been a real 'negotiating' process, as developing countries made considerable concessions in agreeing to the higher levels of protection of IPR demanded by industrialised countries," [241] and "the TRIPs Agreement itself has built-in asymmetries." [242] In addition, developing countries were particularly vulnerable having starched to the limit of their negotiating capacity. [243] Unsurprisingly, the negotiating position of developing countries was almost always passive and defensive, since these countries lacked not only the necessary access to information but also the exports who understood the game of global trade. [244]

Offer by "Top-up" – Deserved Compensation

As has been noted, TRIPs is largely suitable for and beneficial to certain group of people as technology exporters, largely ignoring the disadvantages of the technology consumers, "and it overlooks many such forms that exist in the countries of the South." [245] In other words, TRIPs is unbalanced in its orientation. Accordingly, there is considerable doubt as to whether developing counties could overcome the inherent incompatibility of the IPR system with their indigenous conditions merely through a process of adaptation or adoption of that system. [246] Indeed, it is neither reasonable nor sustainable to set forth a same standard for two nations at different stages of development. Figuratively, they are "boxers" from different "heavyweight division." This gives credence to the view that the interests of developing countries would best be served by rejecting the international IPR system as inapplicable until they can pass through the necessary stage of industrialisation and scientific and technologi-

---

[238] *The TRIPs Agreement: A Guide for the South*, *supra* note 196, at 6-7.

[239] *Ibid.*

[240] Percy F. Makombe, "Are We Embarking on Disastrous TRIPs? A case for TRIPs Review," *SEATINI Bulletins*, *available at* <http://www.seatini.org/bulletins/>.

[241] *The TRIPs Agreement: A Guide for the South*, *supra* note 196, at 7.

[242] *Ibid*, at 10.

[243] *Ibid*, at 8-9.

[244] *Ibid. See*, also Carlos M. Correa, *Intellectual Property Right, the WTO and Developing Countries-The TRIPs Agreement And Policy Options* 5 (2000).

[245] Alan Story, "Burn Berne: Why the Leading International Copyright. Convention Must be Repealed," 40 *Univ. Houston L. Rev.* 793 (2003)(mentioning that Berne Convention as a major international copyright treaty is "unbalanced and lopsided in its orientation").

[246] Correa, *supra* note 146, at 5.

cal advance,[247] however these developing countries cannot afford to be isolated within the existing global trade system.

Since the TRIPs Agreement as a "service package" has been accepted by the international community, it appears unrealistic to unwind the TRIPs norms at present and in the foreseeable future. Any bargaining mode between developed and developing countries can only be conceived and implemented within the existing TRIPs framework. It seems true that to require developing countries to adopt the higher standard without reasonable concessions, reducing tariffs for instance, would be just an official line of developed countries. The most practical policy is to provide with more technical support to those developing states that have made firm commitment to implementation of TRIPs minimum standards. Developed countries could in turn "go a long way towards raising enthusiasm for TRIPs if they would actively implement their 'best efforts' commitments to encourage technology transfer to the least developed countries and to provide technical and financial assistance for developing countries."[248] As noted by Lai and Qiu, developed nations should compensate developing nations in an appropriate way and on a reasonable scale as a price for the promotion and harmonisation of the IPR standard.[249] If the extra surplus generated from strengthened IPR protection benefited developed nations solely, developing countries should under no circumstances have implemented and enforced the IPR willingly.[250]

In the meantime, developing countries may continue to leverage all possible flexibility within present TRIPs structure before the necessary revision of the agreement were to be made. Developing countries are advised to "operate at the lower limits" of the TRIPs standard.[251] In addition, the fact that the TRIPs is subject to periodic review gives developing countries the opportunity to coordinate their negotiation positions, taking into account their own development objectives. Making full use of this flexibility to find a dynamic balancing of interests will be beneficial not only to developing nations, but also, in the long term, to developed nations.

---

[247] *See generally*, Assafa Endeshaw, *supra* note 199, at 116.

[248] *See* "Intellectual Property: Balancing Incentives with Competitive Access," *Global Economic Prospects*, World Bank 147 (2002).

[249] Lai and Qiu, "the North's Intellectual Property Rights Standard for the South?" *supra* note 45, at 199, 203 (demonstrating, "[t]o make the TRIPs Agreement incentive-compatible for the South, the North, which is the beneficiary region, has to compensate the South[.] for its increase in IPR protection").

[250] *Ibid,* at 203.

[251] "Intellectual Property: Balancing Incentives with Competitive Access," *supra* note 248, at 147.

Exploring the "Grey Area" – Feasible Solutions

The TRIPs Agreement is an integral part of the WTO Agreements involving *inter alia* some degree of "grey area" of implementation. Although members of the agreement have to implement the requirements of TRIPs in good faith, some crucial areas of the TRIPs appear to leave reasonable flexibility for domestic interpretation.[252] In addition, some TRIPs provisions serve as an apparatus for determining the scope of content of national legislation.[253] While the TRIPs Agreement sets forth minimum standards, it provides such flexibility in a number of areas and developing countries should be afforded the opportunity to "operate at the lower limits."[254] This may take relieve some of the tension between developed and developing world.

TRANSITION PERIODS

In light of the budgetary and institutional aspects of standardisation, "least-developed countries should be afforded latitude in exercising delays in implementation of TRIPs," especially in the politically sensitive and technically complex areas such as pharmaceutical protection in the developing world.[255] The feasible option is to tailor the current IPR regime to the characteristics in each country. At the moment developing and the less-developed countries have each been granted transition periods in which to adapt to and fit in with the harmonised standards. A further extension can also be granted by the WTO Council for TRIPs.[256]

COMPULSORY LICENSING

Second, developing countries are entitled to grant compulsory licensing (CL) to ensure medicines and other essential goods and services are available and affordable to the society. CL is a useful and suitable mechanism for developing countries to take advantages of policy options and to safeguard public interests relating "other use without authorisation of the right holder."[257]

---

[252] *The TRIPs Agreement: A Guide for the South, supra* note 196, at 26.

[253] *Ibid*, at 61.

[254] *See* "Intellectual Property: Balancing Incentives with Competitive Access," *Global Economic Prospects, supra* note 248, at 147.

[255] *Ibid.*

[256] *See* TRIPs Agreement Article 66.1 (which stipulates that "[i]n view of the special needs and requirements of least-developed country Members, their economic, financial and administrative constraints, and their need for flexibility to create a viable technological base, such Members shall not be required to apply the provisions of this Agreement, other than Articles 3, 4 and 5, for a period of 10 years from the date of application as defined under paragraph 1 of Article 65. The Council for TRIPS shall, upon duly motivated request by a least-developed country Member, accord extensions of this period").

[257] *See* TRIPs, Article 31.

In Doha Ministerial Conference (DMC), where the Declaration on TRIPs and Public Health in Doha (DTPH) was adopted, Ministers reached a consensus that "each WTO Member has the right to grant compulsory licences and the freedom to determine the grounds upon which such licences are granted."[258] This Article allows members to "decide the grounds, which warrant issue of a CL,"[259] although WTO members are obliged to keep in line with the terms and conditions of Article 31 of TRIPs in formulating these grounds, and providing efficient and equitable procedures for granting such licences. [260]

Further to this point, the DTPH clarifies the "national emergency" or "other circumstances of extreme urgency" where, under the TRIPs Agreement, limitations can be waved and a CL can be issued to address theses "emergency" or "urgency," such as HIV/AIDS. Fast-track procedures are available for developing or less-developed states suffering such "emergency" or "urgency."[261] In such cases affected states can issue a CL without a licence agreement being finalised in the first instance.[262]

These clarifications of DTPH provide reasonable flexibility by which governments in developing countries can legislate public health measures sufficient to use CL for expanding access to patented medicines at reasonable cost either when they are in short supply or only available at an unaffordable price. This also allows domestic industry to develop by meeting the demand whilst at the same time recognising the proprietary interests of the patent holder. However, the wording permitting compulsory licensing is still somewhat difficult to operate in practice and there are specified conditions to be filled.[263]

SPECIAL AND DIFFERENTIAL TREATMENT

There has been a significant controversy over the role of IPR in modern society.[264] As stated in the Report of CIPR, the TRIPs provisions "should not be

---

[258] "Declaration on the TRIPs Agreement and Public Health," adopted on November 14, 2001, Article 5 (C).

[259] C. Rammanohar Reddy, "Technology Policy Issues at the WTO," 1 (1) *Technology Policy Briefs* 3 (2002).

[260] "TRIPs in the Context of the Doha Ministerial Declaration," Speech by Paul Vandoren, Head of Unit for New Technologies, Intellectual Property, Public Procurement DG Trade, January 6, 2002.

[261] *See* "Implementation of Paragraph 6 of the Doha Declaration on the TRIPs Agreement and Public Health," Decision of the General Council of 30 August 2003, *available at* <http://www.wto.org/English/tratop_e/ trips_e/implem_para6_e.htm>.

[262] *See* TRIPs Article 31(b).

[263] *See* Lord Sydney Templeman, 1 (4) "Intellectual Property," *J. Int'l Econ. L.* (1998), at 603-606.

[264] *See, e.g.*, Ricardo Meléndez-Ortiz and Ali Dehlavi, "Sustainable Development and Environmental Policy Objectives: A Case for Updating Special and Differential Treatment in the WTO," *ICTSD Publication, available at* <http://www.ictsd.org> (suggesting that, "the notion of development embedded in the international trade system, including the multilateral regime of the WTO and the regional integration schemes which are increas-

pressed on developing countries without a serious and objective assessment of their development impact." [265] "In the majority of developing countries there is considerable dependence on technical assistance, [...]. Thus, because the policymaking process is complex and technical, governments may seek to short circuit the process, particularly in the face of international agreed deadlines."[266]

One approach to ameliorating the problem is to draw on the entitlement to special and differential treatment.[267] Developing states accept and implement provisions at a time they can afford – ordinarily this means that the developed world offers flexibility and subsidise the developing world on a temporary basis. As has been noted, "[f]lexibility as to when developing countries should assume WTO obligations reflects an appreciation of the adjustment costs of change as well as administrative and infrastructural capacity needs that might be associated with implementation." [268]

2.4 Conclusion

Conventional perceptions from economic perspective tend to believe that a strengthened IPR regime annexed to the WTO is a propeller of economic growth. However, since the establishment of the global trading system, it still remains controversial as to whether and how the introduction of the international IPR regime and its infrastructure would generate significant economic growth as originally expected. Developing countries accepted TRIPs agreement with various policy goals. However, the new regime is asymmetric in the sense that it mainly benefits industrialised countries. IPR can either trigger or stifle innovation, and can either promote or hinder economic growth, depending on different national circumstances. Evidence also shows that the full in-

---

ingly subjected to GATT principles and rules, is anachronistic and has proven to be delusive and ineffective. The 'transit period' and 'special and differential' treatment are among their target").

[265] "Integrating Intellectual Property Rights and Development Policy," *supra* note 62, at v-vi.

[266] *Ibid*, at 154.

[267] The Special and Differential Treatment is designed as a mechanism that enables developing and less-developed countries to integrate in the global trading system with reasonable flexibility. *See* "Work on Special and Differential Provisions," in *Development: Trade and Development Committee*, WTO, *available at* <www.wto.org/english/tratop_e/devel_e/dev_special_differential_ provsions_e.htm>.

[268] *See* "Special and Differential Treatment in the WTO: Why, When and How?" Staff Working Paper ERSD-2004-03, May, 2004, WTO Economic Research and Statistics Division, *available at* <http://www.wto.org/english/res_e/reser_e/ersd200403_e.doc>, at 30.

teraction between stronger IPR protection and higher-level technology transfer remains untested.

From a legal perspective, concern remains about the 'universal' standard of harmonisation which lacks flexibility for developing countries. In a comparative law context, legal transplants of foreign countries have proved practicable over the past decades in some developing countries, but a "fitting-in" process is usually essential to ensure effectiveness of a transplanted law in a unique socioeconomic environment. While legal transplants are feasible, cultural adaptation is essential. In the arena of world intellectual property, intellectual property law has posed as a radically new form of legal transplant in developing countries since it usually has no counterpart in the indigenous legal traditions. However, the success of transplanted IPR infrastructure depends largely on how indigenous tradition of that imported law is remade in the image of its original model. This reception process in launching a brand-new legal system is, to a great extend, a process of indigenisation of the foreign law, and this process cannot be simplified when a cultural gap is significant.

In the context of political economy, the TRIPs Agreement represents a successful culmination of several attempts by developed states to consolidate their monopoly position over the global economy. The role of developing states within the TRIPs regime has been vulnerable and the concessions they have made should be enumerated in appropriate ways, such as providing financial aid and offering technical assistance.

Based on the theoretical ground, we will uses the prism of EU-China trade relations to suggest ways to reconcile the minimum standards imposed by international IPR regime and the specific conditions of particular states, and provide insight into the unresolved issues. To achieve this goal, we need to assess Chinese response to the TRIPs agreement and the shortcomings of the IPR enforcement, which are what will be discussed in the following chapter.

3 China's Response to the Multilateral Context of TRIPs

As the biggest developing country and the only Communist member of the WTO, China's role in the global trading system is unique. Having laid out the theoretical ground for exploring feasibility of reconciling the IPR international standards and the specific conditions of particular states, this chapter will expand on insight into China's experience with the WTO and the TRIPs Agreement, and the IPR enforcement problems that have been undermining China's credibility and threatening the relations with its Western trading partners.

3.1 Tortuous Journey towards WTO Membership

In discussing China's response to the multilateral context of TRIPs, a logical starting point is to examine and understand China's role in the global trading order. Through almost twenty years of economic reform and openness (*gaige kaifang*), China had clearly developed into a major participant in the global trading system. As a result, China had shown an increasing incentive to join the WTO. However, the path to the WTO that China has taken turns out to be tortuous and "the trajectory of China's reform process over the past two decades mirrors China's lengthy process of joining the WTO."[1]

In fact, China was one of the 23 original contracting parties to the GATT. The Republic of China (ROC), the predecessor of the People's Republic of China (PRC), signed the 1947 Protocol on May 21, 1948,[2] but the Chinese civil war between the Chinese Communist Party and the Chinese Nationalist Party (Kuomintang) during the mid 1940s resulted in its withdrawal.[3] Al-

---

[1] Karen Halverson, "China's WTO Accession: Economic, Legal, and Political Implications," 27 *BC Int'l & Comp. L. Rev.* 320 (2004).

[2] Susanna Chan, "Taiwan's Application to the GATT: A New Urgency with the Conclusion of the Uruguay Round," 2 *Ind.J.Global Legal Stud.* 277(1994).

[3] After the Chinese Communist Party established the PRC on the mainland China and the Kuomintang retreated to Taiwan, the ROC government in Taiwan announced its withdrawal from the GATT in 1950. *See* generally, Robert P. O'Quinn, "How to Bring China and Taiwan into the World Trade Organisation," *Asian Studies Centre Backgrounder* No. 140 (Mar. 22, 1996); Jeffrey L. Gertler, "The Process of China's Accession to the World Trade Organization," in *China in the World Trading System* (1998),

though the PRC has maintained that Taiwan is an integral part of its sovereign territory and has never recognised the withdrawal of Taiwan from the GATT, the PRC framed its policy on the basis of "readmission".[4] Following the Uruguay Round, China embarked on an ambitious plan to resume its status as a GATT contracting party.[5] China followed a devious route to attain an observer status with GATT in 1982.[6] However, it was not until March 1987 that the GATT Council established a Working Party to renegotiate the terms of China's membership.[7]

During the WTO accession negotiation, the issue of IPR appeared to be one of the most complicated and sensitive issues over the negotiations between the United States and China. The Memorandum of Understanding on the Protection of Intellectual Property (MOU)[8] signed on January 17, 1992 between the two governments committed China to update its IPR regime significantly. In responding to the requirements of the MOU, China joined the Berne Convention and the Geneva Phonograms Convention.[9] China also established its credentials by updating its laws and regulations to provide strengthened protection of IPR.

During the period 1994-1995, following a Section 301 investigation, the United States announced 1.08 billion dollars in trade sanctions to be imposed against China, resulting in another accord which was reached between the two

---

at 65-66; Michael N. Schlesinger, "A Sleeping Giant Awakens: The Development of Development of Intellectual Property Law in China," 9 *Journal of Chinese Law* 135 (1995); Ramona L. Taylor, "Tearing Down the Great Wall," *supra* note 16, at 154-5.

4   *See* David Blumental, "Reform" or "Opening"? Reform of China's State-owned Enterprises and WTO Accession - the Dilemma of Applying GATT to Marketizing Economies," 16 *UCLA Pac. Basin L.J.* 262 (1998).

5   O'Quinn, *supra* note 328, at 65-66.

6   For an official account of the chronology from the Chinese side, *see* "Bilateral Agreement on China's Entry into the WTO between China and the United States," Ministry of Foreign Affairs of China, November 17, 2000.

7   *See* Taylor, *supra* note 3.

8   The MOU 1992 was a direct result of the United States' threat to impose the "Special 301" investigation into China's IPR practice. The MOU covers a broad range of issues including copyright, patent, trademark, anti-unfair competition and trade secret protection. Under the MOU, the Chinese government committed, *inter alia*, to fulfilling the obligations set out in the Paris Convention and acceding to international copyright conventions such as the Berne Convention. For a precise account of MOU, *see* Loke Khoon Tan, "U.S., China Sign Important Memorandum of Understanding," 9 (6) *The Computer Lawyer* (1992). *See* also "China-United States: Agreement Regarding Intellectual Property Rights [February 26, 1995]," 34 *International Legal Materials* 881-907 (July 1995).

9   *See* Graham J. Chynoweth, "Reality Bites: How the Biting Reality of Piracy in China Is Working to Strengthen Its Copyright Laws," 2003 *Duke L & Tech. Rev.* 9 (2003).

countries. [10] This aggressive investigation made China's accession to the GATT much more unpredictable. [11] Influenced by external pressure, from 1997 to 2001, China National People's Congress (NPC) initiated a new phase of legal reform by introducing new laws, implementation regulations, as well as judicial interpretations towards IPR protection.

The U.S.-China agreement signed in November 1999 in Beijing[12] set a milestone for China's protracted journey towards entering the WTO.[13] As noted by Chinese top negotiator Long Yongtu, China hailed it as a good "win-win" deal.[14] When the trade agreement between EU and China was signed one year later, it seemed China was standing on the threshold of the WTO. On December 11, 2001, China at last became a WTO Member.

Despite the hurdles in its endeavour to gain admission to the WTO, China's membership gave rise to much controversy in China. While China's accession is viewed by domestic commentators as "a strategic choice of importance for the state to actively participate in the economic globalisation,"[15] and applauded internationally as one of "the most momentous events in recent history whose importance far transcends the realm of world trade,"[16] some opponents do not agree to the view as to "merging into the mainstream of the world economy."[17] Nevertheless, as the largest economic engine to be built among developing country members, China's accession to the WTO is historically significant, and will have a profound impact on China's economic, legal, and political transitions,[18] including the transformation of the IPR regime.

---

[10] "Historical Summary of Selected Countries Placement for Copyright-related Maters on the Special 301 List," Appendix E, International Intellectual Property Alliance, February 2005.

[11] See Schlesinger, "A Sleeping Giant Awakens, supra note 3, at 137.

[12] For details about the US-China bilateral agreement concerning China's accession to the WTO, see USTR Press Releases, available at <http://www.ustr.gov/Document_Library/Press_Releases/2001/June/USTR_Releases_Details_on_US-China_Consensus_on_China's_WTO_Accession.html>.

[13] John Wong, et al, Sino-US Trade Accord and China's Accession to the World Trade Organization 15-23 (2000).

[14] See "Major Breakthrough Made in China's Entry into WTO," People's Daily, Wednesday, November 17, 1999 (stating that China and the United States reached an agreement on the basis of mutual benefits).

[15] Han Rongliang, "Entry into WTO, an Important Choice for China to Merge into Global Economy," People's Daily, November 06, 2001.

[16] A Maturing Partnership – Shared Interests and Challenges in EU-China Relations (Updating the European Commission's Communications on EU-China Relations of 1998 and 2001), Commission Policy Paper for Transmission to the Council and the European Parliament, Commission of the European Communities, Brussels, 10/09/03 COM (2003) 533 finial.

[17] "Interview: Long Yongtu on China's WTO Entry," People's Daily, November 12, 2001.

[18] Halverson, supra note 1, at 320.

3.2 Implementation

The essential function of the WTO is described as providing a means to "resolve conflicts of interest *within, not between*, nations." [19] In this context, the WTO serves as a lever for domestic reform.[20] Indeed, in order to meet the requirements for its WTO accession, China launched the most ambitious campaigns towards its legal reform long before its accession. This is a one-way process and China's reform will continue.

3.2.1 Law Reform Programme

A Brief History

For hundreds of years China has been described as a "sleeping oriental giant lion" removed from the rest of the globe. China awoke from this complacent isolation during the last quarter of the twentieth century and since then has gradually, but persistently, liberalised its trade and investment regimes to emerge as the nation with considerable potential for challenging the economic leadership of the West. [21]

China's contemporary IPR legislation can be traced back to the 1920s. The precursor of China's intellectual property law was enacted in the first quarter of the twentieth century. [22] The ROC promulgated the Trademark Law in 1923,[23] and a new version of the law crafted subsequently in 1931.[24] The ROC enacted its Copyright Law in 1928[25] and Patent Law in 1944. [26] These intellectual property laws formed as integral part of the Republic's "Six Codes" (Liu Fa Quan Shu).[27]

---

[19]   *Ibid*, at 333 (quoting Frieder Roessler, "The Constitutional Function of the Multilateral Trade Order," in Meinhard Hilf & Ernst-Ulrich (eds), *Essays on the Legal Structure, Functions & Limits of the World Trade Order* 109 (2000)).

[20]   *Ibid*, at 333.

[21]   *See* Per Gahrton, "China in the WTO – In Whose Interests? European Parliament," Brussels, Belgium, Released from a workshop of EU-China Programme in Antwerp, May 2000.

[22]   Mingde Li, "The Intellectual Property System in the Modern Chinese Social Development," *National Institute of Law*, China, November 11, 2003, *available at* <www.iolaw.org.cn/>, last visited March 12, 2004.

[23]   Prior to the Trademark Law, there was a Trial Regulations Trademark Registration introduced in 1904. *See* Mingde Li, *ibid*.

[24]   *Ibid*.

[25]   In 1910, the Qing government enacted China's first copyright law which had never been implemented due to the prompt overthrow of the Qing Dynasty (A.D. 1644-1911). *See ibid*.

[26]   Mingde Li, *supra* note 22.

[27]   Since the beginning of the twentieth century, Chinese law evolved into a legal regime modeled upon modern Japanese law, which, interestingly, was transplanted from the

Upon the establishment of the PRC in 1949, the legal regime of the ROC reflected in the so-called "Six Codes" was purged completely.[28] As a consequence, prior to the implementation of China's reform programme commenced in 1970s, China experienced a lengthy period of "legislative vacuum" and had no legal system in the modern sense. During that period, disputes between enterprises and individuals were usually resolved through administrative channels, as part of the national planning system.[29]

The Launch of the Legal Reform Programme

China's ambitious programme of reform, which commenced in the late 1970s, enabled "law to gain in unprecedented importance in Chinese society."[30] In 1978, Deng Xiaoping (*Teng Hsiao-P'ing*) was rehabilitated after being disgraced twice during the Cultural Resolution and returned to power.[31] Based on his belief that a comprehensive legal system was a prerequisite for the political stability and the economic recovery, Deng initiated "a major overhaul of the nation's legal system."[32]

Among a complex array of legal reforms aimed, the envisioned intellectual property legislation is a radically new legal transplantation because intellectual property in the modern sense bears no resemblance to the Communist collectivist ideology.[33] After the Cultural Revolution, the government started introducing and implementing the first wave of legislation that laid the foundation for a comprehensive IPR regime whereby the legal guidelines on IPR took shape in the 1980s.[34] These included the Trademark Law (1982), the Patent Law (1984) and the Copyright Law (1990), representing "the backbone legislation governing IPR."[35] The State Council also enacted separate regulations on the implementation of the above laws.[36] In addition, the General Principles

---

German law. China's intellectual property laws were included in the Code of Administrative Law which formed one "code" of the "Six Codes".

[28] Mingde Li, *supra* note 22.

[29] *See* Taylor, *supra* note 16.

[30] *See* Stanley Lubman, "Bird in a Cage: Chinese Law Reform after Twenty Years," 20 *Nw. J. Int'l L. and Bus.* 383 (2000).

[31] *The Cambridge History of China*, Vol.15, Denis Twitchett and John K. Fairbank (eds.) 350-51 (1991).

[32] *See* Geoffrey T. Willard, "An Examination of China's Emerging Intellectual Property Regime: Historical Underpinnings, The Current System and Prospects for the Future," 6 *Ind. Int'l & Comp. L. Rev.* 420 (1996).

[33] *See* "A Square Peg in a Round Hole: Individual Rights Protection under Collectivist Ideology", *infra* § 3.4.1.

[34] Dittmer Lowell, *China under Reform* 91 (1994).

[35] "IPR Protection Makes Steadfast Progress," *China Daily*, May 17, 2004, at 5.

[36] *Ibid.*

of the Civil Law in 1986,[37] a cornerstone of China's civil code,[38] "devotes an entire section to IPR under the chapter on civil rights," not only providing explicit recognition to the proprietary rights involving intangible properties, but also establishing equitable remedies for infringement.[39]

The 1990s witnessed a further wave of significant legal reform. This reflected the growing appeal to establish an effective legal basis from which to engage the global trading system and to achieve the goal of accessing the WTO. As will be seen in the next section a Copyright Law was legislated in 1990, and Patent and Trademark Laws were significantly amended in 1992 and 1993 respectively. During this period China has also involved in active participation in IPR conventions and activities sponsored by related international organisations, and considerably intensified its cooperation with various countries and NGOs concerning IPR protection.[40] Additionally, in order to satisfy China's treaty obligations, the NPC enacted the Decision on IPR Protection in 1994, the Regulation on Customs Protection of Intellectual Property in July 1995, the Regulation on the Protection of New Plant Varieties in 1997,

---

[37]   Zhonghua Renmin Gongheguo Minfa Tongze [General Principles of the Civil Law of the People's Republic of China] (1986). For full text of the General Principles of the Civil Law, see Laws & Legislations Databases, National People's Congress of China, available at <http://www.npc.gov.cn/englishnpc/news/Legislation/node_2763.htm>.

[38]   China's first Civil Code is still being drafted at present and is expected to comprise around 1,000 to 1,500 articles, make it the most voluminous legislation in the country so far. It is estimated to receive final approval by 2010. See "China's First Draft Civil Code Submitted for Review," People's Daily, December 24, 2002, available at <http://english.people.com.cn/200212/23/eng20021223_108978.shtml>.

[39]   See "New Progress in China's Protection of Intellectual Property Rights (2005)," official White Paper, available at <http://www.china.org.cn/e-white/20050421/index.htm>.

[40]   Chronologically, China joined the World Intellectual Property Organisations in 1980 and acceded to the Paris Convention for the Protection of Industrial Property in 1985; It signed the Treaty on Intellectual Property in Respect of Integrated Circuits in 1989 and the Madrid Agreement Concerning the International Deposit of Industrial Designs in 1989; China acceded to the Berne Convention for the Protection of Literary and Artistic Works in 1992, the Convention for the Protection of Producers of Phonograms against Unauthorised Duplication of Their Phonograms in 1993, the Patent Cooperation Treaty in 1994, and the Nice Agreement Concerning the International Classification of Goods and Services for the Purposes of the Registration of Marks in 1995; It acceded to Budapest Treaty on the International Recognition of the Deposit of Microorganisms for the Purposes of Patent Procedure in 1995, and applied for membership of Protocols of the Madrid Agreement Concerning the International Deposit of Industrial Designs, which made the agreement come into effect in 1995; China join into the Locarno Agreement on Establishing an International Classification for Industrial Designs in 1996, and a the Strasbourg Agreement Concerning the International Patent Classification in 1997; China participated in the entire TRIPs negotiations and initialled the final text, which has been effective since China's accession to the WTO. See Zhongguo Canjia de Duobian Guoji Gongyue [The Multilateral Agreements That China Has Ratified or Signed], Ministry of Foreign Affairs, available at <http://www.fmprc.gov.cn/chn/wjb/zzjg/tyfls/tfsckzlk/zgcjddbty/t70814.htm>, last visited October 23, 2006.

and the Regulation on the Protection of the Layout and Design of Integrated Circuits in 2001.[41] These multi-level provisions further strengthened the legal framework overseeing IPR.[42]

Since 2001, the Supreme People's Court issued a series of judicial interpretations on how to handle cases brought under the trademark law.[43] While the legal system for IPR protection was established rather late in China,[44] within only two decades or so, a comprehensive legal system that covers a wide range of subjects and that is in line with international norms has taken shape.[45] This progress in implementing international IPR at domestic levels is extraordinary because it was accomplished within a relatively short period of time which had taken developed countries decades or centuries to achieve.[46] Although deficiencies still remained, these cumulative changes brought China into compliance with global standards of IPR by the time it acceded to the WTO. What remained, however, was a subsequent "fitting in" period to allow implementation of domestic legal rules to become fully consistent with international requirements.[47]

3.2.2 Emergence of the Intellectual Property Regime

Chinese intellectual property legislative regime mainly consists of Copyright Law, Trademark Law and Patent Law. In addition, there are certain statutes which do not directly grant legal exclusive rights but which are intimately allied with the practical protection of IPR in China, such as the Anti-unfair Competition Law, the Anti-monopoly Law, the Consumer Protection Law, the Product Quality Law,[48] the Foreign Trade Law,[49] and the Scientific and Tech-

---

[41] "New Progress in China's Protection of Intellectual Property Rights (2005)," *supra* note 39.

[42] "IPR Protection Makes Steadfast Progress," *supra* note 35, at 5.

[43] *Ibid.*

[44] "New Progress in China's Protection of Intellectual Property Rights," *supra* note 39.

[45] *Ibid.*

[46] *Ibid.*

[47] *See* "Judicial Interpretation towards Chinese Intellectual Property Protection," *available at* <www.chinaiprlaw.com/flfg/flfglm2.htm>.

[48] The Product Quality Law defines the liability relating to the quality of products. According to the product quality law, "[i]t is prohibited to forge or fraudulently use authentication marks or other product quality marks; it is prohibited to forge the origin of a product, or to forge or fraudulently use the name and address of another producer; and it is prohibited to mix impurities or imitations into a product that is manufactured or for sale, or pass a fake product off as a genuine one, or pass a defective product off as a quality one." In this context, fake goods, or products involving illegitimate use of origin such as fake company names or addresses, are routinely dealt with under the product quality law. *See* Article 5, The Product Quality Law, NPC Laws & Legislations Databases, *available at* <www.npc.gov.cn/englishnpc/Law/2007-12/12/content_1383813.htm>.

nological Progress Law.[50] This section, however, will focus on the law of the copyright, trademark and patent.

The Copyright Law

Chinese copyright legislation was in a state of vacuity before 1990s, and was the least developed of the recognised forms of intellectual property.[51] Coincidently, the one area the Western countries would most like to see improve in terms of China's IPR regime is the area of copyright.[52] The Western world has been particularly sensitive to what is perceived as the frangibility of enforcement of China's copyright laws, particularly in cases of copyright infringement involving widespread piracy of compact discs and computer software.[53] Indeed, China has long been depicted by the West, particularly the U.S., as one of the most rapacious offenders of the copyright laws and international treaties.[54] To some extent, copyright protection has been regarded as a "touchstone" to assess the efficiency of the integrated IPR enforcement mechanism.

Up to the end of the 1980s, China had made "slow, but consistent, progress" towards establishing a substantial copyright protection system.[55] The early 1990s at last witnessed tremendous changes when the Copyright Law of the People's Republic of China (Copyright Law (1990)) became a milestone in China's path to protection of literary, artistic and scientific works in China.[56] According to Article 1, the Copyright Law (1990) was designed, in accordance with the Constitution, to protect copyright of the authors and the copyright-related rights and interests over various forms, and to encourage the creation and dissemination of works contributing to the development and prosperity of the socialist culture.[57] The 1982 Constitution[58] set the tone for the

---

[49] China revised its Foreign Trade Law on April 7, 2004 in conformity with its WTO TRIPs commitments. A new chapter entitled "Protection of Trade Related Intellectual Property Rights" was inserted into the law. *See* The Foreign Trade Law, *available at* <http://www.npc.gov.cn/englishnpc/Law/2007-12/12/content_1383624.htm>.

[50] The newly approved Law of Scientific and Technological Progress is due to take effect from on July 1, 2008. *See infra* § 6.4.2.

[51] *See* Willard, *supra* note 32, at 419.

[52] Schlesinger, "A Sleeping Giant Awakens: The development of Intellectual Property Law in China," *supra* note 3, at 119.

[53] *Ibid.*

[54] *See* John W. Hazard, Jr., *Copyright Law in Business and Practice* § 1:67.50 (rev. ed.).

[55] Schlesinger, *supra* note 3, at 119.

[56] Willard, *supra* note 32, at 423.

[57] According to Article 1, "[t]his law is enacted, in accordance with the Constitution, for the purposes of protecting the copyright of authors in their literary, artistic and scientific works and the copyright-related rights and interests, of encouraging the creation and dissemination of works which would contribute to the construction of socialist moral and material civilisation, and of promoting the development and prosperity of the socialist culture and science." *See* Article 1, Copyright Law.

copyright legislation and the enactment of General Principles of the Civil Law laid the groundwork for the creation of the copyright law.[59] While seen as a creditable effort to strengthen the Chinese IPR system, the Copyright Law (1990) was of "somewhat limited utility to foreigners," which was criticised for its inconsistency with the WTO principle of national treatment.[60] The Copyright Law (1990) failed to provide sufficient protection to the unpublished works of foreigners.[61] Although Chinese authors were protected no matter whether their works were published in China, in the absence of any treaty granting more extensive rights, foreign authors had to be published in China to gain protection.[62]

In keeping with undertakings given to the United States, shortly after the enactment of the Copyright Law (1990), China acceded to the Berne Convention and the Universal Copyright Conventions in October 1992,[63] and ratified

---

[58] Article 47 of the Constitution stipulates that [c]itizens of the People's Republic of China have the freedom to engage in scientific research, literary and artistic creation and other cultural pursuits. The State encourages and assists creative endeavours conducive to the interests of the people that are made by citizens engaged in education, science, technology, literature, art and other cultural work." For full text of the Chinese Constitution, see Constitution, NPC Laws & Legislations Databases, available at <http://www.npc.gov.cn/englishnpc/Constitution/node_2830.htm>; for a detailed introduction and interpretation of China's four Constitutions, see Ann Kent, "Waiting for Rights: China's Human Rights and China's Constitutions, 1949-1989," 13 Human Rights Quarterly (1991).

[59] Willard, supra note 32, at 423 (noting that, under the Civil Law, Chinese citizens and legal persons became entitled to rights of authorship and could seek compensation and injunctions in cases of infringement).

[60] Ibid, at 372.

[61] Paul B. Birden, Jr., "Trademark Protection in China: Trends and Directions," L.A. Int'l & Comp. L.J. 438 (1996).

[62] See Willard, supra note 32, at 424. While there remains criticism that the copyright law does not provide sufficient protection to foreign copyright holders, there is a persuasive argument contrary to this opinion, asserting that Chinese law goes too far to protect foreign copyrights. This situation is ironically described by some Chinese scholars and commentators as Super National Treatment. See Hong Xue and Chengsi Zheng, Chinese Intellectual Property Law in the 21st Century, Hong Kong: Sweet and Maxwell Asia 12 (2002).

[63] As mentioned above, in 1992, China and the United states entered into a Memorandum of Understanding, which committed China to adopt Berne-compatible regulations to its copyright law and to adopt the Berne Convention and the Geneva Phonograms Convention under the terms of the MOU. 3(1) of the MOU stipulates that "[t]he Chinese Government will accede to the Berne Convention for the Protection of Literary and Artistic Works (Berne Convention) (Paris 1971). The Chinese Government will submit a bill authorising accession to the Berne Convention to its legislative body by April 1, 1992 and will use its best efforts to have the bill enacted by June 30, 1992. Upon enactment of the authorising bill, the Chinese Government's instrument of accession to the Berne Convention will be submitted to the World Intellectual Property Organisation with accession to be effective by October 15, 1992." See Memorandum of Understanding be-

its accession to the Geneva Phonogram Convention in April 1993.[64] Pursuant to the requirements of these conventions, China made substantial amendments to the copyright law.[65] Apparently, it was by joining these international agreements that China was committed to bringing its laws into line with international standards, which "signalled its intention to provide greater protection to copyrighted works."[66]

During a similar period of time and under a similar circumstance, China was subjecting itself to a similar ordeal from the U.S., having been urged to move swiftly towards adequate protection for computer software developers and manufacturers from the U.S. against massive pirating operations based in China.[67] Again, China's responsiveness was remarkable. Only three days after enacting the Copyright Law (1990), Chinese authorities released its Regulation for the Protection of Computer Software which was built in the template of copyright law.[68] These rules enumerated specific rights of software copyright holders including rights relating to jointly developed software, and software developed by those working on commission or during the course of their employment.[69] The protection period was set at twenty-five years with a one-time extension for a further twenty-five years.[70]

Naturally enough, the software regulations yielded a number of pitfalls and called forth a good deal of criticism. Similar to the copyright law, the regulations made Chinese citizens eligible for protection wherever they released their software, whereas for foreigners, the first release of their programmes should have taken place in China to be eligible for protection.[71] Also, an exception allowed authorities to engage in teaching, scientific research, or carrying out state duties, to make a limited number of copies of protected pro-

---

tween the United States and China (1992), *available at* <http://untreaty.un.org/unts/144078_158780/4/4/12279.pdf>.

[64] Article 3(2) further confirms that "[t]he Chinese Government will accede to the Convention for the Protection of Producers of Phonograms Against Unauthorised Duplication of Their Phonograms (Geneva Convention) and submit a bill to its legislative body authorising accession by June 30, 1992. The Chinese Government will use its best efforts to have the bill enacted by February 1, 1.993. The Chinese Government will deposit its instrument of ratification and the Convention will come into effect by June 1, 1993." *See* US-China MOU 1992, *ibid.*

[65] Birden, *supra* note 61, at 438-9.

[66] Willard, *supra* note 32, at 424.

[67] *See, ibid*, at 426.

[68] *See ibid* (explaining that, as a burgeoning industry, computer software in China was in its initial stage; China had no precedent from which to work but to build its software protection regime in the template of copyright).

[69] *See* Jisuanji Ruanjian Baohu Tiaoli [Regulations on the Protection of Computer Software] (1990), Article 13.

[70] *Ibid*, Article 15.

[71] *Ibid*, Article 6.

grammes for "non-commercial" purposes.[72] In defining what constitutes legitimate copying, Article 22 adopted subjective terms such as "necessary" and "state duties," through which authorities were given vast discretionary powers.[73]

Despite China's impressive legal reform programme, the United States was apparently not satisfied with China's *status quo* and pressure towards greater protection was not eliminated. With the signing of the so called "last minutes" agreement, the U.S. and China reached further consensus on both substantive and procedural matters of China's copyright legislation,[74] resulting in the U.S.-China Agreement Regarding Intellectual Property Rights in February 1995,[75] which paved the way for a new version Copyright Law in October 2001 (Copyright Law (2001)). Interestingly, this new copyright law was promulgated only one week before China signed its WTO accession documents, which was considered to be more than coincidental.[76] Of the 56 articles of the Copyright Law (1990), more than 20 articles were revised or abolished in an effort to bring copyright protection into full compliance with relevant international conventions.[77] The most notable amendment falls in the provisions ensuring non-discriminatory treatment to foreigners and stateless persons based on reciprocal arrangements and international treaties.[78] In addition, while the old version of copyright law only granted protection towards exploitation and remuneration, the new law created complete categories of various exclusive rights enumerated in the Berne Convention.[79]

---

[72] Copyright Law (2001), Article 22.

[73] *Ibid.*

[74] *See* Reiko R. Feaver, China's Copyright Law and The TRIPs Agreement, *J. Tran'l L. Pol.* 437 (1996).

[75] This agreement takes the form of an "action plan (*xingdong jihua*)" by which the Chinese government will "effectively crackdown on infringement of intellectual property rights in China." *See* Annex I, Action Plan for Effective Protection and Enforcement of Intellectual Property Rights, 4 *J. Int'l L. & Prac.* 416 (1995).

[76] Martin Wolff, "Best IP Protection is Through Education, Not More Enforcement Actions," 1 *TESOL L. J.* 47 (2006).

[77] *See* "Judicial Interpretation towards Chinese Intellectual Property Protection," *supra* note 48.

[78] According to Article 2(2), "[t]he copyright enjoyed by foreigners or stateless persons in any of their works under an agreement concluded between China and the country to which they belong or in which they have their habitual residences, or under an international treaty to which both countries are parties, shall be protected by this Law." *See* Article 2(2) of the Copyright Law (2001), NPC Laws & Legislations Databases, *available at* <http://www.npc.gov.cn/englishnpc/Law/2007-12/12/content_1383888.htm>.

[79] According to Article 10, the term copyright includes: the right of publication; the right of authorship; the right of alteration; the right of integrity; the right of reproduction; the right of distribution; the right of rental; the right of exhibition; the right of performance; the right of showing; the right of broadcast; the right of communication of information on networks; the right of making cinematographic work; the right of adaptation; the

The turn of the new century also witnessed the revisions to the Regulation for the Protection of Computer Software.[80] To take into account the equipments of relevant international agreements, the new regulations brought into effect a number of important revisions. For example, the legal entitlement for unauthorised copying has been restricted to the use of the software for purposes of the user's own personal study, research or appreciation.[81] The controversial provision for "non-commercial use" was removed. Also, the previous software regulations allowed for compulsory licensing of software developed by the State-owned enterprises, which was corrected in the new version regulations.[82]

The Trademark Law

Although Chinese began to use trademarks to identify a product's manufacturer in *Northern Zhou* Dynasty (556-580 A.D.),[83] and there is a good case to be made that mark of *White Rabbit* for trading needles from the *Song* dynasty (960-1279 AD) was arguably the first trademark in the world,[84] it is overall a consensus that the trademark law in 1982 represented "China's first modern experiment in intellectual property protection" in the contemporary Chinese history.[85]

Subsequent to the establishment of the PRC, the former "Six Codes" of the ROC, including the trademark law, were removed and a new soviet style trademark legislation was enacted in 1950 and 1963, with the 1963 legislation

---

right of translation; the right of compilation as well as any other rights a copyright owner is entitled to enjoy. *See* Article 10, the Copyright Law (2001), *ibid.*

[80] "New Progress in China's Protection of Intellectual Property Rights (2005)," *supra* note 39.

[81] *See* Jisuanji Ruanjian Baohu Tiaoli [Regulations on the Protection of Computer Software] (2001), Article 17 (stipulating that "[a] piece of software may be used by its installing, displaying, transmitting or storing for the purposes of studying or researching the design ideas or principles embodied therein, without permission from, and without payment of remuneration, to the software copyright owner").

[82] Chiang Ling Li, "The New PRC Regulation for the Protection of Computer Software", *J. World Intell. Prop.* 493 (2001).

[83] Charles D. Paglee, "Chinese Trademark Law Revised: New Regulations Protect Well-Known Trademarks," 5 *U. Balt. Intell. Prop. L.J.* 38(1997).

[84] Willard, *supra* note 32, at 413-4 (quoting William Alford, "Don't Stop Thinking About...Yesterday: Why There Was No Indigenous Counterpart to Intellectual Property in Imperial China," 7 *J. Chinese L.* 165 (1993)).

[85] Willard, *ibid*, at 421(mentioning that The Trademark Law 1982 was China's first reform-era initiative in IPR law); *see* also, Jill Chiaing Fung, "Can Mickey Mouse Prevail in the Court of the Monkey King? Enforcing Foreign Intellectual Property Rights in the People's Republic of China," 18 *L.A. Int'l & Comp. L.J.* (1996), at 624 (noting that China's first intellectual property law since its ambitious economic reform programme was the trademark law adopted in 1982).

taking effect in 1980 as part of its efforts to accede to the WIPO.[86] China abrogated the 1980 version and enacted a brand new trademark law at the Twenty-fourth Session of the Standing Committee of the Fifth NPC on August 23, 1982;[87] China issued a set of detailed measures for the implementation of the trademark law in the succeeding March.[88]

The Trademark Law was designed "for the purpose of improving the administration of trademarks, protecting the exclusive right to the use of a trademark, and encouraging producers and dealers to guarantee the quality of their goods and services and preserve the credibility of trademarks, so as to protect the interests of consumers, producers and dealers and promote the development of the socialist market economy."[89] Through the new regime, the trademark law was intended "to put an end to the indiscriminate use of marks, a practice that marred the old system." [90]

The first amendment to the trademark law was commenced in 1993 in compliance with the Paris Convention.[91] Subsequent to the first revision, in October 2001, the Standing Committee of the NPC enacted the revised Trademark Law (2001), which brought the law into line with the TRIPs Agreement at the eve of China's accession to the WTO.[92] During this revision, 47 amendments and changes were incorporated into the Trademark Law (2001).[93] Unlike the previous trademark laws, the new law applies equally to both natural persons and legal entities.[94] Collective marks, certification marks and geographic indi-

---

[86] Birden, *supra* note 61, at 433; *see* also Maria C.H. Lin, "China After the WTO: What You Need To Know Now," 817 *Practising Law Institute: Commercial Law and Practice* 186 (2001)(noting that the main purpose of the trademark law 1963 was merely to reinforce government control over the manufacturing units through a set of unified quality standards achieved in the process of trademark registration, and the law did not actually provide ownership rights to trademark holders).

[87] *Ibid.*

[88] *See ibid*; *see* also, "Zhongguo Shangbiaofa de Sanci Xiugai [Three Amendments of China's Trademark law]," *available at* <www.chinaiprlaw.com/yycj/yycj46.htm>.

[89] Article 1, Trademark Law 2001, NPC Laws & Regulations Databases, *available at* <www.npc.gov.cn/englishnpc/Law/2007-12/13/content_1384018.htm>.

[90] Fung, *supra* note 85, at 624.

[91] "Ten Years of Enforcement in China," Judicial Protection of IPR in China, *available at* <http://www.chinaiprlaw.com/english/news/news26.htm>.

[92] "Shangbiaofa Xiugai de Biyaoxing he Zhengti Silu [The Necessity and Strategy for the Revision of the Trademark Law]," the CAIC Official Documents, *available at* <www.saic.gov.cn/redshield/lt/2000/lt10.htm>.

[93] *See* Min Shi, "Towards the Amendment of China's Trademark Law," *Sina Net*, January 15, 2003, *available at* <http://chanye.finance.sina.com.cn/zf/2003-01-15/131264.shtml>.

[94] According to Article 4, protection has been extended to "any natural person, legal person, or other organisation that needs to acquire the exclusive right to the use of a service trademark for the services." According to the previous law, however, only the Chinese legal entities and organisations are entitled to file an application for registration. *See* Article 4, *supra* note 89.

cations were brought under protection to ensure conformity with the Paris Convention.[95]

According to the new trademark law, "[w]here a trademark bears a geographical indication of the goods when the place indicated is not the origin of the goods in question, thus misleading the public, the trademark shall not be registered and its use shall be prohibited. However, where the registration is obtained in goodwill, it shall remain valid."[96]

It is also worthwhile mentioning that the new trademark law granted protection to "well-known trademarks,"[97] which had long been the subject of heated debate in China.[98] The restrictions were introduced in accordance with the Paris Convention.[99] From 2002 to 2006, the Supreme Court affirmed 187 well-

---

[95]   According to Article 3, registered trademarks "refer to trademarks that are registered with the approval of the Trademark Office, including trademarks for goods and services, collective trademarks and certification trademarks." See Article 3, ibid.

[96]   Article 16, ibid.

[97]   Article 13 stipulate that "[w]here the trademark of an identical or similar kind of goods is a reproduction, imitation, or translation of another person's well-known trademark not registered in China and is liable to cause public confusion, no application for its registration may be granted and its use shall be prohibited. Where the trademark of a different or dissimilar kind of goods is a reproduction, imitation, or translation of another person' well-known trademark not registered in China and it misleads the public so that the interests of the owner of the registered well-known trademark are likely to be impaired, no application for its registration may be granted and its use shall be prohibited." See Article 13, ibid.

[98]   In practice, China provided certain protection to well-known trademarks under the "Interim Provisions on Well-known Trademark Authentication and Administration" promulgated by SAIC, which oversees the Trademark Office. See "Chengming Shangbiao Rending he Guanli Zan Xing Banfa (1996) [Interim Provisions on Well-known Trademark Authentication and Administration (1996)]", available at <www.hzgs.gov.cn/FGZX/gsfg/sbzcgl/52_011.html>.

[99]   China's trademark law prohibits registration of any mark that is substantially identical with, or deceptively similar to, an official symbol unless otherwise authorised. Article 10 contains various prohibitions on registration, including those identical with or similar to the State name, national flag, national emblem, military flag, or decorations, of the People's Republic of China; those identical with the names of the specific locations that are seats of central state organs; or those identical with the names or designs of landmark buildings; those identical with or similar to the state names, national flags, national emblems or military flags of foreign countries, with the exception of those the use of which is permitted by the government of the country concerned; those identical with or similar to the names, flags or emblems of international inter-governmental organisations, with the exception of those the use of which is permitted by the organisation concerned or is not liable to mislead the public; those identical with or similar to an official mark or inspection stamp that indicates control and guarantee, except where authorized; those identical with or similar to the symbol or name of the Red Cross or the Red Crescent; those having the nature of discrimination against any nationality; those constituting exaggerated and deceitful advertising; and those detrimental to socialist ethics or customs, or having other unwholesome influences. See Article 10, supra note 89.

known trademarks including foreign brands. [100] By affirming well-known trademarks, Chinese courts have strengthened judicial protection for the intangible assets of the right holders. [101]

Timely procedural reforms were also made, with the most noteworthy reform being the stipulation that all the administrative decisions should be subject to judicial review.[102] Unlike the previous trademark law which mandated the Trademark Review and Adjudication Board (TRAB) to make final decisions towards trademark disputes, the new law transferred the ultimate adjudication from TRAB to the judicial body,[103] which constituted an unprecedented step towards strengthening the vision of rule of law in China.

In September 2005, China's SAIC promulgated the new Trademark Review and Adjudication Rules which came into effect on October 26 2005.[104] The new rules have made further changes to the TRAB practice.[105]

The Advent of Patent Law

Similar to the history of Chinese trademark, the patent in China came into existence nearly three millennia ago in the *Zhou* Dynasty.[106] However, patents as interpreted in a modern sense did not appear in China until approximately the end of the nineteenth century.[107] In the modern era, China experienced a period of social upheavals during which patent was seen as a critical element of capitalism against the ideal of communism. Shortly after the "door" was opened to the outside world, the Chinese leaders realised that a patent protection system was necessary "[i]n order to nurture and continue absorption of advanced technology from abroad and develop a technological infrastructure in China."[108]

Based on this awareness, in 1980, China joined the World Intellectual Property Organisation and since then has established a close working relation-

---

[100] *See* "China's Courts Affirm 'Well-know' Trademarks to Curb IPR Infringement," *People's Daily*, January 18, 2007.

[101] *Ibid.*

[102] The law stipulates that "[w]here the party is dissatisfied with the ruling of the Trademark Review and Adjudication Board, he [or she] may, within 30 days from the date the notification is received, bring a suit in a People's Court. The People's Court shall notify the other party involved in the trademark adjudication proceedings to take part in the legal proceedings as the third party." *See* Trademark Law, Article 43(2), *supra* note 89.

[103] *See* Trademark Law, Article 32, 33, 43 and 49.

[104] *See* "Shangbiao Pingshen Guize [Trade Mark Review and Adjudication Rules]," *available at* <www.gov.cn/ziliao/flfg/2005-10/10/content_75527.htm>.

[105] For a detailed introduction and comments on the new Trade Mark Review and Adjudication Rules, *see ibid.*

[106] Willard, *supra* note 32, at 415.

[107] *Ibid.*

[108] Fung, *supra* note 85, at 626.

ship with WIPO.[109] As an integral component of the strategic policy, the first wave of professionals with political, legal and scientific backgrounds were sent to various developed countries to study and receive training in patent law and practice.[110] After a few years preparation, on March 12, 1984, the NPC enacted the Patent Law,[111] which was largely modelled on German and Japanese laws.[112]

On March 19, 1985, China joined the Paris Convention for the Protection of Industrial Property.[113] Pursuant to the commitments made in the 1992 U.S.-China MOU, the Patent Law was subsequently amended on September 4, 1992, which evidenced a commitment on the part of China to integrate its national market to the global economy.[114] Unlike the pre-amendment law under which patent owners were required to manufacture their products in China or were vulnerable to compulsory licensing,[115] the new patent law extended the term of patent protection to 20 years, clarified and intensified the compulsory licensing requirements, and extended the scope of protection to include pharmaceuticals, agricultural goods and chemical products.[116] According to the patent law, claimants may seek both injunction and compensatory damages against patent infringements.[117] Since the law in particular addressed several concerns voiced by the U.S. in the MOU, the Patent Law (1992) contained a number of provisions which are similar to the American standards.[118]

Pursuant to the requirements for its WTO accession, on August 25, 2000, Chinese patent law underwent its second amendment, leading to the establishment of the State Intellectual Property Office of the People's Republic of China (SIPO) as the national patent administration authority to oversee the implementation of the patent law.[119] The Patent Law (2001) includes substan-

---

[109] The SIPO in China and the WIPO signed a protocol on May 21, 2002 in an effort to achieve their mutual goal of protecting copyright and patents. *See* "China's Patent Cooperation with WIPO to Improve," *China Daily*, May 22, 2002.

[110] Fung, *supra* note 85, at 626.

[111] *See* Patent Law (2001), China NPC Laws & Legislations Databases, *available at* <http://www.npc.gov.cn/englishnpc/Law/2007-12/13/content_1383992.htm>.

[112] Lin, *supra* note 86, at 189.

[113] "Paris Convention for the Protection of Industrial Property", China SIPO, *available at* <http://www.sipo.gov.cn/sipo_English/specialtopic/IPManual/200801/t20080117_2308 55.htm>.

[114] Substantial amendments were introduced to the patent law as a result of U.S.-China MOU 1992. *See* Tan, *supra* note 8; *see also* Birden, *supra* note 61, at 443.

[115] Birden, *supra* note 61, at 444.

[116] *See* Guanghua Yang, "Zhong Mei Zhishi Chanquan Tanpan de Yingxiang he Qishi [Reflections on the Impact of Sino-US Intellectual Property Negotiation]," *available at* <http://www.saic.gov.cn/redshield/xw/2000/zx/zx62.htm>.

[117] Patent Law, Article 60, *supra* note 111.

[118] *Ibid.*

[119] The SIPO (Chinese Patent Office as its predecessor) was established with the vision that it would coordinate and merge the patent, trademark and copyright offices under its unique authority. However, this goal has not yet been achieved. *See* "Protecting Your

tial amendments and modifications covering judicial review, property reserva-
tion and other significant aspects.

For example, under the new version patent law, "[w]here the applicant for
patent is not satisfied with the decision of the Patent Re-examination Board,
he or it may, within three months from the date of receipt of the notification,
institute legal proceedings in the people's court."[120] In a event that "any patentee or interested party has evidence to prove that another person is infringing or will soon infringe its or his patent right and that if such infringing act is
not checked or prevented from occurring in time, it is likely to cause irrepara-
ble harm to it or him," the patentee or interested party "may, before any legal
proceedings are instituted, request the people's court to adopt measures for ordering the suspension of relevant acts and the preservation of property."[121]

Anti-unfair Competition

The main purpose of the anti-unfair competition law is to "shore up a major
breach" in the IPR protection.[122] The Anti-unfair Competition Law, which was
promulgated in 1993, "is formulated with a view to safeguarding the healthy
development of socialist market economy, encouraging and protecting fair
competition, repressing unfair competition acts, and protecting the lawful
rights and interests of business operators and consumers."[123] Prior to the enactment of the Anti-unfair Competition Law, China had no laws to deal with
improper acquisition or disclosure of business secrets.[124] As a result, foreign
companies pursuing protection for the confidentiality of proprietary information had to rely solely on the contractual agreements negotiated with their
Chinese trading partners.[125] However, it was not unusual that those who infringed trade secrets had no contractual relationship with the owners of the secrets and, accordingly, relying on contractual rights remained unreliable and
unpredictable.[126] In addition, contractual provisions had been suffering difficulties in putting into practice due to the dominant position of the state-owned
enterprises.[127]

Intellectual Property Rights (IPR) in China: A Practical Guide for U.S. Companies,"
U.S. Department of Commerce, International Trade Administration, January 2003.
[120] *See* Article 41 (2), *supra* note 111.
[121] *See* Article 61, *ibid.*
[122] Birden, *supra* note 61, at 447.
[123] *See* Law of the People's Republic of China Against Unfair Competition, Article 1,
China NPC Laws & Legislations Databases, *available at* <http://www.npc.gov.cn/eng-
lishnpc/Law/2007-12/12/content_1383803.htm>.
[124] *See* Fung, *supra* note 85, at 631.
[125] *Ibid.*
[126] *Ibid.*
[127] Lin, *supra* note 86, at 193.

China's Competition Law aims to remedy this deficiency through preventing and suppressing monopolistic practice. A notable feature of the law is the availability of the civil and criminal penalties against inappropriate practices such as false advertising, price fixing, and commercial bribery. For example, article 31(2) stipulates that "if the circumstances are serious, business licence [of the violator] may be revoked; and if the commodities sold are fake and inferior, and the case constitutes a crime, he shall be investigated for criminal responsibility according to law."[128] However, the implementation of the law has encountered certain obstacles, which constituted a reason for the authorities to initiate and expedite the legislative process of the antitrust law.[129]

Civil Procedure and IP Litigation

Civil procedure has an indirect but significant impact on intellectual property litigation in China. Although the provisions provided by the Civil Procedure Law are "not compliant, or not explicitly compliant in terms of IPR protection,"[130] by laying down a conflict rule, Article 238 of the Civil Procedure Law provides a catch-all clause.[131] This article states that, "[i]f an international treaty concluded or acceded to by the People's Republic of China contains provisions that differ from provisions of this Law, the provisions of the international treaty shall apply [as priority], except those on which China has made reservations."[132] This provision has created a two-tier system of laws, which gives an additional guarantee to foreign IPR proprietors who rely on the provisions of the international treaty.[133] Technically, as far as the Civil Procedure Law is not in conformity with the TRIPs Agreement, Article 238 can be used as leverage to promote China's compliance with its WTO obligations.[134]

3.2.3 Legal Reform Evaluation

Over the past decades since China initiated its legal reform programme, propaganda and mass media have demonstrated the central government's ap-

---

[128] *See* Article 31 (2), *supra* note 123.

[129] Birden, *supra* note 61, at 449.

[130] Douglas Clark, "IP Rights Will Improve in China – Eventually," *The China Business Review*, May-June 2000.

[131] *Ibid.*

[132] Part IV of the Civil Procedure Law of China contains special provisions for civil procedure for cases involving foreign elements. *See* Civil Procedure Law of the People's Republic of China, China NPC Laws & Legislations Databases, *available at* <www.npc.gov.cn/englishnpc/Law/2007-12/12/content_1383880.htm>.

[133] Carolyn Morton, "the Accession of the People's Republic of China to the WTO and Protection of Intellectual Property," Paper of New Zealand LAWASIA Biennial Conference New Zealand 4-8 October 2001.

[134] Douglas Clark, *supra* note 130.

preciation of an established IPR regime. Chinese leaders have explicitly recognised that the lack of IPR protection is a constraint on the development of a
knowledge-based economy, and have laid much emphasis in updating the IPR
protection regime. While there are still numerous obstacles, there is no doubt
that China "is diligently trying to amend its current laws and affirm its international obligations, putting a positive spin on the piracy issue."[135]

Persuasive Figures

Since China emerged from more than ten years of darkness of political turmoil
and economic chaos, its legal reform and economic achievements have been
continuously impressive. For example, from 1994 to 2000, the average annual
increase in Chinese patent applications was 14.6 percent while foreign applications increased by 22.3 percent.[136] Prior to China's accession to the WTO,
there were 25,346 Chinese patent applications and 30,343 foreign applications,[137] showing an upward tendency. This indicates a rapidly growing domestic demand for a more effective patent system. Statistics also show that by
the end of 2004, China had registered a total of 1,255,499 patents.[138] A rough
extrapolation of these figures suggests that, overall, China has drastically
amended its intellectual property laws and has been on the right track of implementing these laws.

Peripheral Responses

As has been noted, China has been enthusiastically engaged in bringing its legal framework of IPR into full compliance with its WTO obligations. As is
claimed in the statement of the former Ministry of Foreign Trade and Economic Cooperation (MOFTEC) spokesman, "China had taken just a few years
to set up the same legislative protection that Western countries had laboured
over for hundreds of years."[139]

China's achievement of its legal reform has also impressed the outside
world. As Arpad Bogsch, Director-General of the World Intellectual Property

---

[135] Jeanmarie Lovoi, "Competing Interests: Anti-Piracy Efforts Triumph Under TRIPS But
New Copying Technology Undermines the Success," 25 *Brook. J. Intl. L.*, 447(1999).

[136] Statistics indicate, in Japan, the annual filing of domestic and foreign patent applications was approximately 400,000. The annual patent applications in the United States
and Germany were 200,000 and 150,000 respectively. *See* "WTO Access Urges Protection of Intellectual Property Rights," *China Daily*, December 28, 2001.

[137] *Ibid.*

[138] Source: China State Intellectual Property Office, *available at* <www.sipo.gov.cn/>.

[139] Gregory S. Feder, "Enforcement of Intellectual Property Rights in China: You Can
Lead a Horse to Water, but You Can't Make It Drink," 37 *Va. J. Int'l L.* (1996), at 252.

clearly stated, "China had accomplished all this at a speed unmatched in the history of IPR protection."[140]

Legislative Blind Spots

As mentioned in Chapter 2, while the TRIPs Agreement has been described as "an imperialist model" of the international protection for IPR, it nonetheless constitutes "the intellectual property component of the WTO."[141] In participating in the global economy, developing countries, including China, had no choice but to make the "maximum adaptation" in domestic application of the international standards set out by the TRIPs.

While China's legal reform has yielded notable results, legislative pitfalls still exist. For example, while the trademark law (2001) has provided protection to well-known trademarks, it does not seem to accommodate Article 6*bis*(1) of the Paris Convention,[142] which extends protection of well-known trademarks to cases in which only "an essential part of the mark constitutes a reproduction of any such well-known mark or an imitation liable to create confusion therewith."[143] In other words, if a well-known trademark is locally unregistered in China, it is only protected when the infringement is based on the mark as a whole rather than as "an essential part." Although Chinese officials have clarified orally that full protection may still be achieved in practice,[144] this article is confusing and may mislead the public, causing damages to the private interests of the registrants of the well-known trademarks.[145]

---

[140] "Intellectual Property Protection in China," Chinese Government's White Paper on Intellectual Property Protection, Information Office of the State Council of the People's Republic of China, June 2004.

[141] Brent T. Yonehara, "Enter the Dragon: China's WTO Accession, Film Piracy and Prospects for Enforcement of Copyright Laws," 22 *DePaul-LCA J.Art & Ent. L.* 405 (2002).

[142] *See* "Review of Legislation: Response from China to the Questions Posted by Australia, the European Communities and Their Member States, Japan and the United States," Council for Trade-Related Aspects of Intellectual Property Rights, IP/C/W/374, September 10, 2002.

[143] 6*bis*(1) of Paris Convention stipulates that "the countries of the Union undertake, *ex officio* if their legislation so permits, or at the request of an interested party, to refuse or to cancel the registration, and to prohibit the use, of a trademark which constitutes a reproduction, an imitation, or a translation, liable to create confusion, of a mark considered by the competent authority of the country of registration or use to be well known in that country as being already the mark of a person entitled to the benefits of this convention and used for identical or similar goods. These provisions shall also apply when the essential part of the mark constitutes a reproduction of any such well-known mark or an imitation liable to create confusion therewith." *See* 6*bis*(1), Paris Convention for the Protection of Industrial Property, *available at* <http://www.wipo.int/treaties/en/ip/paris/trtdocs_wo020.html>.

[144] *See* "Review of Legislation: Response from China to the Questions Posted by Australia, the European Communities and Their Member States, Japan and the United States,"

In addition, the TRIPs Agreement Article 27.3(b) requires members to provide certain forms of intellectual property protection for animal inventions and the protection of plant varieties.[146] In addition, Paragraph 19 of the Doha Declaration has broadened the scope of protection to include traditional knowledge and biodiversity.[147] Since biodiversity is under threat of erosion and becomes undervalued in China with the inappropriate use of modern industrial and agricultural methods, China is expected to provide timely and necessary protection towards biodiversity in its future legislation.

3.3 Enforcement Shortcomings

Over the past two decades or so, China has demonstrated a strong desire to be involved in the global trading system and has established a sound legal framework for the IPR protection. As illustrated above, the gap between TRIPs and China's intellectual property laws has been greatly narrowed and China has, in general, met the international standards for IPR protection. Some commentators have given even more optimistic appraisals, asserting that China's intellectual property laws have approached an advanced level in the world.[148]

An extensive theoretical literature has examined the impact of TRIPs standards on Chinese IPR legislation and the stepped-up efforts China has endeavoured to make in bringing its domestic laws into conformity with its WTO commitments. While it has been accepted that "China has implemented its WTO obligations on time, and in some cases ahead of schedule,"[149] the testing of empirical evidence as to effectiveness of enforcement has been little-explored. A broad consensus is developing amongst academics and practitioners that it is the enforcement rather than legislation that prevents China from fulfilling its TRIPs obligations. As some scholars have pointed out, it has become less persuasive for the Chinese government to point merely to the existence of legislation as proof of China's compliance with its WTO commit-

---

Council for Trade-Related Aspects of Intellectual Property Rights, IP/C/W/374, September 10, 2002.

[145] *See* Jay Sha, "Summary of Changes of Chinese Trademark Law," Jeekai & Partners, Beijing China (2001) (on file with the author).

[146] *See* "TRIPs: Reviews, Article 27.3(B) and Related Issues," WTO, *available at* <http://www.wto.org/english/tratop_e/trips_e/art27_3b_background_e.htm>.

[147] *Ibid.*

[148] *See, e.g.,* Willard, *supra* note 32, at 435 (stating that "China's intellectual property laws are now among the world's most comprehensive and modern").

[149] *See* "European Business in China Position Paper 2005," European Union Chamber of Commerce in China.

ments.[150] This chapter of the book thus aims to complement the standard empirical literature, which has conventionally focused on legislative implementation.

Technically, upon the WTO accession, Chinese intellectual property laws as a whole are adequate for the prevention of the IPR infringement. However, as shown in the USTR Annual Report, the problem of counterfeiting and piracy in China remains out of control.[151] As a consequence, "Washington's warnings against Chinese piracy of films, music, software, medicine and machines have become a diplomatic mantra."[152] At present, China is still considered to be one of the world's largest exporters of counterfeited and pirated goods.[153] Much has been done in an attempt to eradicate the problem, but the counterfeiting and piracy seem to have become a persistent ailment.

The sticking point is clear: laws without enforcement are waste paper as are rights without remedy.[154] No panacea for counterfeiting and piracy is available. China will have no option but to gear up to fulfil its international obligations and it is to the related difficulties to which we now turn.

3.3.1 Cultural Perspective

A Square Peg in a Round Hole: Individual Rights Protection under Collectivist Ideology

In contrast to Western notions of property rights, Communism, the unprecedented socialist experiment calling for equality and freedom in the twentieth century,[155] substantially influenced cultural perceptions in modern China.[156] As Robert Weatherley has noted, Karl Marx deemed the individual as a "species being" who exists as an intrinsic part of the society to which he or she was born.[157] Upon the establishment of the PRC in 1949, China abolished the entire

---

[150] Donald Clarke, "Private Enforcement of Intellectual Property Rights in China," 10 *NBR Analysis*, No 2, 32 (1999).

[151] *See* "2005 Report to the Congress on China WTO Compliance," USTR, *available at* <http://www.ustr.gov/assets/Document_Library/Reports_Publications/2005/asset_upload_file293_8580.pdf>.

[152] *See* Chris Buckley, "On Piracy, an Advocate for China's progress," *International Herald Tribune*, Tuesday, October 4, 2005, *available at* <http://www.iht.com/articles/2005/10/04/business/IPRjudge.php>, last accessed October 19, 2006.

[153] *See* Robert Marquand, "China's Pirate Industry Thriving," *The Christian Science Monitor*, January 9, 2002.

[154] *See* Willard, *supra* note 32, at 435.

[155] *See A Dictionary of Marxist Thought*, Tom Bottomore (ed), Blackwell 102-05 (1983).

[156] *See* Brigitte Binkert, "Why the Current Global Intellectual Property Framework under TRIPs is Not Working," *Intell. Prop. L. Bull* 147 (2006).

[157] Robert Weatherley, *The Discourse of Human Rights in China: Historical and Ideological Perspectives* 93, 104 (1999) (examining the relationship between individual rights

corpus of existing legal regime and began to introduce a new legal system based on the Soviet template.[158] While IPR is an outcome of a market economy, Marxism-Leninism provides a basis for a theory that "private capital is a means to exploitation." [159] As a consequence of the ideological predisposition, the mentality of sharing wealth became dominant, and the IPR regime was deeply embedded in the notion that "individual rights are most readily defended as effective means to state ends."[160] Accordingly, China's IPR protection regime was built upon the foundation that sustains "the balance between collectivist and individualist thought,"[161] and "the harmony of interests between individuals and the state they belong to."[162] Since collective dominance has outweighed the interests of individual rights for decades,[163] in order to maintain a harmonious community, citizens are usually encouraged to consciously, and sometimes unconditionally, give up any rights in favour of the society.[164] Not surprisingly, collectivist ideology is apt to undermine IPR as a form of individual right.[165]

As a result, while China's economic reforms have been remarkable, the transplanted IPR system is like "a square peg in a round hole," making it "more of a wish list for foreign investors than a realistic and effective system" of global enforcement for IPR.[166] Although the law has been introduced and implemented, there is an inertial way of thinking among some of China's leaders to view IPR as a barrier to obtain modern technologies necessary for continued economic development.[167] Indeed, it is still a dominant discourse in

---

and the superiority of collective interests, and harmony of interests under the Marxist ideology).

[158] See Willard, *ibid*, at 372.

[159] Yonehara, *supra* note 141.

[160] Weatherley, *supra* note 157, at 128.

[161] Robert Bejesky, "Investing in the Dragon: Managing the Patent versus Trade Secret Protection Decision for the Multinational Corporation in China," 11 *Tulsa J. Comp. & Int'l L.* (2004), at 446.

[162] Weatherley, *supra* note 157, at 95-6, 126-8 (explaining that, in Marxist thinking, individuals are not expected to exercise their rights in a way that fulfils a perceived need to protect themselves from the authority of the state, since the interests of individuals and the state are basically identical).

[163] See Randall P. Peerenboom, "Rights, Interests, and the Interest in Rights in China," 31 *Stan. J. Int'l L.* (1995), at 359, 367 (noting that "[i]n the dominant western conception, individual rights precede interests and the balancing process. By contrast, the Chinese conception of rights as interests to be balanced more readily lends itself to the view that rights are [...] granted by the authorities"). See also Robert Weatherley, *supra* note 157, 105-6 (1999).

[164] Weatherley, *supra* note 157, at 105-6.

[165] Bejesky, *supra* note 161, at 447.

[166] See Scott J. Palmer, "An Identity Crisis: Regime Legitimacy and the Politics of Intellectual Property Rights in China," 8 *Ind. J. Global Legal Stud.*, at 450.

[167] Andrew J. McCall, "Copyright and Trademark Enforcement in China," 9 *Transnat'l Law* 591(1996).

China that in accepting reluctantly the incompatible standards for the protection of foreign IPR, China, together with other developing countries, are being exploited and dominated.[168] Ironically, while the American critics depict China as a "land of unethical pirates," some Chinese see the U.S. as a "land of money-grabbing monopolists."[169]

In addition, China's perception towards IPR has been influenced by inherent nationalist sentiments.[170] To a great extent, this nationalist sentiment was an actual reaction to the long-standing indignities and humiliation that China suffered at the hands of far more powerful Western imperialism,[171] particularly after China's decisive defeat in the Opium Wars which commenced in the mid nineteenth century.[172] It is much more apparent when it comes to the distinction and interaction between what is "foreign" and what is "domestic," in a state that had long been isolated from the outside world. Fuelled by socio-economic torment and nationalist sentiments, Chinese instinctively vented their grievances on foreign enterprises.[173]

Since the principle of intellectual property contravenes the fundamental beliefs of collectivist society and the protection towards foreign proprietors arouses nationalist sentiments, implementation of IPR is thus undertaken with reluctance. Although the "door" has been opened for decades, and China has obtained membership of the WTO, public ownership remains dominant and China is still a Communist country in terms of constitutional ideology.[174] The

---

[168] *Ibid* (mentioning that the developing nations view the importation of intellectual property as a means of the developed nations to dominate and explore the developing world); *see* also, J. Cheng, "China's Copyright System: Rising to the Spirit of TRIPs Requires an Internal Focus and WTO Membership," 21 *Fordham Int'l L. J.* (1998), at 1982 (discussing that "China shares economic disincentives to the vigorous enforcement of intellectual property rights with many other developing countries").

[169] Alexander C. Chen, "Climbing the Great Wall: A Guide to Intellectual Property Enforcement in the People's Republic of China," 25 *AIPLA Quart. J.* 8 (1997).

[170] Peter Yu, "Piracy, Prejudice, and Perspectives: An Attempt to Use Shakespeare to Reconfigure the U.S.-China Intellectual Property Debate," 19 *Boston Univ. Int'l L. J.* 26 (2001).

[171] *Ibid.*

[172] The Opium War, also known as the First Anglo-Chinese War, took place between Great Britain and the Chinese Qing Empire from 1839 to 1842 with the aim of protecting British opium trade in China. The Anglo-Chinese War initiated a long history of Chinese political and social chaos and their antipathy to European imperial hegemony that arguably still has remnants. *See China: A Historical and Cultural Dictionary* 237-8 (Michael Dillon ed., 1998). *See* also, Yongnian Zheng, *Discovering Chinese Nationalism in China: Modernization, Identity, and International Relations*, Cambridge University Press (1999), at 154.

[173] Yu, "Piracy, Prejudice, and Perspectives," *supra* note 170, at 26.

[174] According to Article 6 of the Constitution, "the basis of the socialist economic system of the People's Republic of China is socialist public ownership of the means of production, namely, ownership by the whole people and collective ownership by the working people. The system of socialist public ownership supersedes the system of exploitation

negative aspects of the notions have not been rooted away entirely and still unconsciously influence comprehension and belief of intellectual property law, at least for some of Chinese leaders.

Strong Legislation and Weak Legal Consciousness

Taking a cultural-historical approach, Professor William Alford demonstrates in his work, *To Steal a Book Is an Elegant Offense*,[175] the evolution and predisposition of Chinese legal tradition. Due to the incipient consciousness of rule of law, and combined with the influence of the dominant socialist ideology, the concept of the rule of law is abstract and remote. As a result, despite the enormous legal apparatus, the gains from others' intellectual property and the profits from piracy are still considered more legitimate than the liberal norm of respecting IPR.[176] Having been embraced for generations, this philosophical conception dies hard and is indicative of a range of influences over how IPR is comprehended and the level of commitment they have exhibited in modern Chinese society.

For instance, in an effort to curb the infringement problems, the revised criminal code defined relevant criminal liabilities for violation of intellectual property laws.[177] However, a large number of citizens, including some officials, do not have a strict belief in adhering to the ethical constraints and legal standards. In this environment prosecutions are pursued reluctantly, adding inertia to entrenched value orientation. Statistics show that, in 2003, there were 37,489 trademark violation cases that were investigated and handled across the country, among which, only 45 cases were eventually transferred to judicial

---

of man by man; it applies the principle of 'from each according to his ability, to each according to his work.'" "During the primary stage of socialism, the State adheres to the basic economic system with the public ownership remaining dominant and diverse sectors of the economy developing side by side, and to the distribution system with the distribution according to work remaining dominant and the coexistence of a variety of modes of distribution." *See* Article 6 of Constitution of the Peoples Republic of China, NPC Laws & Legislations Databases, *available at* <http://www.npc.gov.cn/zgrdw/english/constitution/constLink.jsp>.

[175] William P. Alford, *To Steal a Book is an Elegant Offence: Intellectual Property Law in Chinese Civilisation* (1995).

[176] Susan K. Sell, "Intellectual Property Protection and Antitrust in the Developing World: Crisis, Coercion, and Choice," 49 (2) *International Organization* 332 (1995).

[177] In November 2004, a joint judicial interpretation was issued by the Supreme People's Court and Supreme People's Procuratorate, which substantially lowered the threshold for criminal liabilities on IPR infringement (150,000 Yuan, equivalent to 18,000 U.S. dollars). The existing Criminal Law imposes a two-year prison sentence and a fine of between 50 and 200 percent of the estimated profits from the illegal activities. For the judicial interpretation, *see* "Interpretation on Several Issues Concerning Legal Provisions Applied in Criminal Cases on Intellectual Property Rights Infringement (2004)," *available at* <www.legalinfo.gov.cn/zt/2004-12/28/content_172931.htm>.

organs for criminal prosecution.[178] The percentage of criminal prosecution cases remains low which mirrors a major barrier for China to strengthen its IPR enforcement mechanism.

Claims of Private Rights under Public Ownership

Private property rights are among the fundamental concepts upon which many Western states are built and IPR was born of a predominantly Western concept of private property rights and benefits.[179] At the international level, the objective of TRIPs is to support liberalisation of the global trading system while protecting the private monopoly rights of intellectual property owners by curbing counterfeiting and eliminating of piracy.[180] The first sentence of the preamble of the TRIPs Agreement highlights these goals by explicitly identifying the need to protect private interests by committing members to a shared objective of "[d]esiring to reduce distortions and impediments to international trade, and taking into account the need to promote effective and adequate protection of intellectual property rights."[181]

However, influenced by communist ideology and collectivist mentality, Chinese society has traditionally viewed private rights as individualisation, which is considered wicked and vicious.[182] Unlike the constitutions in most developed countries which hold sacred the private rights, emphasising their abstract and universal nature, the Constitution of China does not explicitly address IPR. [183] It does, in contrast, place a strong emphasis on the public interest in terms of rights and responsibilities.[184] In addition, Chinese justice is "geared towards the settlement of specific disputes rather than defining the claims for private rights."[185] Although Marxist fundamentalism has been loosened by the

---

[178] *See* "Report on the Protection of Intellectual Property Rights in China in 2003" (Abstract), State Intellectual Property Office (SIPO), SAIC, National Copyright Administration of China (NCAC), April 13, 2004, *available at* <http://www.sipo.gov.cn/sipo_English/gfxx/zyhd/t20040414_33974.htm>.

[179] Eric M. Griffin, "Stop Relying on Uncle Sam! – A Proactive Approach to Copyright Protection in the People's Republic of China," 6 *Tex. Intell. Prop. L.J.*182(1998).

[180] Agreement on Trade-Related Aspects of Intellectual Property Rights, April 15, 1994, Marrakesh Agreement Establishing the World Trade Organisation, Annex 1C, Legal Instruments-Results of the Uruguay Round, 33 *I.L.M.* 81 (1994).

[181] TRIPs Preamble, *ibid.*

[182] Indeed, in Chinese society, values to the individual are secondary to the values that would accrue to the communities. While China is gradually re-introducing notions of private ownership, the process is likely to be lengthy and tortuous.

[183] Derk Bodde & Clarence Morris, *Law In Imperial China*, Harvard University Press (1967), at 18-21.

[184] China's existing Constitution emphasises the "public interest" in terms of expropriation and requisition of land and private properties. *See* Article 10 (3) and Article 13, Constitution, PNC Laws & Legislations Databases, *available at* <http://www.npc.gov.cn/englishnpc/Law/2008-01/24/content_1381976.htm>.

[185] Fung, *supra* note 85, at 615.

new "pragmatic" Chinese leadership, the legacy of communitarian thought has a certain amount of inertia. It is still a prevailing point of view in China that rights are bestowed by the State rather than being natural, inalienable rights enjoyed by individuals.[186] As Weatherley explains, one possibly significant point to be drawn from the Chinese practice of defining rights is the unequivocal rejection of the concept that rights are universal.[187] In a similar vein, Palmer observes that, a notable characteristic of China's legal landscape is "the government's establishment of the interrelated doctrines of legal equality and political inequality in the context of civil obligations."[188] It is apparent that Chinese people do not, or dare not believe that "individuals are endowed with rights that they are entitled to assert," particularly "with respect to those in positions of authority."[189] The comprehension of general private rights is nascent and, as such, the legislation for protecting them is in some senses rudimentary. Despite the introduction of a 2004 amendment to China's Constitution that would provide protection to private property,[190] China still has a long way to go to fully protect private rights, such as integrating the amended provisions into existent laws and regulations. The lack of rights consciousness illustrates, at least to some extent, how Western legal concepts are incompatible and incommensurable with Chinese traditions and aspirations.[191]

By contrast, China has been engaged in intellectual property protection for over two decades, which has resulted in comprehensive and substantive legislation.[192] The protection of IPR preceded recognition of the general private rights. China has thus spawned a modern amalgam – China's remarkable intellectual property regime has been inoculated whereas the notion of private rights is still in its infancy.

Within this context, the commitment to protection of IPR cannot be regarded as unalterable. Establishing a substantive private rights system in China and giving its citizenry private property rights are by no means a quick

---

[186] Weatherley, *supra* note 157, at 113.

[187] *Ibid.*

[188] Palmer, *supra* note 166, at 456.

[189] *See* Alford, *supra* note 175, at 117.

[190] On March 14, 2004, China's NPC adopted a series of landmark amendments to the state Constitution, including special provisions that deliver protections to human rights and private property rights. For example, Article 33 of the amended Constitution has a third paragraph inserted, which reads "The State respects and preserves human rights." *See* the forth amendment of the Chinese Constitution approved on March 14, 2004 by the Second Session of the Tenth NPC, PNC Laws & Legislations Databases, *supra* note 184.

[191] Palmer, *supra* note 166, at 475-76.

[192] For example, Chinese copyright law was legislated in 1990, and patent and trademark laws, which were promulgated one decade ago, were significantly amended in 1992 and 1993 respectively. For a recent and comprehensive account of Chinese intellectual property laws, *see* Peter Ganea, *et al*, *Intellectual Property Law in China*, Kluwer Law International (2005).

or easy solution to China's IPR enforcement problem. They should be regarded as long-term policies that need to be underpinned in order to create a sound basis for further economic development.

Dynamic Intellectual Property under Rigid Education Model

The educational regime in China often acts in a negatory manner in promoting the evolution of collectivist mentality and instilling an ethos hostile to counterfeiting and piracy. On the contrary, it fuels the perception that the concept of intellectual property is exotic (*bolaipin*) and that intellectual creation is the property of human civilisation.[193] As a result, while intellectual property has become a popular jargon in China, the overwhelming majority of Chinese officials and citizenry do not genuinely comprehend the general principles of intellectual property law and would be antithetical to theories about the role of the intellectual property law in encouraging creativity and contributing to economic well being.[194]

Moreover, the special Chinese education model is largely built on faultless recitation of classical works in a process of rote learning,[195] which is typically considered as mechanical memorisation.[196] Those who can recite the classical works and cram for their examinations are usually assured academic success and public recognition.[197] In such a force-fed environment, students are ingrained with a plenitude of information and treated as subservient repositories of knowledge. This education model arguably hinders original thoughts and fosters a tendency of imitation rather than creation.

3.3.2 Institutional Perspective

Ossified Bureaucracy and Decentralised Responsibilities

It is an interesting phenomenon in that the management of counterfeiting and piracy has, in many circumstances, outstripped official punitive measures.[198]

---

[193] Lingdi Zhu, "Cong Majang Duize de Bentuxing Kan Zhongguo Zhishi Chanquan Fa Yizhi [Legal Transplant of Intellectual Property Law in China: Reflections from the Indigenous Nature of the Rule of *Majang*]," *Legal Daily*, December 2, 2004, *available at* <http://www.china.com.cn/chinese/OP-c/719075.htm> (last visited June 19, 2007).

[194] Cheng, *supra* note 168, at 1998.

[195] Eric M. Griffin, "Stop Relying on Uncle Sam!" *supra* note 179, at 183.

[196] *See* N. Wingrove, "China Traditions Oppose War on IP Piracy," 38(3) *Research-Technology Management* (1995), at 6-7.

[197] Eric M. Griffin, *supra* note 179, at 183.

[198] *See* "Transitional Review Mechanism of China, Communication from the European Communities and their member States By means of a communication from the Permanent Delegation of the European Commission," the World Trade Organisation, IP/C/W/371, August 29, 2002, at 2.

Regardless of the financial aspect, the low efficiency of the entrenched bureaucracy is an important reason. The continued rhetoric of those who lobby for external pressure against China over a strengthened domestic enforcement reveals an overwhelming degree of ignorance about the "Chinese exceptionism" in implementing international norms through the conservative and bureaucratic colossus.[199]

Effective enforcement calls for optimal allocation of responsibilities and resources among different authorities to ensure transparency and accountability at various levels. Unfortunately, China's vertical administrative structure provides significant scope for overlapping jurisdictions between enforcement institutions, which exhibit a substantial degree of heterogeneity across regions and result in parallel enforcement mechanisms.[200] A notable challenge in practice falls in the determination as to who asserts jurisdiction over the enforcement, which, in many circumstances, results in continuous bureaucratic turf battles among various national ministries and between central and local government agencies. For instance, the Ministry of Commerce (MOFCOM) – Chinese chief negotiator equivalent to the United States Trade Representative (USTR) – acts merely as a coordinator over enforcement agencies and has no direct authorities over domestic enforcement as the USTR does. This has led to instances where effective enforcement has been frustrated and counteracted by bureaucratic rivalries.[201]

Having accomplished its mission of promoting a positive result of the WTO negotiations through the domestic bureaucracy, MOFCOM has "exhausted its political capital" and has little goodwill on which it can draw to ensure effective implementation of the result.[202] Accordingly, it has entered into a new stage of implementing these agreements, and thus it is the turn for other ministries such as the State Administration for Industry and Commerce (SAIC) to translate the agreements into action.[203] However, due to the lack of expertise and because of the departmental protectionism, the later is liable to impede appropriate initiatives and therefore slow down working efficiencies.[204]

Thus the Trademark Office still remains under the control of SAIC, rather than being brought within the responsibility of the State Intellectual Property

---

[199] Andrew C. Mertha, *The Politics of Piracy, Intellectual Property in Contemporary China* 2, 22-34 (2005)(noting that "[t]he application of foreign pressure, always present as diplomatic tool," has to be tailored into China's circumstances due of its unique "cultural and historical legalities").

[200] Daniel C.K. Chow, "Enforcement Against Counterfeiting in the People's Republic of China," *Nw J. Int'l L. & Bus.* 454(2000).

[201] *Ibid*, at 543.

[202] Mark L. Clifford, "China's Fading Free-Trade Fervor," Business Week, June 5, 2002, *available at* <http://www.businessweek.com/bwdaily/dnflash/jun2002/nf2002065_48 30.htm>, last visited July 7, 2006.

[203] *Ibid*.

[204] *Ibid*.

Office,[205] which oversees only the patent matters.[206] The Trademark Review and Adjudication Board (TRAB),[207] which should be independent from the Trademark Office, is nevertheless under the control of SAIC.[208] For example, "prior right" or malicious anticipatory registration of marks of fame is stipulated in the Trademark Law (2001)[209] in an effort to prohibit the registration of any mark copying or imitating other prior lawful rights.[210] These "prior rights" are recognised and accepted by some authorities but not by all. The registration of business names, for instance, is managed at different administrative levels and, at a local level, limited to a certain geographical area.[211] The business name registration remains separate and the resistance to recognition of such "prior rights" still exists among local AICs which are in charge of the registration.[212]

The Administration for Quality Supervision, Inspection and Quarantine (AQSIQ), which replaced the former State Bureau of Quality and Technical Supervision, is also empowered to handle infringements of registered trademarks as part of its duty to ensure Chinese product quality and standards.[213]

---

[205] The Chinese Patent Office was established in 1980 and renamed as the State Intellectual Property Office in 1998. *See* Introduction to the State Intellectual Property Office, Central People's Government of People's Republic of China, *available at* <http://www.gov.cn/banshi/qy/rlzy/2005-09/02/content_29008.htm>.

[206] Sha, *supra* note 145.

[207] The TRAB, an administrative organ established by SAIC, is responsible for the review and adjudication of trademarks in respect of the determination of the attribution of the trademark, exercising the right of final adjudication on matters of trademark review and adjudication. *See* Rules for Trademark Review and Adjudication, Article 2, *available at* <http://www.ipr.gov.cn/ipr/en/info/Article.jsp?a_no=2199&col_no=119&dir=200603>, last accessed January 5, 2006.

[208] Sha, *supra* note 145.

[209] *See* Trademark Law, Article 9, 31.

[210] Sha, *supra* note 145.

[211] In China, the SAIC is responsible for the approval of business names containing such indications as "Zhongguo" or "Zhonghua" (both meaning China), "Guojia" (State) or "Guoji" (international), as well as those excluding geographical indications. Accordingly, local AICs are responsible for the approval of business names containing a certain geographical indication at the same level. *See* Provisions for the Administration of Business Name Registration, Article 5.

[212] Sha, *supra* note 145.

[213] In order to keep pace with international standards in light of the accession to the WTO, a new legal and administrative enforcement organ named the General Administration of Quality Supervision, Inspection and Quarantine was established in April of 2001 through the merger of the existing State Administration for Entry-Exit Inspection and Quarantine and the State Quality and Technical Supervision Bureau. The AQSIQ, in turn, created the Standards Administration of China (SAC) and the China National Regulatory Commission for Certification and Accreditation (CNCA), both of which operate under the supervision of AQSIQ. The AQSIQ also supervises the WTO TBT Inquiry Centre, which operates as a liaison between China and the WTO. For more information, *see* AQSIQ, *available at* <http://english.aqsiq.gov.cn/AboutAQSIQ/>.

However, since the AQSIQ can only enforce the Product Quality Law, the most an IPR proprietor can expect is the fake goods being confiscated or destroyed without remedy.

Similar problems can be seen with regard to copyright. The National Copyright Administration (NCA) of China, the State Council's copyright administrative control department, is responsible for, *inter alia*, the implementation of national copyright laws and international treaties, investigation of infringement cases, administration of external copyright relations and guidance for local authorities.[214] However, the NCA shares a "two in one" administrative system with the General Administration of News and Publication. The operation of this dual structure has inevitably led to insufficient resources and expertise of copyright and its arbitrary and incoherent performance. Moreover, some enforcement bodies, such as SAIC and the NCA, have seen cutbacks in staff and resources over the past years in light of the streamlining and restructuring efforts.[215] For example, as of early 2005, China's Trademark Office, which had a backlog of 20,000 cases of trademark dispute, was still dealing with complaints filed in 1999.[216]

In July 1994, the Chinese government established within the State Council the Intellectual Property Executive Conference (IPEC), with similar subordinate committees at both the ministerial and provincial levels.[217] The IPEC is intended to address major IPR issues and related strategies, decision-making, legislation and enforcement, and international consultation.[218] However, evidence has mounted that it lacks necessary resources to carry out its organisational mandate. The Acting Office of IPEC was initially attached to the Ministry of Science and Technology and was soon transferred to the renamed State Intellectual Property Office in 1998. Since then, the IPEC ceased to function at the sate level.

Ten years later, in 2004, the State Council set up another similar IPR enforcement mechanism named National Working Group for IPR Protection (NWGIPR), where Vice Premier Yi Wu was nominated as the Director.[219] This "Working Group" is composed of various administrative and judicial authorities, namely the Supreme People's Court, Supreme People's Procuratorate, Ministry of Commerce, Ministry of Public Security, State Administration for Industry and Commerce, National Copyright Office, State Intellectual

---

[214] *See* "Responsibilities of NCA," *available at* <http://www.ncac.gov.cn/introduce/znfw.jsp>.

[215] Chris Buckley, "Pushed on Patents, China Shoves Back," *International Herald Tribune*, January 14, 2005.

[216] *Ibid.*

[217] Ruichun Duan, "China's Intellectual Property Rights Protection towards the 21st Century," 9 *Duke J. Comp. & Int'l L.* 217 (1998-1999).

[218] *Ibid.*

[219] *See* "Chinese Vice-premier on China's IPR Protection," *People's Daily*, January 14, 2005.

Property Office and General Administration of Customs.[220] NWGIPR is intended to enhance cooperation and coordination of IPR enforcement throughout the country and oversee the handling of major cases involving IPR protection.[221]

One significant development, compared with the IPEC, is that, under the uniform deployment of the NWGIPR, a cross-department IPR enforcement collaboration mechanism has been established to maximise communication and coordination among different dimensions.[222] The Acting Office of the NWGIPR, in conjunction with other relevant departments, has formulated and released China's Action Plan on IPR Protection 2006, and China's Action Plan on IPR Protection 2007.[223] Under the uniform leadership of the central government, the NWGIPR has initiated a national wide publicity campaign, aiming at altering and reshaping public perception towards IPR protection.[224] Pursuant to the requirement of the central government, all provinces, autonomous regions and municipalities have established their own branches of NWGIPR as state executive agencies overseeing the enforcement of IPR in various regions.[225]

To form such a cross-ministry entity comprising a several competent ministries and judicial authorities is without doubt a major undertaking. As a sign of greater efforts to protect IPR, subsequent to the establishment of the NWGIPR, the State Council launched a prolonged anti-infringement campaign scheduled from September 2004 to August 2005.[226]

During the campaign, special attention was given to seven areas where large amounts of fake products were identified – Beijing, Shanghai, Zhejiang, Jiangsu, Shandong, Guangdong and Fujian.[227] According to the statistics, only during the first two months of this campaign, the police investigated more than 1,000 IPR infringement cases, involving 550 million Chinese Yuan (equivalent to 66.5 million U.S. dollars).[228] Meanwhile, the Beijing Administration for

---

[220] Ruichun Duan, *supra* note 217.

[221] *Ibid.*

[222] Yi Wu, Vice Premier of China's State Council, "Speech at the China-US IPR Roundtable," Beijing, January 13, 2005.

[223] *See* "China's Action Plan on IPR Protection 2006," MOFCOM Documents, *available at* <http://bzb2.mofcom.gov.cn/aarticle/speechactivity/200603/20060301681736.html>, last visited August 19, 2006; "China's Plan on IPR Protection Action 2007," *available at* <http://english.gov.cn/2007-04/06/content_574197.htm>.

[224] "Marked Progress was Made in IPR Protection Work in China," MOFCOM Documents, *available at* <http://preview.english.mofcom.gov.cn/aarticle/counselorsreport/europereport/200501/20050100015005.html>.

[225] *Ibid.*

[226] *Ibid.*

[227] "2005 Daji Daoban Yinxiang Zhipin Zhuanxiang Xingdong Chuzhan Gaojie [The Cracking Down Campaign Has Met its First Goal]," SHDF, *available at* <http://www.shdf.gov.cn/newshtmt.html>.

[228] *See* "China Resolved to Protect IPR," *Xinhua News Agency*, January 13, 2005.

Industry and Commerce (AIC) recently cracked down on Xiu Shui Market, a renowned tourist spot adjacent to embassy area where many named brands were available at a fraction of the normal retail price.[229] However, this kind of anti-infringement campaign is normally policy-oriented in response to the external diplomatic pressure, and thus has only intermittent and temporary effect.

Seeking Transparency in "Camera Obscura"

Transparency is an important WTO principle,[230] and, to this end, maintenance of a case-reporting system for both administrative and judicial mechanisms is a necessity.[231] Without such a system, powers are apt to be abused and efficiency hindered.[232] Transparency as a WTO principle had been anticipated to be leverage to promote predictability and significantly alter the image of China's legal system upon its WTO accession. While China has been implementing systematic reform towards its legal system, this expectation appeared to be over-optimistic.

Indeed, despite the necessity of building rule of law-based administration and judiciary, the transparency in both administrative and judicial institutions in China remains elusive. For example, the government's legal gazette often fails to provide updated notice of changes in administrative rules and regulations and the public has no steady and direct access to the legal databases.[233] Moreover, the particular nature of China's legal system is largely reflected in what is categorised as internal (*neibu*) provisions and interpretations, which are normally unavailable to the public and which may be in contradiction with published laws and regulations.[234]

The lack of transparency, to a large extent, can be attributed to the Chinese preference for organising systems by human relationship rather than regulation. Political compromise and consensus are usually reached in "smoke-filled rooms" rather than in a public arena. In a system driven by personal favours characterised by "attaining objectives in camera obscura" (*anxiang caozuo*), transparency becomes problematic. As a consequence, the enforcement of IPR by relevant agencies has become a major structural problem within the bureaucracy, a system with a high degree of discretion based largely on "back

---

[229] *See* "Xiu Shui Partially Demolished," *People's Daily*, November 14, 2004.

[230] Key WTO transparency provisions include GATT Article 10, GATs Article 3 and TRIPs Article 63, which contain substantively similar obligations involving trade in goods, services and intellectual property respectively.

[231] Yonehara, "Enter the Dragon," *supra* note 141, at 100.

[232] *Ibid*, at 101.

[233] *See* Feaver, *supra* note 74, at 455-6.

[234] Patrick H. Hu, "The China 301 on Market Access: A Prelude to GATT Membership?" 3 *Minn. J. Global Trade.* (Minneapolis) (1994), at 144.

door" political manipulation,[235] which provides a raw portrayal of the Chinese bureaucracy. The intention of circumventing the excessive bureaucratic red tape leads to reluctance in addressing the IPR infringements, and many IPR proprietors have to seek assistance without recourse to legal system.[236]

Central Government is Ambitious Whereas Local Authorities are Ambiguous

With its comprehensive legislative structure, China has good will to eliminate infringements, but the central leaders sometimes have difficulties convincing local authorities and controlling their commercial behaviour.[237] In local regions, the saying goes, "the mountains are high, and the Emperor is far away (*shan gao huangdi yuan*)." [238] The vast extend of land and the sheer size of population constrains effective monitoring of implementation of the national strategy towards IPR protection.[239]

The intractability encountered by Chinese central policy makers in bringing their initiatives into full play has been a common problem in China.[240] Ironically, the massive spread of regionalism may have been inadvertently fostered by the central government in Deng's era,[241] as a short-term strategy to encourage certain people and certain regions[242] to prosper before others.[243] Since the end of the 1970s when the "open-door" policy was initiated, Chinese leaders have viewed the devolution of central authority to local regions as a necessary

---

[235] *See* Stanley Lubman, "Bird in a Cage: Chinese Law Reform after Twenty Years," 20 *Nw J. Int'l L. & Bus.* (2000), at 390-391.

[236] Susan Tiefenbrun, "The Piracy of Intellectual Property in China and the Former Soviet Union and Its Effects upon International Trade: A Comparison," 46 *Buff. L. Rev.* 11 (1998).

[237] Gregory S. Feder, "Enforcement of Intellectual Property Rights in China," *supra* note 139, at 253.

[238] Yonehara, "Enter the Dragon," *supra* note 141, at 82.

[239] *Ibid.*

[240] Donald Clarke, *supra* note 150, at 33.

[241] In 1978, the landmark Third Plenary Session of the Tenth Central Committee of the Communist Party encouraged local political autonomy and the economic decentralisation as a strategy to recover the national economy. *See e.g., China Deconstructs: Politics, Trade and Regionalism*, David S. G. Goodman and Gerald Segal (eds.), 5 (1994) (noting that "[d]ecentralisation and the introduction of market force suggest in general terms that the centres of the economic power are moving away from the centre to the localities and away from the CCP and the government").

[242] This differentiated policy reflected Deng Xiaoping's well-known motto, "allowing certain part of the country to be developed first (rang bufen diqu xian fu qi lai)." Coastal and border areas were encouraged to make full use of their geopolitical locations and comparative advantages in an effort to attract foreign trade and investment. *See ibid*, at 2.

[243] *See* Willard, *supra* note 32, at 372.

means of fostering economic growth.[244] Local authorities have been equipped with considerable decision-making power in establishing necessary institutions and conducting independent economic activities.[245] It is the policy of decentralisation and differentiation that fuels the emergence of the Special Economic Zones (SEZ) in the southern provinces.[246] Within more than a decade since the SEZ was set up, "the Chinese political structure was transformed from one that was once reputed for its high degree of centralisation and effectiveness into one in which the centre has difficulty coordinating its own agents' behaviour."[247] When the central government released its rigid control over the local authorities in an effort to facilitate economic growth, the steady growth of regional power bases and the gradual erosion of the central authority turned out to be a nightmare that Chinese leaders would never have considered possible.

In this context, it is not surprising that central government works in earnest while local authorities remain unconvinced that result will follow. As a result, central government is naturally facing domestic resistance in its effort to promote IPR protection.[248] Driven by economic interests vested in different regions, relevant organisations and departments are more or less playing the role of conniving with the spread of the counterfeiting and piracy. Cutting off the profit chain behind the counterfeits is key to curbing the problems.

The central government has attempted to "delocalise" (*shouquan*) the power over the past years. In September 2006, Liangyu Chen was ousted from his position as the Party Commissioner of Shanghai.[249] This has been arguably interpreted as a concrete step of the central government to tackle regionalism.[250] While measures are being taken, doubts still remain as to whether local protectionism can be eradicated eventually. Here little is possible without creating a truly independent legal system immune from administrative interference. There has, however, been little hint for making this a reality in the near future.

---

[244] Goodman & Segal, *supra* note 240, at 2; *see* also Jeffrey W. Berkman, "Intellectual Property Rights in the PRC: Impediments to Protection and the Need for the Rule of Law," 15 *UCLA Pac. Basin. L. J.* (1996), at 17.

[245] Goodman & Segal, *ibid*, at 2-5.

[246] *Ibid*, at 2.

[247] Lubman, *supra* note 30, at 385 (quoting Shaoguang Wang, "The Rise of the Regions: Fiscal Reform and the Decline of Central State Capacity in China," in Andrew G. Walder (ed.), *The Waning of the Communist State: Economic Origins of Political Decline in China and Hungary* 87 (1995)).

[248] J. Cheng, "China's Copyright System," *supra* note 168, at 1979.

[249] *See* Zhong Wu, "Out from under Jiang's Shadow," *Asia Times*, September 27, 2006 (mentioning that Chen's removal "certainly is a great help in checking the increasingly rampant regionalism enabling Beijing's macroeconomic control policy to be faithfully carried out at the local level").

[250] *Ibid*.

Struggle of the Judiciary in Adhering to "the Correct Political Orientation"

In China, the standards adopted by the courts for calculating economic damages tied to piracy – an essential factor for making ultimate prosecutorial decisions – are normally based on the value of the infringing products in the pirate market rather than the value in the legitimate market.[251] As a result, the low value of judicial fines and penalties are frequently viewed as "paltry" and regarded by infringers as "mere cost of doing business." [252] As has been reported, Microsoft has prevailed in taking legal actions against infringements, resulting in an award for compensation of only 2,600 U.S. dollars, which is controversially low.[253] Sega Enterprises claimed for punitive damages and a permanent injunction and was awarded 3,000 dollars as compensation.[254] The lack of commitment towards punishing infringers has only encouraged them to become bolder and put a premium on committing infractions.[255]

More importantly, it is part of traditional culture that infringers can "openly flaunt the law by relying on protection from friends [and relatives] in government."[256] Personal networks with influential individuals are usually more important than legal provisions in seeking appropriate remedies.[257] Indeed, as the Chinese proverb goes, "having friends in government is key to quenching everything intractable (*chao zhong you ren hao banshi*)." Although anecdotal, social network (*guanxi*) does play a significant role in shaping a typical Chinese society. When encountered difficult problems, people tend to seek solution through personal relationship rather than legal support, particularly pursuing network as the avenue of first recourse.[258] The use of such network to influence judicial decision is common in China through which certain cases are specifically categorised as "*guanxi* cases," which are expected to receive differential treatment.[259]

---

[251] *See* "Excerpt from the IIPA Special 301 Recommendations, February 24, 1997, People's Republic of China," at 5, *available at* <http://www.ipr.gov.cn/cn/zhuanti/meiIP zhuanlan/1997interIP301material.doc>.

[252] "The International Intellectual Property Alliance 2001 Special 301 Report, People's Republic of China, Executive Summary," at 29.

[253] *See* Chen, "Climbing the Great Wall," *supra* note 148, at 16.

[254] *Ibid.*

[255] *See* "Education Key to Protecting Inventors' Interests," *China Daily*, July 26, 2004.

[256] Willard, *supra* note 32, at 430.

[257] *See* Bejesky, *supra* note 161, at 474 (mentioning that "[p]ersonal connections with key individuals in emerging market countries are often more important than the written law").

[258] *Ibid.*

[259] Lubman, "Bird in a Cage," *supra* note 30, at 396.

Moreover, the judicial system in China is still dependent upon local administration in finance and personnel.[260] As Palmer describes, the judicial organ continuously serves as "an abiding stronghold of politicised administration of law" as it was before legal reform.[261] Under "unified leadership of the Party," a judge in China is *de facto* a governmental official, and it is apparent that most of the judges are more than complacent about the political *status quo*.[262] As a consequence, courts are still expected to follow instructions articulated by the Party Committee and the government, notably in the interim campaigns against crime, including anti-counterfeiting campaigns, which have proved to be a palliative rather than a cure.[263] Indeed, there is a slogan which has been given wide publicity within the Chinese judicial system: "keeping firmly to the correct political orientation of the judiciary (*jianchi shenpan gongzuo de zhengzhi fangxiang*)."[264] Succumbing to pressures from the local government, judges may appear partial to local parties.[265] In addition, some unethical judges solicit and take bribes in exchange for rewarding judgments (*quan qian jiaoyi*).[266] According to a survey conducted by the author in 2003, seventy-four percent of businessmen tend to believe that bribery is necessary for them to deal with Chinese officials and judges when seeking protection of their IPR.[267]

3.3.3 Economic Perspective

Huge Profits with Little Capital: An Irresistible Temptation

The most striking economic feature of counterfeiting and piracy is that the original products which are being counterfeited and pirated are expensive to

---

[260] Palmer, *supra* note 168, at 452; *see* also J. Cheng, "China's Copyright System," at 1992 (discussing the problems of Chinese judicial system due to its "inability to render impartial judgments").

[261] *See* Lubman, *supra* note 30, at 394.

[262] *See ibid.*

[263] *Ibid.*

[264] For example, Xiao Yang, the President of Supreme People's Court, gave emphasis during an interview that the Court must respect the leadership of the Party conscientiously and keep firmly to the correct political orientation. *See* Xiao Yang, "Kexue Fazhan Fayuan Shiye, Tuoshan Chuli Shi Ge Guanxi (Improving Judiciary through Coping with Ten essential Relationships)," *Xinhua News Net*, January 5, 2006, *available at* <http://news.xinhuanet.com/politics/2006-01/05/content_4014729.htm>, last visited September 26, 2006.

[265] J. Cheng, "China's Copyright System," *supra* note 168, at 1992-3.

[266] *See, e.g.*, Yonehara, "Enter the Dragon," *supra* note 141, at 92-3.

[267] *See* the List of Semi-structured Interview Questions (question 5) and the responses illustrated in the following List of Charts at the Appendices of this book.

create but inexpensive to copy.[268] At the same time, a significant gap exists between the retail prices of the pirate and the legitimate products which make it possible for the infringers to usurp market share from the legitimate producers.[269] Under this scenario, it is no exaggeration that counterfeiting and piracy have developed into a nationwide shadow economy that contributes to the national economy.[270] Eliminating this shadow economy would mean depriving communities of literally hundreds of jobs.[271] The temptation of large profits, little capital, and vast opportunities for employment is a difficult combination to resist.[272] By some estimates, piracy directly or indirectly employs three million to five million people, and provides national income of between nineteen and twenty-four billion dollars.[273] Mainly due to economic decentralisation, the infringement of counterfeiting and piracy occurs especially at the local levels, where it supports local economies.[274] Shutting down counterfeiting and piracy means, in many instances, cracking down a pillar of a cornerstone industry that will bring about economic tension or social turmoil, which are problems that the Chinese government monitors closely.[275]

It is worthwhile mentioning that the above aspects affecting IPR enforcement are both inter-related and inter-dependent. For instance, the inadequate judiciary is associated with inherent defect of the political system and, if there were independent judicial authority, the problem with local protectionism would be solved readily. It is an interesting and demonstrable fact that the political transition, *inter alia*, is a decisive factor and therefore acts as a pivot.

---

[268] Glenn R. Butterton, "Norms and Property in the Middle Kingdom," 15 *Wis. Int' L.J.* (1997), at 281, 293.

[269] *Ibid*, at 294.

[270] *See* China-U.S. Trade Issues, Congressional Research Service, July 1, 2005, at 12.

[271] Alexander Chen, "Climbing the Great Wall," *supra* note 148.

[272] *See* WTO Council for Trade-Related Aspects of Intellectual Property Rights, "Transitional Review Mechanism of China, Communication from the European Communities and their Member States," IP/C/W371 (August 29, 2002).

[273] *See* Robert Marquand, "China's Pirate Industry Thriving," *The Christian Sci. Monitor*, January 9, 2002, at 6. By contrast, according to the Report of China State Council Development Research Centre, the estimated market value of counterfeit goods made in China was from 19 billion dollars to 24 billion dollars in 2001, which could well be a conservative figure. *See* "China Faces Uphill Battle Against Counterfeits," *People's Daily*, July 23, 2003.

[274] Willard, *supra* note 32, at 429-30 (illustrating the role of regionalism and impact of infringing activities by government owned entities).

[275] *See* Berkman, *supra* note 228, at 19 (mentioning the local authorities remain unwilling to enforce laws against local business pillars which serve as important sources of local revenue).

3.4 Conclusion

As the instrument establishing the standard of international IPR protection, TRIPs serves as the benchmark for evaluating the adequacy of China's IPR laws.[276] According to this benchmark, China's IPR legislation is consistent with international standards.[277] While China has notably upgraded its IPR legal regime, an unwillingness regarding enforcement remains a significant problem. Since enforcement procedures form essential part of the TRIPs Agreement,[278] China's claim to TRIPs consistency rings hollow should there be no corresponding enforcement measures.[279] The mystery behind the predicaments entails China's cultural uniqueness, institutional impediments and economic insufficiency, and these are knotty points that we now turn.

---

[276] *See* Terence P. Stewart, *The GATT Uruguay Round: A Negotiating History (1986-1992)*, 2249 (1993) (introducing TRIPs as the cornerstone of the global IPR infrastructure).

[277] *Ibid.*

[278] The enforcement procedures are mandated by Part III of TRIPs, comprising no less than 20 articles (Article 41-61) on the enforcement of IPR.

[279] *See* Lubman, *supra* note 30, at 413.

4 Cultural Perplexity in Intellectual Property: How to Undo the Gordian Knot[1]

China is conventionally depicted as one of the main offenders in the international IPR arena with a strong perception of legislative shortfalls. However, China has established a full panoply of IPR legislation and institutions.[2] It is the enforcement of IPR that is contrastingly fragile. This has indisputably emerged as the central and essential issue when reviewing China's IPR.

The last chapter examined the theoretical literature addressing Chinese IPR enforcement and involved a multidisciplinary and interdisciplinary approach to do so. What was not explored there but is the focus of the current section is whether the conventional interpretation has accurately focused on the real systemic issues which have allowed the problem to arise and make it hard to address. This is what current chapter seeks to address.

There is an extensive theoretical literature examining the IPR enforcement problem in China. Confucianism is the concept most frequently cited by commentators, while the literature criticising Confucian philosophy as the root of China's IPR enforcement problems is plenteous.[3] However, current main-

---

1   This chapter of the book draws upon Wei Shi, "Cultural Perplexity in Intellectual Property: Is Sealing a Book an Elegant Offense?" 32 (1) *N.C. J. Int'l L. & Com. Reg.* 1-48 (2006).

2   *See e.g.*, Robert Bejesky, "Investing in the Dragon: Managing the Patent versus Trade Secret Protection Decision for the Multinational Corporation in China," 11 *Tulsa J. Comp. & Int'l L.* 487 (2004)(mentioning that "China has eagerly consummated international treaties and has adopted strong [domestic intellectual property legislations] [...] to attract technological innovations"). *See* also Warren Newberry, "Copyright Reform in China: A 'TRIPs' Much Shorter and Less Strange Than Imagined?" 35 *Conn. L. Rev.* 1446 (2003)(concluding that China's "reform brought China's copyright regime into compliance with the TRIPs Agreement and the Berne Convention").

3   *See, e.g.*, Alford, *To Steal a Book is an Elegant Offense*, at 8, 19-22 (1995) (discussing how the Confucian culture militated against copyright protection and did not allow intellectual property protection to take root); "The Second Coming of Intellectual Property Rights in China," 11 *Benjamin N. Cardozo School of Law Occasional Papers in Intellectual Property* 44 (2002) (contending that "the culprit behind the Chinese piracy problem is the Confucian beliefs ingrained in the Chinese culture," which contradicts intellectual property rights"); Alexander C. Chen, "Climbing the Great Wall: A Guide to Intellectual Property Enforcement in the People's Republic of China," 25 *AIPLA Quarterly* 10 (1997) (mentioning that "Confucianism [...] provided [a] strong barrier[] to the idea of 'intellectual property' [...].."); Andrew Evans, "Taming the Counterfeit

stream legal epistemology links China's enforcement problem to Confucian values, which is confusing and misleading. It is a mainstream point of view that Chinese cultural and philosophical history and Confucianism in particular provide a pervasive and unconscious influence on their comprehension of, and commitment to, intellectual property laws. This argument levels criticism at the phrase "to steal a book is an elegant offence" (*qie shu bu suan tou*) which indicates that traditional Chinese culture does not consider copying to be "wrong." Under the dominating theory of this point of view, Confucianism is a cultural predisposition leading to a lack of consciousness of intellectual property rights,[4] and the creed of "elegant offence" is likely to have a continuing influence on attitudes towards IPR protection. One cynical commentator has even assert that "until it abandons its twisted Confucianism, the [Asian] region will trail the West," and allege that it is time to "deconstruct Confucius."[5] In this chapter, the author aims to raise a challenge to this mainstream perception and demonstrate the genuine causes of China's IPR enforcement problems.

This chapter considers the enforcement insufficiency via a discussion of the evolving cultural phenomena associated with the fundamental systemic weakness to China's institutional problems. Apart from exploring the origin, evolution and impact of Confucian values on the modern Chinese society, this chapter extends beyond China to focus on the global IPR regime and also to compare China with other economies that have emerged in Asia, such as Japan and Korea. By tracing and comparing development trajectories of different economies, it concludes that counterfeiting and piracy are not problems caused

---

Dragon: The WTO, TRIPs and Chinese Intellectual Property Laws," 31 *Ga. J. Int'l & Comp. L.* 587, 588-90 (2003)(suggesting that Confucian ethics has been a philosophical obstacle to combating Chinese counterfeiting and piracy); Jill Chiang Fung, "Can Mickey Mouse Prevail in the Court of the Monkey King? Enforcing Foreign Intellectual Property Rights in the People's Republic of China," 18 *L.A. Int'l & Comp. L.J.*(1996) at 613, 616-24 (1996) (mentioning that "the modern Chinese laws have incorporated the pure Confucian ideas inherent in traditional Chinese legal thinking," which has especially influenced the development of China's intellectual property laws); Eric M. Griffin, "Stop Relying on Uncle Sam! – A Proactive Approach to Copyright Protection in the People's Republic of China," 6 *Tex. Intell. Prop. L.J.*169, 182 (1998)("[M]ore important than the lack of protective influence by the state is the influence of Confucianism [...]."); Ann Kent, "Waiting for Rights: China's Human Rights and China's Constitutions", *1949-1989*, 13 *Hum. Rts. Q.* 170, 174 (1991) (stating that the Chinese view of rights is attributable to the "traditional concepts of society, the state, and the law," and these concepts, in turn, are deeply rooted in Confucian philosophy and ideology).

4   Brent T. Yonehara, "Enter the Dragon: China's WTO Accession, Film Piracy and Prospects for Enforcement of Copyright Laws," 22 DePaul-*LCA J. Art & Ent. L.*, at 74-80 (2002)(ascribing China's IPR enforcement problem to cultural and historical predispositions).

5   Sin-ming Shaw, "It's True. Asians Can't Think," *Time International*, May 31, 1999, at 23.

by the Confucian ethics, as the mainstream view states, but rather common inevitable consequences of inadequate economic development, and a by-product of a unique set of socioeconomic crises deriving from the development of a dysfunctional institutional regime.

In view of the fact that both legal and non-legal factors interact in shaping Chinese attitudes towards IPR protection, the analysis comes from a prismatic lens, from cultural to institutional, from institutional to overtly economical.[6] It is however worthwhile to mention that none of these factors alone may be sufficient to account for China's institutional variables which directly or indirectly affect China's IPR enforcement. This section is intended to provide a penetrating insight into the environment needed to enable development of an effective IPR enforcement mechanism.

4.1 Focusing Accurately on the Targeted Problems

The theoretical literature of the last chapter has examined the reasons for IPR enforcement problem in China. One potentially interesting testing ground that has not been empirically explored in much depth is how to identify the dominating aspect and focus accurately on the targeted problem. This section challenges the mainstream viewpoint by providing clues to the genuine Chinese cultural underpinnings and further creates a new cultural perspective. In addition, it examines the copying phenomenon through insights into the economic sphere and seeks to assess the link between economic development and IPR protection.

4.1.1 Confucius Confusion: Is Stealing a Book an Elegant Offence?

Look through the Confucian Values

PRINCIPLES OF CONFUCIANISM

Confucianism is an ancient Chinese way of thought that spread through much of the neighbouring Asian region, including Japan, Korea, Taiwan, and Vietnam.[7] As a systematic code of interpersonal behaviour, Confucianism is a

---

[6]   The lines between these conceptual categories are blurred in practice.

[7]   It is debatable whether Confucianism should be described as a religion, or a quasi-religion. While it involves much ritual, little of it could be construed as worship or meditation in a formal sense. Whether Confucianism should be considered a religious tradition or not is part of the question of how to define Confucianism. The interpretations of Confucianism are contrastingly divergent. *See* Xinzhong Yao, *An Introduction to Confucianism* 38-39 (2000).

practical, political, and social doctrine, rather than a religion or a quasi-religion.[8]

As a philosophical system, Confucianism has been developed from the writings attributed to the Chinese philosopher Confucius (551-479 BC).[9] Born in *Lu*, a small state in current Shandong Province,[10] Confucius lived in ancient China during the chaotic period of feudal rivalry known as the Warring States Period (*Zhanguo Shidai*).[11] He is credited with numerous books, the best-known of which is *The Analects*, a collection of his sayings which was compiled into its modern form during the Han Dynasty (206 BC-24 AD).[12] His writings and beliefs did not become popular until well after his death[13] and international recognition and study of Confucianism did not occur until the sixteenth century.[14]

Confucian thought is based on varying levels of moral quality in connection with which the rituals of Confucianism evolved over time and matured into the four forms: *li* – ritual (which originally meant "to sacrifice"); *xiao* – filial piety; *zhong* – loyalty; *ren* – humaneness.[15] The *li* is roughly analogous to the Western concept of natural law.[16] It governs people's conduct and proper etiquette with regard to interactions with family, political establishments, and society at large, and emphasises virtue and model behaviour.[17] In Confucianism, the ultimate goal is to strive for a harmonious society, as "everyone all over

---

[8]   *See China: A Historical and Cultural Dictionary* 62 (Michael Dillon ed., 1998). *See also* Yongming Chen, Ruxue Yu Zhonggue Zongjiao Chuantong [Confucianism and China's Religious Tradition], in Religious Culture Press 109-131 (2003)(stating that, as an orthodox philosophy, Confucianim contains few characteristics found in religions).

[9]   His Chinese name was Master Kong *(Kung Futze / Kong Fuzi)*, which was Latinised to Confucius by Italian Jesuit Matteo Ricci (1552-1610) in order to portray Chinese society to Europeans. *See* Yao, *supra* note 7, at 1-2, 21-22.

[10]   Patricia Buckley Ebrey, *The Cambridge Illustrated History of China*, Cambridge University Press 42 (1996).

[11]   *See, China: A Historical and Cultural Dictionary, supra* note 89, at 62-63 (explaining that Confucianism had no priesthood or liturgy and Confucius himself was not treated as *god*).

[12]   Written by his pupils, *The Analects* is regarded as the chief text of Confucianism. It contains sayings and conversations between the Teacher and his disciples. For a full text and comprehensive interpretation of The Analects, *see, Confucius, The Analects* (Raymond Dawson trans., 1993).

[13]   *See, China: A Historical and Cultural Dictionary, supra* note 8, at 204.

[14]   *See* Yao, *supra* note 7, at 2 (mentioning that, by introducing Confucianism to Europe, Jesuit Matteo Ricci became a pioneer of Confucian studies in the West).

[15]   *See,* Hyung Kim, *Fundamental Legal Concepts of China and the West: A Comparative Study* 30-31 (1981).

[16]   *Ibid*, at 57.

[17]   *Ibid*.

the world ought to be brothers."[18] Confucianism has shaped the Chinese perceptions, which have been fostered and developed over the tens of centuries.[19]

One of Confucius's most important doctrines is that there is a proper order to all things in the universe, including human society, which is described as "harmony."[20] Confucius illustrated this doctrine as "let a ruler be a ruler, a subject a subject, a father a father, and a son a son (*jun jun chen chen fu fu zi zi*)."[21] Through the definition of "five cardinal relationships," Confucius provided a simple guide for ordering the family and society. The five moral disciplines that govern the five cardinal relationships are: (1) Justice and righteousness should mark the relations between sovereign and subject; (2) A proper rapport should be maintained between father and son; (3) Division of duties between husband and wife; (4) The younger should give precedence to the elder; (5) Faith and trust should reign over relationships between friends.[22] Confucius's "five cardinal relationships" reflect a hierarchical order based on a set of norms and virtues.[23] As Confucius emphasised, within and through this traditional order, peace and harmony can be achieved if every person plays his or her proper role in society and strives to uphold the responsibilities of that role.[24] In this context, Confucianism advocates the virtues of honesty and loyalty in an effort to create a harmonious social order.

CONFUCIAN VALUES AND INTELLECTUAL PROPERTY

As the oldest continuous civilisation in the East, China has long been regarded as an "exceptionally creative and inventive" nation and has enjoyed a remarkable history of technological and creative enterprise.[25] It is common knowl-

---

[18] *See, Confucius, The Analects* 44-45, bk. 12, chp. 5 (1993).

[19] Yonehara, *supra* note 4, at 74; *see also* Hyung Kim, *supra* note 15.

[20] In Confucianism, "harmony" is deemed as "the highest virtue," and is closely related to nature, politics, ethics and daily life, and is regarded as a moral standard to cultivate order and peace internally and externally. *See* Yao, *supra* note 7, at 172; *see also* Pamela A. Newman, "The Confucian Ethic: A System of Ideals in Korea," *Social Studies, Comparative Religion*, at 49, *available at* <http://www.koreasociety.org/>.

[21] Confucius, *supra* note 12, at 46, bk. 12, chp.11. When Duke *Jing* of *Qi* consulted Confucius about government, Confucius replied that the only way such a doctrine could be made to function effectively and efficiently was for each person to behave according to the prescribed societal norms. That is, let everyone play his proper role in the natural order, and all will be well.

[22] *See, RoutledgeCurzon Encyclopedia of Confucianism* 501-03 (Xinzhong Yao ed., 2003).

[23] *Ibid. See also* Ronald J. Troyer, "Chinese Thinking about Crime and Social Control," in *Social Control in the People's Republic of China* 45, 51-52 (Ronald J. Troyer *et al.* eds., 1989)(claiming that Confucian philosophy has designated the importance of particular actors in society by placing the state first, the collective second, and the right of the individual last).

[24] *RoutledgeCurzon Encyclopedia of Confucianism, supra* note 22, at 501.

[25] John R. Allison & Lianlian Lin, "The Evolution of Chinese Attitudes toward Property Rights Invention and Discovery," 20 *U. Pa. J. Int'l Econ. L.* 735, 742 (1999).

edge that the Chinese invented a number of items prior to their "invention" or use in the West.[26] The famous four great inventions, namely papermaking, typography, the compass, and gunpowder,[27] have profoundly impacted the world's economy and the human culture. Trademarks in China can be traced back to the *Tang* Dynasty (618-907 A.D.), when traders "started using marks and logos to distinguish goods."[28] With the advent of printing technology in the *Tang* Period, China also saw the first "substantial, sustained efforts to regulate publication and republication."[29] During the *Ming* and *Qing* Dynasties, an "informal system of guild registration and protection of [trade]marks was instituted, where a manufacturer could register his trade mark with other guilds."[30] As early as the Imperial Period, beginning in 221 B.C.,[31] Chinese rulers issued decrees criminalising the copying of certain works,[32] although these decrees could hardly be characterised as copyright in the modern sense.[33] Not surprisingly, the historical record dealing with intellectual property in China appeared very early.

At least to some extent, Confucius can be viewed as a popular international synonym of China, and Confucianism has been acknowledged as the foundational philosophy of oriental civilisation and culture.[34] In contrast to most Western societies, Confucian philosophy is characterised by a collection of "individuals" and their "interconnections and interdependencies."[35] Accordingly, Confucian ethics place a relatively low value on terms based on individuals and profit, but it does place value on the concept of communal property.[36] This is at significant variance with the dominating personal rights and property bases that are important to Western ideas. The Western concept of property is closely associated with the philosophy of natural law originated

---

[26] *Ibid.*

[27] *See ibid.* For a detailed introduction of the Chinese innovations, see generally Joseph Needham, *Science and China's Influence on the World, in* The Legacy of China, Raymond Dawson (ed.) 234(1971); Robert K. G. Temple, *The Genius of China: 3,000 Years of Science, Discovery, and Invention* (1986).

[28] Hamideh Ramjerdi and Anthony D'Amato, "The Intellectual Property Rights Laws of The People's Republic of China," 21 *N.C. J. Int'l L. & Com. Reg.* 169, 172 (1995).

[29] Gregory S. Feder, "Enforcement of Intellectual Property Rights in China: You Can Lead a Horse to Water, but You Can't Make It Drink," 37 *Va. J. Int'l L.* 223, 230 (1996)(quoting William P. Alford, *supra* note 32, at 13).

[30] Charles Baum, "Trade Sanctions and the Rule of Law: Lessons from China," 1 *Stan. J. E. Asian Aff.* 46, 51 (2001).

[31] The year 221 B.C., which marks the shift from state to empire, represents the beginning of the imperial era, a period that lasted until the fall of the Qing Dynasty in 1912. *See China: A Historical and Cultural Dictionary, supra* note 8, at 154.

[32] Baum, *supra* note 30, at 50 ("Han dynasty regulations (circa 200 B.C.), *for example*, barred the unauthorised reproduction of the Confucian Classics").

[33] *See* Allison & Lin, *supra* note 25, at 743.

[34] Hyung Kim, *supra* note 15.

[35] Ming-Jer Chen, *Inside Chinese Business: A Guide for Managers Worldwide* 72 (2001).

[36] Hyung Kim, *supra* note 15, at 90.

from the Greek Stoics[37] and later interpreted and codified by Roman philosophers and jurists,[38] while Confucianism reflects the natural order and emphasises the obligations necessary to maintain it.

Nevertheless, this unique philosophy has played a positive role in fostering innovation and entrepreneurship over the centuries in China and other Eastern nations. Confucianism does not reject personal rights, but affords protection in a different way. Its emphasis on "personal development, in contrast to personal gain, helped create a culture in which the individual was viewed as quite important, but primarily so because of his or her contribution to society."[39] It would therefore be inaccurate to state that Confucianism and technology cannot coexist, or that Confucianism has served to hold back technological development.[40] Under the set of Confucian ethics there appears no credible evidence of a link between "honesty and loyalty" and "counterfeiting and piracy."

DIMINUTION OF CONFUCIAN VALUES

The influence of Confucian values has been diminishing and, although widely thought to be the most important basis of Chinese culture, the sage's ideas were severely criticised during the "Cultural Revolution" [41] as the "superstructure of feudalism."[42] During this period, statues at the Confucians' Temple were regarded as feudal relics and seriously damaged by the "Red Guards."[43] Although the broken statues were later carefully mended, this was more to

---

[37]   Ellis Washington, "Excluding the Exclusionary Rule: Natural Law vs. Judicial Personal Policy Preferences," 10 *Deakin L. Rev.* 772, 775 (2005).

[38]   *Ibid*

[39]   Allison & Lin, *supra* note 25, at 744.

[40]   *See generally,* David J. Thorpe, "Some Practical Points about Starting a Business in Singapore," 27 *Creighton L. Rev.* 1039 (1994) (demonstrating the extent of economic development in Singapore).

[41]   The Cultural Revolution, more precisely known as the "Great Proletarian Cultural Revolution," was a massive attempt by Mao Zedong to inculcate the younger Chinese generation with his ardour for totalistic iconoclasm. The so-called "Four Olds", especially the traditional religions and philosophies, which were relegated to the sphere of feudal superstitions, were attacked and destroyed. For a comprehensive account of the Cultural Revolution, *see, The Cambridge History of China*, Vol.15, 305-6, 660-5, Denis Twitchett and John K. Fairbank (eds.)(1991). *See* also Tony H. Chang (Compiler), *China During the Cultural Revolution, 1966-1976: A Selected Bibliography of English Language Works* (1999).

[42]   *See* Willem Van Kemenade, *China, Hong Kong, Taiwan, Inc.*, Diane Webb trans., (1998).

[43]   The Red Guards in China were composed of high school and university students and young workers, and were formed during the conflict within factions of the Chinese Communist Party during the Cultural Revolution in the 1960s. The name was borrowed from the *krasnaya gvardia*, who protected Lenin after the October Revolution. *See The Cambridge History of China, supra* note 38, at 84-85. *See also, China: A Historical and Cultural Dictionary, supra* note 8, at 260-61.

preserve historical heritage than to demonstrate a widespread reconciliation between Confucianism and current beliefs.[44]

From that time on, the influence of Confucian values has been diminishing. Now, in modern day China, attitudes towards traditional Confucian values tend to fall into two attitudinal categories, which are based on age, education and experience.[45] Older generations tend to adhere to practices steeped in Confucianism and think of ethical behavior as a long-term commitment. By contrast, younger generations – born in the 1960s and 1970s – influenced by modern culture are apathetic and give little thought to traditional values.[46] Unlike old generation, young people are quick to accept new things and are spiritually distanced from Chinese traditional values. For example, they are not afraid to use the legal system if they think it will help them. Thus, the Confucian tradition is fading and dwindling gradually, despite the attempts of many scholars to interpret Confucian ethics as a spiritual resource for the emerging global community.[47]

Kong Yi Ji as a Harlequin

One important element of the misunderstanding of Confucian values is the intentionally or unintentionally misattributed proposition "To Steal a Book is an Elegant Offence" (*Qie Shu Bu Suan Tou*). This is a concept unknown to Confucianism and was only popularised with the 1919 publication of the popular fiction *Kong Yi Ji*, written by the famous novelist Lu Xun.[48] In his fiction, the

---

[44] *Ibid.*

[45] *See* Mengxi Liu, "Lun Chuantong Wenhua de Liushi yu Chongjian [the Erosion and Reconstruction of the Traditional Culture]," *Contemporary Philosophy*, *available at* <http://www.contemphil.net/articles/news/lwhctdlsycj.htm>.

[46] *Ibid.*

[47] In the last two decades, a number of "leading [Neo-]Confucian thinkers in Taiwan, mainland China, and Hong Kong independently concluded that the most significant contribution the Confucian tradition can offer the global community is the [conception] of the 'Unity of Heaven and Humanity' [*tian ren he yi*]…" Tu Weiming, "The Ecological Turn in New Confucian Humanism: Implications for China and the World," 130 *Daedalus J. Am. Acad. Arts Sci.* 243, 243 (2001). In mainland China, in keeping pace with the so-called Neo-Confucian revival movement [*Guoxue fuxing yundong*] which has emerged in East Asia, Chinese scholars and commentators seek to explicitly promote Confucian values in society in an effort to strengthen the legitimacy of the Party. *See ibid.* at 243-64.

[48] Lu Xun (1881-1936), pseudonym of Zhou Shuren, was a short-story writer, essayist, critic, and literary theorist. He is arguably one of the greatest writers of modern China, and is considered a revolutionary pioneer by Chinese Communists. In some of his works, Lu Xun contrasted the hypocrisy of upper-class intellectuals with the suffering of the lower-class individuals and condemned the traditional Confucian culture. For a comprehensive introduction to his work, *see* James Reeve Pusey, *Lu Xun and Evolution* (1998); Jon Eugene von Kowallis, *The Lyrical Lu Xun: A Study of His Classical-Style Verse* (1996).

author attempts to examine the obsolescence of a pathetic literature and exemplifies his belief that literature should be socially relevant, and avoid the "clichés" of traditional Chinese linguistics that, in his view, had hampered and restrained people's creative thinking for centuries. In Lu Xun's portrayal, Kong Yi Ji was depicted as a poor harlequin, who was "a big, pallid man whose wrinkled face often bore scars," and was made fun of by everybody.[49] He earned a living from copying manuscripts for rich patrons and sometimes stole books to trade for wine. His behaviour drew on his being soundly beaten. *To Steal a Book Is an Elegant Offence* was his augment when he was taunted. His personal character and his way of thinking are thus far removed from Confucian values. However, he shares the same Chinese surname with Confucius (*"Kong"*), and this did much to cause and perpetuate confusion in the popular mind. Indeed, the phrase "To Steal a Book Is an Elegant Offence" was unknown to Chinese until Kong Yiji as a fictional character appeared in the early twentieth century and, interestingly, it was unpopular to foreigners until Professor Alford's book made its debut in the mid 1990s.

The Paradox of Confucian Determinism

When it comes to intellectual property enforcement problems in China and other Asian countries, Confucianism is commonly identified as the root of the problem. This suggests a question: in the current legal and political environment, where intellectual property is to be respected under the law, should Confucian values restrain people from breaking the law, or remain a passive influence allowing it to be broken?

As previously noted, Confucian ethics promote social order and ethical behaviour. Confucius emphasised that each person has responsibilities to live up to within the natural order and social hierarchy they are in.[50] Traditionally, in China, ethical and moral obligations formed the basis for personal and commercial communications and, as a result of Confucian philosophy, moral obligations may well have a greater influence on Chinese attitudes than Western thought may perceive.[51]

It is apparent that the predominant commentary on Confucian philosophy serves to obscure rather than illuminate the situation. This is true because it is difficult to comprehend the prevalent theft of intellectual property in China as an inevitable outcome of an ethic that advocates "honesty," unless of course the ethical concepts derived from Confucius have somehow been subverted. "To steal a book" is not an "elegant offence." Rather, it is, from a Confucian

---

[49] Lu Xun, "Kong Yiji," in *Na Han [Outcry]*, Renmin Wenxue Chubanshe [People's Literature Press], 20-25 (1973).

[50] Yao, *supra* note 7, at 1-23.

[51] Yingshi Yu, *Zhongguo Chuantong Sixiang de Xiandai Quanshi [The Modern Interpretation of Chinese Traditional Thought]* 130 (1987).

viewpoint, an act that is against the "natural order." Confucius has been a convenient scapegoat of a misleading theory. Now it is the time to rehabilitate Confucianism and identify more compelling causes.

Empirical evidence has also been seen through a recent survey conducted by the author.[52] In this survey, approximately fifty-eight percent interviewees see IPR infringement as an "inelegant offence," with additional twenty-two inclined to share the same belief.[53] In addition, fifty-nine percent of interviewees state that there is no negative impact of Confucian philosophy on their altitude towards IPR protection.[54] Correspondingly, fifty-five percent of foreign businessmen who involved in the interview do not view the cultural environment very seriously.[55] This contributes the belief that the "famous" but meretricious Chinese proverb may not be widely accepted, at least among government officials and business persons.

4.1.2 New Cultural Perspective

Utilitarianism: By-product of the Mere Economic Reform

As previously discussed, Confucianism has arguably faded in mainland China in recent decades. As a result, older Chinese ethics have been eroded and replaced by more pragmatic and self-serving utilitarian ideas,[56] which found fertilisation in a set of socioeconomic crises that originated from a haphazard and dysfunctional institutional regime.

LORD YE'S FONDNESS OF DRAGONS: DILEMMA OF DEMOCRACY IN CHINA

In ancient China, a county magistrate in Chu Kingdom was called the Lord Ye (*Ye Gong*) who was known widely as a great lover of dragons. The Lord of Ye was so fond of dragons that the dragons were painted or carved on his walls, pillars, beams, furniture, window lattices and ceilings. In addition, all his robes and bed nets were embroidered with different images of dragons. The dragon in heaven was moved and, in a stormy night, descended to earth to

---

[52]   *See infra* Appendices.

[53]   *See* the List of Semi-structured Interview Questions (question 3) and the responses demonstrated in the following List of Charts at the Appendices of the book.

[54]   *See* the List of Semi-structured Interview Questions (question 2) and List of Charts.

[55]   *Ibid* (question 6).

[56]   Philosophically, utilitarianism is an ethical doctrine that prescribes the quantitative maximisation of good consequences for society at large. *See generally*, John Plamenatz, *The English Utilitarians* (1958) (providing a comprehensive discussion of utilitarianism). The ethical theory proposed by Jeremy Bentham and James Mill states that all action should be directed towards achieving the greatest happiness for the greatest number of people. *See ibid.* To examine the utilitarianism in a philosophical perspective is beyond the scope of this book. Here this term is only used to describe the dominating self-serving phenomena of losing ethical constrains in China.

visit him. The dragon glided down to Lord Ye's house, poked its head into the window, leaving its long tail out in the yard. At this sight, the Lord Ye fled in panic.[57] This story shows that Lord Ye was not genuinely fond of dragons but merely *images* of dragons – he professed love of what he actually feared (*ye gong hao long*).

Chinese central leaders are in such an ambivalent and self-contradictory position in terms of China's political transition. Many critics have linked economic changes to greater political freedom in China.[58] But the reality is that China is currently standing at an ideological, social, and political crossroads: the intersection of a splendid economic landscape marred by lagging political reform.[59] Like two lines askew, China's economic and political structures are contrastingly divergent. The assumption that the spread of Beatles music and Mercedes Benz cars throughout China is representative of the triumph of Western democracy is only a myth.

On one hand, Chinese leaders genuinely believe that the Western style of democracy is not suitable for the fundamental realities (*guoqing*) of China.[60] This may be either because they have learned from China's modern history [61] and the recent history of the former Soviet Union that it will lead the country to social chaos and state fragmentation, [62] or because they may be afraid that the Communist Party will lose its status as the ruling party if radical democratisation commences. [63] Political reform has thus been characterised by incrementalism and progress made only by the "trial and error method,"[64] carrying on through "existing political institutions within the one-party framework." [65] The stated objective of the Communist Party to implement political reform is often just a way to strengthen its own legitimacy.[66] Despite pious declarations

---

57   *See* Xiao Min, *Classical Chinese Idioms 1: Lord Ye's Fondness of Dragons* [Jingdian Chengyu Gushi 1: Ye Gong Hao Long], Northeast Normal University Press 1-156 (2001).

58   Allison & Lin, *supra* note 25, at 774.

59   *See* Wei-Wei Zhang, "China's Political Transition: Trends and Prospects," 7 *EurAsia Bulletin*, Publication of European Institute for Asian Studies 11 (2003)(asserting that Chinese economic reform may better be described as "great economic reform with lesser political reform").

60   Information Office of the State Council of the People's Republic of China, Building of Political Democracy in China § 1 (October 19, 2005), *available at* <http://english. people.com.cn/whitepaper/democracy/democracy.html.>

61   *Ibid.*

62   *See* Mu Bai, "Sulian Jubian Gaosu Women Shenme [What the Collapse of the Soviet Union Tells Us]?" *People's Daily*, November 3, 2004.

63   *Ibid. See* also Yongnian Zheng, "Political Incrementalism: Political Lessons from China's 20 Years of Reform," *Third World Quarterly* 1160 (1999).

64   Information Office of the State Council of the People's Republic of China, *supra* note 50, at § VI. *See* also Yongnian Zheng, *ibid*, at 1160-1.

65   Wei-Wei Zhang, *supra* note 59, at 3.

66   *See* Anthony Saich, "Beijing's Balancing Act on Reform," *The Financial Times*, November 4, 2002 (mentioning that substantive political reform would strengthen the le-

of good intentions about political reform, the process of democratisation seems to have stagnated.[67] Those in competing political parties continue to draw fire against themselves.

On the other hand, however, there have been growing concerns that the ongoing economic reform may have opened a Pandora's Box of unintended consequences. Harry Harding, a leading China expert, has suggested that while "dismantling many of the totalitarian institutions of the past, the Chinese Communist party is not yet prepared to move equally rapidly towards the creation of new institutions that could permit the articulation or aggregation of political demands."[68] This dilemma has made Chinese leaders solicitous in initiating substantial political reform. Although the principle of democracy has been introduced into the Constitution, China likes democracy in the way of Lord Ye: China accepts the fame of democracy but does not embrace the spirit of it. While China has committed itself to a socialist "rule of law" state,[69] without the spirit of liberal democracy, "rule of law" in China will unsurprisingly remain symbolic and problematic.

SPECIAL POLITICAL ECOLOGY AND SOCIO-ECONOMIC CRISES

The enormous transformation of the political, social and economic landscape has fundamentally reshaped the beliefs and values of Chinese citizens.[70] Economic reform has not only brought about greater prosperity, but also created "unprecedented opportunities for people to pursue their own interest and shape their own destiny."[71] Individual aspirations of the citizens are widespread, but they are released without a corresponding regulation system. In this context, the intellectual enforcement problem in China is a unique political phenomenon resulting from the systemic dystrophy fundamental to the institutional development and, in a broader sense, it may be the source for recasting and strengthening legal enforcement in China as a whole.

Having failed to bring its political evolution into comprehensive correspondence with its economic development, the Chinese government runs the risk of precipitating the social instability and civil strife that Chinese leaders have

---

gitimacy of party rule, and a "more democratic system would provide a residual legitimacy that might help the regime to negotiate the difficult transition ahead"), *available at* <http://www.ksg.harvard.edu/news/opeds/2002/saich_reform_ft_110402.htm> (last visited September 8, 2006).

[67] *See* Xianglin Xu, "Yi Zhengzhi Wending Wei Jichu de Zhongguo Jianjin Gaige" [China's Political Reform is Preoccupied by Incrementalism], 5 *Strategy and Management* (2000).

[68] Harry Harding, "Political Reform" in Mark Borthwick (ed.), *Pacific Century – the Emergence of Modern Pacific Asia*, Westview Press, Boulder 423 (1992).

[69] *See* Chinese Constitution Article 5(1)(stating that the People's Republic of China "practices building a socialist rule of law system").

[70] Harding, *supra* note 68, at 403.

[71] Wei-Wei Zhang, *supra* note 59, at 11.

sought to avoid by means of rigid political control.[72] Against the backdrop of economic transition, Chinese leaders have found themselves in a great quandary and have to confront the grievous crises that rapid economic development is bringing in its wake: regional disparities, rampant income gaps,[73] rising unemployment,[74] widespread official corruption and, arguably the most serious, a collapse of traditional values.[75]

Since the economic reform was initiated in the late 1970s, crime and violence have risen, provoking widespread concerns about social stabilities and personal securities.[76] China's socioeconomic disorder has been accentuated by the erosion of traditional values. The "rules of the game" by which Chinese citizens planned their lives for generations have been undermined, producing an altered set of winners and losers.[77] The seamy side of society that socialism was designed to eliminate over the past decades – including landlordism, unemployment, criminal mafias, and prostitution – are abundant and are appearing on the scene once again.[78]

---

[72] *Ibid.*

[73] According to official statistics released by the International Poverty Reduction Centre in China, the absolute number of the poor people and the poverty rate remain staggeringly high despite the overall economic prosperity. By the end of 2004, the number of the poor rural residents who were unable to feed themselves adequately reached 26.10 million. The gap of income between the rich and the poor continued to widen. From 1992 to 2004, the ratio between the income of the urban residents and that of the rural residents increased from 2.33:1 to 3.2:1. *See*, Gao Hongbin (Deputy Director General of the State Council Leading Group Office of Poverty Alleviation and Development), "Regional Policy Seminar on Pro-Poor Growth and Scaling Up Poverty Reduction in East Asia," May 18, 2005, *available at* <http://www.iprcc.org.cn/item/2006-09-25/50547.html>. China's income gap widened in the first quarter of 2005, with 10 percent of its richest people enjoying 45 percent of the country's wealth, while China's poorest 10 percent had only 1.4 percent of the nation's wealth. *See* "Income Gap in China Widens in First Quarter," *China Daily*, June 19, 2005, *available at* <http://www.chinadaily.com.cn/english/doc/2005-06/19/content_452636.htm>.

[74] In March 2005, 11 million urban residents, including those entering the workplace for the first time, ex-servicemen and college graduates, were awaiting employment. There are now 13 million unemployed and laid-off urban workers, and large numbers of surplus rural labourers need to find jobs in urban areas. *See* "China Expects Higher Urban Unemployment Rate in 2005," *China News Net*, March 6, 2005, *available at* <http://www.chinanews.cn/news/2004/2005-03-06/2238.shtml>.

[75] Anne F. Thurston, "Muddling toward Democracy Political Change in Grassroots China," Peaceworks No. 23, United States Institute of Peace (1998), *available at* <http://www.usip.org/pubs/peaceworks/thurst23/thurst23.html>.

[76] *See* Stanley Lubman, "Bird in a Cage: Chinese Law Reform after Twenty Years," 20 *Nw. J. Int'l L. & Bus.* 383, 390-91 (2000).

[77] *See* Martin King Whyte, "Chinese Popular Views about Inequality," *Asian Program Special Report* 5 (2002), *available at* <http://www.wilsoncenter.org/topics/pubs/asiarpt_104.pdf>.

[78] *See ibid*, at 5-6.

Disparities in income and wealth are observed as growing intensively, and are not justified by national needs or meritocratic efficiency.[79] China's accession to the WTO has accelerated market reform and expanded the private sector, thereby exacerbating income inequality.[80] Many of the benefits of the reforms are seen as "monopolised by a handful of rich and powerful [overnight millionaires], whose gains are due to corruption and connections, rather than to entrepreneurship, intelligence, hard work, or contributions to social welfare."[81] Profound demoralisation is widespread among officials and the broader citizenry.[82] A great variety of satiric doggerel verses criticising social evils and political scandals are spread privately through dinner conversation, Internet forums,[83] and mobile messages as limited means of airing grievances.

SPROUTING AND GROWING OF UTILITARIAN IMPULSE

The cascading societal and political problems have, in many circumstances, frustrated the efforts of ordinary Chinese citizens to earn their living through normal channels.[84] In order to survive the upheaval, people have to contemplate every possible approach they deem workable. Hedonism, money worship, and utilitarianism now dominate many people's minds throughout the country and "money for power" exchanges have been an increasing game throughout the country.[85] As China scholar Stanley Lubman has stated: "Relations among Chinese are changing, as new networks of personal relationships appear as [a] means of getting things done."[86] The shift is exacerbated by the weakness of ethical constraints and the shared personal standards that might otherwise have provided a normative framework for interpersonal communications and market transactions. Ironically, the money fetishism[87] that Karl

---

[79] *Ibid*, at 6.

[80] *See* Karen Halverson, "China's WTO Accession: Economic, Legal and Political Implications," 27 *B.C. Int'l & Comp. L. Rev.* 322 (2004).

[81] Whyte, *supra* note 77.

[82] Yongqi Zhao, "Yong Daode Guifan Quan Shehui [Strengthen the Morality of Our Society]", *People's Daily (Overseas Edition)*, January 29, 2002, at 2 (describing different forms of demoralisation in Chinese society).

[83] Those satiric doggerel verses, usually by anonymous authors, can be easily found inside the chatrooms of the major Chinese web portals such as Sina and Sohu.

[84] Whyte, *supra* note 77, at 5.

[85] Yi-min Lin, "State and Markets under China's Transformation: Rethinking China's Economic Transformation," 29 *Contemp. Soc.* 608, 609 (2000)(Reviewing He Qinglian, *Xiandaihua de Xianjing: Dangdai Zhongguo de Jingjin Shehui Wenti [Pitfalls of Modernization: Economic and Social Problems in Contemporary China]* (1997) (mentioning that a large number of active players (*e.g.* enterprise leaders) in China's new economic game are increasingly engaged in "reap[ing] enormous benefits through a money-for-power exchange with officials for the embezzlement of states assets").

[86] Lubman, *supra* note 76, at 404.

[87] Money fetishism attributes powers to an alien force that dominates social affairs. It is the illusion that money has its own productive powers, particularly in politics, and is fetishised to the extent that its power to solve problems is considered as inherently natu-

Marx criticised over a century ago may now have been adopted as the credo of many people who are, or used to be, his faithful disciples.

All these issues call for a more sophisticated and accountable government and hence a more liberalised political system, which would be a better way of tackling some of the new inequalities than such current outbursts of rioting and demonstrations.[88] However, many commentators are pessimistic about China's commitment to adhering to the rule of law[89] and "creating an ambiance for which enforcement of laws can flourish."[90] The only practical way to influence the process of democratisation in China is to work cooperatively with the Central government but even here the consequences remain uncertain.

From Marx's Atheism to "Belief Vacuum"

The father of modern international law, Hugo Grotius, asserted that, in the same sense that international law maintains religious toleration, religious toleration sustains a stable international order.[91] Freedom of religion is considered by many to be a fundamental human right.[92] As an entrenched interna-

---

ral, believing that money is a "radical leveller" invading all spheres of social life. *See* Karl Marx, *Capital,* Friedrich Engels (ed.) 31-37 (1952).

[88] Anthony Saich, "Beijing's Balancing Act on Reform," *supra* note 66.

[89] Indeed, over the past years, flurries of expectant hopes have been repeatedly dashed by the eventual resurgence of conservative forces, raising a perennial question: how could China be able to continue transforming itself into a more liberalised and democratic country? *See* Halverson, *supra* note 80, at 319, 363-65 (demonstrating the intractability and inflexibility of China's political reform).

[90] Yonehara, "Enter the Dragon," *supra* note 4, at 107-108.

[91] Myres S. McDougal, *et al.,* "The Right to Religious Freedom and World Public Order: The Emerging Norm of Nondiscrimination," 74(5) *Mich. L. Rev.* (echoing the sentiments of Grotius that "[t]he trends toward religious freedom and equality within national communities have […] have brought about transnational expectations of religious liberty that, in turn, have strengthened national practice. Building upon the doctrine of natural rights as a source of transnational authority, Hugo Grotius (and other prominent international lawyers after him) emphasised that, in the same sense that international law is important to the maintenance of religious toleration, is religious toleration indispensable to a stable international order).

[92] The Universal Declaration of Human Rights adopted and proclaimed by the General Assembly of the United Nations on December 10, 1948, at the Palais de Chaillot in Paris, France defines freedom of religion and belief as follows: "Everyone has the right to freedom of thought, conscience and religion; this right includes freedom to change his religion or belief, and freedom, either alone or in community with others and in public or private, to manifest his religion or belief in teaching, practice, worship, and observance." *See* "Universal Declaration of Human Rights," Articles 2 and 18. The International Covenant on Civil and Political Rights, a UN treaty based on the Universal Declaration of Human Rights created in 1966, expands its prior statement to address the manifestation of religion or belief. Article 18 of this Covenant includes four paragraphs relating to religious belief: 1) Everyone shall have the right to freedom of thought, conscience and religion. This right shall include freedom to have or to adopt a religion or

tional human right, it is recognised in all the important international human rights treaties and remains the focus of debate in a variety of international human rights bodies. [93]

CONSTITUTIONAL RIGHTS OF RELIGION

The Chinese Constitution explicitly guarantees citizens' right to "freely choose and express their religious beliefs" and make clear their religious affiliations.[94] Accordingly, both the Party and the government are obligated to create the legal mechanisms necessary to enforce this constitutional guarantee. However, the gap between rhetoric and reality is enormous.

THE GAP WITH REALITY

The Chinese government has demonstrated a continued reluctance to be flexible in its religious policies and provide minimum guarantee for religious freedom. Dominated by socialist atheism, the government views religion as a perpetuation of feudal superstitions, treats religious groups as a threat and places strict limitations on religious organisations.[95] National regulations require that religious organisations and individual places of worship register with the Religious Affairs Bureau, a ministry-level component of the Chinese government.[96] Local regulations and provisions are more restrictive and protective

---

belief of his [or her] choice, and freedom, either individually or in community with others and in public or private, to manifest his religion or belief in worship, observance, practice and teaching; 2) No one shall be subject to coercion which would impair his freedom to have or to adopt a religion or belief of his [or her] choice; 3) Freedom to manifest one's religion or beliefs may be subject only to such limitations as are prescribed by law and are necessary to protect public safety, order, health, or morals or the fundamental rights and freedoms of others; 4) The States Parties to the present Covenant undertake to have respect for the liberty of parents and, when applicable, legal guardians to ensure the religious and moral education of their children in conformity with their own convictions. *See* International Covenant on Civil and Political Rights, *available at* <http://www.unhchr.ch/html/menu3/b/a_ccpr.htm>.

[93] Leonard M. Hammer, *A Foucauldian Approach to International Law: Descriptive Thoughts for Normative Issues* 73 (2007).

[94] Chinese Constitution Article 36 stipulates that "citizens of the People's Republic of China enjoy freedom of religious belief. No state organ, public organisation or individual may compel citizens to believe in, or not believe in, any religion; nor may they discriminate against citizens who believe in, or do not believe in, any religion. The state protects normal religious activities. No one may make use of religion to engage in activities that disrupt public order, impair the health of citizens or interfere with the educational system of the state. Religious bodies and religious affairs are not subject to any foreign domination."

[95] *See* "Congregational-Executive Commission on China, Annual Report", 16-20 (2002), *available at* <http://www.cecc.gov/pages/annualRpt/2002annRptEng.pdf>.

[96] *See* "Regulations on Managing Places for Religious Activities [Zongjiao Huodong Changsuo Guanli Tiaoli]," issued on January 31, 1994.

than their national-level counterparts.[97] While some local officials encourage foreign religious groups to supply basic social services in their communities,[98] authorities are extremely sensitive for fear of foreign domination over domestic religious affairs.[99] On July 29, 2006, Christian residents in Hangzhou's Xiaoshan District at China's eastern Zhejiang province clashed with police after authorities sought to demolish a church that was deemed as unlawful.[100] This illustrates the government's ambivalence towards religion.

Consequently, many religious practitioners in China "reject the validity of worshipping in religious institutions that fall under the auspices of a government controlled by the officially atheist Communist Party."[101] Under such circumstances, some practitioners have no choice but to abjure their beliefs.[102] The tight control over religious practice has isolated Chinese religious believers from the rest of the religious world, which in turn largely accounts for the lack of ethical belief among a large percentage of the population, particularly the younger generation.

As a result, a large percentage of the population, particularly the youth, lacks religious beliefs and the ethical support that those beliefs provide. At the same time, with the disintegration of Communism as a means of meeting social aspirations, there are few followers of the principles of Marxism, resulting in a situation where China has entered upon a period of a "belief vacuum". This is a precarious moment indeed, a time of doubt when the law can do nothing but wait powerlessly for the advent of real leadership, with no other ethical system to alleviate the strain.

SYLLOGISTIC IMPLICATION

As stated in Galatians:

[A] person is justified not by the works of the law but through faith in Jesus Christ. And we have come to believe in Christ Jesus, so that we might be justified by faith in Christ, and not by doing the works of the law, because no one will be justified by the works of the law.[103]

The freedom of religious belief is a universal and essential human right. Although religion and law are usually viewed as two elements of moral values with distinct social identities, in reality, religious faith and legal order inevita-

---

[97] "Congregational-Executive Commission on China, Annual Report," *supra* note 95, at 17.
[98] "International Religious Freedom Report 2004 (China (includes Tibet, Hong Kong, and Macau))," Released by the Bureau of Democracy, Human Rights, and Labor, U.S. Department of State.
[99] *See* "Regulations on Managing Places for Religious Activities," *supra* note 96, Article 4 (2).
[100] *See* "China's Christians Resist Church Demolition," *Reuters*, July 31, 2006.
[101] *Ibid.*
[102] *Ibid.*
[103] *Galatians* 2:16.

bly interact.[104] Of course whilst it is too arrogant to assert that morality would be impossible without religious belief, it may be true that, under religious principles, individuals are more inclined to adhere to an ethical code and bind themselves by social, legal or moral tie. The imposition of law by its own force or momentum is tenuous. Without religious belief and faith, there would be no developed multidimensional systems to provide a firm foundation to enable an enduring belief in law and, as such, no self-disciplining consciousness to constrain counterfeiting and piracy.

Press Control Policy: "Coin It In Silence"

Freedom of speech is a fundamental personal liberty, and is regarded as one of society's most cherished rights.[105] However, while China has undergone dramatic economic and social changes, the central government has endeavoured to maintain rigid control over the media as a means of stifling social discontent.[106] China employs an extensive licensing system to restrict publication of news and opinions on matters of public concern, and the authorities place severe restriction on imported movies, books and audiovisual products.[107] Chinese mass media, which is criticised as the mouthpiece (*houshe*) of the Party, has been squeezed into the mission of issuing propaganda. A recent example is the proposed national emergency law which has drawn a great deal of attention in China since June 2006. This proposed law, which has the alleged objective of enhancing disaster responsiveness and ensuring administrative responsibility,[108] includes a media clause that would impose heavy fines on news media reporting without authorisation on natural disasters, public health incidents or industrial accidents.[109] A major controversy was stirred up over this

---

[104] Harold J. Berman, *Faith and Order: The Reconciliation of Law and Religion* 209-220 (1993).

[105] Frank S. Sengstock, "Achieving A Workable Definition of Free Speech: A Symposium on the Nature and Scope of the Constitutional Guarantee of Freedom of Expression," 47 *J. Urb. L.* 395, 396 (1969-1970)(mentioning that freedom of speech is essential to democracy).

[106] Although people in China are generally free to express their discontent with their government, anyone wishing to publish sensitive information or ideas may face legal and economic barriers. *See* CECC Report, *supra* note 95.

[107] For a precise discussion of the rules and regulations of information control policy in China, *see, generally*, Anna S.F. Lee, "The Censorship and Approval Process for Media Products in China," in Mary L. Riley (ed.), *Protecting Intellectual Property Rights in China* 127 (1997); Mary L. Riley, "The Regulation of the Media in China," in Mark A. Cohen *et al* (eds.), *Chinese Intellectual Property: Law and Practice* 355 (1999); Peter Yu, "Piracy, Prejudice, and Perspectives, An Attempt to Use Shakespeare to Reconfigure the U.S.-China Intellectual Property Debate," 19 *B. U. Int'l L.J.* 1, 28-32 (2001).

[108] *See* "China Mulls Emergency Management Law," *Xinhua News Agency*, June 24, 2006.

[109] Article 57 stipulates that "news media making bold to report the development and handling of emergencies without authorisation, or releasing false reports, would be fined between 50,000 Yuan (6, 250 dollars) and 100,000 Yuan if the reports lead to serious

media clause of the emergency law, particularly for those approaching this issue from the standpoint of liberal press theory.

Apart from traditional media, the government has a longstanding set of
policies restricting information and has particularly attempted to implement
controls to prevent the public's access to politically sensitive information by
the method of internet filtering and blocking.[110] The National People's Congress (NPC) has passed an Internet censorship law, and the enforcement of
this provision appears to be discretionary and *ad-hoc*.[111] A typical example of
this is the government's blocking or filtering of Chinese internet users' access
to Google, AltaVista [112] and Wikipedia.[113] Recently, Microsoft acknowledged
that it was working, at Chinese government's request, with the Chinese government to censor its new Chinese-language Web portal and Web log tool,
MSN Spaces.[114]

In China, "freedom of speech" is theoretically protected under the Constitution.[115] However, it is not an individual liberty in practice, but rather a tool for
citizens to sing a collective song of praise. According to the Congressional-
Executive Commission on China's report, China's legal system "discourages
the free flow of information, not only by erecting barriers to non-government-
controlled institutions, but also by encouraging individual self-censorship by
not clearly defining what constitutes protected speech."[116] Those who are allowed to publish confront a legal system that obscures the boundaries of freedom of speech, so that many Chinese are vulnerable to publish information
that authorities might deem sensitive. [117] As a result, "coin it in silence" (*men*

---

consequences." *See* Shangwu Sun, "Law 'Will Ensure Accurate Info,'" *China Daily*,
  July 14, 2006.
[110] *See* Jonathan Zittrain & Benjamin Edelman, "Empirical Analysis of Internet Filtering in
  China," *available at* <http://cyber.law.harvard.edu/filtering/china> (last visited October
  29, 2006).
[111] *See* "Decision of the Standing Committee of NPC Regarding the Safeguarding of Internet Security," Adopted on December 28, 2000 by the Nineteenth Session of the Standing Committee of the Ninth National People's Congress of China, *available at*
  <http://www.chinaeclaw.com/english/readArticle.asp?id=2386>.
[112] *See* Jason Deans, "Chinese Government Backs down on Google," *The Guardian*, September 13, 2002 (describing how the China's government ended its two-week block on
  Chinese subjects using U.S. Internet search engine Google).
[113] *See* "Blocking of Wikipedia in Mainland China," *available at* <http://en.wikipedia.org/
  wiki/Blocking_of_Wikipedia_in_mainland_China>, last visited on August 1, 2006.
[114] Kelley Beaucar Vlahos, "U.S. Tech Firms Help Governments Censor Internet," *Fox
  News*, July 19, 2005.
[115] According to Article 35 of Chinese Constitution, Chinese citizens "enjoy freedom of
  speech, of the press, of assembly, of association, of procession and of demonstration."
  See Constitution Article 35.
[116] "Congregational-Executive Commission on China, Issue Report on Information Control
  and Self-Censorship in the PRC and the Spread of SARS," 10 (2003), *available at*
  <http://www.cecc.gov/pages/news/prcControl_SARS.pdf>.
[117] *Ibid.*

sheng fa da cai), which means making fortunes quietly without being associated with politics, has been a motto for many Chinese in their attempts to survive and adapt in an unsafe world. In this circumstance, unless genuine effort is being taken by the government, it would be naturally assumed that people are well positioned to reap the benefits of piracy as a means of "making fortunes quietly."

Due to this stringent information control policy, the media business and the publishing industry remain the most heavily regulated industries in China.[118] For example, China's restrictions allowing only 20 foreign movies per year to be imported for greening on a revenue-sharing basis has handicapped the distribution of the products through legitimate channels and created a huge demand for illicit products.[119] As such, consumers have to settle for black market products, which can saturate the cultural market.[120] Even though the market is finally open, it will need much time to overcome entrenched inertia of old custom.

4.1.3 Insight into the Economic Spectrum

As prior chapters have demonstrated, the pirating of intellectual property fuels economic development until the country reaches the stage where IPR protection becomes economically advantageous to a sufficiently strong set of domestic vested interests.[121] Within the global trading system, if a country has not obtained endogenously generated impulse to change their economic behaviour, any radical strategy for stronger demands of IPR protection will only turn into a tragic legal failure.[122] Apparently, China remains a consumer of intellectual property and is therefore not in a position to see gains from the vigorous protection of IPR, instead profits will result from the imitation of existing products.[123]

---

[118] *See* Lee, *supra* note 107, at 127.

[119] China's WTO Implementation: An Assessment of China's Fourth Year WTO membership, Written Testimony of US-China Business Council, September 14, 2005, at 6 (*available at* <http://www.uschina.org/public/documents/2005/09/ustr_testimony.pdf>).

[120] Peter K. Yu, "The Second Coming of Intellectual Property Rights in China," *supra* note 3, at 31.

[121] *See, e.g.,* Stefan Kirchanski, "Protection of U.S. Patent Rights in Developing Countries: US Efforts To Enforce Pharmaceutical Patents in Thailand," 16 (2) *L.A. Int'l & Comp. L. Rev.* 598 (1994); Frederick M. Abbott, "The WTO TRIPs Agreement and Global Economic Development," in *Public Policy and Global Technological Integration* 3, 4-12 (1997).

[122] *See* Robert E. Hudec, *Enforcing Intellectual Property Law: The Evolution of the Modern GATT Legal System* 364 (1993).

[123] Michael Yeh, "Up Against a Great Wall: The Fight against Intellectual Property Piracy in China," 5 *Minn. J. Global Trade* 516 (1996).

An Ethnicity and Indigeneity Approach: A Socio-Economic Analysis

Whilst singling out the cultural reason for the IPR enforcement problems in China, it is worthwhile to examine the development of counterfeiting and piracy as a major economic activity. In the mid-1980s, there were generally no home-produced counterfeit products on sale in China,[124] although, after China opened up to foreign investment in the early 1980s, the counterfeit products from Taiwan and Hong Kong began to rush through the doors. [125] At that time the counterfeiting products were viewed as "exotic goods." Even in the early 1990s the counterfeiting industry in mainland China was still in its infancy.[126] Since the early 1990s, the production export, and domestic sale of counterfeit products started to increase dramatically.[127] This variation has been attributed to a number of historical circumstances.

First, this phenomenon is an actual result and unintended consequence of the continued liberalisation of China's economy, which offered domestic companies much freedom to participate in the self-determined manufacture and sale.[128] Whilst China opened up its distribution channels, a sensitive industrial sector given the huge number of people employed, state trading monopolies began to break down.[129] Due to the phenomenal economic growth, such infringing activities became so widespread and anti-counterfeiting measures so ineffective, that it became virtually impossible to combat counterfeiting and piracy at the retail level.[130] It is inconceivable that if the planned economy were still dominant in China, counterfeiting would have developed as an uncontrolled epidemic. Of course, this is not to assert that the infringement is a necessary consequence of economic liberalisation.

Secondly, the establishment of manufacturing facilities by the companies of Great Southern China,[131] including counterfeiters, fuelled further growth of China's wholesale markets, which have already seen explosive expansion in both size and influence of markets over the past two decades.[132] Historically, residents in Hong Kong normally have their ancestral home in Guangdong

---

[124] Douglas Clark, "IP Rights Will Improve in China – Eventually," The China Business Review, May-June 2000.

[125] Ibid.

[126] During that period, small quantities of counterfeit products, especially wine, soft drinks and cigarettes, could be found in some open markets of much developed southern regions such as Guangdong and Fujian. See Clark, supra note 124.

[127] Ibid.

[128] Ibid.

[129] Ibid.

[130] Geoffrey T. Willard, "An Examination of China's Emerging Intellectual Property Regime: Historical Underpinnings, The Current System and Prospects for the Future," 6 Ind. Int'l & Comp. L. Rev. 347(1996).

[131] Greater Southern China includes Taiwan, Hong Kong, and China's southern provinces of Guangdong and Fujian.

[132] Clark, supra note 124.

Province; similarly, residents in Taiwan normally have their ancestral home in Fujian Province. The companies of Hong Kong and Taiwan supply the capital and the know-how by investing in Guangdong and Fujian Province, and thereby take advantage of different territories of Hong Kong and Taiwan as umbrellas to elude law enforcement and detection.[133] A channel convening counterfeit and pirate goods was finally established.

In addition, this phenomenon demonstrated a growing appreciation within China of the commercial value of foreign direct investment (FDI) and transfer of technology.[134] China's economic growth over the decades of the 1980s and 1990s has been fuelled in large part by FDI from industrialised countries. In the 1990s in particular, China emerged as the world's second largest recipient of FDI after the United States and, in 2003, China attracted 53.5 billion dollars worth of FDI, surpassing the United States as the top global destination for foreign investment.[135] In view of today's global knowledge-based economy, the IPR component of FDI has become the most noticeable characteristic of the foreign investment. China has thus gained unprecedented access to the most sophisticated technology and valuable intellectual property.[136] In the process of the transfer of technology through FDI that is being absorbed into China's legitimate economy through joint ventures and foreign-invested enterprises, some of the intangible assets are being diverted simultaneously into China's illegitimate economy.[137] This offers optimal environmental conditions for growth and development of counterfeiting and piracy in China.

Stage Theory for IPR Protection: A Historical Overview

The emergence of counterfeiting and piracy is a natural consequence of market equilibrium, where demand meets supply. An economy must reach a certain stage of overall development before it can commit substantial resources to R&D and embark on a genuine effort to protect IPR.[138] In light of this acknowledgement, many countries insist on an appropriate level of IPR protection because of varying stages of economic development.[139] Looking back at

---

[133] *Ibid.*

[134] *Ibid.*

[135] *See* "UNCTAD World Investment Report 2004: The Shift Towards Services," *available at* <www.unctad.org/en/docs/wir2004_en.pdf>.

[136] Daniel C.K. Chow, "Intellectual Property Protection as Economic Policy: Will China Ever Enforce its IP Laws?" Congressional-Executive Commission on China, *available at* <http://www.cecc.gov/pages/roundtables/051605/Chow.php>, last visited December 12, 2005(stating that China is the world's largest recipient of FDI and a main source of intellectual property counterfeiting and piracy).

[137] *Ibid.*

[138] Allison & Lin, *supra* note 25, at 775.

[139] *See* Thomas.G. Rawski, "Chinese Industrial Reform: Accomplishments, Prospects and Implications," 84 (2), *Am. Econ. Rerv.* 271-72 (1994) (stating that IPR protections are normally weaker in emerging markets than in developed markets).

national economic development in the international balance of payments structure, countries are normally technological followers of more industrialised countries, and usually pass through stage of cycle in the balance of payment.[140] The primary stage of development is largely characterised by imitation rather than innovation, given the fact that the divergence between the "haves" and "have-nots" in the information age is still significant.

In this context, China is "not alone in its apparent inability to surmount obstacles to effective intellectual property protection,"[141] and the counterfeiting problems in China today are not unique.[142] Arguably all developing countries pass through a stage of development where imitation of foreign products is widespread.[143] As Barbara Ringer noted, until the Second World War, "the United States had little reason to take pride in its international copyright relations, but rather, had a great deal to be ashamed of."[144] Teresa Watanabe also demonstrated that the United States passed a stage in copying European technology in its early years of economic growth.[145] The development of the U.S. in the nineteenth century was largely based on adoption of technological, economic, and legal policies from England and France.[146] In the case of Japan, Watanabe stated that "the total price Japan had to pay for the Western technology it needed to transform itself from a nation of "rice paper and bamboo" to "transistors and skyscrapers" was a bargain-basement 9 billion dollars.[147] American domestic entrepreneurs were "notorious pirates of British works of intellectual property,"[148] as were the Japanese.

---

[140] *See* R.J. Ruffin and P. R. Gregory, *Principles of Macroeconomics*, Addison Wesley 729 (2001).

[141] Warren Newberry, *supra* note 2, at 1445, 1447.

[142] Clark, *supra* note 124.

[143] *See* Assafa Endeshaw, "A Critical Assessment of the US-China Conflict on Intellectual Property," 6 *Alb. L. J. Sci. & Tech.* (1996), at 295, 300(demonstrating the fact that the industrialising countries usually "borrow, often without public acknowledgment, policies, technologies, as well as legal concepts" from the industrialised countries). *See also* Douglas Clark, *ibid.*

[144] Barbara A. Ringer, "The Role of the United States in International Copyright – Past, Present, and Future," 56 *Geo. L.J.* (1968), at 1050, 1051. *See also* Pat Choate, *Hot Property: The Stealing of Ideas in an Age of Globalization* (2005) (arguing that the United States, the major promoter of establishment of the world intellectual property regime, "is not blameless in the realm of idea theft" in a historical perspective).

[145] Teresa Watanabe, "Japan Sets Sights on Creativity," *L.A. Times*, June 10, 1990, at A1.

[146] Endeshaw, *supra* note 143, at 266, 300.

[147] *See* Watanabe, *supra* note 145.

[148] Griffin, *supra* note 3, at 187.

China's Current Stage of Economic Development and Its IPR Policy

Despite the rapid economic growth over the past two decades, China still heavily relies on the importation of intellectual property and is thus not in a position to see benefits from upgrading its IPR enforcement mechanism.[149] In order to harness the weak purchasing power of low-income citizens, Chinese authorities often turn a blind eye on counterfeiting because it is an insurmountable problem in the early stages of development.[150]

The experience of imitation in China was similar to that of European countries before the emergence of the contemporary notion of authorship in the eighteenth century, as well as the United States in the nineteenth century and Japan in the twentieth century.[151] Despite its dramatic economic development, China's per capita GDP of 5,000 dollars ranks one-hundred and twenty-second in the world.[152] At such an undeveloped level, there is no exception to passing through this stage in China, although it may be possible to gain faster development and thus accelerate the process of transition.

Prospectively speaking, there should be an adaptive phase before China's WTO accession will eventually result in the removal of the various impediments to an effective IPR enforcement regime and lead to a noticeable decrease in IPR infringements. [153] In the short term, some predict that there may be an increase in the number of infringements,[154] since China's efforts to create an internationally competitive free market economy have simultaneously created an illegal market of counterfeits,[155] and "unleashed a flood of products, both genuine and counterfeit, into the world market."[156]

At this transitional period in its development, China will need time to phase-in effective policies. During this period, "if no politically influential domestic constituency favours the new policies, one can only expect non-

---

[149] Yeh, *supra* note 123, at 516.
[150] *See e.g.*, Seth Faison, "China Turns Blind Eye to Pirated Disks," *N.Y. Times*, March 28, 1998, at D1 (noting that Chinese custom officials pose little threat to copyright pirates).
[151] *See generally* Mark Rose, *Authors and Owners: The Invention of Copyright* (1993); Martha Woodmansee, *The Author, Art, and the Market: Rereading the History of Aesthetics* (1994).
[152] *See, Central Intelligence Agency, The World Fact Book* 115 (2004).
[153] Clark, *supra* note 124, at 130.
[154] "EU Strategy to Enforce Intellectual Property Rights in Third Countries - Facts and Figures," European Commission Press Releases, *supra* note 174 (noting that around fifteen to twenty percent of all brand products sold in China are fakes, and that the portion has risen significantly in recent years). *See also* "Study of the Impact of Movie Piracy on China's Economy," Chinese Academy of Social Sciences Report, *available at* <http://www.uschina.org/public/documents/2006/07/cass_piracyimpact_e.pdf> (showing that 61 percent believed that piracy will continue to increase while 39 percent believed that piracy levels will remain steady and none expects the market for pirated movies to shrink in the immediate future).
[155] Peter K. Yu, "The Copyright Divide," *25 Cardozo L. Rev.* (2003), at 372, 373.
[156] Clark, *supra* note 124, at 130.

implementation and robust domestic resistance."[157] In future periods, however, China's WTO accession should lead to a decrease in the infringement of IPR. This decrease is likely because the growth of intellectual property infringement in China has "paralleled the growth of China's economy and Chinese companies' greater access to domestic and international markets" – both of which will continue to grow with WTO membership.[158] When economic growth creates the development of more sophisticated and competitive home grown enterprises, and the domestic enterprises display entrepreneurial enthusiasm to protect their own IPR, the intellectual property infringement levels will reach a plateau and start to decrease.[159]

4.2 Experience of Japan

As another Chinese phrase says, "the stones from other hills may serve to polish the jade." (*ta shan zhi shi ke yi gong yu*), which means advice from others may help one overcome the shortcomings.[160] East and Southeast Asian countries are heavily influenced by Confucian values and have also been the "scene of a tremendous shift of technology and wealth from West to East."[161] Accordingly, this section of the book draws on the experience of other regional states, which not only share the same, or similar, cultural values to those found in China, but have also developed domestic standards of IPR protection. Of these, Japan and Korea are notable for their cultural similarities with China and their high levels of intellectual property protection. On one hand, Confucian norms of social harmony and moral precepts have permeated the intellectual life of Japanese citizens and have played a pivotal role in moulding Japanese culture as it exists today. On the other hand, Japan's economic development trajectory is significantly characterised by its variable intellectual property policies in accordance with different stages of the development. If China is to start a new process for its IPR protection, it is worthwhile to model its process after those who have had similar experience.

---

[157] Susan K. Sell, *Power and Ideas: North-South Politics of Intellectual Property and Antitrust* 177 (1998).

[158] Clark, *supra* note 124.

[159] *Ibid.*

[160] *See*, Grand Chinese Dictionary (Hanyu Da Cidian), V1, 1155, Shanghai (1994).

[161] *See* Richard E. Vaughan, "Defining Terms in the Intellectual Property Protection Debate: Are the North and South Arguing Past Each Other When We Say 'Property'? A Lockean, Confucian, and Islamic Comparison," 2 *ILSA J. Inl'l & Comp. L.* 346 (1996).

4.2.1 Analysis of Japan's IP Law and Policy

In Japan, economic development has been linked from the very start to the introduction of industrial property rights. [162] The Meiji regime established in 1868 quickly discarded the feudal system and launched a comprehensive programme of reform that significantly altered the political ecology and institutional landscape of the Japanese society.[163] During the Meiji Restoration, a revolution in Japan which "restored" imperial rule and transformed Japan from a feudal into a modern state, legal systems, sciences, and technology were mainly introduced from Western Europe and North America.[164] The rapid growth of the 1960s was made possible by the introduction of foreign technology.[165]

While the Japanese regime in 1721 issued a decree that made inventions a criminal offence, the first statute of monopolies was introduced in 1872 after Emperor Meiji had declared that the whole administration and the entire population in Japan should commit themselves to making Japan an advanced nation.[166] At the end of the nineteenth century, Japan became a member of both the Paris Union for the Protection of Industrial Property and the Berne Union for the Protection of Literary and Artistic Works.[167] Japan thus paved the way for systemic legislation that indicated that IPR should play an important role in the country's national industrialisation and cultural renaissance.

In views of the legislation, although Japan has enjoyed the longest tradition of IPR in Asia, it only serves to illustrate the early development of the Japanese economy.[168] In fact, it is not surprising that Japan's IPR legal regime had

---

[162] Christopher Heath, "Intellectual Property Rights in Asia – Projects, Programmes and Developments," Online Publication of Max Planck Institute for Intellectual Property, Competition and Tax Law, *available at* <http://www.intellecprop.mpg.de/Online-Publikationen/Heath-Ipeaover.htm>.

[163] *Ibid.*

[164] Carol Gluck, *Japan's Modern Myths, Ideology in the Late Meiji Period* 17-23 (1985).

[165] *See* Michio Morishima, *Why Has Japan 'Succeeded'? Western Technology and the Japanese Ethos* (1982) (stating that, since the Meiji Restoration, Japan has had extensive contacts with the European countries, through which Japan "broke with a long history of isolationism and paved the way for the adoption of western technologies").

[166] *See* Heath, *supra* note 162.

[167] Consensus on an appropriate international mechanism to enable this was initiated in the last quarter of the nineteenth century with the main pillars being the Paris Convention for the Protection of Industrial Property (originally signed in 1883), and the Berne Convention for the Protection of Literary and Artistic Work (originally signed in 1886). *See* "The Paris Convention for the Protection of Industrial Property," July 14, 1967, 21 *U.S.T.* 1583; "Berne Convention for the Protection of Literary and Artistic Works," September 9, 1886, 25 *U.S.T.* 1341, 828 *U.N.T.S.* 211 (last revised at Paris, July 24, 1971). For a detailed introduction concerning these two unions, *see* Robert J. Pechman, "Seeking Multilateral Protection for Intellectual Property: The United States 'TRIPs' Over Special 301," 7 *Minn. J. Global Trade* 179, 181-84 (1998).

[168] Heath, *supra* note 162.

long been characterised as a diffusion of knowledge rather than a facilitating innovation. [169] The first Director-General of the Japanese Trademark Registration and the Patent Office, Korekiyo Takahashi, who became Prime Minister in 1921, wrote in his autobiography when visiting the United States Patent Office in Washington DC, around the year 1900: "We have looked about us to see what nations are the greatest, so that we can be like them. We said: 'What is it that makes the United States such a great nation?['] And we investigated and found that it was patents and so we will have patents."[170] Interestingly, the major driving force for developing a Western-style IPR legal system in Japan during the *Meiji* Period was to promote Japan to becoming "an advanced nation," as Emperor Meiji wished, or facilitate it into "a greatest nation," as Premier Takahashi expected. The nationwide transplantation of an exotic intellectual property system in Japan was virtually a massive copying activity reflected by an ingrained habit of imitation.

Due to the lack of economic underpinnings for a strong IPR protection, during the early phase of economic development, compulsory licensing was frequently required for a patent holder and, until 1938, a patent was liable to expire in practice if it was not in use by the patent holder.[171] In 1960s, the United States Patent Office normally approved or disapproved an application for patent within eighteen months.[172] By contrast, it took the Japanese Patent Office (JPO) an average of five to seven years,[173] with the Kilby patent case being a typical example.[174] Also, the JPO required "full disclosure of the technology submitted in the application for the accommodation of imitation."[175] In addi-

---

[169] Koichi Hamada, "Protection of Intellectual Property Rights in Japan," Working Paper, April 1996, Council of Foreign Relations (maintaining that Japan's IPR related legal system emphasised the "diffusion of foreign knowledge rather than creating its own").

[170] David Vaver, "The Future of Intellectual Property Law: Japanese and European Perspectives Compared" (Working Papers of Oxford IP Research Centre, Working Paper No. 09/99), *available at* <www.oiprc.ox.ac.uk/DVWP0999.pdf>. *See* also "Intellectual Property Policy Outline," Strategic Council on Intellectual Property, July 3, 2002, *available at* <www.kantei.go.jp/foreign/policy/titeki/kettei/020703taikou_e.html.> (demonstrating that the ambitions and strategies of the Japanese government are to make Japan "a nation built on intellectual property").

[171] Hamada, *supra* note 169.

[172] Vaughan, *supra* note 161, at 347.

[173] *Ibid.*

[174] In 1961, the electronic giant Texas Instruments obtained the basic patent in Japan covering the integrated circuit, known as the "Kilby patent" under the name of Nobel laureate Jack St. Clair Kilby. Texas Instruments was then required by the JPO that the application be divided into fourteen segments of which twelve were ultimately rejected. It took approximately seventeen years for the first patent to be granted after it was filed, "during which time the Japanese semiconductor industry copied and export large quantities of chip products, earning billions of dollars in profit." For a substantive introduction of and comment on the Kilby case, *see* Dana Rohrabacher and Paul Crilly, "The Case for a Strong Patent System," 8 (2) *Harv. J. L. & Tech.* (1995), at 263, 265.

[175] Vaughan, *supra* note 161, at 347.

tion, although Japan had joined the Paris Union on July 15, 1899, as recent as in 1990s, the duration of patents in Japan was less than twenty years, which is the minimum duration set out in the TRIPs Agreement.[176] It was not until 1994 that the patent law was amended and improved to guarantee at least 20 years after the application for the patent.[177]

A strong IPR protection only came into being in Japan when external pressure was created by the United States and a lobbying pressure was raised by the domestic industrial sectors. In this sense, it was only recently that Japan substantially came into harmony with the international standards and embarked on a national undertaking with a view to the construction of a nation built on intellectual property.[178]

4.2.2 Confucian Values and the Intellectual Creation

The cultural evolution in Japan has illustrated a continuing vitality of Confucianism. In Japan, Confucianism tended to be overshadowed by Buddhism in early nineteenth century but soon regained its dominant ethical position.[179] In the 1950s and 1960s, Confucianism was perceived as "an obstacle to modernisation", but it reconfirmed its status as a "facilitator" in 1980s.[180] In Japan today, although not adopted and practised as a religion, Confucianism has deeply influenced Japanese culture and custom,[181] and these unique ethical values continue to permeate modern Japanese society and affect Japanese thinking.[182] As noted by Reischauer and Jansen, "[a]lmost no one consider himself a Confucianism today, but in a sense almost all Japanese are."[183] Ac-

---

[176] Hamada, *supra* note 169.

[177] *Ibid.*

[178] Since 2002, Japanese government has initiated various institutional reforms in the area of intellectual property rights. The work has been promoted in accordance with the "Intellectual Property Policy Outline" in July 2002 and the "Strategic Program for the Creation, Protection and Exploitation of Intellectual Property" in July 2003, which defined concrete measures the government should take and priorities in establishing a "nation built on intellectual property" where intellectual property is used to create high-value added products and services with the aim of revitalising the economy and society. *See* "Intellectual Property Outline," *supra* note 170; "Strategic Programme for the Creation, Protection and Exploitation of Intellectual Property," Intellectual Property Policy Headquarters, July 8, 2003, *available at* <http://unpan1.un.org/intradoc/groups/public/documents/APCITY/UNPAN017539.pdf>.

[179] Edwin O. Reischauer and Marius B. Jansen, *Japanese Today: Change and Continuity*, Harvard University Press 204 (1995).

[180] *See* Gavan McCormack and Yoshio Sugimoto (eds), *The Japanese Trajectory: Modernization and Beyond*, Cambridge University Press 5 (1988).

[181] *See, Japan: A Country Study*, Ronald E. Dolan and Robert L. Worden (eds) 103-4 (1992).

[182] Reischauer and Jansen, *supra* note 179, at 204.

[183] *Ibid.*

cording to Reischauer and Jansen, while Japan has widely adopted democratic doctrines and embraced liberal values, strong Confucian traits still run deep in Japanese consciousness, and "Confucianism probably exerts more influence on Japanese than does any other of traditional religions or philosophies."[184]

In Japan, identifiable signs of Confucian values are widespread. The Japanese believe in a social and hierarchical order and collectivist ideology.[185] As Gluck observed, the character of Confucianism is more significant than that in China.[186] For example, in Japan an employer can be treated as the author of a work that is completed by an employee on the job, whereas in Europe this would be unacceptable.[187] The European employer will, as in Japan, usually own the copyright, but the status of author is reserved to the human being who creates the work rather than the entity which pays for the creation.[188] As Morishima has noted, the European view underscores the individual, rather than the organisation to which he or she belongs,[189] but the "Japanese rule emphasises the importance of the organisation, cooperation[,] and teamwork, rather than the individual."[190] Each view delineates a distinct logic shaped by the culture in which it is embedded. However, within the diversity of its culture, each economy attempts to reach the same goal by different routes. The infrastructure of Confucian philosophy, based on the cardinal relationship and hierarchical order, has played a significant role in Japanese economic development[191] and contributed substantially to its "economic miracle" subsequent to the Second World War.[192] What Japan's economic success tells us is that Confucian values can act and have acted as a positive role in its economic and cultural prosperity.[193]

4.2.3 Tolerant IPR Policy and the Economic Blooming Up

After the Second World War, Japan received foreign aid from Western Europe and the United States and had to rebuild from the ashes of war. This aid enabled Japan to obtain necessary investment and technology without having to

---

[184] *Ibid.*

[185] Troyer, *supra* note 23, at 45, 51-52. *See also* Gluck, *supra* note 157, at 258-59.

[186] Gluck, *supra* note 164, at 259.

[187] Vaver, *supra* note 170.

[188] *Ibid.*

[189] *See* Morishima, *supra* note 165 (illustrating the weak reception of liberalism and individualism as an important factor of Japan's economic success).

[190] Vaver, *supra* note 170.

[191] *See* Gluck, *supra* note 164, 258-59, 286.

[192] Morishima, *supra* note 165.

[193] *See* Morishima, *supra* note 165 (explaining the importance of the role played in the creation of Japanese capitalism by Confucian ethical doctrines as transformed under Japanese circumstances, in particular, the Confucian ethics of complete loyalty to the firm and to the state to which an individual belongs).

build a sound intellectual property environment. Japan has "garnered the lion's share of this wealth" transfer from the West and has "accomplished this while in the course of converting itself from a country devastated by allied bombing during World War II into an industrial giant."[194]

During the rehabilitation period, Japan's "meteoric technological rise was not based on Japanese innovation, but on the imitation of Western ideas."[195] Based on this, Japan enjoyed a high level of prosperity by "providing cheap, high-quality, mass-produced products to the world."[196] During the two big oil crises in 1973 and 1975, Japan showed remarkable resilience.[197] Japan has "carefully orchestrated its economy to keep out foreign imports while encouraging the copying of Western technology."[198]

Within this context, the Japanese government applied a relatively tolerant intellectual property enforcement policy and, as a result, counterfeiting and piracy were very common. Counterfeit products were usually protected by the Registered Trade Mark and Design Law.[199] It was during this period that Japan seized a valuable developmental opportunity. In 1953, less than a decade after the war, the Japanese were able to overcome the devastation of the war, and exceed pre-war levels of prosperity.[200] At the beginning of the 1960s, the Japanese Prime Minister Hayato Ikeda launched his ambitious "doubling the income" plan.[201] Then, at the centennial of the Meiji restoration, when China was under a violent storm of Cultural Revolution, Japan's GNP climbed dramatically to become the second largest in the world, surpassing West Germany.[202] It comes as no surprise that Japan did nothing different than the U.S. in copying European technology in its early years.[203]

The era of Japan's economic miracle led to a transition towards stronger IPR protection in response to lobby groups within specific domestic sectors.[204] As a major example, Yoshida Kogyo KK, famous maker of YKK zippers, discovered counterfeit YKK imported from Korea and initiated a protracted six-year lawsuit against the copiers.[205] Although the Japanese plaintiff lost the case, the setback aroused enthusiasm for enhancing IPR protection. Since then, the Japanese Ministry of Finance has organised the "Customs Informa-

---

[194] Vaughan, *supra* note 161, at 346. *See also* Gluck, *supra* note 164, at 258-9.
[195] *Ibid*, at 346.
[196] *See* "Intellectual Property Policy Outline," *supra* note 170.
[197] *See* Edwin O. Reischauer, *Japan: The Story of A Nation* 270-75 (1989).
[198] Vaughan, *supra* note 161, at 316.
[199] *See* Morishima, *supra* note 165.
[200] Hamada, *supra* note 169, at 4. *See also* Shotaro Inshinomori, *Japan Inc.: An Introduction to Japanese Economics* (Betsey Scheiner trans.)(1988)(introducing the post-war Japanese economic miracles).
[201] *Ibid*, at 7.
[202] *Ibid*.
[203] Vaughan, *supra* note 161, at 316-17.
[204] *See* Inshinomori, *supra* note 200, at 3-4.
[205] *See* Vaughan, *supra* note 161, at 349

tion Centre," a "watchdog unit to monitor illicit copying" and to "combat IPR infringement."[206] This gradually became more pervasive, and counterfeits of Japanese origin had almost entirely disappeared by 1970 due to the stringent efforts of the Japanese government to crack down on counterfeit goods and the steady growth of the local economy.[207] However, a period of reversal was noticeable in the mid-1970s when Japan "faced a resurgence of counterfeit goods that flooded into the Japanese market."[208] It is interesting to observe that the rebound phenomenon occurred during the recession, on the heels of the oil crisis in the 1970s.

4.3 Experience of Korea

4.3.1 "Eastern Decorum" and Economic Miracle

Like Japan, Korea is what might be called a typical Confucian country. Confucianism was introduced into Korea during the era of the Three Kingdoms (57 BCE - 668 CE),[209] and became the official ideology of the Korean state with the establishment of the *Yi* dynasty (1392-1910 CE).[210] According to Slote and De Vos, Confucianism in Korea is a conservative tradition, which has strongly captured people's minds and imposed rules, models, and beliefs, while serving as a blueprint for integrating Korean's social lives.[211]

Confucian Values as a Contribution to Industrialisation

Korean culture retains a strictly observed Confucian element. The traditional Confucian social structure, although changing, is still prevalent in modern Ko-

---

[206] *Ibid.*

[207] Masashi Kurose, "Law Strengthened to Fight Flow of Counterfeit Goods," in *Managing Intellectual Property* 12 (2004).

[208] *Ibid.*

[209] In Korea, Confucianism has been integrated into Korean culture for a long time. The Three Kingdoms, Koguryo (37 BCE-668 CE), Paekche (18 BCE-660 CE) and Silla (57 BCE-935 CE), all left records that indicate the early existence of Confucian influence. *See* Key P. Yang and Gregory Henderson, "An Outline History of Korean Confucianism: Part I: The Early Period and Yi Factionalism," 18 *J. Asian Stud.*, No. 1, 82-4 (1958).

[210] The Confucianism which the *Yi* dynasty adopted is known as Neo-Confucianism. The Neo-Confucianism began in the period of the Song dynasty (960-1279 AD) in China. *See China: A Historical and Cultural Dictionary, supra* note 8, at 230.

[211] Walter H. Slote and George A. De Vos, *Confucianism and the Family in an Interdisciplinary, Comparative Context*, Albany: State University of New York Press 33 (1998). *See* also Denise Potrzeba Lett, *In Pursuit of Status: The Making of South Korea's "New" Urban Middle Class* 14 (1998)(providing a detailed account on contemporary South Korean society in the context of Confucian traditions).

rean society.[212] As Connor has pointed out, "nothing has shaped Korean society as much as Confucian philosophy."[213] According to Connor, children in Korea are educated before the age of ten that their lives do not belong to themselves but to their families.[214] As Donald Clark observes, it is unusual and unacceptable for a young Korean to make a seemingly important decision without taking into account the opinions of his parents.[215] Confucianism has been accepted so eagerly and in so strict a form that the Chinese themselves regarded the Korean adherents as more virtuous than themselves.[216] The Chinese see Korea as the "country of Eastern decorum," referring to the "punctiliousness with which the Koreans observed all phases of the doctrinal ritual."[217]

As noted by Choong Soon Kim, Koreans value harmony, social stability, a respect for cultivation, and motivational force, and tend to be obedient in hierarchical orders, which appears to be compatible with dynamic entrepreneurship in Korea.[218] Confucian philosophy provides comprehensive sets of moral standards by which social behaviour is interpreted and evaluated in Korea.[219] As Chaihark Hahm comments, it is a common point of view in Korea that the deeply ingrained Confucian notion of social hierarchy and natural order is still a predominant factor in interpersonal relations, organisational structures and economic life.[220] As a developing nation, Korea has obtained a positive response based on its accomplishment to retain traditional values while establishing its domestic industries.[221] As Tu Wei-ming observes, it is an interesting

---

[212] *See* Kyu Ho Youm, "Libel Laws and Freedom of the Press: South Korea and Japan Reexamined," 8 *B.U. Int'l L.J.* 53, 78 (1990) (describing Confucian ethics in Korea as still prevailing).

[213] Mary E. Connor, *The Koreas: A Global Studies Handbook* 180 (2002).

[214] *Ibid.*

[215] Donald N. Clark, *Culture and Customs of Korea* 32 (2000).

[216] *See* Potrzeba Lett, *supra* note 211, at 14; *see also* Pamela A. Newman, "The Confucian Ethic: A System of Ideals in Korea," *Social Studies, Comparative Religion*, at 225-227, *available at* <http://www.koreasociety.org/>.

[217] *See* "A Window on Korea: Belief, Philosophy and Religion," *ASNIC Online*, <http://asnic.utexas.edu/asnic/countries/korea/beliefsystem.html> (last visited September 5, 2005).

[218] Choong Soon Kim, *The Culture of Korean Industry: An Ethnography of Poongsan Corporation* 57-59 (1992)(asserting, through an empirical study of Poongsan Corporation, that cultural characteristics of the Korean industrial success originate from Confucianism).

[219] Chaihark Hahm, "Law, Culture, and the Politics of Confucianism," 16 *Colum. J. Asian L.* 257, 268, 271 (2003)(asserting that Confucian values, which have constituted a part of Korean culture, are playing an active role in the modern Korean society).

[220] *Ibid*, at 267-70 (having demonstrated the decline and rejuvenation of Confucianism since the 1880s in Korea, Hahm alleged that "the persistence of the Confucian tradition is often noted as an important factor in describing or explaining contemporary Korean society").

[221] *Ibid*, at 267(noting that the Confucianism is "not only compatible with, but also positively advantageous for, economic development [in the East Asian region, including

phenomenon that "the upsurge of interest in Confucian studies in South Korea, Taiwan, Hong Kong and Singapore during the last four decades has generated a new dynamism in the Confucian tradition," paving the way for the emergence of the "'third epoch' of Confucian humanism."[222]

Weak IPR Protection and "Development Policy"

Traditionally speaking, Korea has not been a nation with an intellectual property notion in the modern sense.[223] Intellectual property that is conceived and developed in Korea had long been regarded as an entrepreneurial device to attract investment and transfer of technology, and, similar to Japan, royalty payments had been a major element of the balance of payment.[224] As a result, the effectiveness of Korea's government in keeping the integrity of IPR had been incoherent. For example, the government required complex and specific product information in order to validate an application of IPR, and this information should have to remain contained.[225]

In addition, the Korean government has applied a flexible intellectual property policy of incorporation of imitation into its "national development" and for a long time been considered as an example of a state in which "piracy" was regarded as merely a benign form of technology transfer.[226] Accordingly, Korea did not establish its effective IPR enforcement mechanism until the late 1980s.[227] For example, during the 1960s and early 1970s, Korea was almost entirely an importer of technology from developed countries, particularly from

---

Korea]"). Indeed, after the 1960s, Korea found its role followed the Japanese example and developed into one of the "Four Mini Dragons." Statistics show that "four decades ago GDP per capita was comparable with levels in the poorer countries of Africa and Asia." Today its GDP per capita is seven times India's, sixteen times North Korea, and is "comparable to the lesser economies of the EU," expecting the emergence of a new era of Confucianism from contemporary Neo-Confucian perspective. *See CIA World Fact Book* 297, 300 (2004).

[222] *See* Tu Wei-ming, "The Confucian Tradition In Chinese History," in Paul S. Ropp *et al* (eds.), *Heritage of China: Contemporary Perspectives on Chinese Civilization* 136 (1990).

[223] Vaughan, *supra* note 161, at 335.

[224] Linsu Kim, "Technology Transfer and Intellectual Property Rights: The Korean Experience," in *Intellectual Property Rights and Sustainable Development* (2003), available at <http://www.ictsd.org/pubs/ictsd_series/IPR/CS_kim.pdf>("Korean firms entered the mature technology stage in the 1960s and 1970s by acquiring, assimilating, and improving generally available mature foreign technology through various mechanisms based on duplicative imitation, and evolved into the intermediate technology stage in the 1980s and 1990s through aggressive efforts to strengthen technological capabilities which enabled creative imitation").

[225] *Ibid.*

[226] *Ibid.*

[227] *Ibid.*

the U.S., Japan and Western Europe.[228] The heavy dependence on Japanese technology has resulted in the fact that Korea shares similar industrial advantages, such as the automobile and electronic industries.[229] Were it not for such tolerant IPR, it would not have been possible for local enterprises to have achieved such substantial results.[230] This practice has made tremendous contributions to Korea's economic boom.

Higher Level IPR System as a Diplomatic Compromise

In the area of IPR protection, Korea has had a similar experience to China and both have been repeatedly criticised by the United States. Korea was elevated to the Priority Watch List in the 2003 Special 301 Report of the U.S. Trade Representatives, which highlighted a series of continued concerns regarding the lack of adequate protection and enforcement of intellectual property rights, particularly the growth of online music piracy and continued piracy of U.S.' motion pictures.[231] Under external pressure, Korea has seen a major overhaul of its IPR regulations influenced by the TRIPs Agreement, and has furnished itself with relatively good intellectual property legislation and reasonable enforcement mechanisms.[232]

4.3.2 From "Breaking" to "Preaching": Role Shift in IPR Protection

Similar to the experience of Japan, the incorporation of piracy into "national development" policies facilitated domestic industrialisation and related economic growth in Korea. However, by accumulating sufficient indigenous capabilities with extensive science and technology infrastructures, these two countries reached the later stage of the technological development where IPR protection became an important element in domestic industrial activities.[233] Japan and Korea "could not have achieved their current levels of technological sophistication if strong IPR regimes had been imposed on them during the early stage of their industrialisation."[234] The same principle applied to the United States and Western Europe during their respective industrialisation phases.[235]

---

[228] Walter Arnold, "Science and Technology Development in Taiwan and South Korea," 28(4) *Asian Survey* 440 (1988).

[229] *See* Linsu Kim, *supra* note 224, at 5.

[230] *Ibid.*

[231] United States Trade Representative Special 301 Priority Watch List (2004), *available at* <http://www.ustr.gov/Docment_Library/Reports_Publications/2004/2004_Special_301/Special_301_Priority_Watch_List.html>.

[232] Heath, *supra* note 162.

[233] Linsu Kim, *supra* note 224, at 5.

[234] *Ibid*, at 7.

[235] *Ibid.*

With the development of greater technological sophistication, more and more Korean companies consider IPR as an essential part of the successful commercialisation of their products and have made considerable investments into research and development.[236] Research and development investment has seen a "quantum jump" from 28.6 million dollars in 1971 to 4.7 billion dollars by 1990, and to 12.2 billion dollars by 2000.[237] During this period, Korean was recognised as one of the world's fastest growing emerging economies.[238] As a percentage of GDP, research and development increased from 0.32 percent to 2.68 percent during the same period, overtaking that of many Western European countries.[239] Korean companies have acted as enthusiastic advocates and effective preachers for appropriate protection for IPR.[240] As Samsung and LG have become globally competitive in the technology sector, the Korean government has at last found leverage to punish counterfeiting and piracy and to protect IPR with a vigorous enforcement mechanism. Korea, one of the long-time leaders in piracy practices, came to understand the bite of illegal copying and has now become a genuine believer and supporter of IPR.[241]

The intellectual property law transplantation which took place in the process of industrialisation in Korea reflected a role shift in IPR protection in the second half of the twentieth century. Korea has performed a miracle in both economic development and legal construction without "abandon[ing] its twisted Confucianism" which has been heavily blamed and criticised.[242] Indeed, at the early stage of economic development, economic interests are always prioritised and the cultural factors are bound to become secondary. In this sense, the shift of this role relies mainly on the development of economic interests rather than cultural defects, which suggests that cultural values are less important than market forces at the initial phase of economic development, contrary to what conventional theory suggests.[243]

Two decades ago, both China and Korea were blacklisted by the USTR.[244] While China still remains on the "watch list," Korea has geared up its efforts

---

[236] For example, for the last decade Samsung invested 35 billion dollars on R&D. Samsung has recently launched an ambitious plan to spend 45 billion dollars over the next five years on R&D, starting in November 2005. *See* "Samsung Group Announces Investment Plan," Associated Press, November 8, 2005, *available at* <http://www.marinelink.com/Story/ShowStory.aspx?StoryID=200804>.

[237] Linsu Kim, *supra* note 224, at 3.

[238] *Ibid.*

[239] *Ibid.*

[240] Alice H. Amsden, *Asia's Next Giant, South Korea and Late Industrialization* 3-5 (1992)(introducing Korea's conversion from a learner to an innovator).

[241] *Ibid.*

[242] *See, e.g.*, Sin-ming Shaw, "It's True. Asian Can't Think," *supra* note 5.

[243] For a comprehensive list of works criticising Confucianism as a cultural barrier for enforcing IPR, *see supra* note 3-5 and the accompanying text. For an analysis of the transplant theory and its relationship with culture, *see supra* § 2.2.3.

[244] *See* Vaughan, *supra* note 161, at 335.

and has endeavoured to establish a sound mechanism of the IPR protection. The different experiences of Korea and China provide a good perspective for comparative analysis. By examining Korea through a multifaceted lens, it provides a useful case for assessing the extent to which a developed economy is helped or hindered by "free riding," and provides China a precedent which may lead to a shortcut to the most direct and appropriate IPR management strategy.

4.3.3 Preliminary Reflections

Misleading Correlation between Confucianism and Piracy

Both Japan and Korea are countries heavily influenced by Confucian philosophy. Unlike Western values which advocate individual rights, Confucian ethic emphasises the virtue of austerity, hard work, teamwork and submission to authority, all of which have contributed to the economic miracle in Japan and Korea.[245] Japanese and Koreans cherish the Confucian heritage since "it goes beyond a religion *per se* – it encapsulates a set of rules that govern daily life".[246] This practice of Confucian ethics has played a positive role in fostering innovation and entrepreneurship over the centuries within the Confucian zone in Eastern Asia. It is therefore inappropriate to assert that Confucianism and intellectual property cannot coexist or that Confucian ethic is a devastating obstacle to innovation and creation.

However, the functionality of the Confucian ethics in promoting innovations depends largely on minimum standards of economic development. In other words, at the early stage of development, cultural effect is manifest above all in fostering domestic economic growth. This is not an isolated phenomenon limited to the Confucian states. Tolerant intellectual property policies are normally applied in almost every country in its immature economic development stage, regardless of economic character and cultural structure.

Apparently, the hypothesis linking IPR violation to Confucian ethics fails to account for the current lower rates of counterfeiting and piracy in Japan and Korea which are equally, if not more, influenced by Confucians value than China. The significant difference is that both Japan and Korea have established stronger IPR regimes because of varying stages of economic development.[247]

---

[245] McCormack & Sugimoto, *supra* note 180, at 5.

[246] Stan Mensik *et al*, "Trends and Transitions in Japanese and Korean Approaches," Paper of the 7th International Conference on Global Business and Economic Development, Bangkok, Thailand, January 2003.

[247] Thomas.G. Rawski, "Chinese Industrial Reform: Accomplishments, Prospects, and Implications," 84 *Am. Econ. Rev.* 271, 272 (1994)(stating that IPR protections are normally weaker in emerging markets than in developed markets).

The Particularity of China Compared with Japan and Korea

However, there is a major difference between China and these two neighbouring countries. First, like Japan, Korea has been "Americanised" to a certain degree since the end of World War II, and the legal regime, also like Japan, has long been heavily influenced by Western Civil Code based on the "rule of law" system.[248] Second, culturally, the unilateral Confucian system in these two countries has developed into a mixed cultural system. Interacted with the other elements of religious scene such as Shintoism and Buddhism, Confucianism in Japan has provided fundamental cultural capital in shaping modern Japanese society;[249] Confucian system in Korea has also developed into a Confucian-Christian system.[250] The westernisation process may have made it much easier for these two countries to make necessary adjustments.

While China shares the Confucian tradition with Japan and Korea, China's unique socialist ideology, administrative decentralisation, inadequate judiciary and huge but inefficient bureaucracy have made intellectual property enforcement rather difficult. As has been analysed in the earlier sections of this chapter, despite the remarkable economic prosperity and applausable legal construction, China's political dilemma in its democratisation process has provided an institutional account for its weak effectiveness of IPR enforcement. China's communist development trajectory which resulted in a lack of effective institutions for enforcement had hindered compliance with the objectives of IPR protection.

Nonetheless, it is important to note that, for practical purposes, any approach to effectively analysing and clarifying IPR issues in China must rest on a balanced interplay of political and cultural fundamentals. In other words, the enigmatic dilemma of socio-political reform has shaped a unique model of Chinese philosophies that have exercised indirect but decisive influence over the effectiveness of the enforcement. Even if it reaches an appropriate stage of economic development, without these "fundamentals," the enforcement infrastructure will be endorsed neither by political will of the authorities nor by the

---

[248] *See* Pyong-choon Hahm, "Korea's Initial Encounter with the Western Law," in Sang-Hyun Song (ed.), *Korean Law in the Global Economy* 61(1996).

[249] John Berthrong, "Confucian Piety and the Religious Dimension of Japanese Confucianism (The Religious Dimension of Confucianism in Japan)," 48 (1) *Philosophy East and West* 67 (1998)(arguing that "[i]n short, Confucianism, along with all the other elements of the Japanese religious scene, provides cultural capital for the formation of modern Japan").

[250] *See* Kang-nam Oh, "Sagehood and Metanoia: The Confucian-Christian Encounter in Korea," 61 *J. Am. Acad. Relig.* 303, 316 (1993)(asserting that Korea "can be considered a particularly favourable laboratory for the Confucian-Christian dialogue"); *see* also, Young-Gwan Kim, "The Confucian-Christian Context in Korean Christianity," 13 *B.C. Asian Rev.* 81-4 (2002)(noting that "Korean Christians tend to identify themselves as Christians, but paradoxically their practices in customs and ethics are based on Confucianism").

cultural perception of the citizenries. The short answer is that only when China has carried out its socio-political reform systemically and integrated into the international institutions will it be possible to ensure the endeavour goes further. From this point of view, it may be right that the dysfunctional institutional regime in China has increased complexity and added cost to the eventual attainment of the effective intellectual property protection system, particularly compared to Japan and Korea. That is also why this book supports policy makers in the West who try to promote the transformation of China in both economic and, probably more importantly, political areas.

If that is the case, it reaches a conclusion that the experience of Korea can be used for reference for both China and the EU. On one hand, it is undoubtedly of significance to give an analysis as to how negotiations backing Korea's significant investment in China had dealt with the inherent and intractable tension between "tolerant IPR policy" and "rule of law" ideas. On the other hand, both the EU and Korea have similar interests for trade and investment in China. It would be valuable for the EU to understand and to learn from Korea as to how it has approached similar problems regarding IPR implementation in China, or whether they have crafted their negotiations with China with cultural diversity taken into account. This would provide the EU with a very useful point of comparison.

The Turning Point of IPR Protection in the Developing Stage

As has been discussed in chapter 2, in developing countries, the package of IPR under the confines of TRIPs is perceived as a mandatory obligation imposed by the interest of the West. However, TRIPs also provides a level of protection for domestic innovators that might not ordinarily have applied until a later stage in a country's development. This stage theory poses an interesting challenge to developing states as to when and how they should engage with international IPR norms whilst ensuring legislation is appropriately balanced between the interests of local innovators and the needs of the societies of which they are a part.

By that logic, it indicates a conflict which not only exists between two different worlds, but one in which the appropriate balance in any one state moves along a continuum as a companion to development. The question here is how this balance should be adjusted with the prospect of accelerated development. The answer may well be that the major incentive to developing states to enforce international IPR norms will be lobbies of domestic inventors, authors, or companies who would benefit from higher IPR enforcement, rather than external threats that may only generate intermittent effects. Both Japan and Korea have gone through such a "turning point" where higher level IPR protection becomes beneficial.

4.4 China's Enforcement Problem: Clues to the Perennial Conundrum

As has been noted, while few would disagree that China has impressively established a sound IPR legislation based on its WTO commitments, it is the enforcement that has been fragile. The enforcement problem in China has developed into a perennial conundrum. Unfortunately, strategic solutions to the existing enforcement problems have been little explored. This section seeks to capture the significance and dilemmas associated with IPR protection in China and to demystify the mysteries of the enforcement problems.

4.4.1 Fostering a Shift in China from Rule by Law to Rule of Law

Political freedom depends on economic freedom while economic freedom over a lengthy period of time serves as a catalyst for the creation of political freedom.[251] China is currently experiencing a critical transition – economic reform has not only given impetus to economic prosperity but also fostered the growth of socio-economic inequality and complexity, such as regional disparities, rampant income gaps, widespread official corruption and the collapse of traditional values. As a result, utilitarianism dominates many people's minds throughout the country. In addition, the restriction of religious belief and the tough control over freedom of speech have exacerbated the instability of the country. In this context, counterfeiting and piracy are by-products of the defective political infrastructure.

Due to this background, it is of great significance for Chinese government to facilitate rule of law system and provide its citizenry minimum freedom of expression and religion. It is a stopgap measure that can easily be undone a strategic policy that encourages the creation of a sound environment for such development.

Nevertheless, China has demonstrated "a desire to join the global stage," which will force China to "undergo a tortuous path [...], as it navigates from an isolated socialist country to a market-oriented, centrally-planned regime"[252] where individual liberty and property rights are protected under the rule of law. The political transition will inevitably continue, driven by China's continuous economic dynamism, social challenges and global integration. [253] While it is still too early to predict the future path of political reform in China, there are some encouraging signs that China's integration with the outside

---

[251] Allison & Lin, *supra* note 25, at 774 (quoting Milton Friedman, "The Relation between Economic Freedom and Political Freedom," in *Capitalism and Freedom* 7-21(1962)).

[252] Yonehara, "Enter the Dragon," *supra* note 4, at 107-108.

[253] Wei-Wei Zhang, *supra* note 59, at 14.

world and the new policy initiatives of building a "harmonious society"[254] might, in time, lead to a stable form of political liberalisation.[255]

The 1990s have brought the beginning of what could well be a significant wave of political reform with Chinese leadership addressing the need to strengthen legal institutions,[256] "that might curb bureaucratic arbitrariness by defining the scope of administrative authority and providing remedies for the exercise of arbitrary power."[257]

During a visit to the United States in April 2006, Chinese President Hu Jintao sent an unusual signal at a press conference with his pledge to adopt democracy in the future.[258] Hu pointed out that, "in the light of China's own national conditions and the will of the Chinese people, [China will] continue to move ahead [with] political restructuring and to develop a socialist democracy."[259] Unlike all the previous statement of Chinese leaders which addressed "China's own national conditions," this time, Hu emphasised both "China's own national conditions" and "the will of the Chinese people."[260] While for the time being it is difficult to decide whether it is a slip of the tongue, a political show, or a consensus of Chinese leaders, the statement at least shows a symbolic purpose.

Moreover, market liberalisation and the widespread availability of information over the Internet[261] have already loosened the government's strength in

---

[254] Proposed by President Hu Jintao, the CPC and the central government of China have made it an important task to build a "harmonious society (*hexie shehui*)," which served the fundamental interests of the people. *See* "Building Harmonious Society CPC's Top Task," *Xinhua News*, February 20, 2005.

[255] Halverson, *supra* note 80, at 363.

[256] As a symbolic move, China's National People's Congress amended the Chinese Constitution in 1999 to insert the "rule of law" into that document as a leading principle. *See*, Constitution Article 5, PNC Laws & Legislations Databases, *available at* <www.npc.gov.cn/englishnpc/Law/2008-01/24/content_1381976.htm>.

[257] Lubman, *supra* note 76, at 392.

[258] At a joint press conference following the Hu-Bush Summit in Washington on April 20, 2006, President Hu noted that China would "continue to move ahead with the political restructuring and to develop a socialist democracy," and it will "further expand the orderly participation of the Chinese citizens in political affairs so that the Chinese citizens will be in a better position to exercise their democratic rights in terms of democratic supervision, democratic management, and the democratic decision-making." Press Release, Office of the White House Press Secretary, President Bush Meets with President Hu of the People's Republic of China (April 20, 2006), *available at* <http://www. state.gov/p/eap/rls/ot/64895.htm>.

[259] *Ibid.*

[260] *See* Dehao Fang, "Hu Jintao Zhenggai Shumoing Cang Xuanji [The Implications of Hu's Statement towards Political Reform]," *Asian Times*, April 24, 2006.

[261] According to the latest figures released by China Internet Network Information Centre (CNNIC) in its Semi-annual Survey Report on the Development of the Internet in China, the number of Chinese Internet users connecting to the Internet over broadband connections rose by 173 percent during 2003. *See* Sumner Lemon, "Broadband Internet

controlling all spheres of society,[262] and the phrase "rule of law" is becoming increasingly popular in Chinese society, particularly among officials and intellectuals. China's integration into the global trading system and its participation in the international rulemaking process will profoundly influence Chinese attitudes and ways of thinking.[263] China has no choice but to burn their bridges and carry out its ongoing reform despite the complexity and uncertainty entailed. China has become an institutional laboratory – the largest of its kind in human history – that is freighted with enormous implications for the future of the rule of law.[264]

4.4.2 Facilitating the Conversion of China from an "IP Imitation" to an "IP Creation" Nation

As has been demonstrated above, if the establishment of an IPR legal system lacks social foundation on which adequate economic values of the system have been fully realised, the incentives of innovation may recede and the underpinnings that sustain creativities may collapse. Unfortunately, this is what has been happening in some developing countries, of course including China, in the area of IPR protection.

Lack of Home-grown Intellectual Property

As Allison and Lin have observed, "China has followed the typical pattern of a developing nation by depending heavily on foreign investment and imported technology before being able to generate internal growth and technological advancement on its own."[265] Indeed, for a long time, China lacked genuine enthusiasm and native intelligence to enforce IPR, since providing substantial IPR protection within the confines of TRIPs Agreement does not render immediate economic benefits to the Chinese economy.[266] For many Chinese

---

Usage Soars in China," January 16, 2004, *available at* <http://www.infoworld.com/article/04/01/16/HNchina netusage_1.html>. In 2003, China was estimated to have 79.5 million Internet users, up 34.5 percent from 59.1 million users in 2002. See "U.N. Conference on Trade and Development, E-Commerce and Development Report 2004," UNCTAD, *available at* <www.unctad.org/en/docs/ecdr2004 ch1_en.pdf>.

[262] Halverson, *supra* note 80, at 364-65 (addressing the widespread availability of information over the Internet as an important factor to limit the government's ability in controlling the public).

[263] *See ibid.* at 332 (stating that China's WTO membership will further deepen its integration into the world economy and strengthen its active role in the international economic arena).

[264] Wei-Wei Zhang, *supra* note 59, at 5.

[265] Allison & Lin, *supra* note 25, at 775.

[266] J. Cheng, "China's Copyright System: Rising to the Spirit of TRIPs Requires an Internal Focus and WTO Membership," *21 Fordham Int'l L. J.* (1998), at 1979.

companies, strengthened IPR protection implies that domestic enterprises are obliged to pay a colossal sum of royalties to foreign proprietors, thereby resulting in escalating production costs and shrinking profit margins.[267] Correspondingly, most Chinese enterprises have been content to making imitation products and have invested little capital and made little effort to develop their own innovative technologies.[268]

However, to create home-grown intellectual property in China is indispensable. Over the years, Chinese companies have suffered huge losses in the international market as a result of lacking independent intellectual property.[269] According to a survey conducted by Deloitte & Touche, a professional services firm, as of 2004, Chinese manufacturers were compelled to pay licence fees ranging from fifteen to twenty-two percent on DVD players that retail for less than sixty dollars.[270] It was also reported that royalty payment to Intel and Microsoft accounted to fifty to seventy percent of the retail price of computers manufactured in China.[271]

Apparently, Chinese leaders and entrepreneurs need to enhance the awareness of protection for indigenous intellectual property. A notable example is China's inadequate protection for traditional Chinese medicine (TCM) – the Chinese "national treasure" which has a history of thousands of years. Though having a comparative advantage in TCM products, China has few TCM brands that have established their dominant positions at domestic and global markets.[272] By the December 2005, the trade value of TCM exceeded forty billion dollars in the global market and is growing at a staggering rate of ten percent annually, whereas China home-made TCM constitutes less than three percent of the total value.[273] By contrast, TCM enterprises in Japan, Korea, Southeast Asia and Western Europe purchase raw herbal materials in China

---

[267] *See* "Changes in China's IPR System, Business Alert – China," Publication of Hong Kong Trade Development Council, Issue 10, 2000, *available at* <www.tdctrade.com/alert/cba-e0010b.htm>.

[268] *Ibid.*

[269] Yahong Li, "The Wolf Has Come: Are China's Intellectual Property Industries Prepared for the WTO?" 20 *UCLA Pacific Basin L. J.* (2002), at 101.

[270] *See* David Schutzman & Evonne Lum, "Technology Firms Risk Losing Advantage as China's Influence on Global Standards Reaches Critical Levels: Deloitte Identifies Four Strategies to Exert Influence on Chinese Standards and Generate Long-term Opportunities," August 4, 2004. *See* also USTR Report 2006, at 111, *available at* <http://www.ustr.gov/assets/Document_Library/Reports_Publications/2006/2006_NTE_Report/asset_upload_file684_9235.pdf>.

[271] Richard P. Suttmeier & Yao Xiangkui, "China's Post-WTO Technology Policy: Standards, Software, and the Changing Nature of Techno-Nationalism" 7 *NBR Special report* 20 (2004)(quoting Sherman So, "Low-cost Chip Is Made for China," *South China Morning Post*, February 17, 2004).

[272] *See* "China Losing TCM Intellectual Property," *China News Network*, December 13, 2005, *available at* <http://www.chinanews.cn//news/2005/2005-12-13/15742.html>.

[273] *Ibid*

and, after rough processing locally in China, transport them into their own countries where the raw materials are refined and the exacts are transmuted into finished products.[274] Such TCM products are not only placed in the foreign market but also resold to the Chinese market at enormously escalated prices.[275] Currently, China's TCM import from Japan, Korea, Southeast Asia and Western Europe is valued as high as more than 100 million dollars.[276]

Due to the lack of independent intellectual property, there has not been much incentive for lobbies of inventors or authors who would benefit from higher IPR enforcement. Correspondingly, the Chinese government has felt little internal pressure to enforce IPR.[277] In other words, Chinese leaders have no explicit political will to substantially enforce IPR. In order to build a healthy ecosystem of innovation, China needs to establish an independent domestic intellectual property industry that is required to move the manufacturing economy up the value chain.[278]

Value Chain Restructuring: from "Made in China" to "Innovated in China"

Enriching, nurturing and rewarding homegrown talent constitute the logic start of the intellectual property value chain. Therefore, it is of great importance to facilitate China's transition from a mere consumer of IPR to a net creator, in other words, from "made in China" to "innovated in China," Construction of a system balancing protection and exploitation is therefore indispensable for the establishment of a cycle of an intellectual creation. It is objectively unlikely that the conversion of China from an "IP imitation" to an "IP creation" nation can be achieved without the process of the innovation capacity building.

Universities and research institutions are expected to harness the potential of their technologies to bridge the gaps of R&D, and to contribute at certain stage in the value chain.[279] In order to make China an "IP creation" nation, it is necessary to establish a mechanism by which universities and research institutes can create independent and internationally competitive intellectual property to be used to the maximum extent possible in the society. Based on such awareness, China needs to put in place measures with the aim of encouraging

---

[274] *Ibid*

[275] *Ibid*

[276] *Ibid*

[277] *See* Tara Kalagher Giunta & Lily H. Shang, "Ownership of Information in a Global Economy," 27 *Geo. Wash. J. Int'L. & Econ.* 331(1993).

[278] A company's value chain is normally defined as "an interdependent system or network of activities, connected by linkages." For further discussion, *see* Michael E. Porter, "Competition in Global Industries: A Conceptual Framework," in *Competition in Global Industries* 15, 20-22 (1986).

[279] Amy Kapczynski *et al*, "Addressing Global Health Inequities: An Open Licensing Approach for University Innovations," 20 *Berkeley Tech. L.J.* 1090-91 (2005).

the creation of R&D assets at universities and research institutes. To this end, China needs to set up an innovative society where IPR is viewed as an essential ingredient. China also needs to reconfigure and revamp its education system for lateral thinking – "thinking out of the box,"[280] instead of traditional rote learning, and strive to evolve the nation into a role of being more of a world innovator than a world manufacturer.

Trend Assessment: "Well Begun Is Half Done"

An old Chinese adage says "well begun is half done". Most encouragingly, there have been signs which may reflect an auspicious beginning for the emergence of a sound IPR enforcement system. China has opened its door, and has initiated the transformation of itself from orthodox Marxism to "socialism with Chinese characteristics (*you zhongguo tese de shehuizhuyi*),[281] and has demonstrated outstanding dedication and commitment towards embracing a strengthened IPR enforcement system.[282]

As Yahong Li suggests, upon its accession to the WTO, Chinese enterprises depending heavily on imitation of foreign products are liable to suffer from losing market share.[283] The fierce competition provides the companies with no options but to innovate or exist, will their business strategies reexamined and their resources reallocated. In order to survive in the fierce competition characterised by technological contests, these companies have to promote industrial transformations and reinforce their innovation capacities.

Based on this awareness, over the past decade or so, a momentum of a rapid and continuous development in IPR protection has been maintained in China. According to the statistics released by SIPO, the total number of applications of three kinds of patents reached 694,153 in 2007, an increase of 473 percent compared to 121,150 in 1998.[284] As the Figure 2 shows below, while there has been less sign of growth among foreign applicants and this may have more or less blurred any clear profile for the transformation of China from an "IP imitation" to an "IP creation" nation, during the past ten years, applications by domestic applicants have shown an increasing trend, and Chinese patent applications have generally increased at a rapid pace every year since 1998. From a perspective of EU-China bilateral trade, China's exports to Europe are conventionally restricted to low-tech labour intensive products, but recent years have evidenced a gradual increase in output of value-added products such as

---

[280] Edward De Bono, *Serious Creativity: Using the Power of Lateral Thinking to Create New Ideas* 205-6 (1992).

[281] *See* Jennifer Fan, "The Dilemma of China's Intellectual Property Piracy," 4 *UCLA J. Int'l L. & Foreign Aff.* 207 (1999).

[282] *See* Weiqiu Long, "Intellectual Property in China," 31 *St. Mary's L.J.* (1999), at 47.

[283] *See* Yahong Li, "The Wolf Has Come," *supra* note 269, at 109.

[284] Sources: State Intellectual Property Office (SIPO), *available at* <www.sipo.gov.cn/sipo/ghfzs/zltj/>.

electronic and information equipments.[285] As of 2005, almost twenty percent of China's exports are classified as high-tech.[286] All these trends imply that the process of China's transferring from an IP consumer to IP producer has started.

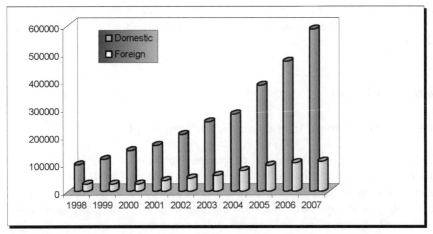

Sources from State Intellectual Property Office (SIPO), Compiled by the author

Figure 2 China's Patent Application (1998-2007)

4.4.3 Promoting Transformation of China from Perceived Infringer to Unfortunate Victim

As has been analysed above, under the current international IPR system, developing nations need sufficient incentives to bring their IPR enforcement systems in line with TRIPs standards.[287] At the same time, however, the recipient countries must be equipped with necessary scientific and technological capacities so that the local economies flourish. This accumulation process is essential and inevitable for a developing country to achieve the point where protection of IPR becomes economically beneficial.[288]

In the case of China, a penetrating strategy entails promoting China's further participation in the global economy and encouraging it to develop its own world class technologies.[289] It is important to encourage an appreciation of the

---

[285] *See* "Zhongou Jingmao Guanxi [EU-China Trade Relations]," *available at* <www.china comeu.org/web3/SINO-EU.htm>.

[286] Larry Elliott, "Bra Wars: Europe Strikes Back," *The Guardian*, August 26, 2005.

[287] Allison Cychosz, "The Effectiveness of International Enforcement of Intellectual Property Rights," 37 *J. Marshall L. Rev.* 1015 (2004).

[288] *Ibid.*

[289] Yeh, *supra* note 123, at 521.

interests that IPR protection can give to Chinese innovators when certain development has been achieved. This will need the establishment of a strong domestic constituency of innovators within China whose interests will suffer both in relation to their own ideas and in terms of access to foreign investment and technology transfer. Only if China continues to protect IPR by its self-sufficient enforcement system without being externally threatened may it be said that the West has found the right key to undoing the "Gordian Knot" and obtaining vigorous enforcement.

4.5 Conclusion

4.5.1 Economic Insufficiency as the Striking Point

Based on the analyses above, it is concluded that the economic factor is one of the important reasons for the IPR enforcement problems in developing countries. While protection of IPR is essential to safeguard innovation, a tolerate IPR policy is indispensable for capacity building in the primary stage of development. To speed up this process will undermine the developmental bulwark, but beyond a certain point, allowing it to continue will also hinder economic growth. This means that the political judgment as to the appropriate balance in any state at any time moves along a continuum as counterpart to development. It may be true, therefore, that the decisive influence towards implementation and enforcement of international IPR norms comes from lobbies of domestic proprietors who would eventually benefit from higher level of IPR protection. In this context, developed countries are best advised to formulate long-term strategies and extend as much cooperation and assistance as possible in order to bridge the economic divide and help developing countries reach the "development stage" and change their "economic behaviour."

China's economic development has not reached the stage where the Chinese leadership has sufficient motivations to fight IPR infringement. However, at this stage of development, China needs time to phase-in its enforcement efforts while adjusting its laws and policies. Not until China's leaders perceive it as harming their own interests to tolerate counterfeiting and piracy will they enforce IPR actively and effectively.

4.5.2 The Paradox of Cultural Determinism

IPR infringement is a common phenomenon that occurs in almost every country, regardless of political factor, economic character and cultural structure. [290] It is incomprehensible that the Confucian system has always been credited

---

[290] Vaughan, *supra* note 161, at 308-310.

when it comes to the inefficiency of the IPR enforcement. However, it is more coincidence than cause that many egregious counterfeits and piracies come from China with Confucian cultural background,[291] as the comparison with Japan and Korea demonstrates.[292] No evidence has been seen to establish causality. To overestimate or even misestimate the influence of Confucian values can create a misleading stereotype and form of "cultural bias."

Although some drawbacks of Confucian ethics may still exist,[293] "Confucian elites have contributed to the social and political achievements of East Asian states such as Japan and Korea in the post-World War II era: rapid and relatively egalitarian economic growth, stable families, and crime-free streets."[294] Confucian ethics have made positive contributions, both in fostering domestic economic development and in maintaining intellectual property in different ways. The important thing is how to preserve the advantages of Confucian ethics while minimising their shortcomings.[295]

The objective of establishing the WTO was to liberalise world trade and to harmonise trade policies to ensure fair access to world markets.[296] While engaging in harmonisation of national trade policies, the world trading system has promoted cultural harmonisation simultaneously, for example, through the transplantation of TRIPs standard.[297] As has been demonstrated in previous chapters, the enforceability and effectiveness of a transplanted law largely depend on how it is culturally filtered into people's minds and how it is adapted to the specific social circumstances.[298] The activation of the IPR enforcement can hardly be achieved by legal means alone but through a complex interplay

---

[291] The "Confucianised" countries were especially designated as Priority Foreign Countries or frequently named to the Priority Watch List. These vulnerable countries include China (Confucian background), Taiwan (Confucian background), Vietnam (Confucian background), Philippines (mixed Confucian-Christian background), and Korea (mixed Confucian-Christian). The IIPA representative stressed that China's trade practice has done the least to address and satisfy the minimum concerns of the United States. *See* <http://www.iipa.com/special301_TOCs/2002_SPEC301_TOC.html> for details, last visited August 28, 2006.

[292] Vaughan, *supra* note 161, at 308-310.

[293] Arguably, it might be true that, while Confucianism demands loyalty, devotion and honour to seniors and ancestors, and advocates human interference to establish social harmony, these concerns in turn place a systemic pressure against argument and disobedience. As such, the role of critical thinking may be somewhat weakened.

[294] Daniel Bell, "The Making and Unmaking of Boundaries: A Contemporary Confucian Perspective," in Allen Buchanan and Margaret Moore (eds), *States, Nations, and Borders: The Ethics of Making Boundaries* 57-85 (2003).

[295] *Ibid.*

[296] *See* TRIPs, 33 I.L.M. 1125 (1994).

[297] *See* TRIPs, *ibid.* As the most comprehensive intellectual property agreement ever, the TRIPs Agreement aims to promote harmonisation and standardisation of approach to protection by providing minimum standards for the member states.

[298] *Supra* § 2.2.3.

of law and culture.[299] In this context, cultural adaptation during legal trans-plantation requires much effort beyond the domain of law in the domestic re-ception process.[300]

However, it seems to be apparent that TRIPs has gone beyond dealing with "trade related" IPR issues within the legal domain and interfered with cultural liberties. As Shin-yi Peng has commented, under the TRIPs regime, a state ini-tially pursues a variety of goals in addition to economic development, such as cultural autonomy, but the compelling rule-based international trade regime restricts the ability of the nation to structure its own domestic laws, which of-ten reflect the cultural values of that nation.[301] For this reason, we cannot ig-nore the fact that, in a multicultural society, it may be an anachronism to strive for a unique cultural environment leading to intellectual property harmonisa-tion.[302] Imposing a superseding international law in the name of trade har-monisation tends to undermine the social values and cultural diversities re-flected in domestic laws.[303]

Like liberal values, which are widely shared by many East-Asian nations, "Confucian values and their political implications may well be applicable in non-Confucian societies that share similar political cultures and face similar political problems."[304] In concrete terms, it might be important to promote a worldwide conception for IPR protection, but it might be equally, if not more

---

[299] The interaction between law and culture has drawn much attention from scholars and commentators. Friedman has demonstrated that, "legal systems [...] reflect what is happening in their own societies." According to Friedman, legal systems "assume the shape of these societies, like a glove that molds itself to the shape of a person's hand." *See*, Lawrence M. Friedman, "On the Emerging Sociology of Transnational Law," 32 *Stan. J Int'l L.* 72 (1996); *See* also Berta Esperanza Hernandez-Truyol, "Glocalizing Law and Culture: Towards a Cross-Constitutive Paradigm," 67 *Alb. L. Rev.* 618, 623. Tamanaha gives another metaphor, stating that law is generally understood to be a mir-ror of society. *See* Brian Z. Tamanaha, *A General Jurisprudence of Law and Society*, Oxford University Press 1 (2005). As noted by Hernandez-Truyol, the relationship be-tween law and culture is mutual or reciprocal. *See* Berta Esperanza Hernandez-Truyol, "Glocalizing Law and Culture: Towards a Cross-Constitutive Paradigm," 67 *Alb. L. Rev.* 618, 621-23 (2003) (examining "a cross-constitutive paradigm of law and culture" and asserting that, in some circumstances, law can change culture but in other circum-stances, "cultural norms can withstand, survive and effectively reject legal change").

[300] *See* Francis Cardinal George, "Law and Culture," 1 *Ave Maria L. Rev.* 4 (2003)(mentioning that the relationship between law and culture is "fragile, more com-plex, and quite problematic").

[301] *See* Shin-yi Peng, "The WTO Legalistic Approach and East Asia: From the Legal Cul-ture Perspective," 1 *Asian-Pac. L. & Pol'y J.* 1, 6 (2000). For an account of interaction between law and culture, *see* Pierre Legrand, "The Impossibility of 'Legal Trans-plants,'" 4 *Maastricht J. Eur. & Comp. L.* 233 (1997); William Ewald, "Comparative Jurisprudence (II): The Logic of Legal Transplants," 43 *Am. J. Comp. L.* (1995).

[302] Shin-yi Peng, *ibid.*

[303] *Ibid.*

[304] Bell, *supra* note 294.

important, to preserve traditional ethics from which indigenous diversity and the intellectual knowledge are rooted.

The IPR enforcement problem is not a cultural problem caused by traditional Confucian philosophy. China has made arduous efforts towards gaining admittance into the international IPR community and has transplanted an elaborate IPR regime that turns out to be "a castle in the air" – the western-style IPR legal system has been built without the political and social foundations to strengthen its adequate enforcement.[305] With enigmatic political dilemmas that rival its economic prosperities, the potential effectiveness and eventual success of the enforcement mechanism depends to a large extent on the intention and volition of the government to pursue systemic political reform. To resolve the IPR enforcement problem, patience, encouragement and technical assistance are essentially required instead of intrusiveness of the culture.

4.5.3 Transitional Dilemma: When Utilitarianism Meets IPR

Due to the precaution of the government in bringing its political evolution into line with its economic prosperity, Chinese central authority runs the risk of precipitating social turmoil and upheaval.[306] As a consequence of the unbalanced reform, traditional values have been eroded and replaced by utilitarianism, which found fertilisation in a set of socio-economic conflicts deriving from the dysfunctional institutional regime development. The peculiar utilitarianism gives rise to moral decline, eroding traditional basis for social cohesion and undermining ethical foundation sustaining IPR protection.

In addition, the government's strict control over the private beliefs and the public press hinders its ability to establish an effective enforcement mechanism. Due to the lack of religious belief and faith, there are no considered and developed ethical systems to provide a firm foundation to enable an enduring belief in law and, simultaneously, no self-disciplining consciousness to constrain counterfeiting and piracy. Also, as a consequence of media restriction, "coin it in silence" has been a motto for many Chinese in their attempts of livelihood. Against this backdrop, it is not surprising that counterfeiting and piracy are pervasive. Limited by economic insufficiencies and cultural dilemma grounded from socio-political impediment, China has much difficulty in fully enforcing international IPR obligations. Having identified China's enforcement difficulties, in the next chapter, we will consider domestic legislation of China and EU in more detail to identify the quality of mutual response towards IPR protection.

---

[305] Scott J. Palmer, "An Identity Crisis: Regime Legitimacy and the Politics of Intellectual Property Rights in China," 8 *Ind. J. Global Legal Stud.* 450 (2001).

[306] Wei-Wei Zhang, *supra* note 59.

5 EU-China Interaction in Normative Integration

China's WTO membership may not only have a considerable impact on its domestic economy, but also on the integration of the global trading system.[1] It is in the interest of the whole world "to see China demonstrating a cooperative and responsible attitude in the international community" and play an active role in various global arenas including the WTO.[2] Among the outside world, the EU has acted as one of the most outspoken supporters of China's WTO membership as in an integral part of China's integration into the international economy.[3] Contrary to the position of the United States, which opposed a fast entry of China into the WTO, the EU supported a quick accession from the mid-1990s on.[4] The European position towards China is "consistently based on stressing cooperation rather than confrontation."[5] China's entry into the WTO significantly improved market access for European companies and fostered the European business competitiveness. As the former European Commissioner Pascal Lamy has noted, "the costs of [EU] exporting will be reduced and the incentives of investing in China will be strongly enhanced by a more attractive and predictable business environment."[6] The EU adopted a flexible strategy in support of China's "transitional membership status,"[7] ignoring the American position that China should enter the WTO with the status of a developed country, and proposing a case-by-case "sectoral" approach to China's accession.[8]

---

[1] Oliver Lembcke, "China's Economic Integration in the WTO: A Test for the Political Integration of the European Union?" Harvard China Review 4th Annual Conference (2001), *available at* <www.harvardchina.org/>.

[2] *See* "A Long Term Policy for China-Europe Relations," A.2: China's Importance for Europe, Communication of the Commission, COM (1995)/279/final.

[3] *See* "Integrating China Further in the world Economy," Commission of the European Communities: Building a Comprehensive Partnership with China, Brussels, 25.3.1998, COM (1998)/181/final. *See* also Lembcke, *supra* note 1.

[4] *See* Lembcke, *ibid.*

[5] *See* Michaela Eglin, "China's Entry into the WTO with a Little Help from the EU," 73(3) *Int'l Aff.* 495(1997).

[6] *See* Speech by Pascal Lamy, European Commissioner for Trade, to the China Europe International Business School, Shanghai, China, December 3, 2001, *available at* <www.delchn.cec.eu.int/en/eu_china_wto/wto1.htm>(last visited October 6, 2004).

[7] *See* "A Long Term Policy for China-Europe Relations," at 10.

[8] *See* Lembcke, *supra* note 1.

Global trade has domestic impacts and IPR infringement has complex international dimensions. However, at the EU level, this situation takes a particular cast due to the significant national disparities with regard to the national means of enforcing IPR.[9] Disparities between national legal systems, penalties in particular, make it difficult for the EU to effectively tackle counterfeiting and piracy negotiations with a non-EU country such as China.[10] In this chapter, we will focus on the domestic legislations of China and the EU in more detail to identify the interactive concerns and mutual response towards IPR protection.

5.1 Introduction

This chapter uses a matrix, showing on one axis current and potential problem areas of one party, and the concerns on the other. It is designed specifically to assist the two parties in both the fight against counterfeiting and piracy, and perhaps in a wider spectrum of related trade issues.

This chapter draws on the experiences and reactions of each side in negotiating trade issues and coordinating domestic standards of IPR protection. The basic presumption is that the problems which each has with the other combine to create a complex negotiating environment and, accordingly, they provide a natural focus which aims to contribute directly to the fostering of constructive cooperation between the two parties. The asymmetrical nature of concerns entails not simply delineating a *via media*, but the more delicate task of manoeuvring seemingly intractable issues, and calming volatile desire of negotiations, in a way that is congruent with the progressive development of the bilateral trade relations between the EU and China.

The first part of this chapter addresses problematic aspects of the EU law and policy as seen from China's perspective; the second part encompasses problematic aspects of the Chinese law and policy as seen from EU's perspective. Together they present contrasting views on EU-China trade relations regarding IPR protection.

---

[9]   Speeches of Mrs. Fientje Moerman, Minister of Economy, Energy, Foreign Trade and Science, on the Occasion of the Annual General Meeting of IFFRO, Brussels, November 12-14, 2003.

[10]   *See* Commission Proposal, COM (2006)168 final.

5.2 Matrix of Concerns within Integrations

5.2.1 EU Integration and its Impact upon China

The EU integration has attracted considerable attention from their Chinese counterpart; however, the legal reality of Europe in respect of trade and IPR enforcement may be different from what Chinese policy-makers expected.[11] The Common Market in many legal respects remains a fragmented "collection of national markets *per se*, which vary in their degree of the European integration depending on the products involved."[12] In such circumstances, there are multiple layers of commercial and political involvement within the EU, and the judicial structure remains dispersed.[13] This unique institutional characteristic of the EU has inevitably created substantial impact on China.

Integration Advantages

The European Union began as the European Coal and Steel Community (ECSC) in 1951, which was the first successful supranational organisation on the road to European integration.[14] The six original Member States – Belgium, France, Germany, Italy, Luxembourg, and the Netherlands – signed the ECSC Treaty which marked the first concrete step towards the unprecedented European integration.[15]

The European Community is the generic term for a collection of the three different European communities: European Coal and Steel Community (ECSC),[16] European Atomic Energy Community (EAEC)[17] and the European Economic Community (EEC).[18] The Treaty of Rome, signed in 1957, known more commonly as the Treaty establishing the European Economic Community, constituted the second of the three treaties outlining the initial profile of the European Communities.[19] With the Treaty of Rome, the original Member States joined together to form a "common market."[20] In an effort to "make war

---

11   *See* Thomas Hays, "Paranova v. Merck and Co-branding of Pharmaceuticals in the European Economic Area," 94 *The Trademark Reporter* 821(2004).
12   *Ibid.*
13   *Ibid.*
14   *See*, David Vaughan (ed.), *Law of the European Communities* 13 (1986).
15   The idea behind this community was originally initiated by the French Foreign Minister, Robert Schuman, after announcing the "Shuman Plan" in 1950. *See ibid. See* also Paul Craid and Grainne De Burca, *EU Law, Text, Cases, and Materials* 8-9 (2003).
16   Also known as Treaty of Paris 1951. *See* Vaughan, at 12.
17   Vaughan, *supra* note 14, at 16.
18   *Ibid*, at 18-9.
19   *See* "Texts of the European Treaties," *available at* <http://www.eurotreaties.com/euro-texts.html>.
20   These original member states of the Treaty of Rome include six states – Belgium, France, Germany, Italy, Luxembourg, and the Netherlands. The United Kingdom, Ire-

unthinkable" in Western Europe,[21] the motivating factor behind this treaty was to strengthen economic interdependence as a basis for peace and prosperity, primarily through trade harmonisation among these Member States.[22] The EC formed the umbrella organisation for these three communities following the signing of the fusion treaty in 1967.[23]

Subsequent treaties extended the scope of the European communities and established various institutions to facilitate the process of integration.[24] The Maastricht Treaty, which was signed on February 7, 1992, renamed the European Community as the European Union[25] by creating what are commonly known as "the three pillars of the EU," namely the European Communities, common foreign and security policy, and cooperation in justice and home affairs.[26] The EU has also embarked on its initiative of developing a common foreign affairs policy and improving cooperation among Member States on justice and home affairs.[27]

The integration of the EU is a driving force for the growth of EU-China bilateral trade, and has started to bear fruit. The most significant example is the arrival of the euro which represents a considerable challenge to the U.S. dollar and has eased China's dependence on the dollar in foreign trade settlements, as well as offered China more flexibility in utilitarian considerations of trade policy.[28]

Institutional Design

However, the institutional hybrid of the EU in respect to trade has, to some extent, counteracted the advantages of the integration. As a unique institutional

---

land, and Denmark acceded to the treaty in 1973, so did Greece in 1981, followed by Spain and Portugal in 1986. These twelve members reached a consensus upon the framework of the Single European Act of 1986, which illustrated the normative basis on what are known as the "Four Freedoms" – the free movement of goods, persons, services and capital. *See* Vaughan, *supra* note 14, at 12-3.

[21] Alec Stone Sweet, *The Judicial Construction of Europe*, Oxford University Press 46 (2004).

[22] Michael J. Graetz and Alvin C. Warren, "Income Tax Discrimination and the Political and Economic Integration of Europe," 115 *Yale L. J.* 1188 (2006).

[23] Vaughan, *supra* note 14, at 22-3.

[24] Graetz and Warren, *supra* note 22, at 1189.

[25] Vaughan, *supra* note 14, at 22-3.

[26] Craid and De Burca, at 48-50. *See* also "Structure of the European Union: the Three Pillars, The ABC of Community Law," *available at* <http://europa.eu.int/eurlex/en/about/abc/abc_12.html>.

[27] Duncan E. Alford, "European Union Legal Materials: An Infrequent User's Guide," *GlobaLex*, September 2005, *available at* <http://www.nyulawglobal.org/globalex/European_Union.htm>.

[28] *See* "China Intend to Buy more Euro to Reduce its Dependence on the US Dollar," *News Digest – Chinese Magazine*, 563 (2002), *available at* <http://www.cnd.org/HXWZ/CM02/cm0201b.gb.html>.

design, duality is one of the most crucial aspects of the EU. The most fundamental dilemma in the process of reforming EU institutions is the underlying tension between fragmentation on the one hand, as each state strives to protect its individual interests and highly competitive economies, and on the other hand,   the cohesion of common policies. [29] As Giovanni Grevi observes, "[w]ithin individual institutions, the desire of each member state to be represented has to be reconciled with efficiency in decision-making."[30] Some commentators state that the duality is a matter of democracy, since the diversity of the EU should be recognised and respected, and reflected in all the constitutional and institutional arrangements that maintain equality and impartiality among Member States.[31] Opponents of this position argue that, as the EU grows, the diversity of interests and the opportunity for limited, issue-based policy-alliances increase exponentially.[32] It is apparent that no consensus has been reached.

Duality Shortfalls

The authority to regulate foreign trade and intellectual property for the EU is two fold: imports are administered at the EU level, whereas exports are partially overseen by individual Member States.[33] In terms of imports, Member States adopt integrated EU criteria on imports while maintaining national policies to foster their exports and monitor their internal markets.[34] As a new creation in the international arena, the EU bears with it the duality of both traditional sovereignty and regional integration, which prescribes the incoherence in its foreign policy, and exerts adverse effects on economies of both the EU and its trading partners.[35]

EU DUALITY AND ITS FOREIGN TRADE POLICY

While China was attempting to establish itself as a coherent national entity, the EU's foreign policy agenda did not necessarily keep pace with those of its

---

29 Craid and De Burca, at 54-65. *See* also, Giovanni Grevi, "The Europe We Need: Time for a Government of the Union," Working Paper, the European Policy Centre, April 10, 2003, at 28.

30 Giovanni Grevi, "The Europe We Need", *ibid.*

31 *Ibid. See* also, Craid and De Burca, at 167-73.

32 Giovanni Grevi, *supra* note 29.

33 Oliver Lembcke, *supra* note 1.

34 Zhengde Huo, "On China-EU Strategic Relationship," *International Studies*, China Institute of International Studies, 2005(2), at 1-17.

35 For a full account of the "layered" institutional structure and its limitations, *see The Evolution of EU Law* (P.P. Craig and Grainne De Burca eds.), OUP (1999); *see also* Huo, *ibid.*

individual Member States[36] – each member state has its own history with China, and some Member States accommodate competing economic interests.[37] There are areas in which the EU was not yet a coherent actor in its foreign policy, which made it difficult for the EU to formulate a common position and arrive at a common policy towards China.[38] For example, in the fundamental area of human rights, while Ireland, Sweden, Finland, Denmark and the Netherlands view the issue as their top priority since their public opinions and parliaments have attached great important to the human rights values, at the other end of the spectrum, the Latin countries seem less concerned, with Germany, the UK and France falling in the middle.[39] As a consequence, China is confronting the dilemma of having to balance its policies towards the EU on one side and its individual Member States on the other.[40]

Stemmed from an incomplete system of regulations flowing from the EU principle of subsidiarity, this dual regime in trade policy enables Member States to "delegate" the powers and inquiries up to EU level, "thereby 'freeing' them from this burden on the national level in order to pursue their individual trade interests."[41] Due to "widespread sense of reliance on and hope in the possibilities of Community action, through the good offices of the European Commission." [42] European member states lack sufficient motivation towards gearing up their national infrastructues in a more active and effective manner. At China's side, the question remains as to how far this situation could be altered by changing the rules in foreign trade of the EU.[43] Here, the EU and the individual Member States need to convey a collective presence in China and act in an identical manner, so that China can pose as an entire platform for Europe to perform cohesively rather than as the sum of individual nation-states projecting themselves in a variety of ways. [44]

The institutional existence of the EU, particularly in respect to IPR, is also different from that which European officials may have envisioned.[45] As has

---

[36] *See EU-China Relation*, Events Reports, European Policy Centre, *available at* <www.theepc.be/en/>, last visited March 21, 2006.

[37] David Gosset, "A Making of a China-EU World," *Asia Times*, July 20, 2005, *available at* <http://www.atimes.com/atimes/China/GG20Ad02.html> (last visited February 5, 2007).

[38] *Ibid.*

[39] Alfredo Pastor and David Gosset, "the EU-China Relationship: A Key to the 21st Century Order," *ARI* 142/2005.

[40] Gosset, "A Making of a China-EU World," *supra* note 37.

[41] Lembcke, *supra* note 1.

[42] *See* "Final Report on Responses to the European Commission Green Paper on Counterfeiting and Piracy," European Commission (1999), at 1(2).

[43] *See* Oliver Lembcke, *supra* note 1 (stating that the "Treaty of Nice has lead [sic] to a number of changes of article 133 of the EC Treaty that concerned the harmonisation of norms" in the area of trade and as well as intellectual property rights).

[44] David Gosset, "The Making of a China-EU World," *Asia Times*, July 20, 2005.

[45] Thomas Hays, *supra* note 11, at 821.

been mentioned above, there are multiple layers of commercial and political involvement and several judicial structures within the Common Market which represents a fragmented combination of national markets.[46] Due to the divergences in national markets for IPR-protected goods, there are price disparities; due to price disparities, parallel trading arises.[47]

EU' DUALITY OF TECHNICAL STANDARDS

Another issue arises from technical standards of the EU. As these are crucial not only to domestic efficiency but also to health and safety concerns, WTO has "exception provisions" providing its members a reasonable level of flexibility, which depends on a set of technical standards.[48] Due to its low technological level, China still finds it difficult to satisfy the EU's technical standards in the short term.[49] The unified currency system has made these standards more complicated, adding more uncertainties and controversies.[50] As noted by China analyst Zhengde Huo, when old European currencies were optional, China was able to adapt the price of products to the different market conditions of the EU Member States; however, after the launch of the euro, the multiple price policy has been unavailable.[51] Furthermore, an integrated euro system enables EU Member States to expand trade gains within an integrated market, instead of with non-EU states, and thus China's export competitiveness has subsequently been weakened.[52]

With regard to the intellectual property in the EU, problems are also accentuated by the cumbrous nature of the duality. Compared to the United States and Japan, the protection of IPR in the EU is characterised by low efficiency and high costs for operation;[53] and the parameters of national competencies and coordination of the different Member States by the EU is cumbersome, resulting in unnecessary and sometimes counterproductive effects.[54] In the pat-

---

[46] *Ibid.*

[47] *See infra* § 5.4.1.

[48] For example, GATT sets forth several measures for general exceptions and national security exceptions. According to Article 20, members of the WTO are entitled to take measures necessary to protect public morals as well as human, animal, or plant life or health. This article also sets out an exception for measures "necessary to secure compliance with laws or regulations which are not inconsistent with the provisions of this agreement, including those relating to [...] the protection of patents, trademarks and copyrights, and the prevention of deceptive practices." Similarly, Article 21 provides a set of exceptions concerning national security. These provisions can be considered as a basis to take exceptions in setting various technical standards.

[49] *See* Huo *supra* note 34, at 1-17.

[50] *Ibid.*

[51] *Ibid.*

[52] *Ibid.*

[53] *See* "IPR in Europe's Safe Keeping," *Innov. & Tech. Transfer* (Innovation Programme, Brussels, Bel.), October 1999, at 11-12.

[54] *Ibid.*

ent area, for instance, while one-third of all patents issued in Europe are American in origin, only fifteen percent of U.S.-issued patents come from Europe, simply because the dual European system is over-complex, expensive, and only partially effective.[55]

EU'S DUALITY AND CHINA'S WTO MEMBERSHIP

The problem with the EU duality also has important implications for China's WTO membership, with a crucial consideration being the conversion of the agreements achieved at the EU level to practical policies of individual Member States.[56] While the bilateral relationship between China and the EU has improved in general terms, technically it deserves to be seen "whether [EU] Member States will be able to agree on a common position if and when disputes between the EU and China arise."[57] From this perspective, the integration of China into the global trading system will prompt questions as to the state of the EU's own integration,[58] and their unique status within the WTO.[59]

5.2.2 China's Integration and its Impact on the EU

Implications of WTO Accession

China's integration into the world economy was strengthened by China's accession to the WTO, and China's participation in the international community reflects its enhanced roles, commitments and responsibilities in global trading system. By obtaining membership, China is directly obliged to comply with the principles and rules prescribed by the WTO.[60] In addition to formal compliance with the general provisions, China is required to adapt to international trade norms, including IPR standards.[61] Since the promotion of China's inte-

---

[55] *Ibid.*

[56] Oliver Lembcke, *supra* note 1.

[57] *Ibid.*

[58] *Ibid.*

[59] Within the WTO, the member states of the EU coordinate their position in Brussels and Geneva, and are represented in the WTO through EU's Trade Commissioner. In this context, the EU remains a WTO member in its own right as are each of its member states. *See* "Understanding the WTO: the Organisation, Membership, Alliances and Bureaucracy," *available at* <www.wto.org/english/thewto_e/whatis_e/tif_e/org3_e.htm>.

[60] China's WTO obligations are set forth in China's Protocol of Accession which contains the terms of membership that China affirms its adherence to the WTO agreements, and an accompanying Report of the Working Party and Goods and Services Schedules. For protocols of accession for membership in the WTO, *see* <http://www.wto.org/english/thewto_e/acc_e/protocols_acc_membership_e.htm>.

[61] In accordance with the TRIPs Agreement, China is obliged to comply with internationally accepted provisions for protecting intellectual property rights. *See* China's Protocol, Part I, 2.A.2., *ibid.*

gration in the multilateral trading system is part of the EU trade strategy,[62] China's embracing of the WTO also reflects its aspirations of strengthening EU-China trade relations.

China's WTO Commitments Towards IPR

According to the WTO non-discrimination rules, WTO members should abide by the principle of most favoured nation treatment,[63] which, in the case of EU-China trade, includes tariff reduction, lifting of import quotas and the easing of market entry criteria and, as mandated in the TRIPs Agreement, strengthening domestic IPR protection.[64]

China's commitments towards IPR were linked to its accession to the WTO in December 2001. As discussed in chapter 3, the Chinese central government has publicly stated that IPR infringement is a priority issue and has tried to establish a State Council level accountability for the anti-counterfeiting and anti-piracy campaign.[65] Chinese leaders have also stressed on different occasions that counterfeiting must be transferred to judicial authorities for criminal investigation and prosecution without delay.[66] Indeed, as has been noted by the Office of the USTR in the "2004 Report to Congress on China's WTO Compliance," China has made tremendous efforts and progress in implementing its WTO commitments, although problems still remain.[67]

---

[62] *See* "Thematic Evaluation of the EC Support to Good Governance," Annexes to the Final Report, Volume 2, March 2006, *available at* <http://ec.europa.eu/comm/europeaid/evaluation/reports/2006/884vol2.pdf>.

[63] The most favoured nation treatment (MFN) constitutes one of the two aspects of the non-discrimination treatment, another aspect being national treatment. *See* GATS Article II & III.

[64] In accordance with the China's WTO commitments, import tariffs and other non-tariff barriers in China are to be reduced significantly and investments by EU companies in China will take place in a more attractive and predictable business environment. For more details about China's accession commitments, *see* "EU-China Agreement on WTO Accession," *available at* <www.europa.eu.int/comm/trade/bilateral/china/wto.htm>.

[65] In 2004, the State Council set up a special IPR enforcement mechanism named IPR Protection Working Group, where Vice Premier Yi Wu was nominated as the Director. *See infra* § 5.3.2.

[66] Chinese authorities made an official announcement in a press conference stressing that all kinds of IPR violations that meet the criminal criteria should be transferred to judicial bodies without delay. *See* "Official Announcement about IPR Enforcement," March 27, 2006, *available at* <www.gov.cn/xwfb/2006-03/27/content_237546.htm>.

[67] *See* "China Has Made Progress on WTO Commitments, But Problems Remain," *available at* <http://www.ustr.gov/assets/Document_Library/Reports_Publications/2004/asset_upload_file281_6986.pdf>.

Impact on the EU

Whilst China's integration process is taking place, the expansion of the Chinese market in the manufacturing, telecommunications, transportation, energy, and environmental sectors is immensely attractive to an EU member state which depends on foreign trade and has a huge surplus capital and advanced technologies.[68] However, since China's WTO accession, EU-China trade relations are no longer the conventional relations characterised by exchanging market for capital and technologies.[69] Rather, from a global perspective, the EU is expected to attach greater importance to China's role in maintaining the stability of and giving an impetus to the global economy.[70] Fundamentally, on the European side, the EU is required to develop a strong and sustainable trading relationship with China by harmonising a common WTO policy – in other words, a common China policy, reflecting a united and coherent Europe.[71]

5.2.3 Same Hierarchy, Different Dimension

While the EU and China share common interests within the process of EU-China negotiations, each has its own objectives and perspectives. China is keen to raise its profile in the EU and to benefit from a strong relationship.[72] This is particularly so with regard to secure the transfer of technology. Simultaneously, the EU is concerned with making the enforcement of IPR a high priority and creating mechanisms to remedy the deficiencies of the existing IPR enforcement.[73] To this end, the EU encourages the integration of China in the world economy.[74]

However, EU's initiative is not, and should not be, limited to the economic interests. Premised on its harmonised and contextualised external policy, the EU is much more engaged in supporting China's transition to an open society based upon the rule of law and the principle of human rights. In addition to

---

[68] Huo, *supra* note 34, at 5-6.

[69] *Ibid.*

[70] *See* "Driving Forwards the China-EU Strategic Partnership," Speech by Javier Solana, EU High Representative for the Common Foreign and Security Policy, September 6, 2005, *available at* <www.delchn.cec.eu.int/en/whatsnew/pren060905.htm>.

[71] Oliver Lembcke, *supra* note 1.

[72] *See* "Zhonguo yu Oumeng Changqi Wending de Jianshexing Huoban Guanxi [Towards a Long-term Reliable and Constructive Strategic Partnership between China and the EU]," Official Document of the Foreign Ministry, November 7, 2000, *available at* <http://www.fmprc.gov.cn/chn/ziliao/wjs/2159/t8999.htm> (stating that China is committed to building and consolidating its credibility as a strategic partner of the EU).

[73] *See* "European Business in China Position Paper 2005," European Union Chamber of Commerce in China.

[74] *See* "Thematic Evaluation of the EC Support to Good Governance," *Annexes to the Final Report*, Volume 2, March 2006, *available at* <http://ec.europa.eu/comm/europeaid/evaluation/reports/2006/884_vol2.pdf>.

acting as an enthusiastic supporter for China's entry into the WTO, the EU also encourages China's participation in the International Convention on Civil and Political Rights in the near future, expecting that China will continue its ongoing institutional and political reform and play a more active role in broad field of bilateral and international affairs.[75]

As has been demonstrated, the problem of counterfeiting and piracy in China is a by-product of a unique set of socioeconomic crises deriving from the development of a dysfunctional institutional regime. Ultimately, the effectiveness of China's IPR enforcement will, to a great extent, depend on how the socio-political predicaments are dealt with. Similarly, "the pace and intensity by which the EU's external trade relations with China will develop in future, depend not simply on the success of the economic reform or the commercial interests of EU member states, but to a large extent on the institutional setting that has been created over more than two decades."[76]

5.3 IPR Enforcement Antitheses

As it has been argued in chapter 3 and 4, it is one thing for a state to demonstrate their legislation on IPR, and another to create an effective and consistent enforcement mechanism. The distinction between the two situations has led to various provisions on IPR enforcement being included, among which the EU IPR Enforcement Directive is an important provision directly affecting EU-China trade relations.

Meanwhile, China has formulated a series of related rules and regulations governing IPR enforcement, whereby it provides more certainty for IPR holders as well as security for foreign investment and technology transfer. While difficult, China has taken the initial step towards strengthening its IPR enforcement mechanism. In the following section, we will focus on the legal framework of IPR enforcement within EU-China trade relations.

5.3.1 IPR Enforcement in the EU

The mid 1990s witnessed the first wave of initiatives of the European Community to handle cross-border IPR infringements, with the Customs Regulation being an essential attempt introducing border control measures against imports of counterfeit goods.[77] In 1998, the Commission adopted the Green

---

[75] "Joint Statement of the 10th China-EU Summit, Beijing," November 28, 2007, *available at* <http://ec.europa.eu/external_relations/china/summit_1107/joint_statement.pd>.

[76] Franco Algieri, "EU Economic Relations with China: An Institutionalist Perspective," 169 *The China Quart.* 77 (2002).

[77] *See* Regulation (EC) No 3295/94.

Paper on Combating Counterfeiting and Piracy in the Single Market.[78] As a result of responses to the Green Paper, the Commission launched an Action Plan in 2000, which has been translated into a directive published in 2004,[79] harmonising the enforcement of IPR within the Community.[80]

EU IPR Enforcement Directive

FACTUAL BACKGROUND

Protecting IPR is considered a valuable and essential approach to pursuing innovation and competitiveness, and this approach was implicitly favoured by the European Commission when a legislative proposal on the enforcement of IPR was introduced on January 30, 2003.[81] It may be interesting to observe here that, the EU was considerably enthusiastic to promote and create a new set of enforcement legal system, setting aside the TRIPs and dispute settlement mechanism within the WTO which had been widely acclaimed. Perhaps, the sentiment of the EU was quite similar to that of the United States before the emergence of the TRIPs regime in the 1970s-80s, complaining the inability of the WIPO and pledging to create a brand-new IPR system. As far as the EU was concerned, it would be insufficient to limit the efforts of the EU to merely monitoring the creation of general legislative frameworks in WTO member countries, and it would be therefore essential that the EU increasingly focuses on efficient and effective implementation of the enforcement legislation.[82]

This directive aims at harmonising legislation through the Member States as a whole relating to the enforcement of IPR and establishing a framework for the exchange of information and administrative cooperation among the Member States.[83] As the Commission emphasised, it is the existing disparity in enforcement legislation among different EU Member States that prevents the EU from effectively dealing with counterfeiting.[84]

---

[78] *See* "Green Paper on Combating Counterfeiting and Piracy in the Single Market," Brussels 15/10/98, COM (98)596 final.

[79] *See* "Directive 2004/48/EC of the European Parliament and of the Council of 29 April 2004 on the Enforcement of Intellectual Property Rights," *Official Journal of the European Union* L 195, 02/06/2004, at 16-25.

[80] "EU Strategy to Enforce Intellectual Property Rights in Third Countries – Facts and Figures."

[81] *See* "IPR – Intellectual Property Rights", *EurActiv*, September 20, 2004, *available at* <www.euractiv.com/main/infosociety/ipr-intellectual-property-rights/article-117513>; for full text of the proposal, *see* <http://europa.eu.int/eur-lex/en/com/pdf/2003/com2003_0046en01.pdf/>.

[82] *See* Annex 1, "Strategy for the Enforcement of Intellectual Property Rights in Third Countries," *Official Journal of the European Union* C 129/3 (2005), at 14.

[83] Directive 2004/48/EC.

[84] *Ibid.*

To achieve these objectives, the directive envisages that a uniform set of enforcement measures should be duly implemented to protect the IPR of the proprietors in each Member State. The directive gives IPR proprietors incredibly powerful tools in safeguarding their rights, and acts as "a political signal which will encourage national courts to apply sanctions and remedies more vigorously."[85]

IPR PROTECTION AND DIGITAL FREEDOM

Following a minor modification, the controversial directive was ultimately adopted in the European Parliament by a large majority amid protests.[86] Although the directive does not harmonise criminal penalties, affected industries will strive to lobby government and the parliament for criminal sanctions at EU level.[87] It is likely that the EU Commission will continue to "add mild support" through proposing appropriate measures on criminal sanctions "in due course."[88]

With a view to harmonising different EU legislation on copyright, trademark, design and other related rights, the European Parliament significantly extended the scope of the directive to cover a broad range of IPR violations.[89] The EU has over time equipped itself with "a thematic approach" to the en-

---

[85] See Robin D. Gross (IP Justice Executive Director), "Protecting Civil Liberties, Competition and Innovation in the EU Intellectual Property Rights Enforcement Directive, IP Justice Statement to the EU Members of Parliament," *available at* <www.ipjustice. org/CODE/eustatement.shtml>.

[86] The original proposal included controversial "anti-circumvention" provisions, which set forth prohibitions against certain types of scientific research and recognise monopolies for dominant media companies over compatible devices. This attracted an international coalition of 50 civil liberties groups and consumer rights campaigns urging European Parliament to abandon the Commission's proposal. Despite the growing concern, the European Parliament's Committee on Legal Affairs and the Internal Market (JURI) introduced significantly more prohibitive "anti-circumvention" measures and an amendment to criminalise non-commercial infringements such as Peer-2-Peer file sharing. See Gross, *ibid.*

[87] John Borland, "Europe's 'DMCA on Steroids' Gets Go-ahead," *ZDNet UK*, November 27, 2003.

[88] As the EU Commissioner Bolkestein stated, "the Commission considers that effective action against counterfeiting and piracy requires criminal sanctions for serious, intentional infringements committed for commercial purposes. We will therefore examine the possibility of proposing in due course further measures providing for criminal sanctions in this field. Moreover, the Directive will not prevent Member States from applying criminal sanctions if they wish to." See "Intellectual property: Commission Welcomes European Parliament Support Against Counterfeiting and Piracy," Brussels, IP/04/316, March 9, 2004.

[89] The Directive falls in broad spectrum covering trademarks, designs, patents for biotechnological inventions, certain aspects of copyright, including computer programmes, and related rights, etc. See Part one (A) of the Directive, "Enforcing the Substantive Law of Intellectual Property", *supra* note 79.

forcement of IPR, thereby "result[ing] in a fragmented body of legislation covering a variety of issues."[90]

The Commission also states that, since the protection of IPR is overseen by various international conventions of which the EU forms a part, such as TRIPs, by adopting the directive, the EU would therefore bring itself into line with its international commitments.[91] However, the directive goes further than international obligations under TRIPs and is therefore controversial with many critics urging that "it would criminalise many innocuous activities, harm consumer choice and impair European competition."[92] The directive has raised concern among politicians, academics and civil liberties groups who claim that academic institutions, internet providers, and ordinary consumers could become innocent victims.[93] For example, the directive could lead to ordinary consumers being at risk of prosecution for downloading and sending a digital photo either through a website or by mobile phone for non-commercial purposes.

The directive fails in distinguishing accurately between unintentional, non commercial infringers and for-profit, criminal counterfeiting organisations. Although the commission "tries to present 'best practice' legislation,"[94] and the enforcement measures would normally excludes acts carried out by "end consumers acting in good faith", the meaning of "indirect economic advantage" is vague and the scope of the directive is not limited to intentional commercial infringements.[95] There is thus concern that the directive appears to be biased in favour of the rights holders who may be able to use the new tougher penalties against consumers.

It is not only non-commercial use that has attracted controversy and criticism, the directive goes further than international requirements in a number of areas thus bringing into play so-called "TRIPs plus" elements.[96] For example,

---

[90] "IPR – Intellectual Property Rights," *supra* note 81.

[91] *Ibid.*

[92] John Borland, "Europe's 'DMCA on Steroids' Gets Go-ahead," *supra* note 86.

[93] *See* "Enforcement of Intellectual Property Rights," *EurActiv*, August 17, 2004, *available at* <http://www.euractiv.com/en/infosociety/enforcement-intellectual-property-rights/article-117513>.

[94] Matthew Broersma, "Music Industry Attacks EU Copyright Proposal," *ZDNet UK*, February 03, 2003.

[95] Matthew Broersma, "EU Anti-piracy Directive Heads for Final Vote," *ZDNet UK*, February 26, 2004.

[96] TRIPs plus represents a set of IPR protections that goes beyond TRIPs Agreement, such as patent terms longer than 20 years, unreasonable limitations on parallel imports, and banning compulsory licensing of patents, all of which are flexibilities legally permitted under the TRIPs Agreement. For an account of the "TRIPs plus," *see* Sisule F Musungu and Graham Dutfield, "Multilateral Agreements and a TRIPS-plus World: The World Intellectual Property Organisation (WIPO)," 3 *TRIPS Issues Papers*, QUNO Geneva/QIAP Ottawa (2003). For a comprehensive discussion of these flexibilities legally permitted by TRIPs, *see infra* § 5.4.

the directive is particularly applauded by large companies which would benefit most from the enforcement measures regarding reverse engineering. This
would arguably affect personal liberty and undermine the digital freedom.[97]
Additionally, the directive could unduly restrain trade by requiring license fees
from companies to produce goods compatible with products such as Microsoft
Windows.[98] Not only would this squeeze small producers but also solidify or
even abuse the monopoly position of the dominant players.

It is therefore not surprising that the directive, which has been criticised as a
"tougher version of U.S. Digital Millennium Copyright Act,"[99] may severely
affect unsustainable small open-source projects and innovative businesses,
while benefiting dominant multinational companies which monopolise IPR.[100]
It is claimed that the directive has become a dangerous "weapon in intellectual
property rights-holders' destructive war on 'piracy.'"[101]

EU AND CHINA: CONTRASTING ATTITUDE

Though controversial, there have been clear signs that the EU will move forward on its endeavour to tackle the enforcement problem. The European
Commission has adopted the directive, thereby establishing a framework to
combat infringements of IPR and "align[ing] national criminal law" to deal
with counterfeiting and piracy.[102]

At the Gleneagles Summit on July 6-8, 2005, the heads of the G8 countries
announced a statement calling for more effective enforcement of IPR.[103] On
July 12, 2005, the Commission's Directorates (DG) General Justice and Home

---

[97] *See* Robert Vaagan, "The LIS Infoethical Survival Kit," 38(1) *Scandinavian Pub. Lib.
      Quart.* (2005), *available at* <http://www.splq.info/issues/vol38_1/06.htm>.

[98] Munir Kotadia, "Copyright Directive 'Will Stifle EU Competition,'" *ZDNet UK*, Au-
      gust 5, 2003.

[99] The U.S. Digital Millennium Copyright Act of 1998 was designed to implement the
      treaties signed 1996 at the WIPO Geneva conference, but included a number of contro-
      versial provisions which left concerns for the public that this Act may serve as the legal
      basis for music companies to sue individuals caught swapping music online. For an of-
      ficial summary of the act, *see* the Digital Millennium Copyright Act 1998, *available at*
      <http://www.copyright.gov/legislation/dmca.pdf>.

[100] According to a recent study conducted by Ross Anderson of the Foundation for Infor-
      mation Policy Research (FIPR) who is associated with the University of Cambridge,
      large companies would be better off under the Directive. For a detailed survey report,
      see Ross Anderson, "The Draft IPR Enforcement Directive – A Threat to Competition
      and to Liberty," *available at* <http://www.fipr.org/copyright/draft-ipr-enforce.html>.

[101] "Weapon in Intellectual Property Rights-Holders' Destructive War," *OUT-LAW News*,
      February 27, 2004.

[102] *See* "Counterfeiting and Piracy: the Commission Proposes European Criminal-law Pro-
      visions to Combat Infringements of Intellectual Property Rights," Brussels, July 12,
      2005, *available at* <http://europa.eu.int/rapid/>.

[103] "Reducing IPR Piracy and Counterfeiting through More Effective Enforcement," *avail-
      able at* <http://www.g8.gov.uk/Files/KFile/PostG8_Gleneagles_CounterfeitingandPi-
      racy.pdf>.

Affairs released "a double proposal" for a Directive and a Framework Decision aiming at more rigorous protection of international IPR against infringements on a commercial scale, including criminal punishments.[104] It is clear that the EU is applying stronger measures to stamp down hard on counterfeiting and piracy within the community.

The directive is based not only on the internal cooperation of the EU Member States, but also on the cooperation between the EU and other none-EU countries including China. For this reason, both the EU and China are enthusiastic in facilitating bilateral cooperation involving IPR enforcement, such as transfer of cases and preliminary injunctions.[105]

However, compared to EU's attitude which is somewhat aggressive and pertinacious, China's attitude towards IPR protection is more equivocal and flexible. While the EU defines the "commercial scale" in a strict sense, Chinese law suggests an ambiguous definition of the threshold. According to Chinese Criminal Code, "huge amounts" of illegal earnings is the threshold of "small violations."[106] In this context, the "commercial scale" is interpreted as "significant amount" comparable to commercial enterprises. This interpretive elasticity provides Chinese authorities much flexibility in adapting to different circumstances and needs. Understandably, as has been analysed previously, this is the defensive tactics that China has to adopt when different interests have to be weighed and balanced at the initial stage of the development.

For this reason, during the recent EU-China Intellectual Property Dialogue in 2007, China put forward a proposal about a specifically designed "two-track enforcement system" and gave reasons for keeping a "double threshold criterion"; regretfully, China's attempt attracted relatively little attention from the EU.[107]

5.3.2 IPR Enforcement in China

The most notable characteristic of China's existing IPR enforcement mechanism is the parallel and multi-layered enforcement system. The IPR enforce-

---

[104] Proposal for a European Parliament and Council Directive on criminal measures aimed at ensuring the enforcement of intellectual property rights, and Proposal for a Council Framework Directive to strengthen the criminal law framework to combat intellectual property offences, Brussels, 12.7.2005, COM (2005)276 final, 2005/0127(COD), 2005/0128(CNS), *available at* <http://europa.eu.int/eur-lex/lex/LexUriServ/site/en/com/2005/com2005_0276en01.pdf>.

[105] *See* "Outcome of the Third Meeting of the EU-China IP Dialogue," Brussels, 15-16 March 2007, *available at* <http://trade.ec.europa.eu/doclib/docs/2007/may/tradoc_134 658.pdf>.

[106] *See supra* § 3.3.3.

[107] *See* "Outcome of the Third Meeting of the EU-China IP Dialogue," *supra* note 105 (mentioning that China presented the two-track enforcement system which was not convincing for the EU).

ment in China is generally divided into administrative enforcement and judicial enforcement. Accordingly, IPR rights holders are able to seek enforcement of their rights through either administrative or judicial channels. As will be demonstrated, China relies too much on administrative instead of judicial measures to combat IPR infringements, which appears to be a noticeable factor that undermines its enforcement effectiveness.

Administrative Enforcement

One of the unique features of the present Chinese enforcement system of IPR is the existence of a parallel system of administrative and judicial enforcement. Various administrative departments also have power to confiscate illicit profits and assets, and impose penalties on those involved in infringement.[108] Administrative enforcement is preferred in China because of its availability of injunctive remedies, rights of appeal and nationwide jurisdiction.[109] Filing a complaint with a relevant local administrative agency remains a common route for IPR holders to seek remedies against infringements.

While the nationwide jurisdiction has a dominating influence, the overlapping jurisdiction occurs frequently in China. Determining which governmental agency has jurisdiction can be a daunting challenge. In most cases, administrative agencies although able to confiscate items, issue penalties, and obtain information about the source of goods being distributed; they are not entitled to award compensation to a proprietor. In addition, jurisdiction is diffused throughout the judicial structure and various government agencies, where roles and responsibilities for enforcement are normally allocated in a way that differs between or among particular statutes or specific areas of laws relating to IPR.[110] The existence of the departmental and regional barriers results in a duplicate structure of jurisdiction, making IPR enforcement more unpredictable. It is suggested that a cross-jurisdictional enforcement procedures be coordinated and created to handle this problem.

---

[108] These agencies include Ministry of Culture, the State Administration of Industry and Commerce (SAIC) and the Administration for Quality Supervision, Inspection and Quarantine (AQSIQ).

[109] Jurisdiction of IPR enforcement in China is allocated among various government agencies, generally depending on the subject matter of the relevant statute establishing IPR protection.

[110] *See* "Protecting Your Intellectual Property Rights (IPR) in China: A Practical Guide for U.S. Companies," U.S. Department of Commerce, International Trade Administration, January 2003.

Border Control

BACKGROUND

Strengthening border control measures is as an essential channel to crack down on international counterfeiting and piracy. Statistics show that the amount of counterfeited and pirated articles seized at the EU's external borders in 2006 reached 250 million euros, representing a phenomenal increase compared with 75 million in 2005 and 100 million in 2004.[111] Counterfeit foodstuffs, medicines, household items and car parts are continuing to grow.[112] In 2006, more than 80 percent of all counterfeit goods seized by EU customs originated from China.[113] In 2007, European manufacturers estimated that IPR infringements may cost them 20 percent of their potential revenues in China.[114]

In 2005, the EU implemented its IPR enforcement directive[115] to reinforce the legal rights of customs. The directive is applicable to the bilateral cooperation between the EU and other countries including China. In recent yeas, the EU and China have reached a number of custom cooperation agreements, giving EU more control over external market relating to Chinese exports.

EU-CHINA CUSTOM COOPERATION

During the 2004 EU-China Summit, the two sides signed the China-EU Customs Cooperation Agreement to facilitate trade and help combat customs violations and fraud such as counterfeiting.[116] The EU-China Customs Cooperation Agreement, which entered into force in April 2005, includes a number of constructive measures such as customs officials exchange to ensure the effectiveness of enforcement in China, particularly at the local levels.[117]

---

[111] *See*, "Customs: Commission Publishes 2006 Customs Seizures of Counterfeit Goods," EC Press Release, IP/07/735, May 31, 2007.

[112] "China, EU Cooperation in Combating Counterfeit," *CIR Online*, November 14, 2005, *available at* <http://en.chinabroadcast.cn/855/2005/11/14/262@30632.htm>, last visited November 19, 2005.

[113] "The EU-China Trade in Facts and Figures," EU External Trade, November 23, 2007, *at* <http://trade.ec.europa.eu/doclib/docs/2007/november/tradoc_136870.pdf>.

[114] *Ibid.*

[115] *See* "Communication from the Commission to the Council, the European parliament and the European Economic and Social Committee," Commission of the European Communities, Brussels, 11.10.2005 COM (2005) 479 final.

[116] *See* "Joint Statement of the 7th China-EU Summit," 8th December 2004, Hague, Netherlands, *available at* <www.fmprc.gov.cn/eng/topics/wenJiabaocxezohy/t174512.htm>, last visited January 30, 2005.

[117] *See* "Agreement between the European Community and the Government of the People's Republic of China on Cooperation and Mutual Administrative Assistance in Customs Matters" [Official Journal L 375 of 23.12.2004], *available at* <http://europa.eu/scadplus/leg/en/lvb/l33309.htm>.

Following the adoption of China's Customs Regulations on IPR Protection in 2004,[118] the Implementing Rules to the regulations came into force on July 1, 2004.[119] Significant changes have been outlined in the rules, for example, protection has been made available without the need for prior recording of rights and the duration of records has been extended from seven to ten years.[120]

Also, customs have now been entitled to impose bond requirements that are below the aggregate value of the goods in question. For example, for goods with acquisition values ranging between 20,000 Yuan (1,500 euros) and 200,000 Yuan (15,000 euros), the bond should be equivalent to half the value of the goods, but no less than 20,000 Yuan.[121] If the value of the goods is more than 200,000 Yuan, the required bond should be equivalent to 100,000 Yuan.[122] Alternatively, a general guarantee of 200,000 Yuan or above has been made available.[123] Finally, the regulations allow the possibility for serious cases to be transferred to judicial organs for criminal liabilities.[124]

CHINA'S BORDER CONTROL REGIME

In China, IPR enforcement is available through customs border measures, which are set out in the Customs Protection of Intellectual Property Regulations in 2004. The regulations, in addition to the implementation measures, establish a legal framework whereby IPR owner can record existing trademark, copyright and patent right with customs nationally and apply to customs to detain the suspected IPR infringing goods which are about to enter or exit the territory of China.[125] The Chinese customs authorities, headquartered in Beijing and including about 40,000 officials across the country, have the power to inspect all the imports and exports and to take necessary measures in the case of violation of IPR.[126]

According to the regulations and its implementation measures, detention of goods is available, subject to the rights owners placing a bond to the equivalent value of the shipment in question.[127] In the event of the suspected infring-

---

[118] "Zhishi Chanquan Haiguan Baohu Tiaoli [Custom Regulations on Intellectual Property Rights Protection]," *available at* <http://www.customs.gov.cn/YWStaticPage/7021/ffafb2ee.htm>.

[119] "Zhishi Chanquan Haiguan Baohu Tiaoli Shishi Banfa [Measures for the Implementation of the Customs Protection of Intellectual Property Rights," 1 March 2004, *available at* <http://www.customs.gov.cn/YWStaticPage/433/d61a3b46.htm>.

[120] *See* "Implementation Measure", *ibid,* Article 9 (former Article 10).

[121] Article 22, *ibid.*

[122] *Ibid.*

[123] *Ibid.*

[124] Article 26, *ibid.*

[125] *See* "Custom Regulation," Article 12, 13.

[126] "Introduction to the Chinese Customs," *available at* <http://www.customs.gov.cn/YWStaticPage/396/a0b4f4e3.htm>.

[127] Custom Regulations, Article 22-25.

ing goods detained by the Customs Offices being identified as infringing goods by the relevant authorities, the Customs may confiscate the goods.[128]

While administrative enforcement is perhaps the most efficient way for the IPR holders to secure protection in China, as Donald Clarke has noted, the effectiveness of this approach is largely dependent upon a number of constraints that make it less effective under the unique Chinese business and cultural environment.[129] First, this kind of enforcement is "subject to perverse incentives" – "the enforcing agencies rely heavily on fines for their operating expenses"; it is therefore not surprising that they have a "vested interest" in safeguarding – or at least not harming – the environment of the infringements.[130] Furthermore, administrative enforcement, as has been mentioned in previous chapters,[131] is prone to the common limitations of lack of resources and "vulnerability to corruption."[132]

Judicial Enforcement

The second track of IPR enforcement is judicial measure. In China, complaints about IPR are heard by specialised tribunals or panels in courts located throughout the country. Since 1993, China has established and maintained Intellectual Property Tribunals (*Zhishi Chanquan Shenpan Ting*) at the different levels of the People's Courts.[133] In 2005, Chinese courts dealt with 16,583 intellectual property cases, an increase of 20.66 percent on 2004.[134] In addition, the Criminal Tribunals at the different levels of the courts heard 3,529 criminal cases in connection with IPR infringements, an increase of 28.28 percent on 2004.[135]

STRENGTH AND WEAKNESS

In general, the judicial system provides a key role in IPR enforcement. However, in modern China, the judicial system is dependent on the government. Although there are no grounds for it to stand superior to government, accord-

---

[128] *Ibid*, Article 21, 22 and 27.

[129] Donald Clarke, "Private Enforcement of Intellectual Property Rights in China," 10(2) *NBR Analysis* 34 (1999).

[130] *Ibid.*

[131] *See* § 3.4.2.

[132] Donald Clarke, *supra* note 129.

[133] Intellectual Property Tribunals were renamed as the No. 3 Civil Tribunals in 2000 at the provincial level. *See* "The No.3 Civil Tribunal of the Supreme Court of P.R.C," *available at* <http://www.ipr.gov.cn/en/services/org/TCT.shtml>.

[134] "Intellectual Property Rights Protection in China in 2005," China SIPO, *available at* <http://www.sipo.gov.cn/ sipo/zcll/zscqbps/200605/t20060509_99482.htm>, last visited October 6, 2006.

[135] Sources from the Network of Judicial Protection of IPR in China, *available at* <http://www.chinaiprlaw.cn/ file/200603277437.html>, last visited October 6, 2006.

ing to the Constitution, it theoretically enjoys independence.[136] However, administrative enforcement has traditionally been the nationwide preferred mode of policy implementation in almost all the fields, and China's judiciary remains subservient to administrative authority that impairs its ability to perform impartially and engage in genuinely independent decision-making.[137] Within IPR protection, there is no exception. The government-oriented approach is still popular and the administrative enforcement therefore remains the preferred channel in China to seek IPR protection.

EMERGENCE OF IPR JUDICIAL SYSTEM

In China at present, all provinces, municipalities and autonomous regions have set up intellectual property tribunals in what are known as "High People's Courts" at the provincial level.[138] The intellectual property Tribunals exercise jurisdiction over the judicial protection of IPR in order to safeguard the rights of the IPR proprietors in China.[139] However, this approach may have unintended effects due to the undue delays of the proceedings caused by the limited resources and expertise. At present, there are no specialised IPR courts which handle criminal IPR infringement cases. These should be considered as it would benefit judicial and administrative officers with requisition of specialised knowledge in IPR. To be effective, such an initiative must include specialised prosecutors and police officers to work in tandem in support.

ESTABLISHMENT OF INTELLECTUAL PROPERTY HIGH COURT

While there are large numbers of intellectual property tribunals attached to the normal courts, in order to enhance the judicial service handling in intellectual property cases, and ensure prompt and effective trial proceedings, it is suggested that a special Intellectual Property High Court (IPHC) be established.

As a "high court," the IPHC is expected to hear cases at first instance which have nationwide influence, appeals against decisions which are made by intermediate courts, and the administrative suits against decisions given by the intellectual property administrations.[140] The cases that are usually brought to High Courts of different provinces shall be transferred to the IPHC upon its establishment. After getting away from interference of local protectionism, IPHC should be in a position to exercise its judicial power independently and impartially.

---

[136] *See supra* § 3.3.2.
[137] Peter Ladegaard, "Programme of Dialogue and Cooperation with China," China Governance Project, Regulatory Management and Reform, Paris, February 3, 2005, CCNM/ CHINA (2004)3, at 21.
[138] "Enforcement of IPR Laws to Improve," *People's Daily*, June 2, 2001.
[139] *See* Alison Cychosz, "The Effectiveness of International Enforcement of Intellectual Property Rights," 37 *J. Marshall L. Rev.* 1012 (2004).
[140] *See supra* § 4.2.

Characteristics of the IPR Enforcement in China

CENTRALISED ANTI-COUNTERFEITING CAMPAIGNS

In order to crack down on IPR infringements, the most common measure is to launch a nationwide campaign. Though intermittent, this has proved to be one of the most effective ways to tackle counterfeiting and piracy in China. Such campaigns are normally initiated by the State Council,[141] which spells out the high level of political awareness. As official statistics show, from 1996 to October 2003, China seized 163 illegal CD production lines; in August 2003 alone, 42 million smuggled and pirated CDs were confiscated and destroyed during a single campaign against smuggled and pirate CDs administered by the Customs General Administration and the State Administration for News and Publications.[142]

In such a country where politics is prioritised and propaganda plays a big part, gearing up the state's massive bureaucratic apparatus and whipping up widespread sentiments and supports are common ways for the party and government to advance a hard-to-discern goal. Within this context, campaigns for IPR protection are normally organised and coordinated by a mixed executive group consisting in key members of different administrative departments, such as the Ministry of Commerce, Ministry of Public Security, Ministry of Culture, and the State Administration of Industry and Commerce. Sometimes, even judicial bodies are included in this "mixed executive group."[143] However, the results of the policy-driven campaigns are, in some circumstances, questionable and unstable.

POLITICAL ENFORCEMENT BODY

In the unique political ecology in China, there is no rigid distinction between law and policy. In keeping the stability of the Party's authoritarian regime, "China's government is organised in a unitary fashion," with its political infrastructure representing a pyramid format.[144] Within such a bureaucracy, both legislative and administrative governmental bodies have the power to fashion

---

[141] The State Council of China (*Guo Wu Yuan*), namely the Central People's Government, is the highest executive organ of State power, as well as the highest organ of State administration. It stands at the head of the executive branch of the central government, oversees more than sixty departments and ministries, commissions, administrations and offices. *See* "the Central People's Government," *available at* <http://english.gov.cn/>.

[142] *See* "Status Regarding China's Enforcement of IPR," Department of Treaty and Law, China MOFCOM, April 12, 2005.

[143] In China, judicial body at the central level consists of the Supreme People's Court and the Supreme People's Procuratorate. *See* Section 7: The People's Courts and the People's Procuratorates, Constitution of China.

[144] Christopher Duncan, "Out of Conformity: China's Capacity to Implement World Trade Organization Dispute Settlement Body Decisions after Accession," 18 *Am. U. Int'l L. Rev.* (2002), at 413-14.

"legislative" enactments, [145] because the Chinese government is not effectively ruled by law - or in other words, has vast discretionary powers.[146] The Chinese government policies can have exactly the same, if not more, effect as formally enacted legislations.

The basis to guarantee an adequate enforcement of IPR is an efficient and independent legal system.[147] However, as has been mentioned, the Chinese government conventionally maintains that "the legal system remain subservient to the political needs of a single party."[148] The balance between "rule of law" and "rule by law" is vulnerable, [149] because laws in China are *de facto* supplementary tools of bureaucrats which make for unpredictable and unforeseeable circumstances.[150] Chinese administrative departments have the power both to issue and to interpret rules in their own capacities and have significant leverage for enforcement of such rules.[151] This power is widespread, if not complete, because "most laws originate in the state bureaucracy rather than the legislative bodies."[152] The broad discretionary power that "Chinese bureaucrats exercise in making and implementing general rules is wielded in a system in which agencies are arrayed in parallel hierarchies of equal [...] authority," resulting in overlapping jurisdictions.[153]

As a notable characteristic, the judicial system is viewed by the Chinese as part of the enforcement arm of such policies in order to improve the enforcement efficiency. While the lack of respect for the "rule of law" principle in China has been a target for criticism, this condition should not be overstressed since it has "overwhelming consequential implications" for the effectiveness of IPR protection.[154] A policy-directed cracking down campaign on IPR violations would take the form not only of increased resources for the prosecution, but also of heavy influences on judicial decisions of the courts.[155]

---

[145] *Ibid,* at 414.

[146] Donald Clarke, *supra* note 129, at 32.

[147] Carlos A. Primo Braga and Carsten Fink, "Reforming Intellectual Property Rights Regimes: Challenges for Developing Countries," *J. Int'l Econ. L.* 549 (1998).

[148] *See* Scott J. Palmer, "An Identity Crisis: Regime Legitimacy and the Politics of Intellectual Property Rights in China," 8 *Ind. J. Global Legal Stud.* 452 (2001); *see* also *supra* § 3.3.2.

[149] Robert Bejesky, "Investing in the Dragon: Managing the Patent versus Trade Secret Protection Decision for the Multinational Corporation in China," 11 *Tulsa J. Comp. & Int'l L.* 474 (2004).

[150] *See* D. Lewis (ed.), *The Life and Death of a Joint Venture in China* (1995), at 44.

[151] Anthony Dicks, "Compartmentalized Law and Judicial Restraint: An Inductive View of Some Jurisdictional Barriers to Reform," in Stanley Lubman (ed.), *China's Legal Reforms* 82, 99-103 (1996).

[152] Stanley Lubman, "Bird in a Cage: Chinese Law Reform after Twenty Years," 20 *Nw J. Int'l L. and Bus.* (2000), at 390-391.

[153] *Ibid,* at 391. *See* also § 4.4 and the corresponding footnotes.

[154] Bejesky, *supra* note 149, at 437.

[155] Donald Clarke, *supra* note 129, at 32.

In other words, a same policy approach to the IPR protection "could either make curbing IP rights infringements difficult or make attaining more effective enforcement probable."[156]

Foster Private IP Investigations

DIVISION OF THE IPR ENFORCEMENT: PUBLIC AND PRIVATE

Although Chinese political and moral traditions contain an inherent preference of public governance, the private consciousness has become a growing phenomenon over the recent years. In this sense, IPR enforcement in China can be divided into two categories: public enforcement and private enforcement. The former includes administrative and judicial measures, and latter refers to a "mechanism whereby policy is implemented through the uncoordinated actions of non-governmental bodies responding to incentives."[157] To a large extent coordinated private enforcement mechanisms are supplementary to public mechanisms, which tend to be more immediately effective, a factor common to a number of developing and transitional countries such as China. However, public enforcement is important as they enable the private enforcement mechanisms to function.

DECENTRALISATION OF IPR ENFORCEMENT

Public enforcement has been swift and effective in combating IPR violations; however, while this approach may yield immediate results, the gains are ephemeral and may ultimately be detrimental to the promotion and development of more stable legal institutions capable of fostering consistent decision-making guided more by the rule of law than government pragmatism.[158] As Donald Clarke points out, it is interesting that foreign IPR holders are pressing the case for protection to the Chinese government more enthusiastically and actively than are domestic IPR holders.[159] This stems from the institutional context in which they can lobby, namely government-to-government negotiations.[160] The unified focus thereby introduced into negotiations facilitates a unified response in the nature of an unequivocal enforcement campaign by a government agency.[161] Ironically, such negotiations are most unlikely to produce a strategic and integrated enforcement mechanism, which is consistent

---

[156] Bejesky, *supra* note 149, at 437.
[157] Donald Clarke, *supra* note 129, at 32.
[158] Michael N. Schlesinger, "A Sleeping Giant Awakens: The Development of Development of Intellectual Property Law in China," 9 *J. Chinese L.* (1995), at 120.
[159] Donald Clarke, *supra* note 129, at 32.
[160] *Ibid*
[161] *Ibid*

and reliable in the long term protection provided.[162] Instead the resulting regime is comprised of *ad hoc* and cumulatively incoherent responses.

PRIVATE IPR INVESTIGATION

Private IPR investigation is an effective means for the IPR enforcement and has remarkable potential for development in China. However, those who suppose to undertake private investigations in China should take every effect to ensure full compliance with existing laws and regulations, which still restrict the scope and duties of private investigations. In practice, however, numerous private investigations firms are registered as certain forms of "market research" investigations on an *ad hoc* basis.

The most significant advantage of the private approach, which decentralised enforcement over administrative enforcement, is that it minimises the layers between policymaking and policy implementation, thereby maximising the effectiveness of the enforcement.[163] Due to excessive bureaucracy, a case should go through multitude of ill-coordinated and overlapping agencies, and the process for a written law to be eventually enforced can be complicated with trivial formalities and petty restrictions. The availability of the private approach makes it possible for right holders to access a shortcut to the dispute settlement and obtain a "club card" in the bureaucratic struggle.

5.3.3 Implications of EU Action Plan towards China

Action Plan: "Third World Version" of the Directive

As has been noted, the new enforcement strategy adopted by the European Parliament is to harmonise the legislation of the EU Member States with regard to IPR protection and generate a uniformly high level of penalties against counterfeiting and piracy. However, strategic implications in the context of EU-China trade relations, particularly when the EU takes aim at third countries, place China on the top of the list.[164] In its newly released Action Plan, entitled "Strategy for the Enforcement of IPR in Third Countries," [165] the European Commission sets high standards for trade policy and grants itself a broad mandate to exert pressure on third countries.

---

[162] *Ibid*

[163] *Ibid*

[164] *See* "Strategy for the Enforcement of Intellectual Property Rights in Third Countries," *supra* note 82.

[165] *Ibid.*

Traditionally, while the EU has introduced legislation harmonising the substance of intellectual property law throughout the Member States,[166] significant differences remain between certain Member States regarding the tools available for enforcing IPR.[167] For example, the protection of commercial confidentiality in the United Kingdom is strong while in the rest of the EU such protection is more limited.[168] There are also differences regarding the availability of court injunctions to curtail the sale of the counterfeit products, the calculation of damages to be awarded to the IPR holders in relation to infringements, and the nature of civil and criminal penalties imposed on counterfeiters.[169] The European Commission considers that these differences may not only undermine the substance of IPR protection in the EU,[170] but also create an impediment when negotiating domestic enforcement norms with non-EU countries.

As the Action Plan indicates, the new enforcement strategy "intends to be a contribution to the improvement of the situation" in developing countries,[171] and the harmonisation of the legislation and tougher action against counterfeit or pirated goods are "logical consequences" of the directive.[172] Thus the Action Plan appears to be the "third world version" of the directive designed to curb the counterfeiting and piracy in third countries including China.

EU' Enforcement Strategy: Unilateral, or Flexible?

However, it can be a daunting task trying to convince policy-makers of the third world of the genuine benefits to tighten IPR enforcement. As the Action Plan acknowledges, "any proposed solutions may only be effective if they are prioritised and considered to be important by the recipient country."[173] According to the objectives set out in the Action Plan, it is not destined for proposing a "one-size-fits-all" approach to promoting IPR enforcement in the developing countries; [174] rather, it adopts a "flexible approach that takes into account dif-

---

[166] For example, the Trademark Directive (89/104/EEC, December 21, 1988) was designed to harmonise national legislation and practice within the EU in light of trademark protection.

[167] *See* "Proposed Intellectual Property Enforcement Directive Condemned as Too Harsh," *Business Alert: EU, General and Market Reports* (TDC), Issue 18 (2003).

[168] Patrick Birkinshaw, "Reform of Information and Openness: Fundamental Human Rights?" 58 *Admin. L. Rev.* 194-95 (2006) (mentioning that the UK, together with the US, enjoys a stronger protection of commercial confidentiality).

[169] *See* "Proposed Intellectual Property Enforcement Directive Condemned as Too Harsh," *supra* note 167.

[170] *Ibid.*

[171] *See* "Strategy for the Enforcement of Intellectual Property Rights in Third Countries," *supra* note 82.

[172] *Ibid.*

[173] *Ibid.*

[174] *See ibid* (stating that the strategy does not intend to "[p]ropose a 'one-size-fits-all' approach to promoting IPR enforcement").

ferent needs, level of development [...] and the main problems in terms of IPR of the countries in question."[175] In this context, the strategy should take every possibility to choose cooperation rather than attempting to impose unilateral solutions to the infringement concerned.[176] It is of particular significance to have a long-term vision for China and avoid pursuing instant benefit, which is destined to be fruitless.

European-styled "Section 301"?

It is clear that any attempt to copy other models of IPR enforcement mechanism, particularly United States "Section 301" approach,[177] would not be wise. Nevertheless, in this Action Plan, the EU Commission set out a target for identifying and focusing on the "most problematic countries" as "priority countries" in terms of IPR violations.[178] These "problematic countries" will be identified according to a regular survey to be conducted by the Commission among all stakeholders and the result of the survey forms the basis for renewing the list of priority countries for the subsequent period.[179] China was considered as one of "the most problematic countries" according to the results of the survey.[180] Although Action Plan attempts to clear up doubts about the strategy, it does provide institutional framework and capacities for the implementation of any actions, including trade sanctions, which are considered to be necessary under certain circumstances.[181] It therefore raises concerns as to whether a European-styled "Section 301" might ultimately be developed.

5.4 Outstanding Issues towards Utilising Flexibilities

It is a hotly contested question as to how to resolve the inherent tension between the rules intended to promote sustainable development for human beings and environment, and the rules governing protection of IPR. While advanced technology and an expanding global marketplace has made the protec-

---

[175] *Ibid.*
[176] *Ibid.*
[177] For a detailed assessment of the U.S. "Section 301" and its effect towards US-China intellectual property debate, *see* "Comparative Analysis: Sino-US Negotiations," *infra* § 6.1.
[178] "EU Strategy to Enforce Intellectual Property Rights in Third Countries – Facts and Figures," *supra* note 80.
[179] "Strategy for the Enforcement of Intellectual Property Rights in Third Countries," *supra* note 82.
[180] *Ibid.*
[181] *See* Part II (5) of the Action Plan (asserting that "[no] rule can be really effective without the threat of a sanction. Countries where IP violations are systematic could be publicly identified").

tion of IPR a critical international priority and thus seen it emerge as a central and essential item on international agendas, the role of IPR in the process of global economic development should not be overlooked. For this reason, both developing and developed countries need to take constructive action to ensure that IPR enforcement does not stall or obstruct development. Considering that substantial amendment to TRIPs looks distant or even unachievable,[182] offering developing countries the benefits of differential and more favourable treatment might be a realistic approach to making the disputed international standards common values embraced by both developed and developing world.

Differential and More Favourable Treatment, also known as the Special and Differential Treatment (SDT), of developing nations has been a fundamental principle of the GATT/WTO, which is based on the premise that developing nations are inherently disadvantaged and subsequently marginalised in their participation in the global trading system.[183] Based on this awareness, the international community has reached consensus that, in general, developing nations may be subject to somewhat different rules and disciplines, such as permission of parallel import and application of compulsory licensing, than those that apply to developed nations; and that the latter may implement their obligations under the WTO in a manner that would allow certain degree of flexibility to the domestic policies of developing world.[184] Since the TRIPs Agreement provides certain exceptions for the exclusive rights conferred to the IPR holders,[185] this section focuses on the specific areas of flexibility and analyses the SDT provisions within the international IPR regime mainly set out in the TRIPs Agreement, and assesses their implementation in light of EU-China trade relations. Parallel imports, compulsory licensing, and fair use provision of copyright are pertinently selected as representative samples in their respective areas of trademark, patent and copyright. The selection of public health has been chosen not merely as an example, but also because the strongest lobbying, both for the original TRIPs Agreement,[186] and subsequently, has come from the international pharmaceutical industry.

---

[182] Developing countries have been keen in restructuring the global IPR system. However, the gap between the perceptions of developing and developed world has been significant. As a result, apart from applying for a systemic amendment of the existing regime, WTO members are seeking maximal adjustment towards relevant articles of TRIPs and making temporarily arrangements. See supra Chapter 2.

[183] See Constantine Michalopoulos, "Special and Differential Treatment of Developing Countries in TRIPs," TRIPs Issues Papers, No. 2, Quaker United Nations Office (QUNO) Geneva, and Quaker International Affairs Programme (QIAP), Ottawa (2003), at 2.

[184] Ibid, at 6.

[185] Article 13, 17, 30 of TRIPs stipulate limitations and exceptions for the exclusive rights of copy rights, trademark and patent respectively.

[186] In light of the special needs of developing countries, the TRIPs Agreement provides a special provision in Article 31, under which countries are authorised to impose compulsory licensing under certain circumstances. See Article 31, TRIPs.

5.4.1 Exhaustion of Rights: Article 6 of TRIPs and Parallel Imports

Whether a country prohibits or accepts parallel imports depends, in principle, on whether the country adopts the principle of international exhaustion.[187] However, both the TRIPs Agreement and the WIPO treaties remain silent on the question of whether, let alone to what extent, national and regional IPR should reinforce market segmentation, and thus outlaw parallel importing, or allow exhaustion of rights at first point of sale. Accordingly they reserve to each member the authority to pursue its own policy.[188] Since developed nations are normally opposed to international exhaustion and related parallel importation, a large number of developing nations have expressed their deep concern that IPR holders in developed nations may take any and every opportunity to block the importation of goods and services legally produced and packed in developing nations for export.[189] If consensus could be established, tension between developed and developing world would be relieved and a large number of trade disputes concerning this issue should be avoided.

Terminology, Definition and Scope

The term parallel importing refers to products that are legitimately produced and marketed in "county A" under license from the proprietor at one agreed price and are subsequently exported for resale into "country B" without the authorisation of the proprietor to the importing country, or their exclusive licensee in "country B" at a lower price that they have set.[190] The significant disparity in market conditions between two countries creates the demand for cross-border parallel trade.[191] Since parallel import is a means by which importers can get arguably genuine products for lower prices by exploiting market segmentation,[192] in economic terms this would seem beneficial to consumers.[193] However, pharmaceutical companies point out that by setting prices to

---

[187] *See* Cindy Wai Chi Wong, "Parallel Importation of Trademarked Goods in Hong Kong and China," 34 *Hong Kong Law Journal* (2004), at 152.

[188] *Ibid.*

[189] Lina M. Monten, "The Inconsistency between Section 301 and TRIPs: Counterproductive with Respect to the Future of International Protection of Intellectual Property Rights?" 9 *Marq. Intell. Prop. L. Rev.* 415 (2005) (stating that the principle of international exhaustion is typically advocated by developing countries).

[190] Carlos M. Correa, "Public Health and Patent Legislation in Developing Countries," 3 *Tulane Journal of Technology & Intellectual Property* 1, 8-9 (2001).

[191] *See* Cychosz, *supra* note 139, at 999.

[192] *See* Wong, *supra* note 187, at 152.

[193] *Ibid*, at 187.

each market (known as Ramsey Pricing), rather than cost of production, developed markets are able to subsidise lower prices in developing states.[194]

The legitimacy of parallel imports has been a much debated issue over the past century which has yet failed to achieve consensus amongst academics and practitioners. The unresolved tension between IPR protection and the doctrine of the exhaustion of IPR are the key to the issue of parallel imports. From the viewpoint of owners of IPR, this is not merely a question of price but also of ensuring consistent quality.

Accordingly, where there are free trade and price differentials in otherwise segregated markets, there will be parallel importing. Within the EU, there exists regional arrangement for acceptance of the exhaustion.[195] As the International Association for the Protection of Intellectual Property (AIPPI) Report shows, in such an arrangement, the fundamental principle for free movement of goods within the single market may call for legitimacy of parallel imports between Member States, resulting in reaching a consensus that such a restriction of the rights of IPR is necessary for the realisation of such a single market.[196] Thus, within the EU, the consumer's interests are placed first and protected by the principle of regional exhaustion. Once sold into the EU, the owner of any licensed rights loses control over parallel trading within the EU. As there are considerable differences of economic conditions within the EU, parallel trading is the "bane of European brand owners" and the competing interests of brand owners and parallel traders have over time established various rules of parallel trading that operate within the EU and form a main agenda item in EU negotiations with other none-EU countries.[197]

TRIPs and Exhaustion

The TRIPs Agreement's treatment of the exhaustion of IPR and parallel imports is somewhat ambiguous and the result of international debate over these controversies has been an implicit manipulation, reflected by Article 6.[198] Article 6 of the TRIPs Agreement stipulates:

---

[194] Patricia M. Danzon, Adrian Towse, "Differential Pricing for Pharmaceuticals: Reconciling Access, R&D and Patents," *AEI-Brookings Joint Center for Regulatory Studies*, Working Paper, May 2003.

[195] *See* Catherine Narnard, *The Substantive Law of the EU: The Fourth Freedoms*, OUP (2004), at 174.

[196] *See* "International Exhaustion of Industrial Property Rights," Q156, AIPPI Report 2001.

[197] Thomas Hays, *supra* note 11, at 821.

[198] Peng Jiang, "Fighting the AIDS Epidemic: China's Options under the WTO TRIPs Agreement," 13 *Albany L.J. Sci. & Tech.* 233 (2002); Catalin Cosovanu, "Piracy, Price Discrimination, and Development: The Software Sector in Eastern Europe and Other Emerging Markets," 31 *AIPLA Quart. J.* 201 (2003).

For the purposes of dispute settlement under this Agreement, subject to the provisions of Articles 3 and 4 above nothing in this Agreement shall be used to address the issue of the exhaustion of intellectual property rights.

Although the TRIPs Agreement does not directly ratify parallel imports, Article 6 provides leverage to connect with the exhaustion doctrine. According to this Article, "once a rights-holder introduces protected goods into the stream of commerce, there is no restriction on how the goods may be further distributed," because their "rights" have been "exhausted." [199]

The TRIPs Agreement provides for (1) a minimum protection in respect of IPR;[200] (2) protection to nationals of Members to the Agreement,[201] that such rights will be enforceable; and (3) equality of protection, on a "National Treatment basis."[202]

By leaving exhaustion to the discretion of the WTO Member States, TRIPs allows states to determine that a right holder loses its exclusive right to import goods after the first sale of the goods.[203] Article 6 has thus been designed so that this provision represents "an agreement to disagree" on the subject of parallel importing, giving members flexibility to adopt their own rules on exhaustion, and subsequently accept, parallel importing.[204]

China's Parallel Imports

BIFURCATED CONTROVERSIES

Theoretically speaking, parallel imports are legally allowed in China because, unlike Chinese patent law which denies parallel imports,[205] Chinese trademark law remains silent with regard to exhaustion.[206] Previously, China lacked eco-

---

[199] Lissett Ferreira, "Access to Affordable HIV/Aids Drugs: The Human Rights Obligations of Multinational Pharmaceutical Cooperation," 71 *Fordham L. Rev.*1146 (2002).

[200] Article 15-20 of TRIPs Agreement for Trade Marks.

[201] Article 1 of TRIPs.

[202] Article 3 of TRIPs.

[203] *See* Ferreira, *supra* note 199, at 1146.

[204] Jiang, *supra* note 198, at 233.

[205] According to Chinese patent law, "after the grant of the patent right for an invention or utility model, except as otherwise provided for in the law, no entity or individual may, without the authorisation of the patentee, exploit the patent, that is, make, use, offer to sell, sell or import the patented product; or use the patented process or use, offer to sell, sell or import the product directly obtained by the patented process, for production or business purposes." In addition, "after the grant of the patent right for a design, no entity or individual may, without the authorisation of the patentee, exploit the design, that is, make, sell or import the product incorporating its or his patented design, for production or business purposes." *See* Patent Law, Article 11.

[206] The Trademark Law (2001), the Anti-unfair Competition Law (1993) and the Foreign Trade Law (1994) constitute the general legal framework for trademark protection which leaves with a lacuna in addressing exhaustion doctrine. *See, e.g.*, Hui Zhang,

nomic grounds for engaging in parallel imports, because it was conventionally known for its low labour and production costs, and prices in China were typically much lower than that in the international market.[207] Constrained by the high import quotas and tough customs duties, parallel imports had not gained adequate space in which to function.[208] Accordingly, it was only with the increase of market-oriented reforms after China's entry into the WTO, that the issue of parallel imports has become significant in China.[209]

Though controversial, as some commentators have suggested,[210] it is unwise for China to adopt any measures aimed at restricting parallel imports under current economic and social conditions.

Firstly, as explained above, both the TRIPs Agreement and the Paris Convention allow for the possibility of parallel imports. Accordingly, there are no international obligations to prohibit or restrict parallel imports in light of trademark protection.[211]

Secondly, the exclusive rights of trademark proprietors tend to be abused, if excessive rights are demanded and granted.[212] Unrestricted use of trademark rights appears to be inconsistent with international norms of competition law curbing monopolies.[213] Since China still lacks an established framework of antitrust law,[214] it is legal and feasible for China to adopt the doctrine of international exhaustion and subsequently introduce parallel imports so as to ameliorate the negative effect of foreseeable monopolisation.[215]

Thirdly, China is still a low-income developing country. If parallel imports were prohibited, Chinese consumers would be unable to get access to quality products at more reasonable and affordable prices, which may result in increased living costs and widening disparities. Furthermore, if parallel importation is not permitted, it is predicted that high prices and lucrative profits in selling products of name foreign brands will lead unscrupulous traders to counterfeit such products.[216] Such a consequence would surely be undesirable for both Chinese leaders and their foreign trade partners.

"Comparative Study on Parallel Imports in Trade Marks," *EU-China Legal and Judicial Cooperation Programme* (2002).

[207] Xiaodong Yuan, "Research on Trade Mark Parallel Imports in China," 25 (5) E.I.P.R. 224 (2003); *see* also, Zhang, *ibid.*

[208] Wong, *supra* note 187, at 164.

[209] Yuan, *supra* note 207, at 224.

[210] *See, e.g.*, Wong, *supra* note 187, at 181.

[211] Zhang, *supra* note 206.

[212] Wong, *supra* note 187, at 180.

[213] *Ibid*, at 180.

[214] While the controversial Antitrust Law (literally translated as "Anti-monopoly" Law) was enacted in August 2007 after lengthy debates, it will not come into force until August 1, 2008; and it may take longer for the law to be implemented and enforced.

[215] Wong, *supra* note 187.

[216] *Ibid. See*, also Yuan, *supra* note 207, at 207.

Moreover, according to the "one country, two systems" policy,[217] China consists of a number of Separate Customs Zones and Legal Territories: Mainland China, Hong Kong, Macao and, arguably, Taiwan. As long as there are trade demands among these four regions, interregional parallel imports and exhaustion of trademark rights are inevitable.[218] Although the four regions have enacted individual trademark laws there is no relevant agreement constraining regional exhaustion of trademark rights.[219] As regional trade becomes more entrenched, so does the pressure from holders of IPR for measures to constrain the possibility of parallel importing. However, over the decision-making process, China should demonstrate its commitment to opening its markets in a regional level and advancing free trade in a global context.[220] China's attempt at fulfilling its regional objective in accordance with its existing trademark law should not portend diminution in its global commitments to facilitating international free trade, which is best served by exhaustion.[221] Since few countries in both developed and developing world have chosen to prohibit parallel imports completely, there is no need for China to treat it imperatively.[222]

JUDICIAL PRACTICE

Although the legislation in China is silent, parallel imports litigation has taken place. The first case of parallel trade, *Shanghai Lever v. Guangzhou Trading Corporation*,[223] took place in 1999, and triggered much debate regarding the Chinese approach to parallel trade.[224] In this case, the brand "Lux" was owned by Anglo-Dutch Company Unilever, and licensed exclusively to the claimant, Shanghai Lever Ltd (China).[225] The scope of the exclusive license was to produce, import and sell the branded products within the territory of Mainland China, excluding Hong Kong, Macao and Taiwan.[226] Owing to the Southeast Asian financial crisis, numerous cosmetic products manufactured in peripheral countries became increasingly cheaper to acquire than those made else-

---

[217] "One country two system " concept was first advanced by Deng Xiaoping in January 1979 and applied in the Kong Kong's returning back to China in 1997.

[218] Yuan, *supra* note 207, at 207.

[219] *Ibid*, at 225.

[220] Zhang, *supra* note 206.

[221] Some countries such as Australia and New Zealand have adopted clear rules permitting parallel imports; other countries such as Japan and Singapore have adhered to the principle of international exhaustion. *See* Wong, *supra* note 187, at 182.

[222] Wong, *ibid*, at 182.

[223] For a detailed interpretation of this case, *see* "Shanghai Lever v. Guangzhou Trading Corporation," *Report of Cases of People's Court* (Commercial and Intellectual Property, 2004), vol. 49, People's Court Press, June 1, 2005.

[224] *Ibid.*

[225] *Ibid.*

[226] *Ibid.*

where.[227] The defendant, the Guangzhou Trading Corporation for Commercial Imports & Exports, thus seized this opportunity to import Lux products from Thailand at lower prices and sell them to consumers in mainland China. The defendant asserted that what had been imported were genuine goods from another market, and insisted that it was a case of parallel imports and the importation was legal.[228]

The Guangzhou Intermediate People's Court ruled that, according to Chinese Trademark Law, the defendant conducted importing and selling the "Lux" branded products in China without furnishing sufficient evidence of the consent of the claimant and thus constituted trademark counterfeiting.[229] This ruling stirred up fierce controversy.

As a general principle, the purpose of trademark law is to prevent confusion over brand names in the minds of the consumers as to "the source or origin of the goods or services – that is, confused as to the designer, manufacturer, selector, or supplier of the goods or services."[230] The way trademark law approaches protecting consumers is by prohibiting "genuine and properly substantiated likelihood of confusion."[231] The core element of determining whether trademark infringement exists is to inquire whether "a reasonably prudent consumer is likely to be confused as to the origin of the good or service bearing one of the marks."[232]

In the case in question, however, the goods produced by the claimant and purchased by the defendant were from the same origin – the Unilever Ltd, which is the proprietor of the trademark. Based on the principle of likelihood of confusion and according to Article 38 of the Chinese Trademark Law, the conduct of the defendant does not constitute infringement.

In addition, although the financial crisis in Southeast Asia resulted in lower sale prices at that time, cheap labour and low consuming levels contributed to the low price of products in China.[233] Also, before China's entry to the WTO, tariffs barriers and quantitative restrictions resulted in high price of imported products.[234] Both factors meant parallel importers under these circumstances had limited chance to achieve large profits and poach on the other's preserves.

---

[227] Yuan, *supra* note, at 207.

[228] *Ibid*, at 225.

[229] "Shanghai Lever v. Guangzhou Trading Corporation," *supra* note 223.

[230] *See* L. Bently and B. Sherman, *Intellectual Property Law*, OUP (2001), at 822-3.

[231] *Ibid*; *see* also Chinese Trademark Law, Article 38, 52, which stipulate similar principles.

[232] *Dreamwerks Production Group, Inc. v. SKG Studio*, 142 F.3d 1127, 1129, 46 U.S.P.Q.2d 1561 (9th Cir. 1998).

[233] Zhang, *supra* note 206; *see* also, Youqun Guo, "Guanyu Tigao Woguo Xiaofeilu de Sikao [Reflections on Fuelling Consuming Standard in China]," 10 *Jingji Wenti* [Economic Problems] 65-7 (2004).

[234] Zhang, *ibid*; *see* also, Yifu Lin and Shudong Hu, "Jiaru Shijie Maoyi Zuzhi: Tiaozhan he Jiyu [Access to the WTO: Challenges and Opportunities]," China Centre for Eco-

Nonetheless, China's accession to the WTO has resulted in a gradual reduction of tariffs and quotas, thereby increasing the potential of Chinese parallel trade, particularly in the field of products relating to public health.[235] To date, parallel import cases in China are frequently driven by brand owning international companies, but the affected companies are most probably the Chinese licensees who have undertaken domestic market development, as in the "Lux" case. [236]

Therefore, in light of China's WTO membership and its subsequent commitments in eliminating trade barriers, "there is still leeway for parallel importers if they can produce concrete evidence that the goods at issue were genuine goods made with the foreign trademark owner's clear authorisation."[237] While the court did not issue a groundbreaking opinion, the ruling did prompt an interesting and a challenging question: what if the defendant were able to provide sufficient evidence of consent at the point of export – would this enable parallel importation?

PRACTICAL SIGNIFICANCE

The conclusion is that, the parallel trade is becoming a global issue at the cutting edge of the debates addressing law and sustainable development - developing countries, including China, may take advantage of parallel trade to "produce patented and trademark products under licence and then re-export them at lower prices to rich countries because of the perceived boost to economic development."[238] In some circumstances, a developing country may produce these licensed goods, particularly pharmaceutical products, and re-export them to other developing countries.[239]

Within EU-China perspective, the significance is two fold. Firstly, in terms of China's imports from the EU, since China does not legally prohibit parallel importation, it is potentially possible for China to obtain EU products from third party states. It is of particular significance for China to obtain generic version of medicines through parallel imports, by which, China's imports from the EU may be subject to competition from parallel imports.

Secondly, in terms of the EU's imports from China, strengthening the monitoring of goods leaving China may be a priority to be addressed. As has been mentioned, due to the institutional duality the EU institutions, the imports and exports of the EU are administered at the different levels. Current monitoring of external trade is periodic and asymmetrical in that the point of

nomic Research, Working Paper Series, March 2000, *available at* <www.ccer.edu.cn/workingpaper/paper/c2000004.doc>.

[235] Lin & Hu, *ibid.*

[236] Zhang, *supra* note 206.

[237] Wong, *supra* note 187, at 168.

[238] Stefan Szymanski and Tommaso Valletti, "Parallel Trade, Price Discrimination, Investment and Price Caps," 20 (44) *Econ. Policy* 714 (2005).

[239] *Ibid.*

entry into the EU can be any Member States whilst negotiations related to Chinese exports are bilateral and handled by the EU. In addition, the export of products to third party states also has a significant impact in the event that they are in turn re-exported to EU Member States.

EU's Parallel Imports

The EU trademark regime, established by the First Council Directive 89/104/EEC of 21 December 1988,[240] is based on the principle of "Community exhaustion."[241] This principle allows any interested party from "country A" to purchase a product legitimately sold in "country B" for resale in "country A", without the consent of the IPR holder. Clearly, to establish a united EU market, this directive does not entitle the proprietor to prohibit onward sale of protected goods within the EU once they have legitimately entered the Community market.[242] According to this directive, trademark rights are exhausted within the EU, while the exhaustion out of the EU is prohibited and still under debate.[243]

The dilemma of implementation of the directive lies in the harmonisation of the exhaustion policy. Technically, within the Member States where the national legislation expressly provided for international exhaustion, the national law should have to be modified to fit in the EU provision.[244] In addition, the national courts of those Member States, which had adopted the wording of the directive on exhaustion, would have to reinterpret the national legislations to keep in line with the decisions of European Court of Justice (ECJ).

In 1999, shortly after the directive was enacted, the Commission organised a meeting with interested parties and discussed the issue as to whether or not to change the current Community-wide exhaustion regime.[245] Meanwhile, a survey of the exhaustion regime from the NERA Institute in London was released, showing that a possible regime change towards exhaustion has only a

---

[240] First Directive 89/104/EEC of the Council, of 21 December 1988, to Approximate the Laws of the Member States Relating to Trade Marks (OJ EC No L 40 of 11.2.1989, p.1), *available at* <http://oami.eu.int/en/mark/ aspects/direc/direc.htm>.

[241] Bently & Sherman, *supra* note 230, at 892-6.

[242] 89/104/EEC, Article 3(1).

[243] However, recent European case law seems to suggest that, within the EU, parallel trade from outside the EU is "prohibited unless there is explicit consent" of the manufacturer. It seems to imply that parallel trade can be viewed as legal movement of products across borders without the explicit consent of the manufacturer. *See* Szymanski and Valletti, *supra* note 238, at 712; for an overview of the relevant case law, *see* European Court of Justice, C-415/99, and Directive 89/104/EEC – Article 7(1).

[244] Craid & De Burca, at 279.

[245] "Parallel Imports and Prices," Seminar of Internal Market and Consumer Affairs Ministers, Lund 27-28 April, MEMO/01/157, Brussels, April 26, 2001, *available at* <http://ec.europa.eu/internal_market/indprop/tm/index_en.htm>.

marginal effect on price.[246] Other elements such as "distribution arrangements, transport costs, health and safety legislation, technical standards and labelling differences may have a greater and more direct impact."[247] Having analysed these information, the Commission concluded that adopting the principle of "international exhaustion will not, at least in the short term, lead to a significant fall in consumer prices."[248]

It seems that the position of the Commission with regard to the exhaustion doctrine as embodied in Article 7(1) of the directive has been generally clear since then.[249] As far as the Commission is concerned, a community exhaustion policy has been designed to "foster integration of the internal market."[250] As the NERA study indicates, the effects of a potential regime change will largely "depend on whether such a change is carried out unilaterally or through bilateral or multilateral agreements."[251] As the Commission reiterates, "[i]f the EU were to introduce an international exhaustion policy, and its trading partners did not do likewise (as seems likely), EU companies would face a competitive disadvantage."[252] It has thus given rise concern for the Commission that a change of regime might potentially inhibit investment in new brands or even make trademark holders withdraw their products from the internal market.[253] The Commission is also concerned lest trademark holders who continue to provide branded goods could choose to reduce the quality of goods or the provision of associated services.[254] So far there is no sign indicating that the Commission would re-evaluate their stance and steer towards international exhaustion.

The issue of parallel imports, commonly referred to as "grey market" imports, has generated considerable case law both among national courts within the Member States and the ECJ.[255] Ironically, two decades have passed since the emergence of the directive, the exhaustion doctrine still "lies at the heart of the debate," and the exclusion of the parallel imports by the trademark holders

---

[246] "NERA and International Trade Issues," *NERA Economic Consulting, available at* <http://nera.com/image/International_Trade_100304.pdf>. *See* also "Communiqué from Commissioner Bolkestein on the Issue of Exhaustion of Trade Mark Rights," *available at* <http://europa.eu.int/comm/internal_market/en/inprop/tm/comehaust.htm>.

[247] *See* "Parallel Imports and Prices," *supra* note 245.

[248] *Ibid.*

[249] *Ibid.*

[250] *Ibid.*

[251] "NERA and International Trade Issues," *NERA Economic Consulting, supra* note 246.

[252] *Ibid.*

[253] Communiqué from Commissioner Bolkestein on the Issue of Exhaustion of Trade Mark Rights, *supra* note 246.

[254] *Ibid.*

[255] Bently & Sherman, *supra* note 230, at 892-6. *See* also Melvyn J. Simburg, *et al,* "International Intellectual Property Rights," 38 *Int'l L.* 299 (2004).

still remains a "grey" area of law, with the Commission now grapping with the issues.[256]

5.4.2 Compulsory Licensing: Daylight Robbery or Timely Help?

The TRIPs Agreement is intended "to reduce distortions and impediments to international trade, and taking into account the need to promote effective and adequate protection of intellectual property rights, and to ensure that measures and procedures to enforce intellectual property rights do not themselves become barriers to legitimate trade [...]." [257] It is, nonetheless, not designed to achieve this goal at the expenses of reducing the range of options available to governments to facilitate social affairs and protect public health. What is of critical importance is how to balance the protection of IPR with social and economic development, "particularly whether or not technical assistance by intergovernmental agencies has allowed developing countries to assess their needs fairly and critically."[258] Based on the fact that the regional disparities and the technological gap are continuing to grow, we should envisage "the need for a short-term perspective to address immediate problems of access, as well as a longer-term approach to issues including capacity building."[259]

As discussed in Chapter 2, TRIPs provides reasonable flexibility for developing and less-developed countries to obtain additional acquisition based on varied economic strengths and technological capacities.[260] For example, Article 31 of TRIPs provides the basis for the legitimate use of the compulsory licensing which involves the freedom for national governments to issue licenses enabling the product to be produced domestically subject only to providing the patent holder with reasonable compensation. As Correa observes, compulsory licensing is used mainly to counter cases of market failure, where the product would otherwise be unavailable or available only at unaffordable prices, and has proved to be an effective tool in reducing pharmaceutical prices.[261]

Doha Agreement

Given the establishment of an international IPR regime that globalisation and digitalisation have engendered, growing criticism has been levelled at the fore-

---

[256] *Ibid.*

[257] Preface of TRIPs, *supra* note 2 in Chapter 1.

[258] Stas Burgiel and Lisa Schipper, "A Summary Report of the Conference on How Intellectual Property Rights Could Work Better for Developing Countries and Poor People," 70 (1) *Sust. Devel.* 5 (2002).

[259] *Ibid.*

[260] Cychosz, *supra* note 139, at 994.

[261] *See* Correa *supra* note 190, at 43-44. *See* also, Jiang, "Fighting the AIDS Epidemic: China's Options under the WTO TRIPs Agreement," *supra* note 198, at 231.

front of the global arena and TRIPs has been specifically identified as the principal target.[262] The most visible manifestation of this challenge comes from the Declaration on the TRIPs Agreement and Public Health, which was adopted as part of the launch of a new round of WTO trade negotiations in Doha.[263]

CONCEPT AND BACKGROUND

Theoretically, the TRIPs Agreement provides developing states with "adequate" provisions to enable them to override protected rights and gain access to essential pharmaceuticals against public health crises through Articles 7,[264] Article 8,[265] and Article 31.[266] In practice, however, many developing states are not in the position to adopt detailed provisions required by Article 31, "particularly the requirement that compulsory licensing be granted only on a non-exclusive and non-assignable basis, with the possibility of judicial review and with adequate remuneration for the patent holder."[267]

In addition, Article 8(1) of TRIPs allows members "to adopt measures necessary to protect public health and nutrition," and "to promote the public interest in sectors of vital importance to their socio-economic and technological development."[268] While this may be "invoked to override a pharmaceutical patent when a member is in urgent need of such pharmaceutical to safeguard public health,"[269] the member state representing the holder of such rights may dispute whether the measures are indeed necessary. It is not surprising that is-

---

[262] *See* Laurence R. Helfer, "Regime Shifting: The TRIPs Agreement and New Dynamic of International Intellectual property Lawmaking," 29 *Yale J. Int'l L.* (2004), at 4-5.

[263] *Ibid.*

[264] Article7 sets forth the overall objectives of the TRIPs Agreement. It provides that the implementation and enforcement of IPR "should contribute not only to the promotion of technological innovation but also to the transfer and dissemination of technology to the mutual advantage of producers and users of technological knowledge in a manner conducive to social and economic welfare and which balances rights and obligations."

[265] Article 8 (1) provides a feasibility that, upon the implementation of the TRIPs Agreement, members may, in formulating or amending their laws and regulations, "adopt measures necessary to protect public health and to promote the public interest in sectors of vital importance to their socio-economic and technological development, provided such measures are consistent with the provisions of the Agreement."

[266] Article 31 of TRIPs provides a series of detailed measures to be followed when issuing a compulsory licence. For an explanation, *See* Alan Sykes, "Public Health and International Law: TRIPs, Pharmaceuticals, Developing Countries, and the Doha 'Solution,'" 3 *Chi. J. Int'l. L.* 47, 55 (2002).

[267] *See* Duncan Matthews, "WTO Decision on Implementation of Paragraph 6 of the Doha Declaration on the TRIPS Agreement and Public Health," 7 *J. Int'l Econ. L.* 79 (2004).

[268] TRIPs, Article 8(1).

[269] *See* Correa, "Public Health and Patent Legislation," *supra* note 190, at 1, 8-11. *See also*, Jiang, *supra* note 198, at 229.

suing a compulsory licence can prove to be a lengthy, complicated and frustrating process.

As a result, the private sector has, in many circumstances, "enjoyed global IPR protection without addressing global health issues."[270] Upon the establishment of the TRIPs regime, WTO members in the developing world have been awkward in balancing two laborious and incompatible tasks: "trying to obtain affordable medical treatment for their AIDS patients while simultaneously upgrading their patent system to provide strict patent protection for pharmaceuticals."[271]

The Doha Ministerial Conference (DMC), which was held in November 2002, did not adopt any new provisions to contribute to the current provisions of the TRIPs agreement that are already in place.[272] Nevertheless, it approved a constructive work programme in the form of two declarations,[273] one of which was the Declaration on the TRIPs Agreement and Public Health (DTPH).[274] The DTPH is a ministerial interpretation of TRIPs, which aims to clarify a number of unanswered issues left by the TRIPs Agreement and provides interpretive meaning to imprecise obligations of TRIPs Agreement.[275] Unlike certain other international fora, the nature of negotiations in the DTPH addresses cooperation rather than confrontation between developed and developing countries.[276] It reduces the issue to a dialogue as to means rather than ends. As such, it has the potential to play a more active role in future dispute resolutions under TRIPs.

Indeed, the DTPH has been recognised as a commendable example of how developing countries should be able to achieve positive results through trade negotiations with developing countries. The DTPH provides unambiguous support for a broad and flexible interpretation of TRIPs, such as strategies to level the playing field in existing IPR standards.[277] During the DTPH negotiation, a bargaining chip of the developing countries was levelled at the fact that TRIPs Agreement did not take measures to protect public health fully into ac-

---

[270] Burgiel & Schipper, *supra* note 258, at 6.

[271] *See* Jiang, *supra* note 198, at 238-9.

[272] Surya P. Subedi, "The Road from Doha: The Issues for the Development of the WTO and the Future of International Trade," 52 *Int'l & Comp. L. Quart.* 425 (2003).

[273] The Doha Ministerial Conference, the fourth WTO Ministerial Conference - the latest round of trade talks among WTO members - was held in Doha, Qatar on 9-14 November 2001. *See* for DMC, *available at* <http://www.wto.org/english/thewto_e/minist_e/min01_e/min01_14nov_e.htm>.

[274] The two declarations include the main declarations and the DTPH. *See* DTPH, *available at* <www.wto.org/english/thewto_e/minist_e/min01_e/mindecl_ trips_e.htm>.

[275] Cychosz, *supra* note 139, at 995.

[276] Subedi, *supra* note 272, at 426-8.

[277] "A Summary Report of the Conference on How Intellectual Property Rights Could Work Better for Developing Countries and Poor People," *supra* note 258, at 5.

count,[278] which "should be interpreted in a manner to provide flexibility," such as compulsory licensing. [279]

Compulsory licensing issues were brought on the agenda of the DMC and the DTPH "opened the door for compulsory licensing of patented pharmaceuticals." [280] In DTPH, members express their concern over "the gravity of the public health problems afflicting many developing and least-developed countries, especially those resulting from HIV/AIDS, tuberculosis, malaria and other epidemics." [281] The Declaration states:

[e]ach member has the right to grant compulsory licenses and the freedom to determine the grounds upon which such licenses are granted. Each member has the right to determine what constitutes a national emergency or other circumstances of extreme urgency.[282]

The most significant flexibility provided by the DTPH is the provision that outlines each member's determination.[283] Although DTPH cannot override the text and substance of the TRIPs Agreement,[284] it does allow members of WTO to clarify, on their own terms, [285] the grounds on which such a licence may be granted.[286]

In practice, although the government or its judiciary in developing countries may use their discretions to issue compulsory licences in cases of national emergency or extreme urgency, the eligible importing countries lacking domestic manufacturing capacity could not avail themselves of this flexibility mainly due to potential pressures from the interested parties.[287] It was not until the subsequent Decision on the Interpretation of Paragraph 6 of the Doha Dec-

---

[278] The Doha Declaration affirms that the TRIPs Agreement "does not and should not prevent members from taking measures to protect public health." *See* Doha Declaration *at* <http://www.who.int/medicines/areas/policy/doha_declaration/en/>.

[279] "A Summary Report of the Conference on How Intellectual Property Rights Could Work Better for Developing Countries and Poor People," *supra* note 258, at 5.

[280] Cychosz, *supra* note 139, at 995.

[281] *See* Correa *supra* note 190.

[282] *See* DTPH Article 5(b).

[283] *See* Jiang, *supra* note 198, at 235.

[284] Alan Sykes, "Public Health and International Law: TRIPs, Pharmaceuticals, Developing Countries, and the Doha 'Solution,'" 3 *Chi. J. Int'l L.* 47, 55 (2002).

[285] *See* DTPH Article 5(c).

[286] Cychosz, *supra* note 139, at 995.

[287] Judy Rein, "International Governance through Trade Agreements: Patent Protection for Essential Medicines," 21 *Nw J. Int'l. & Bus.* 389 (2001).

laration[288] reached by WTO Members on August 30, 2003 that paved way to improve access to essential medicines in developing countries.[289]

PUBLIC HEALTH EMERGENCY IN CHINA

In January 2006, an official statistics was released jointly by Chinese Ministry of Health, Joint United Nations Programme on HIV/AIDS (UNAIDS), and World Health Organisation (WHO).[290] This statistics estimated that, in 2005, 650,000 people were living with HIV in China, including about 75,000 AIDS patients; during 2005, there were around 70,000 new HIV infections and 25,000 AIDS deaths.[291] Chinese officials openly acknowledged that "China is facing a very serious epidemic". Although Chinese authorities predicted that China would meet its goal of keeping the number below 1.5 million by 2010, according to the estimates of UNAIDS, "China could have between 10 to 15 million HIV cases by the year of 2010."[292]

Upon the WTO accession, China has an obligation to abide by the various WTO agreements, including TRIPs Agreement, under which, China is obliged to have patent protection in place for pharmaceuticals.[293] While the compulsory licence should be available, it only remains valid over limited time with complicated application formalities.[294] China's HIV crisis and its WTO obliga-

---

[288] For a detailed introduction to this agreement, *see* "Implementation of Paragraph 6 of the Doha Declaration on the TRIPS Agreement and Public Health," Decision of the General Council of 30 August 2003, WT/L/540 and Corr.1, WTO GENERAL COUNCIL, September 1, 2003, *available at* <http://www.wto.org/English/tratop_e/trips_e/implem_pa ra6_e.htm>, last viewed September 6, 2006.

[289] *See* Harvey E. Bale, "Access to Essential Drugs in Poor Countries – Key Issues: the Industry Perspective," Workshop on Differential Pricing and Financing of Essential Drugs, World Health Organisation and World Trade Organisation, 8-11 April 2001, Norway, *available at* <http://www.wto.org/english/tratop_e/trips_e/hosbjor_ presentations_ e/06bale_e.doc>. Harvey E. Bale, "Drugs in Poor Countries – Key Issues," Director General, International Federation of Pharmaceutical Manufacturers Associations President, Pharmaceutical Security Institute, *available at* <http://www.ifpma.org>.

[290] *See* "2005 Update on the HIV/AIDS Epidemic and Response in China," *available at* <http://data.unaids.org/publications/ExternalDocuments/rp_2005chinaestimation_25jan 06_en.pdf>.

[291] *Ibid.*

[292] *See* "Current Overview of HIV/AIDS in China," *available at* <http://www.casy.org/overview.htm>.

[293] Under the TRIPs Agreement, all Members are committed to making patents available for pharmaceutical inventions in their countries. Article 27(1) of the TRIPs Agreement requires Members to make patent protection available to "any inventions, whether products or processes, in all fields of technology." Moreover, Article 70(8) makes explicit reference to patent protection for pharmaceutical products. *See* Article 27(1), Article 70(8).

[294] For example, Article 31 of TRIPs consists of a specified set of conditions, including, among other things, the need to grant compulsory licensing on a case-by-case-basis and

tion have contradicted each other and thus posed a significant policy dilemma for China.

New Development of TRIPs Amendment

On December 6, 2005, the WTO Members approved the proposed protocol to the TRIPs Agreement "making permanent a decision" on patents and public health originally adopted on August 30, 2003.[295] It is a landmark resolution that a core WTO agreement was amended in response to the concerns and suggestions of developing countries.[296] The WTO General Council has submitted the proposed amendment to the WTO Members for ratification. Once accepted and in force, this amendment will complete a process that has been undertaken since 2001 with the Doha Declaration.[297]

This amendment allows any WTO Member to gain access to essential pharmaceuticals made under compulsory licence for the purpose of supplying developing nations with no or insufficient manufacturing capacities in the pharmaceutical sector.[298] This new provision will be formally incorporated into the TRIPs Agreement and may take into force when two thirds of the WTO Members have ratified the amendment. In the meantime, the waiver decision remains active for each Member until the amendment becomes effective for that Member.[299]

Example of EU-China in the Area of Public Heath

EU CHINA CONSENSUS ON PUBLIC HEALTH ISSUES

In the area of public health, EU and China have marked a milestone in their comprehensive strategy to promote collaboration. Both sides have committed to implementing relevant provisions concerning HIV/AIDS set out in the Doha Declaration.[300] Given the global nature of the epidemic, both the EU and China have recognised the importance of increased cooperation to combat HIV/AIDS as well as other newly emerging infectious diseases, and on

---

the requirement of a prior request to the patent holder on reasonable commercial terms. *See* TRIPs Article 31.

[295] *See* "Members OK Amendment to Make Health Flexibility Permanent," WTO: 2005 Press Releases, Press/426, December 6, 2005.

[296] "The European Commission's Press Release," Brussels, April 27, 2006.

[297] *Ibid.*

[298] For full text of the amendment, *see* "TRIPs Amendment," IP/C/41, *available at* <http//www.wto.org/english/news_e/news05_e/trips_decision_e.doc>.

[299] *Ibid.*

[300] *See* "Joint Statement, 7th EU-China Summit, the Hague, 8 December 2004," Council of the European Union, Brussels, December 8, 2004, 15065/04 (Presse 337), Para 21, *available at* <http://ue.eu.int/ueDocs/cms_Data/docs/press Data/en/er/82998.pdf>.

strengthening the capability of global public health to meet such challenges.[301] Both the EU and China position recognise and emphasise the importance of the increasing availability of anti-retroviral drugs and the necessity of preventive measures, including development of vaccines and microbicides, harm reduction approaches and promotion of safer and responsible sexual behaviour.[302] As a positive response to the EU, China has adopted its newly revised "Law on Diseases Prevention and Control" covering non-discrimination against persons with infectious diseases, pathogeny carriers and persons with suspected infectious diseases as a concrete step to counter stigmatisation and judgmental approaches to persons at risk or infected.[303]

EU's Contribution towards Doha Agenda

In April 27, 2006, the European Commission adopted a proposal that European Member States accept EU ratification of an amendment to the WTO Agreement on Intellectual Property to allow developing countries to benefit from exported generic medicines.[304] WTO Members agreed on the amendment on December 6, 2005, just before the WTO Ministerial Conference which took place in Hong Kong on 13-18 December 2005. The EU played an important part in these negotiations concerning the amendment. This amendment completed a process that began at the Doha Ministerial Conference, and made permanent a provisional decision on compulsory licensing adopted by the WTO in 2003.[305] The acceptance of the amendment to the TRIPs Agreement, in addition to the new "Regulation Implementing the WTO Decision" will confirm the EU's commitment to the process aiming at facilitating access to medicines for poor countries.

EU-China Cooperation Bears Fruit

Combating the HIV/AIDS epidemic is common responsibilities incumbent on the governments of both the EU and China. As the seventh EU-China Joint Statement has acknowledged, both EU and China recognise the importance of increased cooperation to curb HIV/AIDS and other emerging infectious diseases, and appreciate the efforts that have been made over the years by both sides in strengthening the capability of global public health.[306] In implementing the Doha Agenda, the HIV/AIDS Programme of the Global Fund recently

---

[301] *Ibid.*

[302] *Ibid.*

[303] *Ibid.*

[304] The European Commission's Press Release, Brussels, April 27, 2006.

[305] "Commission Welcomes Changes to EU law to Allow Export of Patented Medicine to Countries in Need," European Commission's Press Release, P/06/550, Brussels, April 28, 2006.

[306] "Joint Statement," *supra* note 116, Article 21.

commenced in China, with the EU being a major financial contributor as a fruitful result of the EU-China Summit.[307]

5.4.3 Fair Use of Copyright: Where is the Bottom Line?

Of all forms of IPR, copyright has been viewed as "the most positive, and as critical to the development of local culture,"[308] "and has emerged as one of the most important means of regulating the international flow of ideas and knowledge based products."[309] However, the actual positions that developed and developing countries have within the global copyright system are divergent. The United States is the world's dominant producer of copyright-protected products,[310] and industrialised countries are the main beneficiaries of the copyrights.[311] By contrast, developing and less-developed countries are primarily consumers of copyrighted works.[312] As it suggests in the UNESCO Information Report, "copyright ownership is largely in the possession of the major copyright corporations."[313] By maintaining monopoly status, the rights-holders "place low per capita income countries and smaller economies at a significant disadvantage."[314] Various solutions are being considered in an effort to remedy this imbalance, among which the fair use of copyright may be a plausible and feasible option.

"Fair Use" Doctrine in the Realm of International Law

"Fair use", as a doctrine of national law, particularly the U.S. Copyright Law,[315] is based upon the fact that "every book in literature, science and art, borrows and must necessarily borrow, and use much which was well known before", and it alleviates the "inherent tension in the need to simultaneously protect copyrighted material and to allow others to build upon it."[316] As a

---

[307] *Ibid.*

[308] Burgiel & Schipper, *supra* note 258, at 4.

[309] "World Information Report 1997/98," UNESCO, Paris (1998), at 320.

[310] Alan Story, "Burn Berne: Why the Leading International Copyright. Convention Must be Repealed," 40 *Univ. Houston L. Rev.* (2003), at 766 (concluding that "the United States is the main producer, seller, and beneficiary of intellectual property exports").

[311] *Ibid*, at 769.

[312] *Ibid.*

[313] UNESCO World Information Report, *supra* note 309.

[314] *Ibid.*

[315] "Fair use" was a unique common law doctrine until it was incorporated into the Copyright Act of 1976. This doctrine exists as "fair dealing" in some other common countries such as the United Kingdom and Australia.

[316] *Luther R. Campbell v. Acuff-Rose Music, Inc.*, 510 U.S. 569, 575, 29 U.S.P.Q.2d (BNA) 1961, 1964 (1994); Acuff-Rose, 510 U.S. at 575, 29 U.S.P.Q.2d at 1964 (quot-

common exception of the exclusive right granted by copyright law, fair use attempts to balance the rights of copyright owners and society's interests as a whole.

"Fair use" in the realm of international law still lacks sufficient legitimacy and calls for justification. As the most influential agreement in international intellectual property law, TRIPs Agreement is playing a role that is unique in the international law arena. TRIPs on the one hand reinforces the protection of copyright and the neighbouring rights; on the other hand, however, the copyright provisions do not go as far as was envisaged by other provisions such as that of patents, in light of developing new international standards of protection which are considered to be beneficial for developing countries.[317] In this sense, developing countries have found themselves in an embarrassing position of being unable to find a legal basis to challenge the defective copyright regime. Some commentators attempted to link the claim of developing countries to theory of fair use, but the opponents argued that, while it stands as a common law doctrine, the doctrine of fair use is not justified in international law.[318]

However, as Ruth Okedji has suggested, "[a]lthough the status of fair use under current international law is at best, uncertain," international law should nevertheless specify such a standard.[319] The TRIPs Agreement represents a significant compromise among the copyright laws of many countries and reflects the treatment of exceptions to copyright owners set out in the Berne Convention. In practice, TRIPs permits an individual member to exercise its discretions and make its own determinations as to the adaptability of TRIPs to the local circumstances.[320] One possible option could be to adopt the doctrine of fair use standard internationally, but this process may take time and "it will not happen without pressure from international community through TRIPs."[321]

Copying and Copyright in Historic Spectrum

Retrospectively, it is generally agreeable that, a flexible copyright policy is more suitable "in almost all the countries at their immature development stage." The case at point may be the United States. As Barbara Ringer, the former Register of Copyrights in the United States and one of the principal ar-

---

ing Filippo M. Cinotti, "Fair Use" of Comparative Advertising under the 1995 Federal Dilution Act, *37 IDEA* 149 (1996)).

[317] Carlos M. Correa, *supra* note 190, at 6.

[318] Eric Allen Engle, "When is Fair Use Fair?: A Comparison of E.U. and U.S. Intellectual Property Law," 15 *Transnat'l Law.* 222 (2002).

[319] Ruth Okedji, "Towards an International Fair Use Doctrine," 39 *Colum J. Trans. L.*, 87-9 (2000).

[320] *Ibid*, at 142.

[321] Engle, *supra* note 318, at 222-3.

chitects of the Copyright Act of 1976,[322] commented four decades ago, "[u]ntil the Second World War the United States had little reason to take pride in its international copyright relations; in fact, it had a great deal to be ashamed of. With few exceptions its role in international copyright was marked by intellectual short-sightedness, political isolationism, and narrow economic self-interest."[323]

As mentioned in the previous chapters, tolerant IPR national policies are almost inevitable at the early stages of economic development.[324] Indeed, as has been critically observed, "[t]he U.S. was long a net importer of literary and artistic works, especially from England, which implied that recognition of foreign copyrights would have led to a net deficit in international royalty payments."[325] In the period before the Declaration of Independence, individual American states embarked on the process of promotion and reorganisation of patent rights, but copyright protection was more or less neglected.[326] Shortly after independence, the domestic market was flooded with imported newspapers, periodicals and books, and "copyright laws were virtually nonexistent."[327] As has been remarked by Zorina Khan, "[d]espite the lobbying of numerous authors and celebrities on both sides of the Atlantic, the American copyright statutes did not allow for copyright protection of foreign works for fully one century."[328] As a result, American publishers and producers felt more than legitimate to pirate foreign literature, art and drama.[329] It was not until 1783 that the first legislation made its debut in Connecticut.[330] Even at that time, the piracy of foreign authors' works was still not regarded immoral.[331] As a result, in the period "between 1800 and 1860, almost half of the best-sellers in the U.S. were pirated, mostly from English novels."[332] It was surprisingly interesting that the U.S. was not interested in the formation of and the

---

[322] *See* official bibliography of Barbara Ringer from the U.S. Copyright Office, *available at* <http://www.copyright.gov/history/bios/ringer.pdf>.

[323] Barbara A. Ringer, *supra* note, "The Role of the United States in International Copyright – Past, Present, and Future," 56 *Geo. L.J.* (1968), at 1050, 1051.

[324] *See supra* § 4.1.3.

[325] B. Zorina Khan & Kenneth L. Sokoloff, "History Lessons: The Early Development of Intellectual Property Institutions in the United States," 15 (3) *J. Econ. Pers.* 237 (2001).

[326] *See* B. Zorina Khan, "Intellectual Property and Economic Development: Lessons from American and European History," Study Paper 1a, Commission on Intellectual Property Rights (2002), at 36, *available at* <www.iprcommission.org/papers/word/study_papers/sp1a_khan_study.doc>.

[327] Peter K. Yu, "The Copyright Divide," 25 *Cardozo L. Rev.* 337 (2003).

[328] Khan, "Intellectual Property and Economic Development", *supra* note 326, at 40.

[329] *Ibid.*

[330] In 1783, Connecticut became the first state to approve an "Act for the encouragement of literature and genius," followed shortly by Massachusetts and Maryland. *See* Yu, "The Copyright Divide," *supra* note 337, at 338.

[331] *Ibid*, at 341.

[332] *Ibid.*

participation in the international IPR regime until after the Second World War whilst the foundation stone of the system was laid by the end of the nineteenth century, implying that the American IPR system was established rather late, lagging largely behind its economic capacity.[333] Today, with its rapidly growing economic strength and technological sophistication, the U.S. has long since moved away from its notorious past and turned over a new leaf. Furthermore, it has converted "from the most notorious pirate to the most dreadful police."[334]

Interestingly, copyright law has, to some extent, represented the interests of the stakeholders. As Professor Jessica Litman points out, the most significant character of copyright laws throughout the twentieth century is that "it is for all of the lawyers who represent the current stakeholders to get together and hash out all of the details among themselves."[335] Over the centuries, international copyright debate has been marked by notion of "copyright rich" versus "copyright poor," and the "haves" versus "have-nots" in the copyright system.[336] The rampant copyright piracy that takes place world-wide can be viewed as a "battle between the stakeholders and nonstakeholders over the change and retention of the *status quo*."[337] The stakeholders would be ardent to maintain their accomplishment and competitiveness, while the nonstakeholders would be enthusiastic to expand their share and in an effort to become stakeholders.[338] However, until these nations developed into stakeholders or potential stakeholders, they may have less sufficient motivations to comply with copyright laws.[339] Based on this understanding, policymakers of the stakeholders are best advised to "help the nonstakeholders develop a stake in the system and understand how they can protect their products and receive royalties."[340] For example, they are expected to help the nonstakeholders gain benefits by developing their own software industry, as demonstrated by the Microsoft's successful strategy in promoting their market in China.[341]

In this context, it is reasonable and acceptable for developing economies to seek to develop solutions that "encourage use of digital technology and promote access to information while preserving the rights of copyright own-

---

[333] *Ibid*, at 421.

[334] *Ibid*, at 353.

[335] Jessica D. Litman, "Copyright, Compromise, and Legislative History," 72 *Cornell L. Rev.* (1987), at 857.

[336] Siva Vaidhyanathan, *Copyrights and Copywrongs: The Rise of Intellectual Property and How It Threatens Creativity*, NYU Press 105 (2001). *See* also, Yu, "The Copyright Divide," *supra* note 337, at 402.

[337] Yu, *ibid*, at 335, 403.

[338] *Ibid*, at 331.

[339] *Ibid*, at 335.

[340] *Ibid*, at 336.

[341] *Supra* § 2.1.3.

ers."[342] In other words, at the early stage of development, every effort should be made to reconcile the interests between private and public. In fact, many communities in the developing world have "more pressing concerns than copyright rules," such as poverty, illiteracy, unemployment, poorly resourced schools and libraries and so on. [343] Attention should be paid to contrast realities between developed, technologically proficient societies and less-developed, rural areas. Special attention should be given to the tension between meeting the public need and respecting commercial interests.[344] If no measures are to be taken, the increasing information gap will exacerbate the disparities in the digital realm.[345] As some scholars have suggested, temporary arrangements, such as appropriate exemptions in copyright regulations and affordable licensing, should be put in place so that the world economy can be developed in a more sustainable and integrated manor.[346] Only in this way can a "copyright poor" or nonstakeholder state be transformed to a "copyright rich" or stakeholder state within foreseeable future.

Open Access: An Inevitable Trend in a Digital Society?

Following the establishment of the TRIPs regime, two international conventions on copyright law, namely the Copyright Treaty and Treaty on Performances and Phonograms were adopted by member states of WIPO.[347] While the purpose of these conventions was to intensify copyright protection, various initiatives have been established on the basis of the concept of "open access".[348] These initiatives aim at making use of the digital technology in a manner that promotes and facilitates freedom of sharing.[349] Some initiatives, which include themes such as free software, open content, open access and open standards, may be implemented under an open and collaborative model of R&D.[350] Meanwhile, there has been an empirical study on a new copyright

---

[342] Burgiel & Schipper, *supra* note 258, at 4.
[343] *Ibid.*
[344] *Ibid.*
[345] *Ibid.*
[346] *Ibid.*
[347] *See* "WIPO Copyright Treaty (WCT) and WIPO Performances and Phonograms Treaty (WPPT)," WIPO Information Resources, *available at* <http://www.wipo.int/copyright/en/activities/wct_wppt/wct_wppt.htm>.
[348] *See*, Carlos M. Correa, "Recent International Developments in the Area of Intellectual Property Rights," at 6.
[349] *See, e.g.*, Tere Vaden, "Policy Options and Models for Bridging Digital Divides: Freedom, Sharing and Sustainability in the Global Network Society," *Global Challenges, of eDevelopment*, December 10, 2004.
[350] *See* Olli Hietanen, "Global Challenges of eDevelopment," From Digital Divided towards Empowerment and Sustainable Global Information Society, Seminar on Global Perspectives of Development Communication, University of Tampere, June 28, 2004, *available at* <http://www.uta.fi/jour/global/hietanen2.pdf>.

licensing model, demonstrating a new approach to using dual licensing for one product, especially on the legal and economic requirements of dual licensing.[351] More importantly, in the recent World Summit on the Information Society, concrete steps were taken to give substance to "the international common desire to build a people-centred, inclusive and development-oriented information society." [352]

Currently there is no separate legal mechanism for an open access data sharing.[353] While functioning as a non-profit and voluntary model, open access as a doctrine is grounded in the current legal framework of copyright law.[354]

Though controversial, as Correa has suggested, open access initiatives may be particularly appropriate in fields of academic research and software development.[355] As an alternative to the restricted access model, open access has gained a growing number of adherents in the software area and achieved understanding of many countries including the United States and the EU who are considering measures to encourage the public procurement of open-source software, such as the Linux operating system.[356] A recent feasibility study conducted by the Swedish Agency for Public Management shows that "open software in many cases are equivalent to – or better than – commercial products."[357]

In Europe, while the European Parliament has endorsed the IPR Enforcement Directive for the prohibition of the wide-spread copying practice, there has been a growing demand for diversity of licensing arrangement and, in practice, varieties of licences, which offer more flexibility than traditional copyright licences, have been available.[358] Among these, the launch of the

---

[351]   Mikko Välimäki, "Dual Licensing in Open Source Software Industry," published in Systemes d'Information et Management 1/2003, *available at* <http://opensource.mit.edu/papers/valimaki.pdf>, (last visited October 17, 2006).

[352]   *See* "Declaration of Principles and Plan of Action," Article 25, *available at* <http://unpan1.un.org/intradoc/groups/public/documents/UN/UNPAN014246.pdf>(stating that "the sharing and strengthening of global knowledge for development can be enhanced by removing barriers to equitable access to information for economic, social, political, health, cultural, educational, and scientific activities and by facilitating access to public domain information, including by universal design and the use of assistive technologies").

[353]   *Ibid*, at 7.

[354]   *Ibid*.

[355]   Correa, "Recent International Developments in the Area of Intellectual Property Rights," ICTSD-UNCTAD Dialogue, 2nd Bellagio Series on Development and Intellectual Property, September 18-21, 2003, at 6.

[356]   *Ibid*.

[357]   *See* "Cases of Official Recognition/Adoption of F/OSS," European's Information Society, *available at* <http://ec.europa.eu/information_society/activities/opensource/cases/index_en.htm>.

[358]   *See* "The Management of Copyright and Related Rights," Consultation response from Professor Ross Anderson, University of Cambridge, and Foundation for Information

Creative Commons, "a nonprofits organisation that offers artists, authors, publishers and musicians the option of creating and defining a flexible copyright for their creative works," is a promising achievement.[359]

More encouragingly, there have been a number of landmark copyright litigations endorsing the validity of the new forms of licence. In the Netherlands, the Creative Commons license was judged in courts and the validity of this alternative copyright license was upheld.[360] This decision was noteworthy because, as the first case about the Creative Commons license, it reinforces the principle that "the conditions of a Creative Commons license automatically apply to the content licensed under it, and bind users of such content even without expressly agreeing to, or having knowledge of, the conditions of the license."[361]

Bridging the Digital Divide: From Apple to Nokia and Ericsson

In order to facilitate the transformation of a state from "copyright poor" to "copyright rich", industries have an important role to play. A good illustration of this strategy is the Apple's iTunes, which has been regarded as "the driving force behind the digital music revolution."[362] In April 2003, Apple Computer unveiled its online music service, the iTunes Music Store, offering low-priced download from recording companies, which may possibly catch on as an alternative to the services that allow costumers to access to music for free.[363] In

---

Policy Research (2004), *available at* <http://europa.eu.int/comm/internal_market/copyright/docs/management/consultation-rightsmanagement/rossanderson_en.pdf>, last accessed April 19, 2006.

[359] *See* "Creative Commons" *at* <http://creativecommons.org/>.

[360] Adam Curry, a famous internet entrepreneur, sued Weekend, a Dutch gossip magazine, for copyright infringement after the magazine published family photos of Curry's daughter without his prior consent. These pictures were published under a specific noncommercial Creative Commons license. The photos also carried the notice that "this photo is public". Curry sued for both copyright and privacy infringements. Weekend defended itself, maintaining that it did not understand the reference to the Creative Commons license. The magazine also claimed there could be no damages, since the pictures on the website were publicly accessible. On March 6, 2006 the District Court of Amsterdam ruled in summary proceedings that the "Weekend" could not republish pictures as Weekend did not seek or obtain prior permission. For a more detailed introduction about the case and its judgment, *see* Mia Garlick, "Creative Commons Licenses Enforced in Dutch Court," March 16, 2006, *available at* <http://creativecommons.org/weblog/entry/5823>.

[361] Ingrid Marson, "Creative Commons Licence Upheld by Court," *ZDNet UK*, March 21, 2006, *available at* <http://news.zdnet.co.uk/0,39020330,39258529,00.htm>, last visited October 16, 2006.

[362] "Belgacom's Skynet Gives Up for iTunes," *Brussels Review*, January 30, 2006.

[363] Laurie J. Flynn, "Apple Offers Music Downloads with Unique Pricing," *N.Y. Times*, April 29, 2003, at C2 (mentioning that Apple Computer plans to offer individual songs for 0.99 dollar each and most albums for 9.99 dollar each).

January 2006, a major Belgian music retailer, Belgacom Skynet, announced a partnership with Apple's iTunes Music Store, further offering their customers 20 free iTunes downloads to promote the service.[364]

As reported by the media, iTune has undoubtedly offered "the first small glimmer of hope that Hollywood and the music industry may actually avert a digital Armageddon in which perfect copies of every artist's work become instantly obtainable online for free."[365] As Joseph Menn, author of *All the Rave: The Rise and Fall of Shawn Fanning's Napster*, commented, iTunes is so far "the best thing that's come along for consumers who would rather not steal."[366]

Another issue in light of fair use is attributed to open standards involving information technology.[367] Digital technology makes distribution of information more affordable so that people can make full use of the opportunities to access information available throughout the world.[368] One characterisation of the global network society requires the freedom to share the information on a reasonable scale.[369] In the EU, the growth of Nokia and Ericsson into global mobile phone giants is to some extent attributable to the early establishment of an open international standard in the Nordic Mobile Telephone.[370] This paved way for the companies to innovate and update the standard efficiency.[371] When the wider Global System for Mobile Communications (GSM) standard was created, the companies had obtained a significant advantage that enabled them to capture the market potential.[372]

The developments in freedom of sharing are of particular importance to developing countries such as China that would like to advance the information society and leapfrog right into the latest and best available technologies.[373] Today, almost all the major international electronics, including Siemens, HP, Nokia and Ericsson, have established their network capabilities in China.[374] Since electronics has been targeted as one of China's pillar industries, the

---

[364] *Ibid.*

[365] "Apple Tunes Out the Pirates," *Telegraph*, May 11, 2003.

[366] *Ibid.*

[367] Vaden, *supra* note 349.

[368] *See* Hietanen, *supra* note 350.

[369] *Ibid.*

[370] Petri Rouvinen and Pekka Ylä-Anttila, "Case Study, Little Finland's Transformation to a Wireless Giant," ETLA, The Research Institute of the Finnish Economy, in The Innovation Alliance: Succeeding in an Evolving Global Economy, August 24, 2004, Berkeley Roundtable on the International Economy (BRIE), at 92-6.

[371] *Ibid.*

[372] Vaden, *supra* note 349.

[373] *Ibid.*

[374] *See* "2006 Kuoguo Gongsi de Zgongguo Yumou: De Zhongguo Zhe De Shijie [The Multinational Companies Resolution in China in 2006: If You Get China You Get the Whole World]," *People's Daily*, March 2, 2006, *available at* <http://mnc.peo ple.com.cn/GB/54823/4156474.html>.

semiconductor market in China has been growing rapidly from 4 billion dollars in 1995 to 500 billion dollars by 2010.[375] With the comparative advantages in electronics, manufacturing and telecommunications, the EU is in a position to provide China for specialised skills and technical assistance. China's development potential has provided an immense space for EU-China cooperation in this area.

5.5 Conclusion

As two major trading bodies, EU and China share mutual benefits. Common interests call for a constructive cooperation; however, there exist institutional challenges for cooperation. The EU's dual regime in trade policy characterised by the lack of cohesiveness at the EU level has been cumbrous with regard to IPR protection, resulting in unnecessary and sometimes counterproductive effects.

Enforcement is much more compelling and convincing than statutes in demonstrating China's WTO commitments. The inefficient protection of IPR in China has led to various provisions on enforcement being included, among which the EU IPR Enforcement Directive is an important provision directly affecting EU-China trade relations. As the "logical sequences" of the directive, the Action Plan intends to be a contribution to the improvement of the situation in developing countries. Thus, through harmonising the enforcement procedures open to IPR holders out of the EU, this directive is expected to tackle infringement problems in China in a more efficient way. However, rather than attempting to impose unilateral solutions to the infringement concerned, policy makers of the EU are advised that, ultimately, any proposed solutions will only function if they are considered to be beneficial by the recipient country. It will therefore be necessary to have a flexible approach that takes into account different needs, level of development, and the main problems in terms of IPR of the countries in question.

Within current WTO regime, developing countries are advised to make full use of the ambiguities within TRIPs. From EU-China perspective, there exist specific areas of flexibility, such as permission of parallel import and the application of compulsory licensing. With regard to parallel import, it is of particular significance for China to obtain generic version of medicines through parallel imports, by which, China's imports from the EU may be subject to competition. With regard to compulsory licensing, the EU has adopted a proposal that European Member States accept EU ratification of an amendment to

---

[375] Michael Kelly and William Boulton, "Electronics Manufacturing in the Pacific Rim," WTEC Panel Report, World Technology Evaluation Centre, May 1997, *available at* <http://www.wtec.org/pdf/em.pdf>.

the WTO Agreement on intellectual property to allow developing countries to benefit from exported generic pharmaceuticals. This has made it probable for the EU and China to set a good example in implementing the Doha commitments.

Having identified institutional challenges and addressed outstanding legal issues between the EU and China, we will move on to the next chapter to assess special characteristics of the EU-China IPR debate and explore feasible approaches to mitigating the counterfeiting menace.

6 Harmony or Coercion? EU-China Trade Relations and IPR

It is widely acknowledged that international influences, treaty-based frameworks, and executive agreements have had a notable impact on the aggregate value of intangible assets worldwide and continue to provide more guarantees.[1] Thus, a cooperative international framework validates and embodies long-term relationship, which provides a stable and reliable platform for a country to enact domestic rule improvements and more effective enforcement of those rules.[2] The important aspect is how to negotiate in good faith and facilitate the attainment of consensus that is mutually acceptable and beneficial for the participating parties.

Based on the understanding that the participation in the global trading system contributes to domestic socio-economic development, China's political leaders have demonstrated a notable desire to involve China in the international rule-making process. To this end, China has expanded considerable effort in building on worldwide cooperation, among which, EU-China relations has been an important priority.[3] The political dialogue mechanism established between the two sides has played a positive role in enhancing mutual understanding and trust, and expanding common ground and cooperation.[4] The contentions between EU and China are based both on the legal framework to provide operational regulations and heightened transparency, and, probably more practical and meaningful, on cultural adaptations.[5]

The year of 2007 witnessed the fifteenth anniversary of official relations between the EU and China. Within EU-China relationship, while the bilateral trade has been growing over the years, the enormous challenge for both sides is that what has been agreed on paper, apparently beneficial in theory, is applied in practice. Coincidentally, the effectiveness of this solution is due to the

---

[1] Robert Bejesky, "Investing in the Dragon: Managing the Patent versus Trade Secret Protection Decision for the Multinational Corporation in China," 11 *Tulsa J. Comp. & Int'l L.* (2004), at 446.

[2] *Ibid.*

[3] Zhengde Huo, "On China-EU Strategic Relationship," *International Studies*, China Institute of International Studies, 2005(2), at 1-17.

[4] "Joint Statement of the 10th China-EU Summit, Beijing," November 28, 2007, *available at* <http://ec.europa.eu/external_relations/china/summit_1107/joint_statement.pd>.

[5] Huo, *supra* note 3, at 1-17.

philosophic culture of Confucianism – "living in harmony". It is possible for the EU and China, as would be expected, to set an example for the world regarding the implementation and enforcement of IPR with an approach that recognises that "there are bound to be short-term frustrations and difficulties but that aims to build confidence in the system."[6]

Peace and development are main themes of the new Millennium. In the international arena, policymakers are seeking to build a sustainable system of relations which are based on the balance-of-power rather than the balance-of-interests, making it possible for the establishment of more flexible cooperative mechanisms. In this connection, this chapter aims to assess IPR debate between the EU and China and offer suggested solutions. It focuses, amongst other things, on the need for China's government to interact with the EU and take constructive steps towards strengthening its IPR mechanism. It also identifies the need for EU policymakers to tailor IPR protection to local circumstances, and thus provide an analytical framework on which EU-China cooperation is based.

6.1 Modalities of Trade Relations

Over the past two decades or so, EU-China bilateral trade has undergone substantial transformation and remarkable growth, which have, in part, been in response to the increasing economic interdependence of the two parties.[7] As far as the EU is concerned, China's exponential growth represents tremendous economic opportunities for the European companies, despite the so-called "China threat" or "China collapse" theory.[8]

Historically, there was the shadow of "China threat" theory in the well-known Napoleon saying of "awakened lion", and the hostile "yellow peril theory"[9] prevalent in Europe in the nineteenth century.[10] However, the current

---

[6]   *See* Speech by Pascal Lamy, European Commissioner for Trade, to the China Europe International Business School, Shanghai, China, December 3, 2001, *available at* <http://www.delchn.cec.eu.int/en/eu_china_wto/wto1.htm> (last visited October 6, 2004).

[7]   *See* Oliver Lembcke, "China's Economic Integration in the WTO: A Test for the Political Integration of the European Union?" Harvard China Review 4th Annual Conference (2001).

[8]   Zhengde Huo, *supra* note 3, at 1-17.

[9]   David E. Mungello, *The Great Encounter of China and the West, 1500-1800,* 125 (2005) (mentioning that Chinese and Japanese were viewed as "yellow peril" in hostile racial terms by the West in the late 1880s).

[10]   *See* "China: Is It a Threat, or an Opportunity?" Interview with Prof. Joseph S. Nye, President of the Kennedy Government School of Harvard University; Qu Xing: Vice-President of the China Foreign Affairs College; Minxin Pei, Director of the China Programme at the Carnegie Endowment for International Peace; David M. Finkelstein, Di-

debate as to whether the so-called "China threat" does exist was, to a large extent, triggered by two articles: Richard Bernstein and Ross Munro's *The Coming Conflict with China* and Robert Ross's *Beijing as a Conservative Power*. [11] After the dawn of the new century, some Western policymakers and media vied with each other to pursue explanatory evidence for the emergence of the "China Collapse" Theory. [12]

While some European commentators support this theory of "China threat" or "China collapse",[13] many Europeans see this theory as an American perception.[14] From the context of national policy, while the United Kingdom has seemingly divergent views on the rise of China, Paris and Berlin believe that a modern China is not a threat to the world.[15] As China scholar Zhengde Huo has noted, Europeans tend to believe that "the momentum of China's growth is irresistible."[16] As the European Commission has officially acknowledged, during China's difficult process of transition, the exchange of experience and information between the EU and China helped facilitate China's efforts to improve the efficiency of its systemic reform, while increasing a European understanding of the modern Chinese economy.[17] As far as China is concerned, the EU's model with its tolerance, diversity, multiculturalism and sustainable

---

rector of Project Asia, the Asian Security Studies Centre at US-based Centre for Naval Analyses; Academician M. L. Titarenko, Director of the Far East Research Institute of the Russian Academy of Sciences. *People's Daily Online*, August 23, 2005, *available at* <http://english.people.com.cn/200508/23/eng20050823204164.html>.

[11] *See e.g.*, Richard Bernstein and Ross Munro, *The Coming Conflict with China* (1997); *see* also Robert Ross, "Beijing as a Conservative Power," 76 *Foreign Affairs* 33-44 (1997). For an official response towards this claim, *see* Xiaobiao Liu, "From Concocting 'Theory of Threat' to Dishing up 'Theory of Collapse,'" *People's Daily* June 11, 2002, at 3. *See* also "China: Is it a Threat, or an Opportunity?" *People's Daily Online*, August 23, 2005, *available at* <http://english.people.com.cn/200508/23/eng20050 823_204 164.html>.

[12] *See* Xiaobiao Liu, "From Concocting 'Theory of Threat' to Dishing up 'Theory of Collapse,'" *People's Daily*, June 11, 2002, at 3. *See* also "China: Is it a Threat, or an Opportunity?" *ibid.*

[13] For "China threat," *see, generally*, M. Weidenbaum, M. and S. Hughes, *The Bamboo Network: How Expatriate Chinese Entrepreneurs Are Creating a New Economic Superpower in Asia*, New York: The Free Press 185, 186-95 (1996); for "China Collapse," *see, e.g.*, Gordon G. Chang, *The Coming Collapse of China*, Random House (2001).

[14] For many Europeans, "China's 'non-rise' could pose a greater threat [to global affairs], as sustainable and smooth economic development would be beneficial to Europe. *See* "EU-China Relations," *Events Reports*, European Policy Centre July 25, 2005, European Policy Centre, *available at* <http://www.epc.eu>(follow "Events Reports" hyperlink). *See* also, Huo, *supra* note 3, at 1-17.

[15] Alfredo Pastor and David Gosset, "the EU-China Relationship: A Key to the 21st Century Order," *ARI* 142/2005.

[16] Huo, *supra* note 3, at 1-17.

[17] *See* "A Long Term Policy for China-Europe Relations," Communication of the Commission, COM (1995)/279/final.

development embodied in its integration is more suitable for the future world than the American model.[18] The EU's rational attitude and flexible approach has provided a cornerstone for the further bilateral cooperation between the EU and China. As Javier Solana, Chief of the EU Foreign Affairs and Security, has commented, China and the EU, as two rising forces, are becoming "strategic partners" [19] and "have potential to become the most active factor in the international relations."[20]

6.1.1 Theoretical Dimensions

One popular theory amongst international relations scholars is the balance-of-power theory, which is one of the major concepts in the theory of realism.[21] Premised on the bipolar and anarchic nature of the international relations, this theory maintains that a state has to choose to engage in either balancing or bandwagoning, through other unilateral initiatives or collective actions, to protect themselves against the aggression of or the threats from other states.[22] In the point of view of Confucius, the balance-of-power approach seeks "superficial assimilation" by force without "harmony." Since the sixteenth century, balance-of-power theories have brought about profound impacts on international relations;[23] however, with end of the Cold War and the increasing prominence of international institutions, scholars and observers have argued that "the balance-of-power theory is [gradually] losing its relevance."[24] In recent years, scholars and policymakers, such as Robert O. Keohane and Joseph S. Nye, have constantly emphasised the need to "replace the balance-of-power theory with a balance-of-interests theory,"[25] asserting that, "in order to govern situations of complex interdependence successfully international regimes must be congruent with the interests of powerfully placed domestic groups within major states, as well as with the structure of power among states."[26]

In contrast with the balance-of-power approach which is confrontational to international relations, the balance-of-interests approach is more conciliatory

---

[18]   Huo, *supra* note 3, at 1.

[19]   "EU and China, Strategic Partners with Global Objectives: Interview, with Javier Solana, Chief of The EU Foreign Affairs and Security," *People's Daily*, March 17, 2004.

[20]   *Ibid*, at 2.

[21]   Mark Brawley, "The Political Economy of Balance of Power Theory," in T.V. Paul, Jim Wirtz, and Michel Fortmann (eds), *Balance of Power: Theory and Practice in the 21st Century*, Stanford University Press (2004), at 66-99.

[22]   *See, generally,* Hans J. Morgenthau and Kenneth W. Thompson, *Politics among Nations: The Struggle for Power and Peace* (1985), at 4-23.

[23]   Brawley, *supra* note 21.

[24]   *Ibid*.

[25]   *See, e.g.,* Robert O. Keohane and Joseph S. Nye, *Power and Interdependence* 197 (2001).

[26]   *Ibid*.

and harmonious.[27] According to Schweller's "balance-of-interests" theory, the most important determinant of alignment decisions is the compatibility of political goals" rather than imbalances of power or threat;[28] thus, the underlying rationale of the balance-of-interests theory is the reciprocal adaptation between two parties.[29] This shift in focus from balance-of-power to the balance-of-interests reflects the "growing popularity of international regimes, which are determined primarily by interests rather than the distribution of power."[30]

In light of the North-South disparity over economic strength and technological sophistication, attempts to bridge the divide have taken place through a variety of international sources such as the United Nations, the Organisation for Economic Cooperation and Development, the G8, and the EU.[31] A most significant development through these sources was the G8 Summit at Kyushu-Okinawa in 2000,[32] which was seen as "the result of a unique international collaboration."[33] With a view to bridging the "digital divide" reflecting the increased economic disparity, the Kyushu-Okinawa Summit adopted the Charter on the Global Information Society and agreed to establish a Digital Opportunity Task-force (DOT).[34] The DOT aimed to bridge the "digital divide" which was "threatening to exacerbate the existing social and economic inequalities between countries and communities,"[35] particularly between the developed and developing world. In light of this, some scholars are calling for a balance-of-development approach in order to reconcile the economic tensions of developed and developing states, taking into account the affordability, sustainability, and other special needs of developing and less developed countries.[36]

---

27 *See* Peter Yu, "Toward a Nonzero-sum Approach to Resolving Global Intellectual Property Disputes: What We Can Learn from Mediators, Business Strategists, and International Relations Theorists," 70 *U. Cin. L. Rev.* 605 (2002).

28 Randall L. Schweller, "Bandwagoning for Profit: Bringing the Revisionist State Back," 19 *International Security* 72, 88 (1994).

29 *Ibid*, at 106. *See* also, Yu, "Toward a Nonzero-sum Approach," *supra* note 27, at 605.

30 Yu, *ibid.*

31 Abdul Paliwala "Digital Divide Globalisation and Legal Regulation," 6 *UTS L. Rev.* (2004).

32 *Ibid.*

33 *See* "Digital Opportunities for All: Meeting the Challenge, Report of the Digital Opportunity Task Force (DOT Force) Including a Proposal for a Genoa Plan of Action," May 11, 2001, *available at* <www.g7.utoronto.ca/summit/2001genoa/dotforce1.html>, last viewed March 23, 2007.

34 For detailed text of the document, *see*, "Okinawa Charter on Global Information Society," Okinawa, July 22, 2000, *available at* <http://www.g7.utoronto.ca/summit/2000okinawa/gis.htm>, last visited August 26, 2006.

35 "Digital Opportunities for All: Meeting the Challenge," *supra* note 33.

36 Salah Hannachi, "Kyushu-Okinawa Summit from Balance of Power to Balance of Development," paper for the 2000 G8 Pre-Summit Public Policy Conference, The Kyushu-Okinawa Summit: A G8-Developing Country Dialogue, July 17, 2000, United Nations University, Tokyo.

In a legal context, the WTO and TRIPs Agreement provide a number of principles and provisions that enable countries to focus on sustainable development and pursue a cooperative approach to resolving issues of the North-South disparity.[37] Article 67 of the Agreement requires developed countries to provide "technical and financial cooperation" to developing and less-developed countries in an effort to "facilitate the implementation" of the TRIPs Agreement.[38] According to this article, assistance should be provided "on request and on mutually agreed terms and conditions."[39] The aim of the cooperation is to provide "assistance in the preparation of laws and regulations on the protection and enforcement of intellectual property rights as well as on the prevention of their abuse, and [...] support regarding the establishment or reinforcement of domestic offices and agencies relevant to these matters, including the training of personnel."[40] These principles and provisions, in a more concrete perspective, provide the legal basis for EU-China cooperation involving IPR protection.

6.1.2 Overview of Trade Relations

Negotiations Retrospection

The EU and China maintained a healthy trade relationship until the Tiananmen Square pro-democracy demonstrations in 1989, resulting in political and economic sanctions being imposed by Western countries against Chinese government.[41] Trade relationship was recovered gradually since early 1990s,[42] when China's frosty relations with the outside world began to thaw out. Since then, the EU and China have sustained an exceptionally high rate of growth in bilateral trade. According to the "long term strategy" of the European Commission towards China, since 1992, EU-China trade negotiations have been framed through the pursuance of the following three interrelated objectives: (i) promoting China's economic and trade reforms, (ii) facilitating China into the multilateral trade system, and (iii) achieving better market access for European goods and services, and the bilateral relationship was institutionalised in 1993

---

[37]   Gary W. Smith, "Intellectual Property Rights, Developing Countries, and Trips: An Overview of Issues for Consideration during the Millennium Round of Multilateral Trade Negotiations," 2 (6) *J. World Intel. Prop.* 969-975 (1999). *See also* Peter Yu, "Toward a Nonzero-sum Approach," *supra* note 27, at 641.

[38]   Article 67, TRIPs.

[39]   *Ibid.*

[40]   *Ibid.*

[41]   Li Wang, "Big Events in EU-China Relations," *China Info Network*, April 29, 2004, *available at* <http://www.china.org.cn/chinese/zhuanti/wjbfo/555953.htm>, last visited June 7, 2005.

[42]   *Ibid.*

by an Economic Trade Working Group.[43] In 1994, the EU adopted its Communication to the Council and the European Parliament relating to the revision and the updating of the principles to be followed in the elaboration of the new scheme to be applied for the period from1995 to 2004,[44] and at the same time, "an ambitious new framework for Bilateral Political Dialogue" was established to "encourage Chinese participation in global affairs in the interests of the two parties."[45] In the same year, a sectoral meeting on IPR was initiated. [46] In 1995 and 1996, the EU passed "A Long Term Policy for China-Europe Relations" and "New Strategy towards China," calling for more importance attached to the role and influence of China and a strategy of "constructive engagement" so as to continue the dialogues and strengthen the bilateral cooperation between the two parties.[47] Symbolically, the landmark 1998 "Building a Comprehensive Partnership with China"[48] enabled China to reach same dialogue relevance with the United States, Russia, and Japan.[49]

In 2001, the "EU Strategy towards China: Implementation of the 1998 Communication and Future Steps for a More Effective EU Policy"[50] and the "Europe and Asia: A Strategic Framework for Enhanced Partnerships,"[51] further highlighted the trade relations between the EU and China. These two documents reflected increasing desire and ability of the EU to solidify and improve its political ties with China and promote bilateral economic, scientific and technical cooperation.

China's WTO entry instills new vigor into the bilateral trade ties and provides coherent institutional framework and legal mechanism for promoting reciprocal cooperation between the two sides.[52] The most straightforward evidence for this improvement lies in the impressive figures for bilateral trade over the last years (see Table 3 below). Due to the mutual efforts made by the two sides, the total two-way trade has increased more than forty-fold since

---

[43]   "A Long Term Policy for China-Europe Relations," COM (1995)/279/final, at 17.

[44]   *See* "An introduction to the Asia–Europe Meeting (ASEM)," European Commission, ASEM 4, Copenhagen, September 22-24, 2002, at 5.

[45]   "Opinion of the Economic and Social Committee on 'Relations between the European Union and China,'" *Official Journal C* 158, 26/05/1997, at 42.

[46]   *See* "Review of China-EU Political Relations," *available at* <http://www.chinese-embassy.org.uk/eng/wjzc/t27065.htm>.

[47]   "A Long Term Policy for China-Europe Relations," *supra* note 17.

[48]   "Building a Comprehensive Partnership with China," COM (1998) 181 final.

[49]   Franco Algieri, "EU Economic Relations with China: An Institutionalist Perspective," 169 *China Quart.* 76 (2002).

[50]   *See* "EU Strategy towards China: Implementation of the 1998 Communication and Future Steps for a More Effective EU Policy," Commission of the European Union, Brussels, 15.5.2001, COM (2001) 265 final.

[51]   "Europe and Asia: A Strategic Framework for Enhanced Partnerships," Commission of the European Union, Brussels, 4.9.2001, COM (2001) 469 final.

[52]   Huo, *supra* note 3, at 3-7.

1978, and risen to over 176 billion euros by December 2004.[53] In 2004, EU-China trade grew more rapidly by twenty-three percent,[54] the enlarged EU became China's biggest trading partner and, according to China's statistics, China became EU's second biggest trading partner, roughly on the same level as the U.S., behind Japan.[55] Between 2000 and 2006, the enlarged EU trade in goods with China grew by more than 150 percent, with exports increasing from 26 billion to 64 billion euros and imports from 75 to 195 billion euros.[56] Moreover, China aims to work with the EU to achieve the goal of becoming each other's largest trade and investment partners.[57] To this end, China has set bilateral trade volume target 190 billion euros by 2013 and 267 billion euros by 2020.[58]

Table 3 EU-China Trade Statistics (€bn)

	2006	Yearly Change	2005	Yearly Change	2004	Yearly Change
Total	€255.13	+21%	€210.13	+20%	€175.65	+22%
EU imports	€191.77	+21%	€158.49	+24%	€127.46	+21%
EU exports	€63.36	+23%	€51.65	+7%	€48.19	+17%
Balance	€128.40	+21%	€106.08	+34%	€79.27	+25%

Source: EUROSTAT, at <http://ec.europa.eu/eurostat>

Strategic Partners

China's gradual economic and institutional transition over the past decades, in particular upon the WTO accession, has become one of the most important driving forces for the comprehensive cooperation between the EU and China. With the handover of Hong Kong in 1997 and Macau in 1999, there has been no more substantial divergence of opinion from both sides.[59] At "Commission Policy Paper for Transmission to the Council and the European Parliament, a Maturing Partnership – Shared Interests and Challenges in EU-China Rela-

---

[53] *See* "Bilateral Trade Relations/China," *available at* <http://europa.eu.int/comm/trade/issues/bilateral/countries/china/index_en.htm>.

[54] *See* "European Business in China Position Paper 2005," European Union Chamber of Commerce in China (2005).

[55] *Ibid.*

[56] "The EU-China Trade in Facts and Figures," EU External Trade, November 23, 2007, *at* <http://trade.ec.europa.eu/doclib/docs/2007/november/tradoc_136870.pdf>.

[57] "China, EU Establish Trade Policy Dialogue Mechanism," *China MOFCOM*, October 9, 2003, *available at* <http://weijianguo2.mofcom.gov.cn/aarticle/activity/200412/20041 200008339.html>.

[58] China pushes for bilateral trade volume to reach 200 billion U.S. dollars by 2013 and 280 billion U.S. dollars by 2020. *See, Xinhua News Agency*, October 31, 2003.

[59] David Gosset, "The Making of a China-EU World," *Asia Times*, July 20, 2005.

tions," EU-China relations were described as "dynamic growth."[60] The European Security Strategy of June 2003 has reinforced the EU's Common Foreign and Security Policy, and perceived the status of China as one of the EU's major strategic partners.[61] As the Commission Policy Paper has explicitly acknowledged, "it is in the clear interest of the EU and China to work as strategic partners on the international scene."[62]

Since the beginning of the new century, China has become increasingly involved in broad fields of world affairs, especially in multilateral fora, and is rapidly emerging as one of the major players in the multipolar global arena, along with the EU.[63] The so-called new "Fourth Generation leadership,"[64] which took office in 2003, has taken the reins in Beijing and, after certain degree of tactical adjustment to its foreign policy, asserted "[to] engage the EU at the highest level."[65] Interestingly, unlike his predecessor, Jiang Zemin, who was criticised for his pro-American tendency in the Chinese political context, the new national leader Hu Jintao attempted to cultivate a sense of credibility to France, Germany and other European countries.[66]

China's preference for a more harmonious EU-China relationship was mirrored in the China's EU Public Policy Paper issued in October 2003.[67] Since this document was coincidently released shortly ahead of the sixth EU-China Summit, some commentators would tend to argue that this document was virtually a symbolic gift for the EU from the Chinese government in order to warm up the negotiation atmosphere of the EU-China Summit. However, the fact that a political dialogue mechanism has since then established and en-

---

[60] *See* "A Maturing Partnership – Shared Interests and Challenges in EU-China Relations," Commission Policy Paper for Transmission to the Council and the European Parliament, Commission of the European Communities, Brussels, 10/09/03, COM (2003) 533 finial. Negotiations on a more comprehensive partnership and cooperation agreement are currently underway. In January 2007, the European Commissioner Ferrero-Waldner visited Beijing for the official launch of the negotiations on a reframed comprehensive partnership and enhanced cooperation. *See* "EU-China Relations: A Timeline," *China Daily*, March 17, 2008, at 6.

[61] *See* "A Secure Europe in a Better World," *European Security Strategy*, Brussels, December 12, 2003.

[62] Commission Policy Paper 10/09/03, COM (2003) 533 finial, *supra* note 60.

[63] *Ibid.*

[64] The seemingly peaceful transformation of national power from the "Third Generation" leader Jiang Zemin to the "Fourth Generation" leader Hu Jintang in China was finalised and Mr. Hu has become the indisputable top leader of the party, state and military in such a huge country with more than 1.3 billion populations. For a brief introduction of the leadership transferring in China, *see* John Cherian, "Leadership Change in China," 20(7) *Frontline* (2003).

[65] *See* "China's EU Policy Paper (2003)," *available at* <http://www.fmprc.gov.cn/eng/wjb/zzjg/xos/dqzzywt/t27708.htm>, last visited February 8, 2007.

[66] Joseph Kahn, "In Candor from China, Efforts to Ease Anxiety," *The New York Times*, April 17, 2006.

[67] *See* "China's EU Policy Paper (2003)," *supra* note 65.

dorsed by the Chinese government was in itself a sign of the enhanced mutual understanding and trust and the expanded common ground for comprehensive cooperation.

At the EU side, facilitating China's transition to an open and plural society based upon the "market orientation" and "rule of law" "remains an essential element of EU policy" towards EU-China trade relations.[68] This is especially pronounced "when China is engaged substantially in its social-economic reforms, whose implementation requires the maintenance of societal stability."[69] Despite the political instability, the irrevocable process of the transition has started and, as the European Commission has observed, "China's accession to the WTO symbolises the crowning point of its improvement."[70] Having assessed progress and future prospects of the EU-China relations, in October 2006, the European Commission reframed its strategy towards China in the communication "EU-China: Closer Partners, Growing Responsibilities."[71] This communication signals the EU's growing commitment to further intensifying its comprehensive engagement with China.[72]

In this context, the EU and China have an "ever-greater interest" to cooperate as strategic partners" in broad fields of bilateral and multilateral affairs.[73] The mutual interests of the two sides converge on numerous international governance issues, including the importance attached to the role of the UN and the WTO, where both EU and China have much to gain from furthering international peace and trade liberalisation.[74]

6.1.3 Pending Challenges

Despite outstanding figures as proof of EU-China bilateral trade relationship bearing fruit, some concerns and dilemmas still remain unresolved. On the one hand, China envisages a higher level of expectation towards EU investment in China. EU companies invested heavily from 2000 to 2004 in China with the actual FDI of around 4.2 billion dollars on average, bringing stocks of EU FDI to over thirty-five billion dollars.[75] While substantial, compared with its annual outward investment of three hundred billion dollars, this constitutes only 1.4

---

[68]   "A Maturing Partnership," *supra* note 60.

[69]   *Ibid.*

[70]   *See* "European Commission – External Trade – Trade Issues with China," *available at* <http://ec.europa.eu/trade/issues/bilateral/countries/china/index_en.htm>.

[71]   "The EU's Relations with China, External Relations, European Commission," *available at* <http://ec.europa.eu/external_relations/china/intro/index.htm>. For full text of the document, *see* "EU-China: Closer Partners, Growing Responsibilities," Brussels, 24.10.2006 COM (2006) 631 final.

[72]   *Ibid.*

[73]   "A Maturing Partnership," *supra* note 60.

[74]   *Ibid.*

[75]   *See* "Nations Hail Sino-European Trade," *People's Daily*, December 15, 2004.

percent of its total investment, indicating a great investment potential.[76] On the other hand, the EU is not totally satisfied with the *status quo* and expects a great deal from China.[77] As a consequence, some companies have lobbied European authorities to address their concerns about Chinese IPR policies which are thought to be inconsistent with international practice.[78]

For example, in the officially published "European Business in China 2005 Position Paper," concerns have been highlighted about technical standards for patent.[79] As the Position Paper claims, in recent years an increasing number of European high-tech companies signed deals for joint ventures with their Chinese trade partners and provided Chinese manufacturers with license terms that are different from the standard international terms;[80] however, Chinese standards' organisations in the high-tech area have a policy requiring mandatory patent pool participation, unreasonable disclosure, and compulsory licensing.[81] These companies complained that Chinese officials frequently prohibit domestic Chinese companies from negotiating royalties by using the key technology in so-called "essential patents" that ensure interoperability of products such as TVs, telecom equipment, and CDs.[82] As far as European companies are concerned, these domestic companies avoid the reasonable payment of royalties thereby enabling them to compete unfairly with their foreign competitors who perform R&D or pay the royalties.[83] They believe that this problem has become far more severe since domestic companies in China have started to export these categories of products in large quantities to the EU at disproportionately lower prices.[84]

By contrast, opinions of Chinese entrepreneurs and specialists differ sharply from that of their European counterpart. Not surprisingly, some practitioners

---

[76]   *Ibid.*
[77]   *See* "EU Strategy to Enforce Intellectual Property Rights in Third Countries – Facts and Figures," Brussels, November 10, 2004 (mentioning that, while progress of enforcement is significant, it is still insufficient).
[78]   *Ibid.*
[79]   *See* "European Business in China Position Paper 2005," *supra* note 54.
[80]   For example, since 2000, Qualcomm, the leading network operator which dominates the technology of CDMA, signed a series of deals to provide some Chinese manufacturers with license terms that are more favourable than its standard rates. *See* Press Release, Qualcomm Inc., "Qualcomm Signs CDMA Intellectual Property Agreement with China Unicom" (February 1, 2000), *available at* <http://www.qualcomm.com/press/releases/2000/press347.html>.
[81]   James M. Zimmerman, "Intellectual Property Protection as Economic Policy: Will China Ever Enforce its IP Laws?" Congressional-Executive Commission on China, at 76, *available at* <http://www.cecc.gov/>.
[82]   Emma Barraclough, "US and EU Pile Pressure on China," *MIP Week*, Hong Kong, September 12, 2005, *at* <http://www.europeanchamber.com.cn/show/details.php?id= 583>, last visited October 19, 2006.
[83]   *Ibid.*
[84]   *Ibid.*

in China maintain that, in high-tech joint venture industries, technical standards are dominated, under most circumstances, by foreign companies whereby IPR could be abused. Moreover, there have been efforts to challenge the "patent pools" in China. Ping Zhang, a professor at Peking University, filed a case to the Re-examination Board at the State Intellectual Property Office in December 2005 requesting to invalidate a patent held by Dutch electronics giant Philips as part of the 4C DVD pool.[85] This pool also includes patents owned by Sony, Pioneer, and LG, and charges 3.5 U.S. dollars for each DVD unit produced, which appears to be touted by the patent pool as a discount price versus individual licenses.[86] Zhang, along with other four intellectual property law academics, challenges this Dutch patent since it is alleged to be nonessential.[87] Zhang argues that patent pools often include "questionable patents" and may impede China's economic development by compelling manufacturers to pay high royalties to foreign right holders.[88] The DVD player industry has been the focus of the attention of Chinese anti-patent pool campaigners because of fierce domestic competition and tight profit margins.[89] Dramatically, before the Re-examination Board would make its decision, an agreement was made by the parties. As a "win-win deal" described by both sides, Philips removed the patent from the pool and, in return, the academics withdrew their claim from the Board.[90]

This case reveals a policy dilemma of China regarding its national IPR strategy, and may indirectly affect EU-China trade relations given the fact that the EU is China's top technology supplier. As Zhang and her colleagues have stated to the media, this nullity request was neither against one particular foreign company nor one particular patent;[91] they wanted to use the case to arouse awareness on the public interest that seems to have been more or less neglected by the society.

6.2 Comparative Analysis: Sino-U.S. Negotiations

As a counterpoint to the EU policy towards IPR protection in China, it is instructive to compare the United States' approach, and China's response, to the

---

[85] *See* "Philips in China Patent Standard Spotlight," *Managing Intellectual Property*, August 1, 2006.
[86] *Ibid.*
[87] *See* "Patent Power," Reports for "WTO: IPRs Issues in Standardization (Beijing) International Forum," April 17-18, Beijing, Report No. 1, *Intellectual Property Protection in China*, March 13, 2007, *available at* <www.ipr.gove.cn>.
[88] *See* "Philips in China Patent Standard Spotlight," *supra* note 81.
[89] *See* "Philips Withdraws Patent from Chinese DVD," *Managing Intellectual Property*, December 1, 2006.
[90] *Ibid.*
[91] *Ibid.*

unresolved issues of how and when China's WTO commitments to IPR protection will be implemented. The United States is relevant because, as is well
documentated, the legislative programme of many developing nations, including China, has developed under external pressure from the United States,
which has threatened to impose trade sanctions against countries for their alleged deficiencies in providing adequate IPR protection towards American
products.[92]

6.2.1 America's Concerns

The chronic piracy problems throughout the world and the United States'
growing trade deficit of 765 billion dollars have forced the U.S. government to
act as harshly as before against countries which have encroached on American
interests due to weak IPR protection.[93] The widening American trade deficit
vis-à-vis China, which reached a record 232.5 billion dollars is one of the
largest.[94] As with previous U.S. efforts to secure stronger IPR protection in
China, a significant aspect of the unresolved issues relates to reaching multilateral agreement on how and when China's commitments will be implemented in accordance with WTO requirements.[95] The U.S. maintains that
China's failure to adequately enforce IPR is a problem which has become
prominent over the years and has created enormous economic impact on U.S.
businesses.[96] Against this background, since the beginning of 1990s, the
United States has frequently leveraged a series of unilateral mechanisms –
trade wars, non-renewal of Most Favoured Nation (MFN) status, and opposition to entry into the WTO – to push China towards stronger protection of the
U.S. IPR.[97]

---

[92] "U.S.: China Has High Rate of Intellectual Property Infringement," Washington File,
USINFO, April 29, 2005, *available at* <http://usinfo.state.gov/usinfo/Archive/2005/
Apr/29-580129.html>.

[93] Stephen S. Roach, "The China Fix: Statement Before the Senate Finance Committee
Hearing on 'Risks and Reforms: The Role of Currency in the US-China Relationship,'"
March 28, 2007, at 1, 13 (highlighting "America's massive trade deficit" and proposing
that the U.S. government should "push more for Chinese progress on the [...] protection of intellectual property rights).

[94] USTR Report 2007, *available at* <http://www.ustr.gov/assets/Document_Library/
Reports_Publications/2007/2007_NTE_Report/asset_upload_file855_10945.pdf>.

[95] *See* Pierre-Louis Girard, Chairperson, WTO Working Party on the Accession of China,
"Summing up by the Chairman: Meeting of the Working Party on the Accession of
China" September 28, 2000, *available at* <http://www.wto.org/english/news_e/
news00_e/chinasum_e.htm> (last visited October 30, 2007).

[96] *See* "China in the WTO – Year 3," A Research Report, Prepared for the U.S.-China
Economic and Security Review Commission, January 21, 2005, *available at*
<http://www.uscc.gov/researchpapers/2005/05_01_21_china_inthe_wto.htm>.

[97] Yu, "From Pirates to Partners, Protecting Intellectual Property in China in the Twenty-
First Century," *50 Am. U. L. Rev.* (2000), at 133.

6.2.2 China's Response

Response to external pressure depends on "domestic political and cultural variables";[98] however, that is what has been neglected by the United States. Faced with United States' pressure, China has invariably given clear and prompt responses, demonstrating that the U.S. strategy has, in theory, been effective in securing compliance with requirements of the TRIPs Agreement.[99] Pirating, however, has continued. The enforcement has been characterised by the intermittent improvement and subsequent rebound,[100] and repeated threats of renewed Section 301 action.[101] Faced with continuous external pressure, China has moved erratically; when the tension is alleviated, however, China appears to be more inclined to choose not to enforce the new policies as previously promised.[102]

With Chinese cultural background, the external pressure is apt to provoke unintended responses and become counterproductive.[103] China has, on the one hand, made continuous promises that appear to presage a stronger protection; on the other hand, however, China appears to be adopting countermeasures that undercut these commitments.[104] It has become more and more apparent

---

[98]   Jonathan M. Miller, "A Typology of Legal Transplants: Using Sociology, Legal History and Argentine Examples to Explain the Transplant Process," 51 *Am. J. Comp. L.* 874 (2003).

[99]   Susan K. Sell, "Intellectual Property Protection and Antitrust in the Developing World: Crisis, Coercion, and Choice," 49 (2) *International Organization* 332 (1995).

[100] *See* Myron A. Brillan & Jeremie Waterman, "China's WTO Implementation: A Three-Year Assessment," U.S. Chamber of Commerce, September 2004, at 2.

[101] China was placed by the USTR on the "priority watch list" in 1989 and 1990, and was designated as a "priority foreign country" in 1991. Leveraging the Section 301, the USTR threatened 1.5 billion dollars in sanctions, which China averted by signing a landmark MOU on IPR on January 16, 1992. China's performance, however, was considered unsatisfactory. In 1994, the USTR placed China back on the "priority foreign country" list and threatened retaliatory tariffs of 100 percent on 1.08 billion dollars worth of Chinese products. China again averted by signing another MOU on IPR on March 11, 1995. The disagreement still remained due to the alleged incompliance with the required standard and, in April 1996, the USTR again put China on the "priority foreign country" list and threatened 2 billion dollars in sanctions. Once again China avoided the trade war by signing a last-minute accord on June 17, 1996. On April 29, 2005, the USTR elevated China to the Priority Watch List again. *See* "Congressional Research Service: Report for Congress," 96-469 E, May 24, 1996, *available at* <http://digital.library.unt.edu/govdocs/crs/permalink/meta-crs-334:1>; "Excerpt from the IIPA Special 301 Recommendations," February 24, 1997, *available at* <http://www.ipr.gov.cn/cn/zhuanti/meiIPzhuanlan/1997interIP301material.doc>; "U.S.: China Has High Rate of Intellectual Property Infringement," *available at* <http://usinfo.state.gov/usinfo/Archive/2005/Apr/29-580129.html>.

[102] Susan K. Sell, *supra* note 99, at 332.

[103] *See* Miller, *supra* note 98, at 874.

[104] For example, in order to shield emerging domestic enterprises from global competition, China has adapted proprietary technological standards that discount foreign IPR, such

that the United States coercive policy towards IPR protection has been con-
ceptually misconceived in obtaining the desired results. Repeated international
threats against China, in the absence of satisfactory enforcement of new IPR
policies, suggests that the trend towards greater IPR protection in China is not
being embraced as ardently as wished.[105]

In 2006, the U.S. Trade Representatives (USTR) elevated China to the Pri-
ority Watch List again for "epidemic" infringements of IPR.[106] In the USTR's
Special 301 Report released on April 28, 2006,[107] the U.S. complained that
China has not provided the U.S. with adequate IPR enforcement to which they
are entitled and, accordingly, China would "remain on the Priority Watch
List."[108] On April 9, 2007, the United States filed two trade complaints against
China at the WTO over deficiencies in China's intellectual property laws and
market access barriers to copyright-based industries.[109] As expected, China expressed "great regret and strong dissatisfaction" at this decision.[110] This cast a
leaping blight on the already fragile relationship between these two old rivals.

In order to achieve desirable enforcement, it is necessary to re-examine the
existing mechanism and conceive a workable approach towards its solution.

6.2.3 Lessons to be Learned

Due to a lack of mutual trust and understanding between the United States and
China, the constant use of trade threats has created a stimulating effect on
China with respect to the creation of the protective immunity against various
coercions.[111] Due to hostility and harassment towards the United States within

---

as IGRS (Intelligent Grouping and Resources Sharing) for connectivity, and EVD (Enhanced Versatile Disc) for recording media. Also, there is a trend towards mandated
unique standards which is a technological alliance. *See* Brillan & Waterman, *supra* note
100, at 2, 18; *See* also "Non-market Oriented Revolution of Standards in China," *China
Economic Net*, December 2, 2004.

[105] Susan K. Sell, *supra* note 99, at 332 (emphasising the gap between the U.S.'s expectation and the reality in terms of China's IPR enforcement).

[106] *See* "U.S.: China Has High Rate of Intellectual Property Infringement," USINFO,
available at <http://usinfo.state.gov/usinfo/Archive/2005/Apr/29-580129.html>, visited
May 26, 2006.

[107] "2006 Section 301 Report," *available at* <http://www.ustr.gov/Document_Library/
Reports_Publications/2006/2006_Special_301_Review/Section_Index.html>.

[108] "2006 Section 301 Report," *id.*

[109] *See* "United States Files WTO Cases Against China Over Deficiencies in China's Intellectual Property Rights Laws and Market Access Barriers to Copyright-Based Industries", *USTR Press Release, available at* <http://www.ustr.gov/Document_Library/
Press_Releases/>.

[110] *See* "US Gets Tough on Chinese Piracy," *Guardian*, April 10, 2007, *available at*
<http://film.guardian.co.uk/news/story/0205361400.html>.

[111] Wei Cai, "Zhengduan Zhong De Hezuo: Zhongmei Zhishi Chanquan Boyi [Seeking
Cooperation over the Confrontation: The Sino-U.S. Game of Intellectual Property],

Chinese government and public circles, the Chinese government became increasingly reluctant to implement necessary reforms and do any more than was necessary in meeting the particular circumstances.[112] Clearly, the high protectionist policy towards IPR protection has negatively impacted China, making Chinese leaders more defensive than receptive in strengthening their IPR enforcement mechanisms. Not surprisingly, coercive measures as a dominant United States' strategy have been unsuccessful in curbing global intellectual property piracy.[113] The failure of this strategy is thought to be due to lack of consideration for cultural differences, and in particular the Confucian values of harmony. In this respect, the United States' strategy provides a good example of what has been tried and failed.

Given the amount of international tension created in the past years over narrowly avoided trade wars, it is to be hoped that the WTO Trade Policy Review (TPR) mechanism and Dispute Settlement Body (DSB)[114] will render unilateral actions largely meaningless.[115] Since China' accession to the WTO, bilateral sanctions are much less appropriate and multilateral remedies should be relied on, at least in the first instance.

6.3 EU-China IPR Negotiations

In a manner similar to their U.S. partners, EU companies have also encountered significant infringement problems caused by the lack of adequate IPR protection in China. To protect their economic interests, some EU companies have constantly lobbied EU institutions to initiate trade sanctions; however, the dominant trend has been towards strengthening bilateral cooperation regarding IPR protection. As the EU Ambassador to China, Mr. Serge Abou, figuratively and vividly commented on March 7, 2007 at a press conference in Shanghai, "the trade conflict between the EU and China is inappreciable, as of "a small tree" in "a dense forest," and a strengthened cooperation remains to be the mainstream."[116] In this section, we will explore the profile and institutional framework of EU-China relations concerning IPR protection.

WTO Jingji Daokan [China WTO Tribune]," issue 3, 2005 (highlighting the strategies for understanding the mentality of the United States and winning the "game" of the IPR disputes)

[112] Yu, "From Pirates to Partners," *supra* note 97, at 134.

[113] Robert C. Bird, "Defending Intellectual Property Rights in the BRIC Economies," 43 *Am. Bus. L.J.* 334-335 (2006).

[114] *See infra* § 6.4.2 & § 6.4.3, "*TPR* and DSB: Additional Forms of Leverage."

[115] Michael N. Schlesinger, "A Sleeping Giant Awakens: The Development of Development of Intellectual Property Law in China," 9 *J. Chinese L.* 138 (1995).

[116] *See* "Oumeng Zhuhua Dashi: Moca Juefei Zhongou Maoyi Zhuliu [the EU Ambassador to China: Conflict is By No Means Mainstream of EU-China Trade Relations]," Xinhua News Net, March 7, 2007.

6.3.1 Characteristics of EU-China IPR

EU-China IPR Debate: Why the EU is Different from the United States?

The advantages that the EU possesses over the United State when it comes to dealing with IPR issues in China are numerous. First, the significant difference between the U.S. and EU attitudes towards China reflects their respective philosophies towards international relations – between realism and liberalism.[117]

A realism approach asserts that nation states are the unitary actors and dominant players in the international relations and all policy is driven by the national interest of these participants,[118] while liberalism[119] sees the primary actors on the international stage as individuals and their relations with the state and extra-national organisations.[120] The concept of the latter "is defined as a social ethic that advocates liberty, in general".[121] Based on the realist approach to foreign relations, Europeans tend to believe that "democracy and free trade secure peace between nations, and that cooperation ultimately enhances freedom."[122]

With regard to international IPR, U.S. policy makes no secret of being propelled, or at least accelerated, by various political considerations.[123] For example, the White House has appealed ardently to mounting anti-China sentiments in Congress[124] concerning the bilateral trade deficits with China by lobbying

---

[117] *See* Vincent G. Sabathier, "Europe and China," *ADASTRA Online, available at* <http://www.space.com/adastra/china_europe_0505.html>, last visited February 16, 2006.

[118] Gideon Rose, "Neoclassical Realism and Theories of Foreign Policy," 51 *World Politics,* No. 1, 144-72 (1998). *See* also Mark V. Kauppi and Paul R. Viotti, *International Relations Theory: Realism, Pluralism, Globalism, and Beyond* 55-6 (1999).

[119] As summarised by Mearsheimer, realism bifurcated into two variations: offensive and defensive realism. According to offensive realism, if great powers want to survive, they should behave aggressively towards each other and take advantage of every chance they obtain to amass as much power as they can; according to defensive realism, states ought to pursue rational strategies as the desirable route to security and act in a reactionary manner to the threat posed by strong powers. *See* John J. Mearsheimer, *Tragedy of Great Power Politics,* at 11–12, 35 (2001). *See* also, Kenneth N. Waltz, *Theory of International Politics* 102-128 (1979).

[120] Sabathier, *supra* note 116.

[121] Serge-Christophe Kolm, "Distributive Justice," in Robert Goodin and Philip Pettit (eds.), *A Companion to Contemporary Political Philosophy* 440 (1995).

[122] Sabathier, *supra* note 116.

[123] This practice, as will be explained in detail below, is a political "tying practice." *See,* "From 'Tying Practice' to 'Undiscounted Policy,'" *infra* § 6.5.2.

[124] Jonathan Weisman, "China's Demands Anger Congress, May Hurt Bid," *Washington Post,* July 6, 2005, D01.

various economic sanctions.[125] The recent WTO complaints against China are the latest move on trade by the Bush administration, under growing pressure from Congress to cut the trade deficit with China.[126] These trade deficits continuously influence U.S. trade relations with China, and China remains the biggest country with which the United States runs a bilateral trade deficit.[127] While the total trade volume in 2006 has reached three hundred and forty-three billion dollars, the deficit with China topped two hundred and thirty-two billion dollars.[128] With regard to EU-China relations, although bilateral trade is also marked by a sizeable EU trade deficit,[129] the EU attributes the deficit to the obstacles in market access in China, and tends to believe that, if China were to further open its market, the EU's bilateral deficit with China would shrink.[130]

Second, unlike U.S.-China relations, the EU and China have maintained harmonious relations on both a political and an economic level. This is largely due to the cultural compatibilities and adaptability between Europe and China. The EU and China enjoy a long history and rich heritage, making outstanding contributions to human civilisations.[131] The Sino-European interaction is of long standing, since cultural traits from China have been embraced by Europeans for over two thousand years.[132] The old "Silk Road" provided a vital link between China and Europe and the millennium has seen a greater consolidation of this relationship.[133]

---

[125] For an account of the U.S. bilateral trade deficit with China, *see US-China Trade in Context*, the Document of the US-China Business Council, *available at* <www.uschina.org/public/documents/2006/06/us-china-trade-context.pdf> (stating that "focusing on the bilateral trade deficit with China misses a bigger story and could lead to poor policy choices.")

[126] *See*, Parija B. Kavilanz, "U.S. Files Piracy Complaint against China," *CNNMoney.com*, April 10, 2007, *available at* <http://money.cnn.com/2007/04/10/news/international/china_piracy/index.htm>.

[127] *See* "Study Documents Negative Impact of U.S. Trade Deficit with China," *available at* <http://usinfo.state.gov/ei/Archive/2005/Jan/12-31762.html>.

[128] *See* "US-China Trade Statistics," US-China Business Council, *available at* <www.uschina.org/statistics/tradetable.html>.

[129] In 2006 the EU trade deficit was 131 billion euros; in 2007 the deficit is expected to reach 170 billion euros. *See* "The EU-China Trade in Facts and Figures," EU External Trade, *supra* note 77.

[130] Huo, *supra* note 3, at 1-17. *See also*, Wei Wang, "EU-China Trade to Benefit Both," *China Daily*, October 9, 2004.

[131] Wei Wang, *ibid*.

[132] Paul Frederick Gressey, "Chinese Traits in European Civilization: A Study in Diffusion," 10 (5) *Am. Soc. Rev.* 5. 595 (1945).

[133] *See* "Joint Statement," Article 22, 7th EU-China Summit, The Hague, 8 December 2004, Council of the European Union, Brussels, 15065/04 (press 337), at 8(stating that both the EU and China "stressed the importance of achieving the Millennium Development Goals and attached considerable importance to enhancing bilateral and multilateral cooperation...").

The rituals of Confucian ethics evolved over time and matured into the four forms: *li* – ritual; x*iao* - filial piety; *zhong* - loyalty; *ren* – humanism.[134] Correspondingly, European cultural values underscore classicism, Christendom, enlightenment and humanism.[135] A common denominator of Chinese and European cultures is humanism. Cultural accumulation has equipped Europe and China with historical maturation to better deal with complexity, uncertainty, and the art of compromise.[136]

Indeed, Europe and America share common historical and cultural roots; however, the apparent similarities between the two sides of the Atlantic "mask significant cultural differences."[137] As has been noted by David Gosset, while "Eurasia" carries and cherishes ancient memories, the America, which evolved into a super-power from the womb of colony within only two centuries since its independence, is indulging in the self-obsessed "American spirit" and "departing culturally from its European decent."[138] Although Europe and China have gradually developed civilisations, as Gosset remarks, "having in common long maturations over millennia, the two old worlds have developed affinities and, despite all the exotic representations, the two edges of Eurasia are closer than they seem."[139] While European and Chinese values may be different, the objective of communication and cooperation between Europe and China is to try to understand each other better.[140]

As Christopher De Vroey, the IPR Director at DG Trade of the European Commission, stated during an interview with the author, the difference between EU and U.S. foreign policy is that the EU "aims to maintain a rational and flexible approach in achieving its long-term strategic goals in terms of intellectual property protection, understanding that counterfeiting and piracy are

---

[134] *See* Hyung Kim, *Fundamental Legal Concepts of China and the West: A Comparative Study* at 30-31 (1981)(introducing humanism as one of the "four forms" of Confucian values); *See* also Tu Wei-ming, "Confucius and Confucianism," in Walter H. Slote and George A. Devos (eds.), *Confucianism and the Family*, State University of New York Press 33(1998) (mentioning the emergence of the "third epoch" of Confucian humanism).

[135] Leopold von Wiese, "What Is European Culture?" 11(1) *Brit. J. Soc.* 5-6 (March 1960) (describing classicism, Christendom, humanism and the enlightenment as the nominating European cultures)

[136] David Gosset, "A Symphony of Civilizations," *Asia Times*, August 12, 2006, *available at* <http://www.atimes.com/atimes/China/HH12Ad02.html>, last visited January 5, 2007.

[137] Lionel Laroche, "The Cultural Differences between the European Union and North America and their Impact on Transatlantic Business," *Paper of ITAP International*, *available at* <http://www.itapintl.com/cultural differenceseuna.htm>.

[138] Gosset, "A Symphony of Civilizations," *supra* note 136.

[139] *Ibid.*

[140] "EU-China Relations," Events Reports, *supra* note 14.

common problems in developing countries."[141] The mutual awareness of fundamental cultural and historical commonalities has deepened the links between the two edges of Eurasia and has "a moderating effect on Washington's imperial hubris." [142] This cultural adaptation has resulted in a better understanding between Europe and China which has been essential "for both sides to take the full measure of what the two ancient civilisations can achieve together."[143] As the EU trade Commissioner Peter Mandelson recently acknowledged, the EU "ha[s] accepted that IPR is a complex issue and that China's commercial culture and legal system need time to absorb change."[144] The perceived "gentleness" of the European style and the "courtliness" of the Chinese style are mutually compatible and have provided an excellent ethical foundation for a constructive bilateral relationship.

Third, an institutional foundation has been established to implement the envisioned "strategic partnership," although substantial work is still required. By May 2006, there were about forty cooperation projects with a total amount of two hundred and seventy million euros operating by various European institutions in China.[145] The EU-China Intellectual Property Rights Cooperation Programme is contributing to the progress with IPR protection reforms and their implementation is a demonstrative aspect. The establishment of the European Chamber of Commerce in China (EUCCC), the EU-China Business Dialogue (ECBD), and the newly established EU-Intellectual Property Dialogue is also a promising institutional arrangement, which will be discussed below in depth. By contrast, the United States has been using Section 301 assiduously in fighting piracy without paying much attention to the economic adaptation and indigenous tradition.[146] Almost all of the U.S.-China bilateral agreements concerning IPR protection were outcomes of a coercive U.S. policy aimed at imposing sanctions upon China, while largely neglecting capacity building and the enhancement for the sustainability.

---

[141] Private interview with Christopher De Vroey, the IPR Director at DG Trade, the European Commission, Brussels, May 28, 2003.

[142] Gosset, "A Symphony of Civilizations," *supra* note 136.

[143] *Ibid.*

[144] Peter Mandelson, "Protecting IPR in China," *Trade Fairs Seminar*, Beijing, November 26, 2007, *available at* <http://trade.ec.europa.eu/doclib/docs/2008/january/tradoc_137 535.pdf>.

[145] Sources from the Delegation of the European Commission in China, *available at* <http://www.delchn.cec.eu.int/en/Co-operation/General_Information.htm>, last visited October 10, 2006.

[146] As has been demonstrated, in the area of world trade involving IPR protection, many developing countries adopted higher standards for IPR protection through coercive approaches, such as Section 301, imposed by developed countries, such as the United States. *See* Miller, *supra* note 98, at 847-8.

Interactive Concerns Towards IPR

CHINA'S STATUS QUO

In China, while progress of enforcement is significant, infringement is still pervasive. According to a survey organised by the European Commission and DG Trade, the EU is a "full-scale victim" of counterfeiting and piracy – European intellectual property is being violated on a considerable scale and the variety of fake products ranges from cereal boxes to plants and seeds, from aeroplane spare parts to sunglasses and from cigarettes to medications.[147] However, the EU has suffered deeply in the trademark area than that of the other.[148] This reflects the comparative advantage of the EU in the trademark-protected products, particularly aeroplane parts, automobiles, electronics, watches, toys, clothes and leather.[149] The counterfeiting problem appears to be especially serious in the car industry, and the European car manufacturers in China were concerned about counterfeit auto parts in the country.[150] As Jean-Claude Germain, PSA Peugeot Citroen's chief China representative complained, the counterfeit body parts sold in China "are made of normal steel instead of high-strength steel, turning the car into a 'guillotine' if it crashes."[151]

In the area of copyright, there is widespread piracy in various formats including CDs and DVDs.[152] In the area of patents, problem includes infringements on pharmaceutical products, electrical domestic appliances, and industrial machinery.[153]

Over the past recent years the EU has repeatedly urged China to improve its enforcement tool, but China's endeavours do not appear to impress the EU. There are indications that the EU is gradually running out of patience over China's failure in delivering concrete results of its IPR enforcement. The EU Trade Commissioner Peter Mandelson recently expressed his frustration: "I am firmly convinced that the most effective solution to effective IPR protection is the legal enforcement that mutual cooperation between the EU and China can and should provide [...]. We have been constructive and we have

---

[147] *See* "Survey on Enforcement of Intellectual Property Rights in Third Countries," European Commission DG Trade, July 2003, *available at* <http://europa.eu.int/comm/trade/issues/sectoral/intell_property/survey_en.htm>, last accessed February 12, 2006.

[148] *Ibid.*

[149] *Ibid.*

[150] *Ibid.*

[151] Tschang Chi-chu, "EU Traders Call for Bite in China's Law," *The Straits Times*, October 16, 2004.

[152] *See* "EU Strategy to Enforce Intellectual Property Rights in Third Countries – Facts and Figures," *supra* note 77, at 2.

[153] *Ibid.*

been patient, but the return we have received on that patience has frankly been too low." [154]

EU's MIXED EMOTIONS: IS IPR PROBLEM A SMALL TREE, OR A DENSE FOREST?

Serge Abou draws his analogy between temporary friction in long-term relationship and "a small tree" in "a dense forest," which is inspirational. Indeed, the disagreement and inconsistency do not constitute the "mainstream" of the EU-China trade relations. In fact, some European entrepreneurs have a mixed feelings and complicated attitudes towards their business in China. The common sentiment is that, to some extent, they are more or less reluctant to do business in China because they are not confident enough about the protection of their interests under the current legal and judicial environment; however, most foreign industries cannot afford to ignore the Chinese market with immense potential.[155] The lure of the huge profit margins and low labour costs is so hard to resist that many would rather take the risk.[156] According to a survey by European Union Chamber of Commerce in China (EUCCC), despite the problems associated with IPR enforcement, ninety percent of the survey respondents acknowledged that they were "optimistic" or "cautiously optimistic" about their overall business prospects in China.[157] Sixty-four percent of participants noted that they expected to be profitable.[158] The EUCCC's most recent survey, which was released in November 2007, indicates that European companies "are generally optimistic" about their business in China."[159] Approximately 76 percent of the survey respondents are "either making a profit or at least breaking even," while 82 percent of the participated companies expect to be profitable within 3 years.[160]

---

[154] See "Mandelson Urges China to Tackle Piracy, Hints at WTO Action", *EU Business*, November 26, 2007, *available at* <www.eubusiness.com/news-eu/1196083921.23/>.

[155] See "European Business in China Position Paper 2005," *supra* note 54.

[156] See Juhan Ke, "Mei Weihe Qianghua Dui Hua Jingji Shiya [Why the United States Intensifies Economic Pressure on China]," *Liaowang Xinwen Zhoukan [Outlook Weekly]*, August 10, 2006.

[157] Tschang Chi-chu, "EU Traders Call for Bite in China's Law," *The Straits Times*, *supra* note 151.

[158] *Ibid.*

[159] The EUCCC has recently released its annual European Chamber Business Confidence Survey, revealing that "European businesses are generally optimistic about their business performance in China [...]. However, many of them are concerned about a series of issues such as [...] insufficient protection of intellectual property rights. *See* "European Companies in China Generally Optimistic," *China CSR*, November 23, 2007.

[160] Lin Guan "European Chamber Business Confidence Survey: Paints A Rosy Picture," *China Daily*, December 22, 2007.

What the EU Can Offer China

BEYOND THE CRACKDOWN CAMPAIGNS: FROM POLITICAL MANIPULATION TO LEGAL IMPLEMENTATION

As mentioned in Chapter 5, historically, the crackdown campaigns have proved to be a potent means to tackle rampant IPR infringements in China.[161] However, this measure has its weakness. In the context of IPR enforcement under external pressure, the launch of a crackdown campaign is usually considered as a means to relieve tension at certain vulnerable point in the ongoing high level negotiations, or a logical response to a threat of trade sanctions. For example, over the previous U.S.-China IPR debate, the genuine objective of crackdown campaigns has been, in large part, to warm up the atmosphere of the forthcoming negotiations, and the campaign itself remains a diplomatic show. Unsurprisingly, this kind of policy-driven campaigns can only generate intermittent effect which is far from sufficient. In addition, crackdown campaigns are monitored on an individual and temporary basis and lacks steady financial resources. At the lower levels of the authorities, even the campaigns can be carried on in general with adequate budget, entrenched bureaucratic inertia may delay or counteract the effectiveness of the enforcement. Economic insufficiencies and bureaucratic resistance have created subsequent reluctance in coordination of these campaigns, which in many instances turn out to be a mere formality.

Contrary to the United States, the EU is in its unique role as a collective negotiator, liaising with its member states to develop a feasible and flexible EU position that not only ensures consistency of the EU policy but also helps progress negotiations with a none-European state such as China. Here, the EU is best advised to understand the bureaucratic nature of the Chinese legal, economic and political regimes that may affect the enforcement endeavours and help China build an effective legal enforcement mechanism. Again, it is worth emphasising that the goal of IPR enforcement in China is achieved, in a great measure, through political advocacy rather than a legal process. It is therefore of particular significance for the EU to foster a shift in China from "rule by law" to "rule of law." In a context of EU-China trade relations involving IPR debate, it may be a daunting task for the EU to interfere the evolution of China's enforcement ecology from political manipulation to legal implementation; however, as has been previously demonstrated, there is no shortcut to mitigating the counterfeiting menace in China. Unlike the United States whose coercive approach makes the Chinese more reluctant to implement their commitments, the EU should find ways to identify real problems and resolve specific difficulties without merely displacing their Chinese counterparts elsewhere.

---

[161] *See* "Characteristics of the IPR Enforcement in China," *supra* § 5.3.2.

ECONOMIC INTEGRATION AND INSTITUTIONAL TRANSITION

In a global perspective, the EU acts as "a model of cooperation between nations," whilst China acts as "an example for developing countries," both sides interact and complement each other.[162]As discussed in Chapter 3 and 4, while China has failed to demonstrate its capacity to implement political reform, Chinese economic integration into the world trading system has been perceived by the West as a welcome premise of prospective political integration. In this context, further economic integration is necessary and the EU is best suited to guide China on this.

More importantly, as has been noted, although China has committed itself to a socialist "rule of law" state, without the notion of the liberal democracy being embedded in people's minds, rule of law in China will unsurprisingly remain symbolic and problematic.[163] China is undergoing a dramatic socio-political transition and the eventual outcome of this transition will have considerable implications for the Sino-EU relations. In this sense, it is in the interest of the EU to understand and assist China towards its unprecedented economic and political reform.[164] China should draw on experience from the EU in institutional building, democratic governance, cultural diversity, social stability as well as regional integration.[165]

REFINE THE LEGAL FRAMEWORK

China has embarked on its ambitious plan for its legal reform and has, in principle, established a well-designed legal system. However, apart from the ineffectiveness of the enforcement mechanism, China's existing regulatory system is not fully compatible with the integrity and sustainability objectives that reflect global dimensions of what most countries around the world are dedicated to achieving. In other words, Chinese laws, while comprehensive, need to be "refined." Here, the EU has a wealth of experience to draw upon. Of critical importance is the need for European assistance in the enactment, amendment and refinement of laws, particularly in difficult areas, such as the balance between unfair competition and intellectual property. Certain rules can be refined and restated, taken into account the legislative experience of the EU and its member states.

In concrete terms, as will be discussed below,[166] it is suggested that a differentiated IPR policy should be applied to fit in different circumstances arising from the regional disparities and industrial divergence. Here, China can benefit from the EU's experience in implementing the EU Directive on Enforce-

---

[162] Pastor and Gosset, "the EU-China Relationship: A Key to the 21st Century Order," *supra* note 15.

[163] *See* § 4.4.1, § 5.3.2.

[164] Wei-Wei Zhang, *supra* note 679, at 14.

[165] *Ibid.*

[166] *See infra* § 6.5.4.

ment of IPR. Since this directive was formally adopted on April 29, 2004, two days before the enlargement of the European Union to twenty-five Member States, the ten new members had therefore no influence on the directive.[167] However, this directive is a "one law fits all" provision,[168] which means that although the member states have flexibility in implementing this directive in their own way and at their own pace, all member states, including the new members as developing states, will eventually have to transpose the directive into their respective national laws. In this context, reconciling the old and the new member states coming from both the developed and developing worlds is an enormous challenge for the EU, and its successful harmonisation of this policy will provide valuable guidance for China in dealing with its own differentiation of IPR standards.

Within EU-China negotiations towards IPR protection, unremitting and concentrated efforts should be made by Chinese IPR enforcement agencies and the related European institutions to fight against IPR infringements together. To achieve this goal, the EU should obtain support from both Chinese leaders and intellectual property holders. This is what we will discuss in much detail in the following sections.

6.3.2 Framework of EU-China IPR

Over the past years, the EU and China have built an impressive cooperation mechanism in the field of IPR protection that has developed in the framework of a structured IPR Dialogue as well as an IP Working Group.

Regarding IPR protection in China, the EU has engaged in a series of negotiations with China over the development and enforcement of the Chinese intellectual property laws.[169] The EU-China Annual Summits, with the first

---

[167] The particularity concerning the implementation of the directive in the ten new Member States is reflected by the fact that the directive was adopted just two days before enlargement was initiated. On May 1, 2004 the EU undertook a new wave of enlargement, bringing the total number of the Member States from fifteen to twenty five. *See* "The Enlargement of the European Union," European Parliament, *available at* <http://www.europarl.europa.eu/enlargement/default_en.htm>.

[168] Each Member State is obliged to implement the directive in a manner which fulfils the requirements of clarity and to transpose the provisions of the directive into national provisions in order to assure a uniform enforcement of these standards across the EU. *See* European Union Case Law, Case 239/85, European Court Reports 1986, at 3645 (stipulating that "[e]ach Member State must implement Directives in a manner which fully meets the requirement of legal certainty and must consequently transpose their terms into national law as binding provisions. A Member State cannot fulfil its obligations under a Directive by means of a mere circular which may be amended by the administration at will").

[169] *See* "China, EU Nod to Talks on Trade Rules, IPR Issues," FOFCOM, *available at* <http://english.mofcom.gov.cn/aarticle/newsrelease/commonnews/200706/2007060478 0905.html>.

meeting launched in London in April 1998, have proved to be important meetings for EU-China leaders "to update each other on progress made in numerous areas, to exchange ideas and to plan for the future."[170] This Annual Summit has set the tone for structural reforms and improvement of EU-China bilateral trade relations involving IPR protection. At the eighth EU-China Summit in Beijing in September 2005,[171] leaders from both sides[172] recognised "the importance of implementing and enforcing intellectual property laws, while safeguarding the interests of consumers in creating a positive business environment for continued economic growth and individual prosperity."[173] The agreement reached at the ninth EU-China Summit in Helsinki in 2006 reflected the intensification of the strategic cooperation "with an extremely positive momentum" between the EU and China.[174] Most recently, at the tenth EU-China Summit, consensus was reached to establish by the end of March 2008 a High Level Economic and Trade Dialogue between the European Commission and the State Council of China which will discuss strategies in a broad area of bilateral trade including the protection of IPR.[175] With this in mind the EU and China agreed to set up the IPR dialogue mechanism, and in particular welcomed the newly established IPR working group,[176] which paved path towards further cooperation concerning IPR protection.

However, the consensus achieved through the EU-China Summit should be advanced and implemented in the concrete terms. Various EU and China governmental agencies and NGOs are responsible, directly or indirectly, for the EU-China bilateral IPR negotiations. On China's side, trade negotiations are officially led by the Ministry of Commerce (MOFCOM) – the governmental ministry overweening both domestic and international trade; at the EU side, negotiations are officially led by Directorate General Trade of the European Commission (DG Trade) – the EU governmental agency overseeing EU's external trade. Nevertheless, the actual negotiations are normally incarnated in

---

[170] "Fourth EU-China Summit, Joint Press Statement," Brussels, September 5, 2001, *available at* <http://ec.europa.eu/external_relations/china/intro/summit4.htm>.

[171] *See* "EU-China Summit: Joint Statement 2005", *available at* <http://ec.europa.eu/comm/external_relations/china/summit_0905/index.htm>, last visited October 1, 2006.

[172] In this summit, Premier Wen Jiabao of the State Council of China attended the meeting on behalf of the People's Republic of China. The EU was represented by the President of the European Council, Prime Minister Tony Blair of the United Kingdom, President of the European Commission, Mr. José Manuel Barroso, and Secretary General of the Council of the EU and High Representative for the EU Common Foreign and Security Policy, Mr. Javier Solana. *See ibid.*

[173] *See* "Joint Statement," 2005, Article 15, *supra* note 171.

[174] Pastor and Gosset, "the EU-China Relationship: A Key to the 21st Century Order", *supra* note 15.

[175] "Joint Statement of the 10th China-EU Summit, Beijing," Article 24, November 28, 2007.

[176] *See* IP/05/1091, Brussels, September 5, 2005, *available at* <http://europa.eu.int/comm/external_relations/news/barroso/sp05_478.htm>.

the following mechanisms, most notably, the EU-China Intellectual Property Dialogue and the IP Working Group.

EU-China Intellectual Property Cooperation Programme

In China, domestic companies' IPR awareness has increased in recent years, although there is still much room to improve. An official survey in 2004 showed that nearly seventy percent of the domestic companies interviewed had participated in IPR training programmes, fifty percent had set up their own IPR systems and forty percent had registered patents for new technologies since 2002.[177] In order to foster the notion of IPR, the EU-China Intellectual Property Rights Cooperation Programme (1998-2004) was launched. This programme came into existence under an agreement signed in 1995 between the European Commission and China as represented by its Ministry of Foreign Trade and Economic Cooperation (MOFTEC), the predecessor of MOFCOM.[178] The programme itself was not a negotiation institution; however, as an important outcome of the former EU-China negotiation, its implementation had indirectly influenced the bilateral negotiations. [179]

The main objective of this programme was to facilitate bilateral trade by supporting China's efforts to develop a modern and effective system for the protection of IPR.[180] This Programme was managed by the European Patent Office, with its headquarter in Munich, on behalf of the European Commission, and was overseen by a Programme Management Unit located in Beijing.[181] The programme was split into one horizontal element covering training of judges and solicitors, administrative enforcement, border enforcement, public awareness building, academic institutes, technology transfer, legislative support, international study tours, and three vertical specialised elements, including patent, trademark and copyright.[182] Various workshops, seminars and conferences were organised in Beijing and in the provinces, involving the different Chinese IPR agencies at the national, provincial and local levels.[183] To meet these objectives, the programme addressed various aspects of legislation, administration and enforcement.

---

[177] Cui Ning & Qin Jize, "IPR Strategy to Define Government's Role," *China Daily*, June 14, 2004, at 5 (source from Centre for Intellectual Property Affairs, the Ministry of Science and Technology).

[178] "Successful Move for Closer Cooperation in the Protection of Intellectual Property Rights," *European Patent Network*, October 24, 2003.

[179] *Ibid.*

[180] *See* "A Maturing Partnership," *supra* note 60.

[181] *See* "Programme Goals and Organisation," EU-China Intellectual Property Cooperation Programme, Programme Technical Overview, *available at* <http://www.european-patent-office.org/intcop/ipr_china/protech1.htm>.

[182] *Ibid.*

[183] *Ibid.*

The programme has, in general, accomplished the anticipated result. For example, as the European Patent Office (EPO) commented, the adoption by the Chinese Patent Office of the EPOQE, a suite of applications used by EPO for patent searches, has been seen as a milestone in China's IPR management history, giving SIPO patent examiners access to the EPO's database of over 60 million patent specifications.[184] The implementation of the programme thus paved way for the modernisation and standardisation of China's IPR system.

This programme was terminated in 2004 and was then included in the EU-China Trade Project (2004-2007).[185] The EU-China Trade Project was replaced by a new programme called IPR II (2007-2011), which was officially launched on November 27, 2007 in Beijing.[186] IPR II addresses common objectives to improve the mechanisms for IPR protection in China through the provision of technical assistance to Chinese legislative, judicial, administrative and enforcement agencies and institutions with special emphasis being focused on enforcement capacity.[187] Similar to the former EU-China IPR Cooperation Programme, the IPT II is administered by the EPO in Munich with a technical assistance team based in Beijing.[188]

Steering Role of the EU-China Joint Committee

With a view to fostering and facilitating bilateral relations, it is imperative for the EU and China to work together with an elaborate and balanced agenda capable of assisting China's compliance with its WTO commitments.[189] In light of the goals and priorities of both sides, the EU-China Economic and Trade Joint Committee was established in 1985.[190] As a bilateral summit between the EU and China in trade and economics, EU-China Joint Committee provides a platform for high level discussion of bilateral trade issues.[191] The Joint Committee, through periodical meetings, serves EU-China relations in three aspects: economy and trade, bilateral agreements and dialogues between the European Commission and the Chinese government, and the EU-China coop-

---

[184] "Twenty Years' Co-operation between the European Patent Office and the Chinese Patent Office: EPO International Projects Focus on Asia," *EPO Press Release*, *available at* <http://www.epo.org/about-us/press/releases/archive/2005/05122005.html>.

[185] "Intellectual Property: IPR in China," *European Commission Sectoral issues*, Brussels, December 6, 2007.

[186] *Ibid.*

[187] *Ibid.*

[188] *Ibid.*

[189] "A Secure Europe in a Better World," *European Security Strategy*, Brussels, December 12, 2003. See also *See* also "A Maturing Partnership," *supra* note 60, at 4.

[190] For a full debrief on the EU-China Economic and Trade Joint Committee, *see* "Global Europe: EU-China Trade and Investment," *available at* <http://europa.eu.int/comm/trade/index_en.htm>.

[191] *Ibid.*

eration programme.[192] However, to achieve these goals, the steering role of the EU-China Joint Committee should be intensified and reinforced so as to address not only the broad issues of trade and cooperation, but also concerns arising from the various sectoral dialogues.[193] In order to monitor bilateral agreements to ensure compatibility, on the EU side, "close coordination of the Union and the Member State policies will be required and China will have to ensure that all branches and levels of its administration are on board."[194]

In the twentieth Committee meeting which was held in Brussels on November 4, 2005, the representatives from both sides of the EU and China discussed the important aspects of the ever-increasing bilateral relationship, focusing on market access, IPR and Doha issues.[195] Bo Xilai, the Minister of MOFCOM represented the Chinese government and EU Trade Commissioner Peter Mandelson chaired the trade section of the Joint Committee.[196] Whilst stressing the importance of respect for and protection of IPR in China, the EU expressed its confidence in the ongoing progress of the collaboration between the EU and China and highlighted "the urgent need to correct the perception that intellectual property rights are not properly enforced in China."[197] As a result, the EU and China agreed on the need to work more strategically and closely on existing issues to ensure IPR is effectively protected.[198]

EU-China Intellectual Property Dialogue

As has been demonstrated in previous sections, the EU is an important contributor to technical assistance and capacity building in the field of IPR in China.[199] These technical assistance activities have been undertaken in the framework of a global trade assistance programme named "Support to China's Integration into the World Trading System."[200] With a view of promoting China's reform process and sectoral cooperation, an agenda was adopted to set up a more dedicated dialogue on EU-China IPR issues, "given the continued pervasiveness of IPR infractions in China."[201] As illustrated in the Joint Statement of the Seventh EU-China Summit, the leaders of both sides "welcomed

---

[192] *Ibid.*

[193] *See* "A Maturing Partnership," COM (2005) 533, *supra* note 60, at 4.

[194] *Ibid.*

[195] "China, EU to Cooperate in Trade, Investment," China MOFCOM, *available at* <http://sl2.mofcom.gov.cn/aarticle/chinanews/200511/20051100750917.html>, last visited on December 12, 2007.

[196] *Ibid.*

[197] *See* "EU-China Economic and Trade Joint Committee Debriefing," Brussels, 4 November 2005.

[198] *Ibid.*

[199] *See* "IPR in China," *Sectoral Issues*, Brussels, December 6, 2007, *available at* <http://ec.europa.eu/trade/issues/sectoral/intell_property/ipr_china_en.htm>.

[200] *Ibid.*

[201] *See* "A Maturing Partnership," *supra* note 60, at 19.

the EU-China Dialogue on Intellectual Property" and made consensus "to explore possibilities for further strengthening cooperation in IPR enforcement, in particular through consultation and cooperation between governments and enterprises, and through a closer cooperation of IPR-related institutions, including staff exchanges." [202]

THE LAUNCH OF IPD

In October 2003, EU and China agreed to launch a structured dialogue – the EU-China Intellectual Property Dialogue (IPD) – to discuss bilateral issues concerning protection and enforcement of IPR, and step up joint efforts to combat counterfeiting and piracy. [203] The IPD covers broad areas concerning IPR protection such as improvements in inter-agency coordination, exchanges with sub-central levels, and international cooperation.[204] It also addresses institutional reform, human and financial resources, as well as enforcement-related areas such as central and sub-central enforcement by customs, police, administrative and judiciary bodies.[205]

WEAKNESS OF IPD

While claimed to be the most important negotiation mechanism in the area of IPR, the structured IPR Dialogue does not necessarily function in a manner compatible with the mutual consensus and operational objectives concerning IPR enforcement. The agreement on the structured dialogue consists of only two articles, setting out very broad standards and principles. At present, the IPD mainly serves as a bilateral forum for the EU and China to discuss IPR issues, and the forum itself constitutes an integral and essential part of the general EU-China Dialogue scheme. Since the establishment of IPD, it has so far remained at the initial stage of tentative plan without any substantial and operational guidelines for the implementation the agreement. Based on the understanding of its weakness and the possible room for further improvement, this section of the book seeks to shed some new light on recasting and strengthening its functions, a point that we now turn.

FUNCTIONS OF IPD: SOME REFLECTIONS

IPR FORUM

The function of the IPD as a forum for high level discussion of IPR issues was a major purpose of the dialogue when it was initiated. While the role of the

---

[202] See "Joint Statement," 7th EU-China Summit, 15065/04, *supra* note 133, at 5.
[203] See "EU-China Intellectual Property Dialogue," *available at* <http://ec.europa.eu/comm/external_relations/china/intro/ipr_291003.pdf>.
[204] Article 1(a), *ibid.*
[205] Article 1(a), 1(b) and 1(c), *ibid.*

IPD needs to be well clarified and enhanced, it is still important to maintain and strengthen the original function to be sure that a platform is provided for policy debate and evaluation.

1. Create Holistic Approaches to Harmonising Public-Private Partnerships

In the area of IPR enforcement, significance has been recognised to encourage private sectors to work together with public authorities through public-private partnerships. However, there are no proper institutions to perform this duty. The newly emerged private enforcement agencies, as mentioned in last chapter, have not been fully developed, and are therefore not strong and experienced enough to undertake this enormous task. In this regard, the IPD is expected as an appropriate channel to formulate objectives and benchmarks with a view to regularly setting targets for improvement, monitoring and assessing enforcement progress, and providing professional advice for particular purposes.[206] Such public-private partnership is essential for identifying priorities of the future technical cooperation as well as effectively combating counterfeiting and piracy.

2. Raise Enforcement Concerns

As has been noted, a notable weakness of the Chinese bureaucracy is the obstructed or congested channel between the government and the masses. Freedom of expression is just a tool for citizens and propaganda to sing a collective song of praise.[207] Government polices may not reflect public opinion and public opinions are not exactly and duly heard by the government. The victims of the IPR infringement are usually hesitated, knowing that making a claim to the authority can be expensive and disruptive with much unpredictability.[208] Under such circumstances, information that the government received could be distorted and misleading. Here the IPD can serve as a "bridge" to transform real and critical information to the government. The IPD can collect and analyse data and pass it on to the relevant authorities. Since the IPD is an integral part of the bilateral dialogue scheme based on reciprocal commitments and

---

[206] This point has been adopted and highlighted in the EU's communication with the TRIPs Council. *See* "Transitional Review Mechanism of China," Article 10, Communication from the European Communities, WTO Council for TRIPs, IP/C/W/435, November 26, 2004.

[207] *See* "Press Control Policy: 'Coin It In Silence,'" *Supra* § 4.1.2.

[208] Indeed, facing a trivial infringement, foreign companies, particularly small ones, are, in many circumstances, hesitated whether to take legal actions. To them, "the infringements are just like 'little wood-nibbling worms,' should they turn a blind eye to them, the worms may eat out a whole table." In practice, they sometimes consider themselves less exposed to risk by accepting the facts and tolerating a certain degree of infringement of their rights, rather than playing a waiting game and risking their likelihood in seeking more rigorous IPR protection. *See*, Li Heng, "Double Standards for Chinese and Foreign Big Brands?" *People's Daily*, September 25, 2002.

benefits, if a feedback is required, a prompt response can be expected. In addition, through the forum function of the IPD, participants can express their concerns of IPR enforcement, thereby problems and concerns can be identified and addressed duly and systematically.

3. Influence Decisions of Policy Makers

In the developing world, policy-makers are frequently lobbied to improve their IPR enforcement mechanisms to meet the international standard; [209] however, the decisions of a policy-maker are determined by multiple factors and not by lobbyists preference alone. [210] What makes a claim unique as a determinant of a decision, however, is that this claim reveals success or failure of a government decision. The IPD involves substantial database and social network, and is dedicated to influencing decisions of policy-makers by improving the quality of debate about IPR, raising awareness of the importance of IPR and convincing policy-makers of genuine benefit in improving IPR protection.

PRE-WARNING FUNCTION

The pre-warning function is a function obtained through the reconfiguration of the present IPD. The pre-warning mechanism aims to deliver information to enterprises periodically and provide guidance on how to promote tactical decision making. To achieve this, a profound coverage and a comprehensive network should be established.

1. Target Key Counterfeiting Territories

If the system is to be properly navigated, it is of particular importance to identify poor enforcement conditions and opt for close surveillance of the implementation process on a "sectorial" case-by-case basis. The focus is expected to be on selected key regions where particular efforts should be made to deal with major cases. The priority territories are east and southeast costal provinces, such as Guangdong, Fujian and Zhejiang. The IPD can thus serve as an "investigator" and a "messenger" in an effort to identify the root causes of the problems and suggest meaningful solutions. Where appropriate, the IPD may act as a "monitor" or an "alarm" on the growing dimension of the counterfeiting and piracy. In case of China's non-compliance with its WTO obligations towards IPR protection, the IPD may encourage the right-holders to take full

---

[209] See, e.g., Laurence R. Helfer, "Regime Shifting: The TRIPs Agreement and New Dynamic of International Intellectual property Lawmaking," 29 Yale J. Int'l L. (2004), at 2. See also supra § 2.1.

[210] Scott H. Ainsworth, "The Role of Legislators in the Determination of Interest Group Influence," 22 Legis. Stud. Q., 517, 528 (1997) (mentioning that "a lobbyist's optimal strategy does not depend simply on legislators' preferences or predilections"). See also Martin Reuss, "The Myth and Reality of Policy History: A Response to Robert Kelley," 10 Pub. Hist. 41 (1988) (stating that a policy making process can only commence when policy-makers recognise a problem).

effect of negotiation before seeking recourse to the WTO and making *ex officio* use of the DSB mechanisms.

2. Monitor Key Markets

As demonstrated above, to prioritise some key regions is an effective way to tackle counterfeiting and piracy problems. However, due to limited resources, not all the enforcement agencies are expected to assume the function and responsibility. In this respect, the system of IPD should bear much upon the key markets with high risk of infringement. As far as the EU-China trade is concerned, the key market in general falls in electronic, automobile, and pharmaceutical markets.[211]

3. Recourse to Transparency Provision

The doctrine of transparency in Article 63 of the TRIPs Agreement refers to the obligation of WTO Members to clearly publish their governmental procedures and regulations regarding the ways IPR is protected to ensure predictability of market access.[212] It allows WTO members to request specific information on relevant judicial decisions or administrative rulings that affect the enforcement of IPR under TRIPs.[213] According to the provisions, openness of the public information is achieved and maintained so that interested parties are aware of the risks of any breach of their obligations and the potential disputes are reduced to the minimum level.[214] In the context of world trade, the rule of transparency serves to illuminate the domestic rules of their foreign trade partners, thereby making global transactions more foreseeable.

In this context, it is of importance to clarify detailed reporting guideline through which the EU can invoke the transparency provisions of the TRIPs Agreement to request that China provide appropriate documentation on certain aspects of IPR enforcement that affect their rights under the TRIPs Agreement. A failure to make adequate progress in implementing this duty would constitute a failure to fulfil its TRIPs obligations and as such could provide grounds for recourse through WTO TPR or DSB.

DISPUTE SETTLEMENT

The dispute settlement within IPD consists of two stages reflecting two different functions. First, IPD represents a structural coordinative mechanism which works in light of international trading system. It acts as an intermediary institution and should not surmount or supersede the present TWO TPR or DSB mechanisms. But this, however, has emerged as an advantage of the system in

---

[211] *See supra* § 6.1.3.
[212] Article 63, TRIPs.
[213] *Ibid.*
[214] *Ibid.*

such a country as China where harmony is highly valued.[215] In practice, this system at the initial stage can bring into play as a "buffer zone" before the TPR and DSB are potentially pursued. In the second stage, however, the IPD can be treated as "bypass valve" through which the EU can make full use of TRP and DSB provisions bestowed by WTO.[216] The artful use of prudence, expedience and shrewdness during the two stages exemplifies a well-known Chinese proverb which purports that "try peaceful means before resorting to force (*xian li hou bing*)."

1. Use Right Balance

Apart from mere dispute settlement, strategy for the right balance between negotiation and technical assistance should be applied. As Christopher De Vroey has noted, the EU is aware of the fact that counterfeiting and piracy are common problems in developing countries and understands that technical assistance should be taken into account as an important pattern of cooperation when negotiating with developing countries.[217]

2. The "Force of Example"

It is said "leading by an example sends powerful message." Through dispute settlement machinery, exemplary effects could be achieved through various dissemination and publication channels, such as case reports for the government departments or news releases to the public. From the timely publicity of the cases people can learn what they should do and what they should not do and accept constraints "guided by principles rather than power."[218]

3. Press Conference

It is also important to make regular official announcement in special press conferences and attempt to influent the "orientation of public opinion (*yu lun dao xiang*)." In so doing, smooth and effective relationships with the propaganda and media are required, particularly in such a country as China where

---

[215] Confucius articulates in his works the importance of maintaining harmony in society. This illustrates the preference of mediation in dispute resolution, which is the logical consequence of harmony. For a detailed account of the cultural aspect of dispute resolution in China, *see infra* § 6.4.1.

[216] *See infra* § 6.4.2. & 6.4.3.

[217] The author's interview with Christopher De Vroey, the IPR Director at DG Trade, European Commission, *supra* note 141.

[218] *See* Anne-Marie Slaughter, "Representative Quotes, America's Role in the World," *available at* <http://www.gii-exchange.org/guide/americas_role/repquotes.shtml> ("We can be the nation that accepts constraints even when it doesn't have to, guided by principles rather than power").

structured network of relationships (*guanxi*) plays an important role in China's commercial world.[219]

6.3.3 Roles of Non-Governmental Organisations

Various Non-governmental Organisations (NGOs), both from the EU and China, can play their active roles in promoting a more effective and efficient cooperation between the EU and China. Given China's existing enforcement dilemmas, China needs to seek reliable allies in its struggle to break through the institutional impediment and establish a feasible and acceptable enforcement mechanism, particularly after its accession to the WTO. NGOs, experienced in IPR protection and sustainable development, are able to help China comply with the provisions of TRIPs, in particular, to guide China for a better understanding of development concerns in the context of global trade.

In the EU, a number of NGOs have demonstrated a dedicated commitment to building China's sustainable capacity and subsequently improving its enforcement mechanism. Within EU-China institutional framework, the most dedicated organisation is the European Chamber of Commerce with the Working Group of Intellectual Property as one of its departments.

Give Reins to the EUCCC

The EUCCC, established with the support of the EU Delegation in Beijing in October 2000, is a non-profit organisation with main offices in Beijing, Shanghai and Nanjing.[220] As a leading exponent of European business interests in China, EUCCC aims to serve member companies by being "the voice of European business in China."[221]

The EUCCC publishes its China Position Paper annually, which assesses the progress of China's evolving business environment and identifies the main outstanding issues and concerns that call for resolution.[222] For example, in the 2005 issue of the position paper, IPR enforcement problems were raised and topped the list of its members' concerns.[223] In this document, the EUCCC recommended that Chinese officials destroy fake products confiscated from counterfeiters as stipulated by the existing trademark law.[224] The EUCCC also urged the government to wave the requirement that power of attorney is legalised and to limit the obligation to notarise documents to cases where there is a

---

[219] *See* "Struggle of the Judiciary in Adhering to 'the Correct Political Orientation,'"*supra* § 3.3.2.

[220] *See* "Introduction to EUCCC," *available at* <http://www.europeanchamber.com.cn/>.

[221] *Ibid.*

[222] *Ibid.*

[223] *See* "European Business in China Position Paper 2005," *supra* note 54.

[224] *Ibid*, at 95

"serious objection to their authenticity."[225] The EUCCC's recommendations have made significant impacts across European companies doing business in China and attracted considerable attention from relevant Chinese authorities. For instance, in responding to the request that Chinese lower the level of criminal liability for IPR infringement, on April 4, 2007, the Supreme People's Court promulgated a new judicial interpretation that halves the threshold for criminal prosecution of copyright infringement.[226]

Make Full Play of IPRWG

The EUCCC consists of over 20 Working Groups (WG), among which is an IPR working group (IPRWG), which encompasses European multinationals and enjoys comprehensive database concerning EU's IPR in China.[227] The IPRWG consists of representatives from European law firms, consultants and companies such as Heineken, Nokia and Roche, and is engaged in anti-counterfeiting activities which enable the WG to monitor IPR developments in China and raise concerns to the authorities of both the EU and China over the enforcement of IPR.[228] The WG, therefore, serves as a "bridge" between the business community and European diplomatic presence in China.[229] As an NGO, its coordinative functionality can be achieved smoothly through the European Delegation and EU Embassies in Beijing.

Since its establishment, the IPRWG has been active in addressing hard-solved questions and suggesting constructive solutions in a broad area of IPR especially the enforcement. In September 2007, the fourth session of the IPRWG meeting was held in Beijing where both sides discussed various IPR issues, such as counterfeiting in retail and wholesale markets, licensing agreements in the ICT sector, protection against unfair use of clinical test data, plant variety protection, trade secrets, trade fairs, domain names, as well as technical assistance.[230] According to the agreement reached in this meeting, both parties are obliged to undertake their best efforts to implement a pilot project for enforcement of IPR in retail markets, specifically in the notorious Silk Market[231] (Xiu Shui Market[232]).

---

[225] *Ibid.*

[226] "Zhongguo Chutai Xin Xifa Jieshi Jiada Zhishi Chanquan Xingshi Sifa Baohu[China Issues New Judicial Interpretation to Crackdown Hard on IPR Crime]," *Xinhua Net*, April 5, 2007, *available at* <http://news.xinhuanet.com/legal/2007-04/05/content_5939 800.htm>.

[227] *See* Introduction to EUCCC, *supra* note 220.

[228] *Ibid.*

[229] *Ibid.*

[230] "Outcome of the Fourth EU-China IP Working Group Meeting," *available at* <http://trade.ec.europa.eu/doclib/docs/2007/december/tradoc_137127.pdf>.

[231] *Ibid*, at 95.

[232] For an introduction to the Xin Shui Market in China, *see infra* § 3.4.2.

6.4 Feasible Approaches: Negotiation Strategies

According to Confucius, "[t]he true gentleman is conciliatory but not accommodating; common people are accommodating but not conciliatory (*junzi he er bu tong, xiaoren tong er bu he*)."[233] This famous quote means that wise persons can have harmonious relationships with others without assimilation, while inferior people, on the other hand, can have superficial assimilation without harmony.

Methods of dispute resolution in any society usually reflect that society's normative practices and legal culture. Within a global trade context, cultural differences regarding the appropriate method often give rise to a "multiplicity of perceptions" affecting outcomes of the negotiations.[234] Differences should be properly handled in line with the principle of seeking common ground while reserving differences. Here, we will explore negotiation strategies, taking into account interactions between cultural orientation and commercial behaviour, in particular, from EU-China perspective.

6.4.1 Cultural Characteristics in Commercial Negotiations

Individual Rights as Priority: European Culture in Negotiations

European culture has traditionally prioritised individual rights, which are enforced through individual legal remedy.[235] Many Europeans believe in the "reality principle," making full use of the modern communicative tools in the battleground of debate and confrontation to achieve their goals without having to worry about "loss of face."[236] To this end, litigation is a popular method in commercial dispute settlements.

Live in Harmony: What We Can Learn from Confucianism

By contrast, "living in harmony" (*he wei gui*) is a typical and essential element of Chinese culture that functions ethically when confronting disputes.[237] A

---

[233] *The Analects of Confucius*, 13:23, translated and annotated by Arthur Waley, London: George Allen & Unwin LTD, 177 (1938).

[234] Tanya Kozak, "International Commercial Arbitration/Mediation at CIETAC (China International Economic and Trade Arbitration Commission)," 1999 Dispute Resolution Award in Law Studies, Canadian Forum on Civil Justice, *available at* <http://www.cfcj-fcjc.org/clearinghouse/drpapers-en.php>.

[235] Franco Moretti, *The Way of the World: The Bildungsroman in European Culture* 38-41 (1987).

[236] *Ibid*, at 95

[237] *See* Hyung I. Kim, *Fundamental Legal Concepts of China and the West: A Comparative Study* 17 (1981) ("the purpose of law is to guide the people's conduct so as to cre-

significant aspect of the Confucian attitude towards dispute resolutions is its emphasis on the principle of harmony and the virtue of "giving way (*lirang*)."[238] According to Confucian philosophy, there is a "natural harmony in human affairs" and the most desirable approach to resolving a dispute is through "moral persuasion and agreement" rather than coercion.[239] This culture is associated with maxims such as "harmony is the gate to riches (*he qi sheng cai*)" and "more harmony more prosperity (*jia he wan shi xing*)."[240]

Chinese cultural and social values reflect a significant relationship between law and other social discourses, and these values, to a large degree, illustrate the basic notion of how Chinese laws function domestically and internationally.[241] Influenced by Confucian philosophy, the primary emphasis in society is upon maintaining harmonious interpersonal and social relations,[242] and the main purpose of law and regulations is to shape social roles and to sustain the cardinal order in daily encounters.[243] This traditional perception contributes substantially to the contemporary Chinese attitude towards dispute settlement.[244]

As has been noted, although the influence of Confucian value has diminished in China over the past decades, it is still apparent that the Chinese tend to comply with authorities and adopt subtle philosophy of moral persuasion and conflict avoidance in most spheres of the personal and commercial relations. Interestingly, modern Chinese ideologies and this traditional cultural perception have coexisted with tranquillity.[245] As a result, there is arguably entrenched social spontaneity and cultural inhibition within Chinese people against launching a formal appeal. Even today, presenting before the court (*dui bu gong tang*) is seen as a last resort. Articulation of grievances is per-

---

ate harmonious social order in accord with the natural order"). *See* also, "Principles of Confucianism," *supra* § 4.1.

[238] *See e.g.*, Jay Folberg & Alison *Taylor, Mediation: A Comprehensive Guide to Resolving Conflicts without Litigation* 18(1984)(discussing the importance of mediation in ancient China where the Confucian emphasis was on harmonious relationships and moral persuasion towards agreement).

[239] *See e.g.*, H. Irving and M. Benjamin, *Family Mediation* 46 (1987)(noting that "Confucius emphasised [...] persuasion and agreement as adjuncts to the natural harmony in human affairs").

[240] *See* "Zhongguo Chuantong 'He' Wenhua yu Goujian Hexie Shehui [Traditional Chinese Harmony Culture and the Establishment of Harmonious Society]," 6 Guizhou Shehui Kexue [Guizhou Social Science] (2005), at 55-58.

[241] Shin-yi Peng, Shin-yi Peng, "The WTO Legalistic Approach and East Asia: From the Legal Culture Perspective," 1 *Asian-Pac. L. & Pol'y J.* 9-10 (2000).

[242] Folberg and Taylor, *supra* note 238, at 18.

[243] Shin-yi Peng, *supra* note 241, at 9-10.

[244] *Ibid*, at 10.

[245] *Ibid*, at 11.

ceived as inelegant, humiliating and "a loss of face" (*mian zi*),[246] and the suppression of disputes is a widely-recognised tactics in handling discord.[247] In this context, it is not surprising that many Chinese prefer to settle disputes through a more flexible, less confrontational process, such as consultation or mediation, through which the relevant parties can maintain an amicable "relationship" during and after the dispute settlement.[248] Heavily influenced by this perception, the Chinese show a stronger preference for mediation, consensus building, bargaining, and conciliation than for adversary and inquisitorial litigation.[249]

Cross-Cultural Interactions

In Chinese philosophy, disputes should be dissolved rather than resolved.[250] Forbearance is therefore expected towards disputes and mutual concessions are encouraged and preferred.[251] In many circumstances, even if a party is believed to be in the right, it is desirable for this party to be decent and merciful to the wrong party and forgive gracefully as courtesy.[252] This is usually a yardstick for measuring whether a person is a "gentleman" or a "common person" as Confucius defines.[253] China's deeply-rooted cultural traditions promote settling disputes by verbal and peaceful negotiation, which differs from the European tradition of dispute resolutions.[254] Economic globalisation has undoubtedly had a significant impact on the extent to which culture can be conceived and managed to generalise interaction. [255] Regardless of any Western influence on dispute resolution in modern Chinese society, it appears that Confucian philosophy continues to have far-reaching effects on the Chinese manner of conduct, dictating a harmonious approach as a preferred method of dispute resolution.[256] The "mediation system" (*tiaojie*), which is arguably considered as successful in China, is a natural result of this culture.[257]

---

[246] In China, *face* represents certain self-image of individuals reflecting various social identity and personal dignity. See e.g., David Yau-Fai Ho, "On the Concept of Face," 81(4) *Am. J. Soc.* 867–84 (1976).

[247] Shin-yi Peng, *supra* note 241, at 9.

[248] *Ibid*, at 13.

[249] *Ibid*, at 10.

[250] Rene David, "Two Conceptions of Social Order," 52 *U. Cin. L. Rev.* 140 (1983). See also, *ibid*, at 10.

[251] Shin-yi Peng, *supra* note 241.

[252] *Ibid*, at 10.

[253] *The Analects of Confucius*, 13:23, *supra* note 233 and accompanying text.

[254] Kozak, *supra* note 234.

[255] *Ibid*.

[256] Shin-yi Peng, *supra* note 241, at 10.

[257] Michael T. Colatrella, Jr., "'Court-Performed' Mediation in the People's Republic of China: A Proposed Model to Improve the United States Federal District Courts' Mediation Programs," 15 *Ohio St. J. on Disp. Resol.* 395-6, 399 (demonstrating that, as

In this context, rather than relying on formal and professional mechanisms for dispute resolution, European companies and policy makers need to bear in mind China's cultural antipathy towards conflict. In China, the order of preference for dispute resolution is as follows: (a) negotiation; (b) mediation; (c) arbitration; (d) litigation and (e) unilateral sanction.[258] Negotiation falls "at the most collaborative end of the spectrum and constitutes any form of communication" where disputes are settled peacefully without resort to arbitration or a trial.[259] Disputants who seek to maintain existing business relationship will tend to rely on a collaborative procedure such as negotiation,[260] since winning a case at the sacrifice of losing business is by no means the best choice. Unilateral sanction, which is at the most aggressive end of the spectrum, manifests arrogant hegemony and may only deepen the estrangement and erode the hard-earned partnership.[261]

6.4.2 TPR: Settling Dispute with Gentleness

The TRIPs Agreement establishes a moratorium in the application of a non-violation nullification or impairment remedy. By making the GATT 1994 provisions applicable to the disputes arising under TRIPs Agreement,[262] Article 64 provides for flexible approaches whereby complaining members can resort to a rule-based mechanism for resolving IPR disagreements regarding the TRIPs Agreement.[263] Such a mechanism, while still being debated, has provided necessary predictability and stability to the international IPR system.[264]

Within the WTO, both TPR and DSB have established a clear process whereby the international IPR disputes could be smoothly "dissolved" or peacefully "resolved". While recourse to both TPR and DSB mechanisms is a two-way process between parties involved, in the context of EU-China trade relations, China's shortfall in meeting its WTO commitments appears to be a more significant issue and, in this respect, TPR and DSB may act as an alternative means of leverage in promoting China towards adherence to international standards. Here we only focus on circumstance in which China is arguably not in compliance with its TRIPs obligations.

---

unique Chinese approach to resolving disputes in a peaceful way, mediation (*tiaojie*) is "grounded in both the cultural values and the historical development of China" and has proved to be the most popular method for resolving disputes in modern China).

[258] Danny Ciraco, "Forget the Mechanics and Bring in the Gardeners: An Exploration of Mediation in Intellectual Property Disputes," 9 *U. Balt. Intell. Prop. L.J.* 53 (2000).

[259] *Ibid.*

[260] *Ibid.*

[261] *Ibid.*

[262] *See* TRIPs Article 64(1).

[263] Yu, "Toward a Nonzero-sum Approach," *supra* note 27, at 638.

[264] *Ibid.*

TPR as A Pragmatic Approach: Understanding Before Trust

In the context of multilateral trading system, a "review" is a process by which the reviewing body assesses the behaviour of a state with regard to a rule of international law. [265] In the WTO, each Member is subject to a periodic of inspections and reports, and the collective process of the TPRs is known as the Trade Policy Review Mechanism (TPRM).

TPRM is one of the basic functions of the WTO, set out at Annex 3 to the Marrakech Agreement Establishing the World Trade Organisation,[266] which is designed to facilitate the smooth functioning of the multilateral trading system through regular monitoring and assessment of the effects of policies on the world trading system.[267] It acts as a mandated exercise in which members' trade-related policies are examined and evaluated at regular intervals.[268] To assist in achieving this objective, governments of members are required to follow WTO rules and to fulfil their commitments, by informing outsiders of a country's policies and circumstances, and by providing critical appraisal to reviewed countries on their performance in the global trading system.[269] In this context, TPR aims at, *inter alia*, enhancing transparency and facilitating predictability of the Members' own trade policies and practices, reflecting one of the most important principles within the WTO.[270]

TPR FOR DEVELOPED STATES: A SOFT SWORD

It is clear that TPR can be used, and has been used,[271] by developed states as an instrument to safeguard interests of their IPR owners. In the event that their intangible rights are alleged to be infringed, they are entitled to recourse to TPR for clarifications and rectifications. However, since it only serves *notifying and monitoring* functions, rather than *compulsory enforcement* functions,

---

[265] William Steinberg, "Monitor With No Teeth, An Analysis of the WTO China Trade Review Mechanism," 6 *U.C. Davis Bus. L.J.* 2 (2005).

[266] *See* Annex 3: Trade Policy Review Mechanism, at 379-381.

[267] "Trade Policy Reviews: Ensuring Transparency," in *Understanding the WTO*, WTO Publication (third edition, 2005).

[268] The interval of review depends on member's geographical size and economic strength. The four members with the largest share of trade, including the United States, the EU, Japan and China, are reviewed every two years; the next 16 largest traders every four years, and the remaining members every six years. *See*, Trade Policy Review Mechanism, April 15, 1994, WTO Agreement, Annex 3, at 379-381. For a brief account of the intervals for review of the trade policies of Members, *see*, Ian F. Fergusson, "The World Trade Organization: Background and Issues," *CRS Report for Congress*, May 09, 2007, at 7.

[269] "Trade Policy Reviews: Ensuring Transparency," *supra* note 267, at 58.

[270] *Ibid.*

[271] While TPR formed part of the Uruguay Round agreement, the review itself had been set up on a provisional basis before the round ended. In this connection it existed as an early result of the negotiations. *See "Understanding the WTO," supra* note 243.

it is not binding in nature.[272] Due to this characteristic, TPR is, in theory, a WTO instrument without "teeth."[273] In this context, TPR is seen as a "soft sword" for developed states which are concerned of their IPR and are calling for stronger protection in the developing world.

However, this does not necessarily mean that TPR is inconsequential for developed countries. In fact, it may serve as a potential prelude of a formal process for the dispute settlement as an attempt to avoid any litigation with a combination of consultation and negotiation.[274] From that perspective, using TPR properly can still put considerable pressure on a government in question and potentially generate influence on the decision making of that country.

TPR FOR DEVELOPING STATES: A HARD SHIELD

While TPR is used by developed states as a useful apparatus to monitor IPR protection, developing states, in turn, are in a position to use it to review distortions in trade being caused by excessively high IPR standards.[275] As discussed in previous chapters, TRIPs has provided reasonable levels of flexibility to the domestic policies of developing states.[276] In a global context, intellectual property protection is more a matter of development than a "trade-related" issue. In light of long-term development strategy reflected in the TRIPs Agreement, developed states are well expected to assess their conduct of trade negotiations with developing states with a view that development objectives remain within the agenda during the negotiations.[277] Indeed, the non-compulsory nature of the system has equipped Members with capacities to exert flexibility and discretion in their decision-making process. As a consequence, public interest exemption from compliance with a compulsory standard may be granted in certain individual cases to achieve broader societal goals, such as addressing issues of access to essential pharmaceuticals, in developing countries.

Given the provisions confined by the TRIPs, TPR is a legal, feasible and flexible way for developing states to keep the balance of TRIPs obligations and domestic requirements and to prevent IPR from being abused. To that extent, the TRP mechanism provides, or at least has potential to provide, legitimacy and leverage to safeguard public interest and development objectives within the present global IPR regime.

---

[272] Steinberg, *supra* note 265.

[273] *Ibid.*

[274] Julien Chaisse and Debashis Chakraborty, "Implementing WTO Rules through Negotiations and Sanction: The Role of Trade Policy Review Mechanism and Dispute Settlement System" 28 *U. Pa. J. Int'l Econ. L.* 179 (2007).

[275] Steinberg, *supra* note 265, at 3.

[276] *See, e.g., supra* § 2.3.2 & § 5.4.2 and the complying footnotes.

[277] Peter Drahos, "Developing Countries and International Intellectual Property Standard-setting" (Study Paper 8) in *Integrating Intellectual Property Rights and Development Policy*, Report of the Commission on Intellectual Property Rights.

SCOPE AND LIMITATION

While the TPR is designed to fulfil the monitoring and supervisory functions of the WTO, it is, however, not intended "to serve as a basis for the enforcement of specific obligations under the WTO Agreements, for dispute settlement procedures, or to improve new policy commitments on Members that should otherwise be done through the multilateral negotiation."[278] TPR by itself is not to assess members' compliance with WTO rules. Legal compatibility with WTO disciplines is not determined by the TPR, but left to members to ascertain.

TRM and TPR: China's Perspective

In addition to commitments set forth in the accession documents and other existing multilateral WTO agreements, China has adopted numerous "obligations above and beyond the usual WTO commitments required of other members."[279] These include, *inter alia*, establishing a mechanism for responding to requests from any WTO member or foreign company for information, or investigating cases of alleged inconsistent application, and agreeing to an additional transitional review mechanism for overseeing its compliance.[280]

One of the significant conditions of China's accession was the creation of a special review process, referred to as the Transitional Review Mechanism (TRM), to monitor China's post-accession compliance with its WTO obligations.[281] The most significant difference between China's TRM and the TPRs of other Members is the frequency of the reviews.[282] According to Article 18 of China's Protocol to Accession, the TRM would occur annually for eight consecutive years commencing from 2002 with a final review in the tenth year.[283] China's WTO implementation and compliance is reviewed annually in 16 WTO committees and councils [284] followed by an overall review by the

---

[278] "Overseeing National Trade Policies: the TPRM, Trade Policy Review: Brief Introduction," WTO, *available at* <www.wto.org/english/tratop_e/tpr_e/tp_int_e.htm>, last visited March 31, 2006.

[279] Sharon Hom, "China and the WTO: Year One," 1 *China Rights Forum* 13 (2003).

[280] *See* "Accession of the People's Republic of China," WT/L/432, WTO Doc. 01-5996.

[281] Steinberg, *supra* note 265.

[282] *Ibid*, at 3.

[283] *See* China Protocol, Article 18(4).

[284] For example, on December 10, 2002, China passed its annual TPR on the first year of its WTO membership. The review covered areas of China's fulfilment of its WTO commitments including, *inter alia*, IPR protection. Sixteen WTO members, including the United States, the EU and Japan, finalised their assessments on China's practice within the WTO. In the review, Japan emphasised the importance of IPR enforcement and addressed their concerns raised by the Japanese business community. *See* "China Passes WTO Trade Policy Review," *Xinhua News Agency*, December 21, 2002.

WTO General Council based on the reports and issues of the subsidiary bodies.[285]

The TRM rigid annual review process with China is unprecedented and unique within the WTO.[286] By contrast, other members receive a TPR every two to six years depending on their "rank" in the world trading system.[287] China's exceptional position reflects its peculiar socioeconomic dilemma, since other "WTO members viewed normal TPR as insufficient to oversee China's implementation of its commitments and pursued the TRM specially."[288] In addition, China's TRM process will not replace the normal TPR reviews, meaning that China will not be exempted from participating in TPR reviews based on the standard WTO schedules.[289] However, since China will be involved in review process more substantially and frequently in its annual TRM reviews, the functions of regular TPR reviews could be somewhat nominal and flexible.[290]

Moreover, the review framework of TRM appears to be more comprehensive and complex than other WTO mechanisms.[291] According to this special annual compliance review, China is obliged to provide detailed information and submit detailed responses to any concerns addressed by both the subsidiary bodies and the General Council,[292] which means that, apart from conducting their annual review encompassing all of the WTO Members together, each of these bodies conducts an annual China-specific review independently via a separate route.[293]

Additionally, Article 18, the provision that shapes basic legal structure of China's TRM,[294] refers to annex 1A, which provides additional provisions for the content of the reviews. This annex takes pains to enumerate 62 commitments concerning economic and trade policy information[295] that China is re-

---

[285] Hom, *supra* note 279, at 13; Steinberg, *supra* note 265, at 2.

[286] Steinberg, *supra* note 265.

[287] *See* "Overseeing National Trade Policies," *supra* note 278. As Steinberg commented, "China would receive a review every four years." *See* Steinberg, *supra* note 265.

[288] *See* "U.S.-China Trade: Summary of 2003 World Trade Organisation Transitional Review Mechanism for China," United States Government Accountability Office, January 25, 2005, *available at* <http://www.gao.gov/new.items/d05209r.pdf>, last visited March 31, 2006.

[289] Steinberg, *supra* note 265.

[290] *Ibid.*

[291] *Ibid.*

[292] Hom, *supra* note 279, at 13.

[293] Steinberg, *supra* note 265.

[294] *See* "Accession of the People's Republic of China," Article 18 (4), WT/L/432, WTO Doc. 01-5996.

[295] Annex 1A, "Accession of the People's Republic of China," *available at* <http://english. mofcom.gov.cn/article/topic/wto/law03.doc>.

quested to provide to various WTO committees during the TRM process, [296] through which China has resigned itself to a stubborn position that commitments must be fulfilled unconditionally. Such dominant and submissive atmosphere could undermine mutual trust and lead to the erosion of the bilateral cooperative relations.

Policy Review and IPR: EU-China Interaction

On November 26, 2004, pursuant to paragraph 18 of the Protocol on the Accession of China to the WTO, the European Commission and the TRIPs Council conducted reviews of the implementing legislation of China as part of China's transitional review mechanism. [297]

In this TRM, the European Commission raised 6 particular questions for China to clarify. [298] For example, the Commission requested that the State Intellectual Property Office (SIPO) provide detailed information to clarify the "National Strategy on IPR" that was declared in April 2004.[299] SIPO was expected to answer questions as to whether this new Strategy would shortly be launched and would "have for main objective to enhance the competitiveness of Chinese businesses in the global economy"; whether the National Strategy "foresaw more transparency in the decision making process" and "accelerated procedures for the registration of patents and trade marks"; whether the National Strategy "included specific measures to reinforce the combat against counterfeiting and piracy," and whether National Strategy included an educational programme to deepen intellectual property knowledge among officials at ministerial and provincial levels.[300]

The EU's efforts began to bear fruit at last. The Standing Committee of the National People's Congress in China has recently approved the amendment to the Scientific and Technological Progress Law on December 29, 2007, [301] a move that signals final preparations of the state before the publication of the long-awaited National Intellectual Property Strategy (NIPS).[302] The NIPS is designed to raise IPR awareness throughout the country, encourage so-called joined-up government by connecting existing IPR policies in different gov-

---

[296] See "U.S.-China Trade: Summary of 2003 World Trade Organisation Transitional Review Mechanism for China," *supra* note 266.

[297] "Transitional Review Mechanism of China," TRIPs Council, Contribution of the European Communities, Directorate-General for Trade, Brussels, 26 November 2004.

[298] *Ibid.*

[299] *Ibid.*

[300] *Ibid.*

[301] The amended Scientific and Technological Progress Law will take into effect from on July 1, 2008. *See* Order of the People's Republic of China No. 82 (December 29, 2007); Article 75, The Scientific and Technological Progress Law.

[302] Peter Ollier, "China Gets Ready for National IP Strategy," *Managing Intellectual Property*, January 14, 2008.

ernment agencies and, in the words of Thomas Pattloch, the Intellectual Property Officer at the Delegation of the European Commission in Beijing, take "a macroeconomic look at IPR protection."[303] Since the National Working Group for IPR Protection (NWGIPR) was set up in 2004,[304] it has been dedicated in coordinating IPR policies and developing a more comprehensive National Intellectual Property Strategy. The promulgation of the new Scientific and Technological Progress Law reflects firm commitments by the Chinese government to facilitate independent intellectual properly, and build an innovation-oriented state. It is estimated that the NIPS is to be published in spring 2008 before it is finally approved by the People's Congress.

6.4.3 DSB: Additional Form of Leverage

A significant feature of the Uruguay Round negotiations was the establishment of a brand new system dealing with international trade disputes, known as the WTO Dispute Settlement Understanding (DSU).[305] Like the TRM, in the event that trade disputes arouse over IPR, the DSU can be used as leverage to a settlement. The only difference is that the former is a mechanism without constraining force while the later is a mechanism containing "teeth."

DSU as A Potent Tool: Looking before Leaping

Within the WTO framework, legal rules are enforced through a specific dispute settlement system which is governed by the WTO Dispute Settlement Understanding (DSU).[306] The DSU is an integral part of the Marrakesh Agreement Establishing the World Trade Organisation, consisting of twenty-seven articles and four appendices of the WTO Agreements, and setting out more substantial rules and procedures for settling international trade disputes among WTO members than the GATT dispute resolution system as its predecessor.[307] As the main proponent of the DSU, the United States, together with other developed countries,[308] expected that the new mechanism for implementing dispute settlement rulings would significantly improve the existing en-

---

[303] *Ibid.*

[304] *See infra* § 3.4.2.

[305] "Dispute Settlement Understanding," in *Understanding the WTO*, WTO Publication (2005), at 87.

[306] Joost Pauwelyn, "Enforcement and Countermeasures in the WTO: Rules Are Rules – Toward a More Collective Approach," 94 *Am. J. Int'l L.* 336 (2000).

[307] For full text and an articulating interpretation of the DSU, *see, Understanding on Rules and Procedures Governing the Settlement of Disputes*, Annex 2 of the WTO Agreement, *available at* <http://www.wto.org/english/ tratop_e/dispu_e/dsu_e.htm>.

[308] Christopher Duncan, "Out of Conformity: China's Capacity to Implement World Trade Organization Dispute Settlement Body Decisions after Accession," 18 *Am. U. Int'l L. Rev.* (2002), at 433.

forcement capacity,[309] and therefore maximise the value and efficiency of the WTO as a whole.[310] In the context of global protection of IPR, the TRIPs Agreement subjects the IPR obligations to the rules-based and self-contained WTO DSU mechanism, thus providing an institutional framework for enforcement and further development of the IPR international standards.[311]

DSB: The Overseeing Body

Under the DSU, the Dispute Settlement Body (DSB) is established as the exclusive body overseeing international disputes involving trade in goods, services and intellectual property.[312] As a one-member-one-vote political organ[313] consisting of representatives from all WTO Members signed on to each particular agreement at issue, the DSB functions as an effective tool for trade dispute settlements,[314] and the recommendations made by DSB should be considered binding legal obligations in the sense of international law.[315] Thus, by imposing the rules based on DSU mechanism, the DSB administers IPR disputes between the Members over compliance with TRIPs obligations with regard to either substantive standards or domestic enforcement procedures.[316]

Implication to EU-China Relations

In the context of EU-China relations, implementations towards the DSB are two fold. On China's side, while China is poised to become a grown engine

---

[309] *Ibid* (noting that, unlike the former GATT system which "allowed a party to 'block' both the formation of a panel and the acceptance of the decision itself," the new mechanism "made adoption of its decisions practically automatic, and reinforced their implementation through severe remedial measures for non-compliance").

[310] *See* Lawrence D. Roberts, "Beyond Notions of Diplomacy and Legalism: Building a Just Mechanism for WTO Dispute Resolution," 40 *Am. Bus. L.J.* (2003), at 525 (mentioning that the DSU is designed to facilitate the goal of the WTO).

[311] Peter M. Gerhart, "Reflections: Beyond Compliance Theory – TRIPs as a Substantive Issue," 32 *Case Western Reserve J. Int'l L.* 358 (2000).

[312] Article 2 of DSU specifies the rules and procedures of the DSB establishing and governing the DSU. *See* Article 2, *ibid.*

[313] Pauwelyn, *supra* note 306 (discussing that, in order to obtain legal validity, the reports provided by member panels and the standing Appellate Body "are referred to, and need to be adopted by, the WTO's dispute settlement body (DSB), a one-member-one-vote political organ").

[314] Duncan, *supra* note 308, at 435.

[315] John H. Jackson, "The WTO Dispute Settlement Understanding - Misunderstandings on the Nature of Legal Obligation," 91 *Am. J. Int'l .L.* 60, 62-3 (1997) (stressing that the DSU "clearly establishes a preference for an obligation to perform the recommendation", and the WTO rulings are binding in the sense of "traditional international law").

[316] For a precise interpretation of the settlement procedure, *see, The WTO Dispute Settlement Procedures, A Collection of the Relevant Legal Texts*, 2nd Edition, WTO Secretariat, Cambridge University Press (2001).

for the world economy, several factors still exist that might potentially inhibit its capacity to undertake the DSB commitments. Potential pitfalls in China's legislative and administrative systems are still noticeable, or even extensive, compared with DSB standards, and China lacks sufficient expertise in dealing with WTO dispute settlement cases.[317] For these reasons, although the Chinese leadership has demonstrated its strong desire to comply with DSB standards, the prospect that these intentions will be realised remains uncertain.[318] In light of the fact that China has not attracted batches of WTO complaints, it would be wise for China to "cast an anchor to windward" by taking necessary preventive measures.

On the side of the EU, it is not unusual that the EU frequently vacillates between aggressive and rational policy positions towards China. Frustrated with the rampant counterfeiting problems, the EU is concerns whether the DSB approach has become the last recourse by which to leverage China's compliance with international standards. As has been noted earlier in this chapter, China's cultural preference for harmony runs deep in Chinese consciousness.[319] In other words, Chinese have cultural repugnance for confrontation. Admittedly, it is a corollary that Chinese cultural tendencies are durable, though flexible. China's integration into the global economy will not fundamentally change these tendencies. In this context, the EU should use prudence to enforce China's adherence to WTO obligations through recourse to the DSB mechanism. Under the DSU mechanism, China's compliance should be "mutually satisfactory," requiring both sides to "work together to manage the challenges of international economic integration."[320] The EU should make deliberate decisions about maintaining cooperation and "creat[ing] synergies with countries sharing its concerns and facing similar problems."[321]

It needs to be addressed that the WTO DSB mechanism has been made optional to the EU right-holders to recourse to. According to "EU Strategy to Enforce Intellectual Property Rights in Third Countries,"[322] it is an enforcement strategy to make use of the Trade Barriers Regulation "in cases of evidence of violations of TRIPs," or to make *ex officio* use of the dispute settlement

---

[317] Duncan, *supra* note 308, at 475.

[318] *Ibid*, at 492.

[319] In Confucianism, the ultimate political goal was to create great harmony in the world. *See* "Principles of Confucianism," *supra* Chapters 4 and Chapter 5.

[320] David Blumental, "'Reform' or 'Opening'? Reform of China's State-owned Enterprises and WTO Accession: The Dilemma of Applying GATT to Marketizing Economies," 16 *UCLA Pac. Basin L.J.* 198, 200 243 (1998).

[321] "Strategy for the Enforcement of Intellectual Property Rights in Third Countries," *Official Journal of the European Union*, C 129/3 (2005).

[322] *See* "EU Strategy to Enforce Intellectual Property Rights in Third Countries – Facts and Figures," *supra* note 77.

mechanisms included in multilateral or bilateral agreements "in case of non-compliance with the required standards of IP protection." [323]

As discussed in the last chapter, the EU Commission set out a target for identifying and focusing on the "priority countries," and China was appointed as one of the most problematic countries. Now China has been brought to the most vulnerable position.

Moreover, the United States, the old rival of China in IPR arena, has announced a comprehensive action plan to deal with Chinese IPR issues.[324] As has been mentioned, on April 9, 2007, the U.S. launched two cases against China at the WTO over deficiencies in China's intellectual property laws and market access barriers to copyright-based industries. [325] The U.S.'s complain is that, China pledged to improve its IPR enforcement in its accession protocol to the WTO, but the IPR enforcement remains pervasive. Since the U.S. arguably acts as "the potent, [and] the omnipresent teacher" in the international arena,[326] it is reasonable to wonder whether some other countries, including the EU, might be "taught" to follow their footstep.

Apparently, after American's complaints, Chinese leaders and trade officials are concerned of a possible "domino effect" leading to a profusion of trade disputes. However, EU's attitude is more than ambiguous. The EU trade commissioner Peter Mandelson has stated recently in Beijing that the EU does not rule out its initiating action at the WTO if the enforcement problem remains pervasive. [327] Mandelson emphasised that "Europe has so far held back from testing China's practice on intellectual property protection in the WTO, preferring to prioritise dialogue and cooperation instead. But the sincerity of our approach is being tested, and I regret this. It is hard to see how much longer our patience can last if treatment does not improve." [328] While some commentators' interpretation is optimistic, suggesting that Brussels is employing astute tactics of good cop to the Washington's bad cop to promote China to make reasonable concessions, it appears to be more of a "confused" cop. [329]

---

[323] *Ibid,* Article 5.

[324] "IPR Case against China?" 7(1) *International Trade Centre (ITC) Newsletter* 3 (January 2006).

[325] *See infra* § 6.2.2 and the accompanying footnotes.

[326] This expression is borrowed from a statement of Justice Louis Brandeis, who says "[o]ur government is the potent, the omnipresent teacher. For good or for ill, it teaches the whole people by its example. Crime is contagious. If the government becomes a lawbreaker, it breeds contempt for law; it invites every man to become a law unto himself; it invites anarchy." *See, Olmstead v. United States,* 277 U.S. 438, 485 (1928)(Brandeis, J., dissenting). As the recognised international police, the U.S. may deserve this epithet as the "potent, [and] the omnipresent teacher" of the world.

[327] Peter Mandelson, "Protecting IPR in China," *Trade Fairs Seminar*, Beijing, November 26, 2007, *available at* <http://trade.ec.europa.eu/doclib/docs/2008/january/tradoc_137 535.pdf>.

[328] *Ibid.*

[329] Peter Ollier, "The End of the Beginning," *Managing Intellectual Property*, May 2007.

Regardless of legal merits of the political considerations,[330] aggravation of the dispute would certainly jeopardise the mutual interests, threatening to worsen the already fragile bilateral relations. As Duncan observes, constant and complex litigations involving WTO TRIPs could contrarily inhibit China's effective compliance with its TRIPs obligations.[331] Spurned by having to respond to a large number of TRIPs disputes, China could be proactive to employ the DSU's retaliation or cross-retaliation enforcement mechanisms to legitimise its own non-compliance in the event that China is in a position to challenge another Member.[332] This trend is apt to be exacerbated with the sparked emotional confrontations leading to a new round of trade wars.

Pros and Cons of DSB

In the context of global trade involving IPR protection, the lack of proper implementation and enforcement of IPR has tremendously affected and seriously undermined the interests of the right holders. The availability of the DSB mechanism to enforce obligations under the TRIPs Agreement is designed to ensure that IPR holders can continue to expand their opportunities and diversify their portfolios, thus reducing business risks and making foreign investment for predictable and manageable.

However, as has been noted, DSB should be applied as a last resort to settle disagreements, particularly in such a unique country as China where harmonisation rather than arbitration presents as a preferred method for resolving difference. This characteristic makes China more amenable to early settlement of what could become a potentially divisive trade dispute.[333] Therefore, a WTO complaint may seem embarrassing or even offensive to China and deteriorate the EU-China bilateral relations. To win a lawsuit at the risk of jeopardising long-term trade relationship is of course not a desirable scenario for a healthily functioning EU-China trade relationship.

6.5 Six-Step Strategy

As discussed in previous chapters, China has made significant progress in establishing and strengthening its IPR protection system and has, to a considerable extent, fulfilled the substantive standards set out by the TRIPs Agree-

---

[330] *See* Christopher Swann, Raphael Minder and James Mackintosh, "EU and US in WTO Challenge to China," *Financial Times*, March 30 2006 (mentioning that certain WTO complains may be attributed to the fervour of protectionism which has become growingly prevalent recently both in the U.S. and in the EU).

[331] *See* Duncan, *supra* note 308, at 481.

[332] *Ibid*, at 482.

[333] *Ibid*, at 496.

ment. However, the unbalanced reform gives rise social-political crisis, resulting in the emergence of the utilitarianism, which eroded traditional basis for social cohesion and undermined ethical foundation sustaining adequate IPR protection. As such, enforcement has often been weak.

To target enforcement shortfalls, this section contemplates a six-step strategy that seeks to reformulate the existing ineffective IPR policy towards EU-China relations. First, this strategy covers actions that are needed to cultivate a stable and harmonious relationship between the EU and China and to foster a mutual understanding, particularly an understanding of China by the EU scholars, entrepreneurs, policymakers, and the general public, and the avoidance of application of the inappropriate "tying policy." Second, the strategy focuses on the long-term efforts that are required to promote a self-sustainable IPR regime in China with creative escalating tactics of regional and industrial expansions.

6.5.1 Step One: Leniency rather than Coercion

Anne-Marie Slaughter has given a most picturesque account of the two contrast approaches towards dispute resolution:

"We can achieve far more through persuasion than bullying, through humility than arrogance, through generosity than sanctions, through the force of example than the example of force." [334]

As has been noted in chapter 3 and chapter 4, repeated campaigns for external pressure against China regarding stronger IPR protection reflects an ignorance of the bureaucratic nature of the Chinese legal, economic and political systems.[335] While such external pressure may lead to a prompt updating of IPR laws and regulations, it is the unique cultural perception and the complex network of bureaucracies that influence the attitude of the citizenries towards IPR and decide IPR policy of Chinese authorities.[336] To cultivate and foster a stable relationship between the EU and China, based on the understanding of the Chinese unique culture, a "leniency" strategy is required.

---

[334] Anne-Marie Slaughter, "Representative Quotes, America's Role in the World," *supra* note 218.

[335] Andrew C Mertha, *The Politics of Piracy, Intellectual Property in Contemporary China* 230-31(2005); *see* also Yiqiang Li, "Evaluation of the Sino-American Intellectual Property Agreements," 10 *Colum. J. Asian L.* No 2 (1996), at 391, 393-94 (explaining the bureaucratic norms of Chinese political infrastructure).

[336] Mertha, *ibid*, at 230-31.

Limitations of the Coercive Policy

Under a coercive approach, a trading party relies on their superiority in various aspects to force another party to do what it might otherwise refuse to do.[337] This approach has been widely practiced throughout the history of international trade,[338] with a prime example being Section 301 of the Trade Act of 1974.[339]

While a coercive approach is arguably effective in demanding immediate compliance and inducing short-term concessions,[340] gains from coercion are usually ephemeral, if not accompanied by instant domestic enforcement of IPR.[341] Coercion tends to invite retaliation[342] and, in many circumstances, invokes emotional "eye for eye, tooth for tooth" response.[343] In addition, as Julia Cheng has commented, coercive strategy in the current new era of cooperative global efforts is anachronistic.[344] Additionally, as has been mentioned above, trade sanctions are against principles and provisions of the WTO.[345] Moreover, the high-profile trade sanctions would tend to undermine the cooperative style of the WTO,[346] converting what should be technical and legal trade issues to the political debates and turning structured legal forum into polarised political battlefield.[347]

Up to this point, the coercive strategy has proved to be inappropriate in achieving its goals. For example, when the U.S. administration immersed itself with criticising China over its IPR enforcement problems, Chinese leaders paid a visit to France and placed an order for an estimated 1.5 billion dollars worth of Airbus planes, instead of Boeing planes, sending a deliberate signal to Washington that Beijing can turn to European partners if the bilateral trade with the United States remains intractable.[348] Arguably this demonstrates a preference in China towards the EU's flexible and cooperative strategy.

---

[337] Yu, *supra* note 27, at 573.

[338] *Ibid.*

[339] *See supra* Chapter 1, note 71.

[340] Yu, *supra* note 27, at 581.

[341] Julia Cheng, "China's Copyright System: Rising to the Spirit of TRIPs Requires an Internal Focus and WTO Membership," *21 Fordham Int'l L. J.* 2007 (1998).

[342] *See* Scott Fairley, "Extraterritorial Assertions of Intellectual Property Rights in International Trade," in George R. Stewart *et al.* (eds.), *International Trade and Intellectual Property: The Search for a Balanced System* 141, 144 (1994).

[343] *See* Yu, *Supra* note 27, at 579, 580 (noting that the coercive approach "rarely succeeds in the long run").

[344] Cheng, *supra* note 341, at 2007.

[345] *See supra* § 2.3.2, § 6.1.1.

[346] Yu, "From Pirates to Partners," *supra* note 97, at 169.

[347] *See,* C. Baum, "Trade Sanctions and the Rule of Law: Lessons from China", *Stan. J. E. Asian Aff.* 64 (2001).

[348] Craig R. Whitney, "China Awards Huge Jet Order to Europeans," *N.Y. Times,* April 11, 1996, at A1.

In addition, there has been growing empirical evidence that the coercive approach does not always reflect the wishes of the transnational corporations.[349] Many entrepreneurs with businesses in China have mixed emotions about being in China.[350] While many companies, particularly in the software, media, and high-tech areas, are lobbying for enhanced IPR protection in China, in general, many companies on the ground are more keen on maintaining the existing business revenues and, therefore, reluctant to confront the Chinese authorities through trade sanction.[351] It seems that, some foreign enterprises, including European companies, are not sending clear signals to their own Governments. According to a recent survey, forty-seven percent of the foreign companies in China view coercive policy completely or highly unpredictable.[352]

Bra War: Sign of Danger

The "bra wars" refer to an unresolved stalemate over EU-imposed sanctions on Chinese textiles in the summer of 2005.[353] After realising that there had been a substantial rise in Chinese exports of some of the liberalised textile product categories, the European Commission launched an investigation and took urgent action on curbing the import of Chinese t-shirts and flax yarn.[354] On June 10, 2005, the European Commission and the Ministry of Commerce of China reached an agreement, which was to have been effective until the end of 2007.[355] This agreement covered ten of the thirty-five textile categories of Chinese imports that were made quota-free on January 1, 2005, in accordance with the new WTO agreement.[356] There has been blistering criticism, however, towards the "bra wars" from scholars and practitioners.[357] Even within the EU,

---

[349] This conclusion is based on a survey conducted by the author in June – August, 2003. *See* the List of Interview (question 3-4) and List of Semi-structured Interview Questions (question 7) as well as the responses at the corresponding List of Charts.

[350] *See* Juhan Ke, *supra* note 156.

[351] *Ibid.*

[352] *See* the List of Semi-structured Interview Questions (question 7) and the responses at the corresponding Charts.

[353] Nick Assinder, "Bra War Threatens Blair China Talks," *BBC News Online*, September 5, 2005, *available at* <http://news.bbc.co.uk/1/hi/uk_politics/4213110.stm>.

[354] *See* "'Bra War' Storms EU and China," *available at* <http://www.domainb.com/industry/textiles/20050903_ bra_war.html#1>.

[355] *Ibid.*

[356] *Ibid.*

[357] Maxine Frith, "Revealed: How Bra Wars Devastate World's Poor," *The Independent*, August 27, 2005. *See* also Kate Rankine and David Rennie, "'Bra wars' May Push up Price of Clothes," *Telegraph*, August 25, 2005 (stating that the "bra wars" will only hurt the struggling European retailers).

there is a significant divide among EU Member States.[358] While a written agreement was reached, the EU Commission's efforts, thus far, to resolve the textiles crisis have borne no tangible results.[359]

In the area of IPR enforcement, there have been claims to apply deterrent sanctions and remedies based on the Directive on the Enforcement of Intellectual Property Rights.[360] The "bra war" was a signal of danger. Vigilant attention is required to prevent trade war from extending to the EU-China IPR debate, which has so far been rational.

Avoid European-styled "Section 301"

In promoting China's IPR enforcement, there are various facilitating and inhibiting factors which may ultimately affect the decision-making process. In view of EU-China trade relations, it is apparent that the effect of pursuing a strategic collaborative approach outweighs the impact of using the trade weapon, which can only solidify China's domestic resistance and result in intermittent and incoherent responses. China's harmonious philosophy and the lessons derived from U.S. sanctions have shown that a coercive policy is ineffective.

The European-styled "Section 301", provided it were so conceived, would not be a desirable solution to settle trade disputes.[361] The EU should therefore avoid utilising harsh trade sanctions and pursue practical and workable approaches to resolving disputes and differences.

6.5.2 Step Two: From "Tying Practice" to Undiscounted Policy

Tying sale is the practice of making the sale of one product conditional on the purchase of a second distinctive product.[362] It is a quota sale characterised by a combination package which is normally regarded as anti-competitive as it is implied that one or more components of the package are sold individually by other businesses as their primary product; thereby this bundling of goods

---

[358] The northern states with substantial retail interests, such as Denmark, Finland, Germany, Sweden and the Netherlands, have expressed their serious concerns that the quotas could lead to layoffs of their retailers' staff and therefore request that quotas should be lifted. Contrary to the northern states, the southern textile producing states – France, Greece, Italy, Portugal and Spain – call for protection against free trade to prevent the European textile market from being saturated. See *"Bra War" Storms EU and China*, *supra* note 327.

[359] *Ibid.*

[360] *See* 2004/48/EC and § 5.3.1.

[361] *See* the List of Interview Questions (question 4).

[362] *See, e.g.,* "European Commission, Glossary: Tying or Tied Selling," *available at* <http://ec.europa.eu/comm/competition/general_info/t_en.html>.

would hurt their business.[363] Through the practice of "tying," the supplier threatens to withhold the key product, thereby increasing sales of products that are undesirable.[364]

In political terms, a "tying sale" refers to a policy which can only be applied in a conditional manner towards a particular country, while for other countries there is no such restriction.[365] This conditional treatment acts as leverage to force or lure a country into accepting an unfavourable political decision or arrangement. Under such circumstances, countries which are being unfairly treated will naturally suspect the sincerity of the motives. Due to lack of mutual credibility, it is difficult to push forward a constructive and cooperative relationship.

A noticeable example is the United States' linkage of human rights to trade with China.[366] In the aftermath of the Tiananmen Square Protests in 1989, many U.S. politicians lobbied to link the normalisation of Sino-American trade to improvements in China's human rights record, and profound social and political reform in China.[367] The U.S. Congress and the Clinton administration continued to grant annual extensions of normal MFN status and Normal Trade Relations Status as leverage to get the concessions they sought from China.[368] In 2004, the EU emulated the United States by linking Market Economy Status (MES) to IPR and refusing to grant China the MES.[369] The

---

[363] *Ibid.*

[364] *Ibid.*

[365] This "conditional" policy has been described by some developing countries as "double standards". *See, e.g.* Randall Peerenboom, "Assessing Human Rights in China: Why the Double Standard?" 38 *Cornell Int'l L.J. 74* (2005)(discussing the human rights double standard as applied to China).

[366] *See e.g.*, Patricia Stirling, "The Use of Trade Sanctions as an Enforcement Mechanism for Basic Human Rights: A Proposal for Addition to the World Trade Organisation," *Am. U. J. Int'l L. & Pol'y*, 28 (1996)(noting that the United States "preferred the use of unilateral actions such as sanctions. These actions have often linked human rights to trade as in the recent China dispute and in numerous other instances"); Robbyn Reichman-Coad, "Human Rights Violations in China: A United States Response," 15 *N.Y.L. Sch. J. Int'l & Comp. L.* 185 (1994)(mentioning that, "[i]n 1993, President Clinton followed through with his campaign promise to be tough with China and issued an executive order which linked human rights and trade benefits. He stated that China's privileged trade status would not be renewed unless the Beijing government significantly improved its human rights record"); *See* also, Evan S. Medeiros, "United States-China Relations: Comparative Security and Foreign Policy Processes," *Delegation Report,* NCUSCR Publication, *available at* <http://www.ncuscr.org/Publications/ Medeiros.html> (noting that "Sino-American relations have been plagued with a number of difficulties that have complicated the expansion [...] of further institutionalization of political, economic, and military ties between Washington and Beijing").

[367] Medeiros, *ibid.*

[368] *Ibid.*

[369] *See* European Commission, "China – Market Economy Status in Trade Defence Investigations," *EU Bilateral Relations*, Brussels, June 28, 2004, *available at*

EU Commission insisted that conditions must be met in order for China to be entitled to the MES.[370]

The "tying practice" also happens in the area of IPR enforcement in China. The Chinese government has made considerable efforts to improve enforcement: the speed and scale of actions would be inconceivable in other countries, either due to prohibitive costs, inadequate judiciaries, or bureaucratic apparatus and, from the perspective of some legal practitioners, the effectiveness of China's administrative relief is to be encouraged and commended.[371] China, however, is much more vulnerable to criticism than some other countries because free trade has been adulterated with political elements.

It is difficult to separate political and commercial considerations in practice; however, looking back to China's previous and current reactions, this "conditional treatment" will only make matters worse. Up to this point, in order to facilitate the process of China's IPR enforcement, the EU is best advised to abandon the conditional treatment, and readjust its strategic mentality to be in line with the present status. But how to handle this is a difficult task that should be treated prudently.

6.5.3 Step Three: "Casting a Long Line to Catch a Big Fish" Instead of "Killing the Goose that Lays Golden Eggs"

The English proverb, "to kill the goose that lays golden eggs", refers to the destruction of a reliable and valuable source of income through stupidity or greed.[372] The expression reflects the practice that some developed countries are eager to pursue immediate benefits without paying much attention to the

---

<http://ec.eurpoa.eu/trade/issues/bilateral/countries/china/pr280604_en.htm>. MES is a technical status granted to a national economy or individual businesses, used by trading partners during anti-dumping investigations, for the purpose of assessing the conditions under which exported goods are produced. *Ibid.* For a comprehensive analysis of MES and Non-Market Economy Status, *see* Joseph A. Laroski, Jr., "NMEs: A Love Story, Nonmarket and Market Economy Status Under U.S. Antidumping Law," 30 *Law & Pol'y Int'l Bus.* 369, 370-71, 394-98 (1999).

[370] *Ibid.* The conditions include: (1) State influence: ensuring equal treatment of all companies by reducing state interference, which takes place either on an ad hoc basis or as a result of industrial policies, as well as through export and pricing restrictions on raw materials; (2) Corporate governance: increasing the level of compliance with the existing Accounting Law in order to ensure […] the usability of accounting information for trade defence investigations; (3) Property and bankruptcy law: ensuring equal treatment of all companies in bankruptcy procedures and in respect of property and intellectual property rights; [and] (4) financial sector: bringing the banking sector under market rules.

[371] Alan Adcock, "Opportunity Knocks for IP Owners in China," *Rouse & Co., Int'l*, February 1, 2004, *available at* <http://www.iprights.com/publications/index.asp>, last visited August 19, 2006.

[372] *See The Oxford Dictionary of Idiom*, Judith Siefring (ed.) 127 (2004).

future interests. In contrast, there is another Chinese proverb, "casting a long line to catch a big fish", implying that patience is profitable.

China is of immense importance and great potential to the world economy. On one hand, China's ascension has drawn world attention and enhanced China's status in the global arena. On the other hand, however, the Chinese economy remains fragile and uneven and patience is required for maximum benefits.[373] Compelling or inducing China to accept a higher standard of intellectual property protection amounts to "killing the goose that lays golden eggs". In order to catch a "big fish", the most sensible thing would be "cast a long line."

In addition, China is still encountering uncertainty in terms of its social stability and sustainable development. In light of this uncertainty, promoting constructive and cooperative relationships with China is an emotional and political investment. Whether the gain outweighs the loss in the long run largely depends on how the cooperation is managed and how it stands to work. In the first instance, it requires altruistic endeavors with an expectation of return benefit in the future. This goal can be accomplished by facilitating China's integration into the global economy. To facilitate and accelerate such integration, the EU may promote the emergence of new political ecology by improving China's standing in the international community, such as supporting its participation at the G8 summits.[374]

Within many foreign pharmaceutical companies, R&D funds are in excess of one billion dollars.[375] On health-related R&D the United States Federal Government invested more than twenty-five billion dollars in 2005.[376] By contrast, the largest amount spent on pharmaceutical R&D in China was only one hundred million Chinese Yuan in 2003,[377] which is just equivalent to twelve million dollars. China's R&D expenditure as a percentage of its GDP was 1.34 percent in 2005.[378] Foundations need to be set up to support innovation and enhance competitiveness. The practical approach to achieving this is to have sufficient financial resources for investing in IP-related industries and research institutions.

---

[373] Sharif Shuja, "The Limits of Chinese Economic Reform," *China Brief*, Volume V, Issue 17, August 2, 2005, at 8.

[374] Yu, "From Pirates to Partners," *supra* note 97.

[375] Cui Ning and Qin Jize, "IPR Strategy to Define Government's Role," *supra* note 177.

[376] For example, the federal government of the U.S. invested more than twenty-five billion dollars on health-related R&D in 2005. *See* "Research and Development in the Pharmaceutical Industry," The Congress of the United States of Congressional Budget Office, October 2006, Pub. No. 2589, *available at* <http://www.cbo.gov/ftpdocs/76xx/doc7615/10-02-DrugR-D.pdf>.

[377] "IPR Strategy to Define Government's Role," *supra* note 177.

[378] China's R&D investment in 2005 accounts for 1.34 percent GDP, China Supply Chain Council, September 18, 2006, *available at* <http://www.supplychain.cn/en/art/?1043>, last visited April 29, 2007.

Today's investment in bridging the economic divide is a wise and logical step towards gaining many rewarding benefits tomorrow through its initiatively implemented IPR policies. The "casting a long line to catch a big fish" strategy should not be an antagonistic "zero-sum game" where it is impossible for both players to win or to lose.[379] Given EU-China relations, it is feasible to set up a strategic EU-China cooperation scheme to help China with technical assistance and capacity building. It is a "cradle" for nurturing and safeguarding the infant interests of the innovation enthusiasm from the domestic enterprises.

Fortunately, there have been encouraging signs towards fostering a microclimate for a stronger IPR protection. In the mid 1990s, China adopted its national strategy of "rejuvenating the nation by relying on science and education (*ke ji xing guo*)."[380] Since then, the percentage of R&D in China has been rising steadily;[381] R&D funding for Chinese universities has increased significantly in recent years,[382] and overseas Chinese scientists and specialists are gradually returning to their homeland.[383] Provided this escalating tendency remains, patience is required until an effective high-value industry and efficient IPR enforcement system comes.

6.5.4 Step Four: From "Massive Offensive" to "Defeat in Detail": Establish the IP Special Regions and IP Special Industries

"Knowledge advances by steps and not by leaps."[384] This rule applies very well to the IPR implementation and enforcement in China. Even at a time when adequate protection of IPR becomes necessary in certain industries or regions, policy-makers should seriously consider differentiation in terms of the level of economic development and technological strengths.[385] Otherwise,

---

[379] Yu, "Toward a Nonzero-sum Approach", *supra* note 27, at 638.

[380] Shirley Ann Jackson, "Security, Innovation, and Human Capital in the Global Interest," *Center for Strategic and International Studies*, Washington, D.C., June 17, 2004. *See* also, "China's New Catalogue for Foreign Investment," 287 *China Science & Technology Newsletter*, The Ministry of Science and Technology, People's Republic of China, February 28, 2002, *available at* <http://www.most.gov.cn/eng/newsletters/2002/>.

[381] *See* "China's R&D Spending to Surpass EU within 5 Years," *Brussels Financial Times*, UK, September 10, 2005.

[382] *See* John R. Allison & Lianlian Lin, "The Evolution of Chinese Attitudes toward Property Rights in Invention and Discovery," *U. Pa. J. Int'l Econ. L.* 735, 779 (1999).

[383] *See* Yahong Li, "The Wolf Has Come: Are China's Intellectual Property Industries Prepared for the WTO?" 20 *UCLA Pacific Basin L. J.* 105 (2002).

[384] *Miscellaneous Writings of Load Macaulay*, T. F. Ellis (ed), London: Longmans, Green 112 (1868).

[385] *See* Linsu Kim, "Technology Transfer and Intellectual Property Rights: The Korean Experience," United Nations Conference on Trade and Development [UNCTAD], Project on IPR and Sustainable Development, Issue Paper 2, June 2003, at 6.

the "one-size-fits-all" approach can be a "recipe for disaster" for a country which has some way to go before it reaches a developed level of economic growth and technological accumulation.[386] Slow and steady wins the race.[387] In this context, the tactics of regional and industrial expansion is of great significance.

Regional Expansion: Establishment of IP Special Regions

Regional economic differences in China are considerable, posing serious challenges to the rate of China's economic growth.[388] Statistics indicate that the income ratio between Shanghai's residents – the highest in China – and urban residents in Guizhou Province, whose combined income remains the lowest in China – was 2.33:1 in 2002.[389] The gap continued to widen, reaching 3.2:1 in 2004.[390] The process of the economic globalisation and trade liberalisation has significantly contributed to the widening of this regional gap,[391] and the disparities cannot be bridged automatically and spontaneously through China's further integration into the global economy.

As has been noted, counterfeiting and piracy fuels economic development until a country reaches the stage where a higher level IPR enforcement becomes economically advantageous to its indigenous industries in general.[392] In light of this, many countries insist on an appropriate level of IPR protection

---

[386] *Ibid.*

[387] Attributed to one of Aesop's well-known fables (The Hare and the Tortoise), *see*, Arthur Mee & Holland Thomason, *The Book of Knowledge* (1912).

[388] Zicheng Liang, "Financial Development, Growth, and Regional Disparity in Post-Reform China," *United Nations University (UNU-WIDER) Research Paper No. 2006/90, available at* <http://www.wider.unu.edu/research/2004-2005/2004-2005-6/cip2/papers/Li ang1.pdf>.

[389] Zhao Huanxin and Fu Jing, "Balanced Progress Planned for Country," *China Daily*, March 8, 2004, *available at* <http://www.chinadaily.com.cn/english/doc/2004-03/08/content_312752.htm>.

[390] *See*, Gao Hongbin (Deputy Director General of the State Council Leading Group Office of Poverty Alleviation and Development), "Regional Policy Seminar on Pro-Poor Growth and Scaling Up Poverty Reduction in East Asia," *supra* note 73 in Chapter 4.

[391] Chia Siow Yue, "Economic Globalization and Equity in East Asia," in Natalia Dinello (ed.), *Globalization and Equity: Perspectives from the Developing World* (2005), at 102, 134 (arguing that "globalization has contributed to the growing divide between the haves and have-nots," and "widened the urban-rural gap" in East Asia including China).

[392] *See, e.g.,* Stefan Kirchanski, "Protection of U.S. Patent Rights in Developing Countries: US Efforts To Enforce Pharmaceutical Patents in Thailand," 16 (2) *L.A. Int'l & Comp. L. Rev.* 598 (1994); Frederick M. Abbott, "The WTO TRIPs Agreement and Global Economic Development," in *Public Policy and Global Technological Integration* 3, 4-12 (1997).

because of varying stages of economic development.[393] China is more of a consumer than a producer of intellectual property, and is not in a position to see sufficient values in intellectual property; however, this does not mean that China should wait until the regional gap is fully bridged. In geographical terms, the public in urban and coastal areas are generally more aware of the importance of IPR protection.[394] In the industrialised regions, conditions have generally been met to apply for strong intellectual property standards.[395] In Shanghai, Guangdong, Jiangsu, Zhejiang, and Shandong, more and more domestic enterprises are desperate for an upgraded IPR enforcement mechanism and are lobbying the government for an appropriate adjustment.[396] To adopt a unique IPR protection system in such a big country with significant economic disparity is becoming a factor restricting economic development.

One approach to tackling this problem may be the creation of IP Special Regions (IPSR) where, according to laws and regulations already in place, special authorities are created to adopt local legislations,[397] or promulgate relatively strict interpretations.[398] For instance, Guangdong may be selected as a pilot of IPSR to enact local legislations such as Measures to Protect Intellectual Property in Guangdong Province.[399] Guangdong's experience, if successful, should then be promoted across a wider area.

---

[393] *See e.g.,* Thomas.G. Rawski, "Chinese Industrial Reform: Accomplishments, Prospects and Implications," 84 (2), *Am. Econ. Rev.* 271-72 1994 (stating that IPR protections are normally weaker in emerging markets than in developed markets).

[394] Sibao Shen, Yongmin Cai, "Lun WTO yu Woguo Fada Diqu Fazhi Jianshe (the WTO and the Legal Construction in the Less-developed Regions)," *Legal Daily*, September 5, 2006, *available at* <http://www.legaldaily.com.cn/zt/2006-09/05/content_402908.htm>, last visited September 8, 2006 (noting that people's sense of law in certain economically developed regions has significantly enhanced over the past years).

[395] *Ibid.*

[396] *See* Jianming Cao, "Nuli Tigao Zhishi Chanquan de Sifa Baohu Shuiping (Improving the Judicial Protection for Intellectual Property Rights in China)," *Judicial Protection of IPR in China*, June 28, 2004, *available at* <http://www.chinaiprlaw.cn/file/200406282165.html>, last visited September 8, 2006.

[397] Local legislation is an important feature of the whole legislative system and has played an important role in the social and economic development in China. For a detailed introduction, *see* "Local Legislation in China," September 28, 2003, *available at* <http://www.china.org.cn/english/kuaixun/76344.htm>.

[398] As a significant characteristic of China's judicial system, the judicial interpretation exemplifies specific judicial documents issued by the national supreme judicial authorities on questions concerning specific application and clarification of laws in the judicial practices based on the authorisation of the NPC. The Supreme People's Court and the Supreme People's Procuratorate, by virtue of the relevant decrees adopted by the NPC, both hold the power of formulating the judicial interpretations. For a comprehensive account of the judicial interpretation, *see* Peter Howard Corne, "Creation and Application of Law in the PRC," 50 *Am. J. Comp. L.*396, 397 (2002).

[399] According to the Chinese Constitution, "the People's Congresses of provinces and municipalities directly under the Central Government, and their standing committees, may adopt local regulations[...]." *See* Chinese Constitution, Article 100.

In achieving this goal, government support of these selected local regions is indispensable and essential for the survival of the special region. Based on this awareness and in an effort to establish a comprehensive legal system by 2010, China has been engaged in implementing its National Intellectual Property Strategy (NIPS) to facilitate innovation capabilities and increase the competitive edge of some leading Chinese companies in the global market.[400] In concrete terms, Chinese authorities at different levels are expected to contemplate multiple financial assistance schemes such as allocating special subsidy to facilitate R&D, granting low interest loans to intellectual property developers and innovators, adopting preferential tariff reductions for the IPR industry, and offering professional training to trade officials and entrepreneurs of these regions.

Within EU-China relations, the EU is expected to fully support this differentiated strategy. Should this be accepted and implemented, the EU would be a major beneficiary and would be amply recompensated, because the foreign business area in China is situated largely in the east and southeast regions, in which the "special regions" are supposed to be established. Nevertheless, institutional innovation is a complicated and systemic task which needs prudence and patience.

Industrial Extension: Creation of IP Special Industries

Similar to the economic disparity within regions of China, there is a vast imbalance between different industries in terms of technological capacities. Although weaker IPR protection would be more beneficial at a stage where China is considered an intellectual property consumer as a whole, different industries may call for different levels of IPR protection to adapt to varying economic conditions.[401] While some industries, such as pharmaceuticals, are concerned that IPR protection standards set out in TRIPs are too high for China and the full implementation means sacrificing the interests of China's infant industries,[402] other industries such as software and electronics are singing a different tune and expressing their growing discontent over the incapacity of the IPR mechanisms.[403]

---

[400] *See* Jianke Jiang, "Shidai Huhuan Zhishi Chanquan: Fang Guojia Zhishi Chuanquan Ju Juzhang Tian Lipu (A New Era Calls for an Improved Intellectual Property: An Interview with Tian Lipu, Commissioner of the State Intellectual Property Office)," 14 *People's Daily*, August 25, 2005 (mentioning that China is endeavouring to implement its national intellectual property strategy of revitalising the state through science and education).

[401] *See* Yahong Li, *supra* note 383, at 81 (mentioning that different industries may need different intellectual property standard to "suit their own pace of development").

[402] *Ibid*, at 80 (arguing that less strong IPR enforcement "allows infant domestic industries ample time to grow by imitating and copying foreign products without compensation").

[403] Jianke Jiang, *supra* note 372.

As mentioned in Chapter 2, the one area the United States and other Western countries would most like to see improvement in terms of China's IPR regime is copyright,[404] an area in which China is most likely to make a breakthrough. It is indisputable that the Western countries have become particularly sensitive to the copyright infringement that is perceived as the weak link of China's IPR enforcement, particularly in cases of copyright violations involving the piracy of computer software and compact movie discs.[405] The recent U.S. complaints to WTO about piracy in China addressed such concerns.[406]

In contrast to other Chinese industries, due to its rapid development, the Chinese software industry may be more receptive to and adaptive in IPR protection than other industries. As observed by Professor Keith Maskus, while the Chinese software industry is still in its infancy, "the domestic software industry is growing rapidly in particular business applications that do not suffer much copying, but has faced obstacles in developing larger and more fundamental program platforms."[407]

As early as in 1995, an organisation named China Software Alliance (CSA) was brought into existence by a few major software firms such as Legend (then called Lenova) and Stone.[408] In the first period of its establishment there were not many members of CSA and their voice was very weak.[409] Now CSA has become the biggest software association in China, with branches in forty major cities.[410] This reflects a growing trend that piracy in China is no longer restricted to foreign-produced software.

The CSA has been keen on cooperating with the Chinese authorities and foreign organisations and promoting the campaigns against piracy.[411] It lobbied the National People's Congress in the mid 1990s to emphasise the significance of introducing a separate software protection regulation, and successfully convinced the legislature to adopt clauses that prohibit purchasers from deciphering encryption algorithms embedded in the software.[412] In an effort to bolster copyright protection for software, the CSA collaborated closely with the Business Software Alliance of the United States to set up and maintain a national hotline for reporting piracy and initiated appeals through public

---

[404] Schlesinger, *supra* note 115, at 119.

[405] *See ibid*, at 119-20 (mentioning that copyright protection in China is an area to which the international community is particularly sensitive).

[406] *See* "United States Files WTO Cases against China over Deficiencies in China's Intellectual Property Rights Laws and Market Access Barriers to Copyright-Based Industries," *supra* note 109.

[407] *See* Keith Maskus, *Intellectual Property Rights in the Global Economy* (2000), at 149.

[408] *See* NCAC Database, *available at* <http://edit.ndcnc.gov.cn/datalib/2003/Organize/DL/DL-72955/>, last accessed September 10, 2006.

[409] *Ibid.*

[410] *Ibid.*

[411] *See* Yahong Li, *supra* note 383, at 100.

[412] *Ibid.*

media to promote public awareness of the enforcement of intellectual property laws.[413]

A similar situation occurs to the movie discs. In this area, evidence also shows that rampant piracy in China is hurting local industries more than foreign companies.[414] According to a recent study by independent research firm LEK Consulting, conducted on behalf of the Motion Picture Association of America,[415] whose member studios include Time Warner, Walt Disney, Sony Pictures Entertainment, and Twentieth Century Fox, China loses ninety per cent of its potential market for movies due to piracy.[416] In 2005, China's domestic moviemakers lost roughly 1.5 billion U.S. dollars to piracy, almost three times as much as MPA member studios' losses of a combined five hundred sixty-five million dollars in China.[417]

As noted by Professor Alford, Chinese industries are becoming victims of the counterfeiting and piracy.[418] With increasing violations that result in losses to Chinese companies and individuals, there will be indigenously fostered enthusiasm calling for better IPR protection; thus, domestic commercial interests in stronger copyrights are now playing an important role in promoting enforcement.[419]

In this context, it is necessary for the policymakers to apply differential treatments and offer special support to such particular industries as the software or movie industries. These fast-growing and well-developed industries can receive relatively higher protection and act as forerunners of the international standard for the IPR enforcement.

6.5.5 Step Five: From "Pierre Cardin" to "Hisense": Promote the Role Conversion

Pierre Cardin and Hisense are two totally unrelated brands from different countries – the former is a French fashion magnet while the latter is a new Chinese star in electronic equipment; however, their similar experiences in China brought them together, and provided a significant theme for study and debate.

---

[413] *Ibid*, at 101.

[414] *See, e.g.*, "Tschang Chi-Chu, "China: Piracy Plague," *The Straits Times*, July 1, 2006.

[415] The Cost of the Movie Piracy, An Analysis Prepared by LEK for the Motion Picture Association, *available at* <http://www.mpaa.org/press_releases/leksummarympa.pdf>, last visited August 18, 2006.

[416] Tschang Chi-Chu, *supra* note 414.

[417] *Ibid*.

[418] William P. Alford, "Making the World Safe for What? Intellectual Property Rights, Human Rights and Foreign Economic Policy in the Post-European Cold War World," 29 *N.Y.U. J. Int'l L. & Pol.* 136 (1997).

[419] *See* Keith Maskus, *Intellectual Property Rights in the Global Economy, supra* note 407, at 174.

Pierre Cardin: Sacrifice of Innocence

Pierre Cardin, the French fashion icon, was one of the precursor foreign companies embracing the Chinese market as soon as the door was opened.[420] In 1979, Pierre Cardin organised a trade agreement with China to produce Pierre Cardin clothes.[421] Since then, Pierre Cardin has been so famous in China that he is sometimes mistaken for the French president.[422]

Some years later, in June 2001, Pierre Cardin was surprised to discover that he had a "twin brother" – the "Italian Pierre Cardin (Hong Kong) International" – at an international fashion show in Nanjing City, Jiangsu Province, which soon turned out to be artificial.[423] Later, Cardin discovered large number of Chinese companies registering corporate names under the Chinese translation of Pierre Cardin (*Pier Kadan*) or similar names, resulting in massive sales of counterfeit Pierre Cardin products in large department stores all over the country. [424] What astonished Cardin the most was the multiplied Cardin counterfeits brands such as London Pierre Cardin Fashion (Shanghai) and Italian Pierre Cardin Fashion Group (Guangzhou), let alone confusing brands such as Pierre Kardin, Piere Cardin or Piekadan.[425]

Cardin made a formal complaint followed by a nationwide crackdown against the counterfeits of Pierre Cardin and other well-known brands.[426] These lawless companies at last received their deserved punishment. The crackdown campaign reverberated as it was meant to; however, it was very unlikely that counterfeits would completely vanish. Cardin became an innocent sacrifice leaving for many violators no lessons but profits.

Hisense: Forerunner of "IPR Victims"

The story of Hisense is somewhat sobering. Hisense Group, a well-known Chinese manufacturer of electronic household appliances, alleged that the German powerhouse Bosch-Siemens stole its trademark and registered it in Germany in bad faith.[427] "Hisense" was officially identified as a well-known

---

[420] *See* "Pierre Cardin: China Could Lead 21st Century Fashion," *People's Daily*, May 20, 2002.

[421] *See* "Pierre Cardin", *Encyclopaedia*, The History Channel, *available at* <http://www.thehistorychannel.co.uk/site/home/>.

[422] Laurence Benaïm, "The Great Name of French Haute Couture," *available at* <http://www.diplomatie.gouv.fr/label_france/ENGLISH/DOSSIER/MODE/car.html>, last visited September 16, 2006.

[423] Ying Ying, "Crackdown Stepped Up Against Counterfeit Merchandise," *China Daily*, June 12, 2004, at 5.

[424] *Ibid.*

[425] *Ibid.*

[426] *Ibid.*

[427] "Siemens Registers 'HiSense' Trademark," *China IP Express*, September 6, 2004, *available at* <www.iprights. com/publications/chinaipexpress/ciex_225.asp>.

trademark in China by the Trademark Bureau under the State Administration of Industry and Commerce (SAIC).[428] What surprised Hisense was that Siemens applied for "HiSense" as the registered trademark for its own commodities.[429] In the same year, Siemens applied for registrations through the channels of the Madrid system and EEC system.[430] In addition, it made a claim for priority, completely blocking Hisense's trademark registration within the EU.[431]

As a result, Hisense had to launch its back-up trademark "Hsense" when selling in Germany.[432] However, at the end of 2004, Siemens launched legal proceedings against Hisense at Cologne Local Court in Germany, claiming that Hisense's backup trademark "HSense" had infringed its trademark "HISense" due to the likelihood of confusion.[433] In retaliation, in December 2004, Hisense Corporation demanded that the German Trademark Bureau rescind the "HiSense" trademark registered by Bosch-Siemens according to law, which soon proved to be in vain.[434] Hisense attempted to settle the dispute through negotiation with Siemens, but was offered a trademark transfer price as high as forty million euros, which was unacceptable to Hisense.[435]

Unlike the Pierre Cardin case, which seemed to go unnoticed in China, the Hisense case reverberated widely. The Hisense executives realised that, under an "eye for eye, tooth for tooth" doctrine, they became an unfortunate victim of a behaviour that most were familiar with. As acknowledged by the general manager of Hisense Import & Export Co. Ltd, the case was a "bitter lesson" for Hisense.[436] While urging the enterprises to "mend the fold after a sheep is lost," Hisense invoked all the counterfeiters to "rein in at the brink of the

---

[428] *See* "Haixin Gongsi Jianjie [Introduction to Hisence]," *China Economic Network*, August 3, 2005, *available at* <http://www.ce.cn/cysc/jiadian/jdmq/hx/qyjj/200508/03/t20050803_4334408.shtml>.

[429] *Ibid.*

[430] "Chinese Trademarks Repeatedly Registered Abroad," *China Economic Information Network*, March 4, 2005, *available at* <http://www1.cei.gov.cn/ce/doc/cep1/200503040799.htm>.

[431] *Ibid.*

[432] "High quote blocking Hisense-BSH dispute," Business Weekly, *China Daily Online*, September 26, 2004, *available at* <http://www.chinadaily.com.cn/english/doc/2004-09/26/content377815.htm>.

[433] "Chinese Trademarks Repeatedly Registered Abroad," *supra* note 430.

[434] *Ibid.*

[435] "Chinese Companies Learn to Protect Their IPR," *MOFCOM News*, April 28, 2005, at <http://english.mofcom.gov.cn/aarticle/counselorsreport/americaandoceanreport/200504/20050400082339.html>, accessed on May 29, 2005. *See* also "Zhishi Chanquan Zhishang – Wulun Shi Ziji de Haishi Taren de – Zhe Jiu Shi Haixin Jiaoxun [Giving Paramountcy to IPR: A Lesson from Hisence]", *Zhongguo Zhuanli Shangbiao Wang [China Network on Patent and Trademark]*, March 13, 2005, *available at* <http://gdipc.ctiwt.com/jsp/main/module/pt/pt_browse_2.jsp?corp_id=20030121151531&ch_id=20050313134631>, last visited October 18, 2006.

[436] "Chinese Companies Learn to Protect Their IPR," *ibid.*

precipice."[437] What is more significant is that the landmark Hisense case has acted as a symbol with potentially far-reaching implications, indicating that China has started the process of transformation from an infringer to a victim of IPR. From the Hisense case, it is fair to expect that the notion of Chinese intellectual property law may have been on the verge of losing its conventional, oxymoronic status.[438]

Buried Quarrel and Shook Hands

As one sign of this transformation, shortly after the news released, many distinguished scholars from the IPR arena, in addition to high-level officials convened by the Ministry of Commerce, gathered in Beijing in February 2005 to hold a "Symposium on Safeguarding the Chinese Trademarks Overseas."[439] A consensus was reached that the intended purpose of Bosch-Siemens' registering of "HiSense" was simply to set up a trade barrier through rush trademark registration strategy in an attempt to block the entry of Chinese enterprises into the international market that Bosch-Siemens already occupied or wanted to occupy.[440]

Hisense's Management Counsel adjusted its strategy in dealing with this difficult case. While posing to confront Siemens in German court, Hisense's think-tank suggested resolving the problem through inter-governmental negotiations with the relevant companies.[441] In March 2005, following lengthy negotiations, the two sides reached a reconciliation agreement.[442] According to this agreement, Bosch-Siemens agreed to transfer its "HiSense" trademark, which was registered in Germany and other European countries.[443] Siemens also withdrew its accusation against Hisense, and Hisense withdrew its application to register the Bosch-Siemens trademark in China.[444] The two big companies buried their quarrel and shook hands at last.

Apparently neither Hisense nor Bosch-Siemens expected that a mere business activity would have triggered such potential impact. Apart from sounding

---

[437] *Ibid.*

[438] Graham Chynoweth, "Reality Bites: How the Biting Reality of Piracy in China is Working to Strengthen its Copyright Laws," 2003 *Duke L. & Tech. Rev.* 3, 3-4 (2003) (noting China's accession to the WTO may lead to copyright violation becoming a reality to domestic companies and that Chinese copyright law "may be on the verge of losing its oxymoronic status").

[439] "Chinese Companies Learn to Protect Their IPR," *supra* note 435.

[440] "Chinese Trademarks Repeatedly Registered Abroad," *supra* note 430.

[441] *Ibid.*

[442] "Hexin Ximenzi Shangbiao Zhengyi Jiean, 'HiSense' Huigui Haixin [Hisense Reaches Deal with Siemens: "HiSense" Trademark Returns Home]," *Xinhua News Agency*, March 9, 2005, *available at* <http://news.xinhuanet.com/fortune/2005-03/09/content_2 672391.htm>.

[443] *Ibid.*

[444] *Ibid.*

an alarm for Chinese enterprises, on the EU side, the Bosch-Hisense case also backed up the principle that Chinese culture cherishes stability and harmony. This is a reality that the European businesses have to envisage when leaping into the Chinese market.

6.5.6 Step Six: From Freerider to Stakeholder: When Beijing Embraces the Olympics

When it comes to IPR enforcement in China, the obvious sentiment is that, since all the countries, including the United States and Japan, have gone through the stage of obtaining huge profits through copying, why should China commit the folly of waiving this bestowed gift? The striking point here is how to avoid the suspicion of the Chinese by convincing them of the potential harm of imitation and larger benefits of innovation. China will embrace IPR as long as they are associated with common interests of intellectual property. Concretely speaking, only when Chinese citizens are aware they are harming their own interests, will they move away from the counterfeiting and piracy and actively combat the infringement problems. As the 2008 Olympic Games approach, China is being provided a new stage to act as an active partner in the global protection of IPR.

The protection of IPR has become a significant feature in the scheme of the Olympics.[445] As the codification of the fundamental principles and rules, the Olympic Charter is aimed at protecting the image and spirit of the Olympic Games and the intellectual property so that the value and integrity of the Olympic brand are maintained.[446] Over the past two decades, the protection of Olympic IPR and other related rights has received great attention nationally and internationally and has formed the principal source of income for the Olympics.[447] As a practice, host countries of the Olympic Games promulgate regulations to prohibit the unauthorised use of confusingly similar phrases, symbols, terminology and graphic design.[448] The legal status of the Olympic IPR and other related rights are defined and implemented over the registration

---

[445] Chris Brockie, "Business Doesn't Play with Games," *The Korea Times*, April 2, 2006.

[446] *See* the *Olympic Charter* (last updated on September 1, 2004), Chapter I, 7-14, *available at* <http://multimedia.olympic.org/pdf/en_report_122.pdf>.

[447] "2008 • Beijing Time • IP Protection in China," *Official Paper*, State Intellectual Property Office, China, April 22, 2005, available by search at <www.sipo.gov.cn/>, last visited January 29, 2006.

[448] *For example*, in the United States, the marketability of Olympic trademarks is protected by the Section 110 of the Amateur Sports Act of 1978. Under this provision, the United States Olympic Committee has been invested certain exclusive right to use such name as "United States Olympic Committee," its symbol and emblem, and the words "Olympic," "Olympiad," "Citius Altius Fortius," "Pan American," "Paralympiad," "America Espirito Sport Fraternite," or any combination or simulation thereof tending to cause confusion. *See* 36 U.S.C. § 220506 (2001).

of trademark and copyright administered by the International Olympic Committee (IOC) and other Olympic organising committees.[449] Almost immediately after the 1993 announcement that Sydney, Australia, was to host the 2000 games, its customs service began planning for how to deal with detecting and combating counterfeit goods which infringed IPR associated with the Olympics.[450] Similarly, in the 2008 Olympic Games, it is estimated that the Beijing Organising Committee will enter into thousands of contracts with the International Olympic cooperative partners, each involving IPR.[451]

Since December 2000, the Chinese government has embarked on the Olympic intellectual property legislation and its enforcement, with particular emphasis being given to the protection of Olympic symbols.[452] In November 2001 and April 2002, "the Regulation of Protection of Olympic Symbol of Beijing" and "the Regulation of Protection for Olympic Symbol" were promulgated respectively by the State Counsel.[453] The promulgation of these Regulations demonstrated China's firm commitment to the successful staging of the 2008 Olympic Games. In addition, by April 1, 2005, the Beijing Organising Committee for the 2008 Games Olympiad had registered more than fifty-eight symbols via the State Administration for Industry and Commerce (SAIC) and the IOC.[454]

In 2004, during the "Press Release on Beijing Intellectual Property Protection" held jointly by the information office of Beijing and the municipal government, the Olympic intellectual property protection campaign was launched.[455] Chinese authorities have made an appeal to the public to buy legitimate Olympic products from authorised sellers or retailers.[456] It was also announced that authorities at all levels would "strictly enforce" the relevant regulations.[457]

The General Administration of Customs and SAIC have also been requested to be on alert throughout the country to prevent any unauthorised use of Olympic-related intellectual property.[458] From 2002 to 2003, the SAIC iden-

---

[449] "2008 • Beijing Time • IP Protection in China," *supra* note 447.

[450] Chris Brockie, "Business Doesn't Play with Games," *supra* note 445.

[451] "2008 • Beijing Time • IP Protection in China," *supra* note 447.

[452] From China's perspective, Olympic symbols include the Olympic five-ring symbol and flag, names of formal Olympics-related issues and slogans of the 2008 Olympics such as "New Beijing, Great Olympics" and "Beijing 2008." *See* "Olympic Symbols Receive Protection," *China Daily*, April 1, 2003, *available at* <www.china.org.cn/english/2003/Apr/60488.htm>.

[453] *See* "the Regulations on the Protection of Olympic Symbols," *available at* <http://www.chinaiprlaw.com/english/laws/laws21.htm>.

[454] "2008 • Beijing Time • IP Protection in China," *supra* note 447.

[455] *Ibid.*

[456] Chris Brockie, "Business Doesn't Play with Games," *supra* note 445.

[457] *Ibid.*

[458] *See* "China Pledges Increased Protection for Intellectual Property," *People's Daily*, April 27, 2002.

tified 144 infringements against Olympic symbols at different levels.[459] Until December 2006, the SAIC in Beijing alone has identified eighty-nine cases of Olympic Symbol infringement and confiscated 3,225 goods with unlicensed Olympic symbols.[460] Statistics also show that, in 2006, more than 4 percent of trademark violations in Beijing were Olympics-related.[461] Recently, 112 advertising companies illegally using the slogan created for Beijing's 2008 Olympic bid, "New Beijing, Great Olympics," were ordered by authorities to cease infringement immediately.[462] Customs officials throughout the country have seized about thirty shipments of export goods illegally using the Olympic symbols.[463]

At the same time, to commemorate the second anniversary of the issuance of the "Regulation of Protection for Olympic Symbol," the authorities organised a series of promotional events concerning the protection of the Olympic symbol, and illustrated how to distinguish the genuine Olympic products from the counterfeits.[464] With the 2008 Beijing Olympics fast approaching, it is clear that China has pledged to step-up efforts to fight any infringement of the Olympic symbols. China's seriousness in enforcing the Olympic intellectual property rights has been unprecedented.

It is likely that the Beijing Olympics will mark a turning point in the development of the intellectual property system in China. It may be true that, since China received the Olympic Flag in Athens in 2004, it has undertaken a special mission to protect IPR. From Athens to Beijing, and from Beijing to London, we have reasons to expect a great change. It is hoped that the EU and China have much to gain in the cooperation. Instead of repeating rhetorical sermons, the EU should try to establish the sense of common interests by bringing China "in the same boat." In order to maintain a sustainable trade relationship where frictions can be avoided or overcome by negotiation, both the EU and China have to foster an environment for genuine mutual trust.[465] Only a shared awareness of rooted cultural commonalities can lead to the deepening

---

[459] *See* "2008 • Beijing Time • IP Protection in China," *supra* note 447.

[460] "Beijing Investigated 89 Olympic Symbols Infringement Cases," News Release from *Intellectual Property Protection in China* (An inter-department institution jointly administered by the State Office of Intellectual Property and the Ministry of Commerce), December 25, 2006, *available at* <http://www.ipr.gov.cn/ipr/en/info/article> (last visited May 9, 2007).

[461] In 2006, the Beijing authorities identified and prosecuted 2,072 trademark violations, 89 of which involved Olympics products. *See* "China Gets Serious about Fake Olympic Merchandise," *International Herald Tribune*, April 26, 2007, *available at* <http://www.iht.com/articles/2007/04/26/news/fakes.php>.

[462] "Olympic Symbols Receive Protection," *supra* note 419.

[463] *Ibid.*

[464] *See* "2008 • Beijing Time • IP Protection in China," *supra* note 447.

[465] Gosset, "The Making of a China-EU World," *supra* note 59.

of links between the two sides.[466] In this scenario, the EU and China are in a position to play their pivotal roles in building a harmonious Eurasia.

It may not be a satisfying mirage to predict that, when the Olympic Flag is handed over to the City of London, it should be an appropriate time for the people to ponder the excellences of the Olympic Games in Beijing and, at the same time, applaud the surprisingly improved IPR system in China.

6.6 Conclusion

6.6.1 US-China IPR Debate: A Cat-and-Mouse Game

In terms of enforcement, the U.S. efforts at improving IPR protection in China failed because of various reasons, most notably, the ignorance of China's cultural uniqueness and its systemic interference with the Chinese legal, economic and political regimes. Due to the lack of genuine understanding of this nature, the United States found themselves overwhelmed and powerless in dealing with China's IPR enforcement problems. The cat-and-mouse game has been carried on continuously in various versions and the IPR enforcement in China remains problematic. It is not surprising that China has hammered out a survival strategy in dealing with threat from the United States.

6.6.2 EU's "Six-Step Strategy"

China's integration into the global economy and its participation in the international rulemaking process is dramatically influencing Chinese attitudes and perspectives.[467] It seems true that China's WTO membership has "acted as a lever for economic and legal reform by locking in reform and making it irrevocable."[468] China has thus no choice but to move forward and burn their bridges. During its critical transitional period, lack of flexibility would exacerbate the extent of China's socio-economic problems and, accordingly, deteriorate the social cohesion sustaining adequate IPR protection. Under this scenario, the EU should apply a leniency strategy instead of a coercive policy.

China has been experiencing a shift in both economic and socio-political domains. Collaboration as a strategic option, unlike an exclusive focus on sanctions, is the most realistic solution to help China find its way forward in shaping their strategies and adapting to the expected standard for the IPR protection. By this logic, the EU should apply a strategy to "cast a long line to

---

[466] Gosset, "A Symphony of Civilizations," *supra* note 136.
[467] *See* Karen Halverson, "China's WTO Accession: Economic, Legal, and Political Implications," 27 *BC Int'l & Comp. L. Rev.* 332 (2004).
[468] *Ibid*, at 319.

catch a big fish" rather than "killing the goose that lays golden eggs." By facilitating and promoting the transformation of China from perceived infringer to unfortunate victim, we will eventually find the key to undoing the "Gordian knot."

6.6.3 Prospective Trend: Smooth Sailing or Choppy Waves?

Unlike Sino-U.S. relations, the EU and China have maintained harmonious cooperation in different spheres. This distinctive consequence is largely due to the historical compatibilities and cultural adaptability between Europe and China. Cultural accumulation has equipped two old worlds with historical maturation to effectively deal with complexity and live in amity. The mutual interest and shared values have paved way for the two parts to carry out productive cooperation.

According to an ancient Chinese proverb, "a journey of a thousand miles begins with a single step." China has taken its first step to test it by putting it into practice. It will continue. By energetically applying a six-step strategy, it is optimistic to predict that new norms for IPR can be established in China in the near future. Tortuous as the road of struggle is, the prospects are bright.

7 Conclusion

Intellectual Property in World Trade: Justification and Harmonisation

International trade law scholars tend to maintain that a stronger IPR regime is catalyst of economic growth by promoting innovations and stimulating transfer of technology. However, over the past years since the establishment of the global trade system, it still remains undecided as to whether and how the introduction of the Western-style IPR regime and its infrastructure would generate significant economic growth as expected in the developing world. IPR can either trigger or stifle innovation. They can either promote or hinder economic growth. While improved IPR protection is a potential benefit for further economies growth in a long run, whether or not we can subsequently set up a cause and effect relationship between stronger IPR protection and economic growth remains economically untested.

In a context of comparative law, while there have been compelling cases for transferability of foreign legal system, a "fitting-in" process is almost always necessary to ensure the enforceability of a transplanted law in a unique socio-economic environment. Legal transplants are feasible, but cultural adaptation is essential. Within the global trading system, intellectual property law has been posed as a radically new form of legal transplant in developing countries. However, the success of a transplanted intellectual property structure depends largely on how the imported law is recast under indigenous tradition. In other wards, the enforceability of a transplant depends on whether this foreign law finds appropriate soil sufficiently hospitable for its growth in an indigenous tradition. In this sense, the process of the globalisation is simultaneously the process of indigenisation – globalisation is the cause of indigenisation, and indigenisation is the cultural guarantee of globalisation.

In the case of China, the contemporary Chinese legal system was not inherited from its traditional legal system but was a result of China's continuous legal reform notably commencing since the end of 1970s. Legal transplantation in China is an inevitable historical phenomenon and an important symbol in the process of its unprecedented industrialisation and modernisation. However, Chinese cultural traits still run deep in the national consciousness. The enigmatic cultural landscape has shaped a unique model of Chinese philosophies that have exercised comprehensive influence over the effectiveness of the transplantation, making the legal reform in China much more complicated and time-consuming. The "fitting-in" process in launching a brand new intellectual property protection system in China and most other developing countries is a lengthy process, and the developed countries are advised to be patient and supportive.

In a global context, protection of intellectual property rights is more a matter of development than a "trade-related" issue. While the WTO was established to focus on a harmonisation of trade and economy between different states, it has also promoted cultural harmonisation, for example, through its TRIPs minimum requirement. The TRIPs provision was expected to be an effective global legalistic system dealing only with "trade related IPR issues" but has encroached arbitrarily on the cultural sphere in practice. As a consequence, a state may pursue a variety of goals in its harmonisation process, but the compelling rule-based international trade regime restricts its cultural autonomy, which represents a condition of its participation in the global trading system. It seems incommensurable with the multicultural paradigm to strive for a unique cultural environment leading to IPR harmonisation.

In this context, it is important for developed countries to formulate long-term strategies and provide developing countries with necessary technical assistance. Only in this way can developing countries surpass the "development stage" and change their "economic behaviour." This claim is consistent with the core WTO mission which advocates for "greater flexibility" and "more privileges" for developing countries. Developing countries, in turn, are in a position to keep the balance of TRIPs obligations and public interest and to prevent IPR from being abused.

Intellectual Property in World Trade: Development and Enforcement

The IPR enforcement problem has its cultural element but cannot be attributable to the Confucian values as the mainstream view presents. The reality of China has, at least to some extent, proves the contrary – the rampant IPR enforcement problem is not due to the existence, but rather, due to the decline of the Confucian values. The IPR enforcement problem is not an actual outcome of Confucian philosophy and "to steal a book" is not an "elegant offence." Rather, the Confucian ethics act as a unique moral foundation for intellectual property protection. Apart from the common reason of insufficient economic development, the IPR enforcement problem in China is a unique political phenomenon resulting from the systemic dystrophy fundamental to Chinese institutional development and, in a broader sense, it may be the source for recasting and strengthening legal enforcement in China as a whole.

China is currently experiencing critical transition – the prospect of a splendid economic landscape with political reform lagged far behind. Although China has committed itself to a socialist "rule of law" state, without spirit of the liberal democracy, rule of law in China may unsurprisingly remain symbolic and problematic. As a consequence, economic reform has not only brought about greater prosperity, but also created grievous crises. The cascading problems have, in many circumstances, frustrated the efforts of ordinary Chinese citizens to earn their living through normal channels. As a result, utilitarianism seems to dominate many people's minds throughout the country. In addition, the restriction of religious belief and the tough control over freedom of speech have contributed to the growing of utilitarian impulse. In this context, there is no exaggeration that the counterfeiting and piracy are byproducts of imperfect political reform.

The reasons for the IPR enforcement problem in China are manifold and are interdependent. However, the political aspect, *inter alia*, plays a decisive role. China has made arduous efforts towards gaining admittance into the international IPR community and has transplanted an elaborate IPR regime that has been proved to be "a castle in the air." It is not surprising that the existing IPR regime has not completely fit in indigenous social political environment and China still lacks potential motivations to fight IPR infringement effectively. With enigmatic political dilemmas that rival its economic prosperity, the ultimate outcome of IPR enforcement largely depends on the political will of the Chinese leaders and the level of their attainment in combating political fragmentation. China's formula for success stems, to a great extent, from the highly authoritarian system and its absorbed promotion of coherent institutional reform and rule of law. However, to carry out such a reform in China's conservative and bureaucratic colossus must be an enormous challenge. Without help, it is unlikely that China will be able to make the appropriate adjustments necessary and build the institutional basis for steady economic development. This is a learning curve for which there is no panacea. Any attempt for quick success and instant benefit may result in giving up halfway.

Intellectual Property in World Trade: Integration and Cooperation

It has been demonstrated that the manner of the legal imposition and transplantation may affect, if not determine, the effectiveness of an importing law. If a law is received passively, this law may lack natural affinity, and the attitude towards enforcing it may be capricious. As a consequence, the transplants of intellectual property law in developing countries are often, if not always, outcomes of political expediency – developing countries accept these laws as an exchange for participating in international affairs with their economic interests being taken into account and their cultural diversities being respected. However, they have found the promise of future benefits elusive and present policy problems a significant burden.

Despite the lack of economic strength and technological sophistication in support of a comprehensive IPR protection system, China has strived to create an elaborate Western-styled IPR regime in an effort to show its commitment to participating in the global economy. During its critical transitional period, lack of necessary flexibility would exacerbate the extent of China's socio-economic problems and, accordingly, deteriorate the social cohesion sustaining adequate IPR protection.

Fortunately, China has initiated a series of unprecedented structural reforms in multiple dimensions. Collaboration as a strategic option, unlike an exclusive focus on retaliatory measures, is the best solution to help China find its way forward in phasing in effective strategies and adapting to the expected standard for IPR protection. Coincidentally, the effectiveness of this solution also draws on the culture of Confucianism. The EU is advised to genuinely understand the multifaceted nature of China's enforcement mechanism. Before China has gone through with its transition from "rule by law" to "rule of law," the objective of IPR enforcement in China should be achieved, to a large extent, via political communication, coordination and intervention, rather than a legal process. By this scenario, the EU is expected to foster and facilitate shifts of China in both economic and socio-political domains.

Unlike Sino-U.S. relationship which has reflected the Sino-American sentimental tie amid strains over IPR enforcement, the EU and China have maintained harmonious cooperation in different spheres. This consequence is largely due to the cultural compatibilities and adaptability between the Europe and China. The shared cultural identity of humanism and similar values of standards have made for an excellent ethical foundation for a constructive bilateral relationship. There is no doubt that the EU, which has been engaged in the European integration, is best suited for giving guidance to China with regard to its further integration into the global economy. EU-China bilateral relations have blossomed into multifaceted interactions with China's emergence on the global economic scene. By energetically applying a six-step strategy, it is optimistic to predict that new norms for IPR can be fostered and established in China in the foreseeable future.

Appendix

Sample for Questions around which Interviews are Conducted

1. What is your overall opinion of IPR protection in China as far as the needs of EU business are concerned?

2. What do you access the cultural impact on attitudes towards IPR protection?

3. What do you access coercive measures that have been applied by the United States, and possibly by the EU? In what degree do you welcome a European-styled "Section 301"?

4. Do you think that views of IPR between China and West, though traditionally different, are not inherently irreconcilable and that such differences which exist can be bridged?

5. What are your opinion and experiences of administrative bureaucrats in intellectual property management in China?

6. When encountered IPR infringements, will you bring the cases to courts or accepting business practices by tolerating a certain degree of infringement? Why?

7. Do you know in advance ineffectiveness of the Chinese IPR enforcement? If so, why did you still log in? Would you still have come here if you had known then what you know now about Chinese IPR enforcement?

8. Do you think the IPR enforcement, though ineffective, will improved and become active eventually? Why?

9. What do you most want to recommend to the Chinese government in terms of EU-China trade relations and IPR?

10. Do you have any other suggestions?

Sample for Questions in Semi-Structured Interviews

1. Laws are [   ] effectively enforced by government officials in China.
A. never   E. mostly
B. rarely   F. always
C. sometimes   G. don't know
D. frequently   H. don't understand

2. China's Confucian ethic has [   ] made IPR protection rather difficult.
A. never   E. mostly
B. rarely   F. always
C. sometimes   G. don't know
D. frequently   H. don't understand

3. In Morden China, to steal a book is [   ] regarded as an elegant offence.
A. never   E. mostly
B. rarely   F. always
C. sometimes   G. don't know
D. frequently   H. don't understand

4. Imagine a dispute is brought into a court in China with the evidence being clearly in
    your favour. The assigned judge can [   ] be trusted to enforce the law objectively.
A. never   E. mostly
B. rarely   F. always
C. sometimes   G. don't know
D. frequently   H. don't understand

5. It is [   ] necessary to use bribery when claiming IPR and dealing with government of-
    ficials in China.
A. never   E. mostly
B. rarely   F. always
C. sometimes   G. don't know
D. frequently   H. don't understand

6. It is [   ] to measure the cultural risk for the foreign firms in China when marketing in
    China, particularly in connection with claiming intellectual property.
A. completely predictable   E. mostly unpredictable
B. highly predictable   F. completely unpredictable
C. fairly predictable   G. don't know
D. frequently unpredictable   H. don't understand

7. The trade sanction is [   ] to promote China's IPR enforcement.
A. completely predictable   E. mostly unpredictable
B. highly predictable   F. completely unpredictable
C. fairly predictable   G. don't know
D. frequently unpredictable   H. don't understand

8.   It is [   ] that counterfeiting and piracy in China are making, and should continue to make a contribution to the national income.

A. *completely predictable*   E. *mostly unpredictable*
B. *highly predictable*   F. *completely unpredictable*
C. *fairly predictable*   G. *don't know*
D. *frequently unpredictable*   H. *don't understand*

9.   Since China is at the critical point of transition, the success of China's IPR policy is [   ] to rely on how the social political reform is carried out.

A. *completely predictable*   E. *mostly unpredictable*
B. *highly predictable*   F. *completely unpredictable*
C. *fairly predictable*   G. *don't know*
D. *frequently unpredictable*   H. *don't understand*

10. Over the long term, China's economic growth should be [   ] to provide opportunities for domestic companies to profit from legitimate activities

A. *completely predictable*   E. *mostly unpredictable*
B. *highly predictable*   F. *completely unpredictable*
C. *fairly predictable*   G. *don't know*
D. *frequently unpredictable*   H. *don't understand*

List of Charts

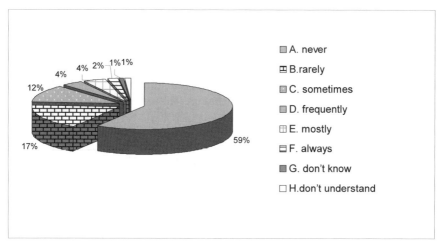

Chart 1 for semi-structured question 1

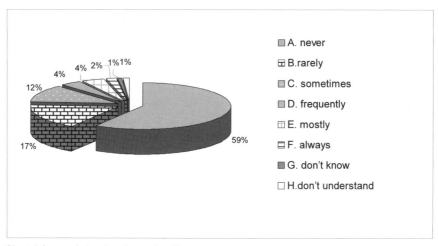

Chart 2 for semi-structured question 2

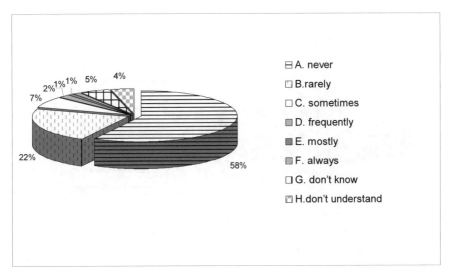

Chart 3 for semi-structured question 3

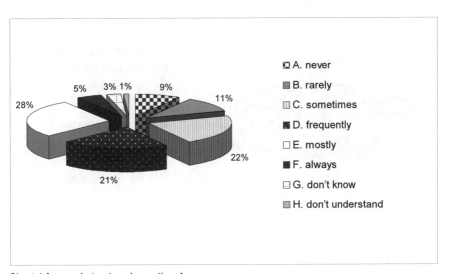

Chart 4 for semi-structured question 4

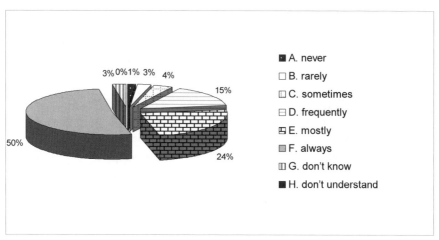

Chart 5 for semi-structured question 5

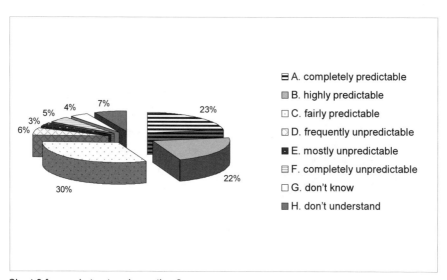

Chart 6 for semi-structured question 6

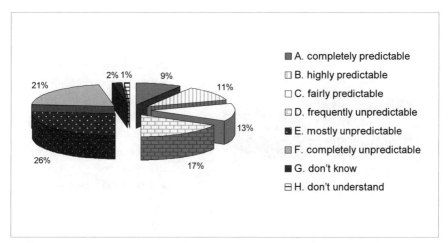

Chart 7 for semi-structured question 7

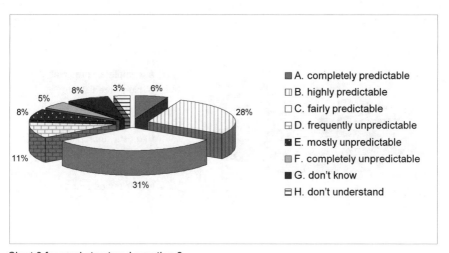

Chart 8 for semi-structured question 8

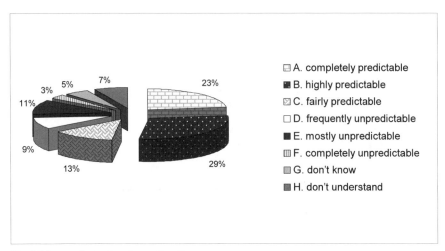

Chart 9 for semi-structured question 9

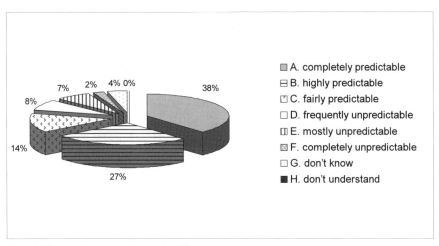

Chart 10 for semi-structured question 10

Selected Bibliography

Books

Abbott, Frederick, Cottier, Gurry & Francis, Thomas, *The International Intellectual Property System: Commentary and Materials*, The Hague; Boston: Kluwer Law International, (1999).

Abbott, Frederick M., & Gerber David J., *Public Policy and Global Technological Integration*, Kluwer Law International (1997).

Alford, William P., *To Steal a Book is an Elegant Offense: Intellectual Property Law in Chinese Civilization*. Stanford: Stanford University Press (1995).

Alikhan, Shahid, *Socio-economic Benefits of Intellectual Property Protection in Developing Countries*, Geneva, WIPO Publication (2000).

Alice H. Amsden, *Asia's Next Giant, South Korea and Late Industrialization* (1992).

Bederman, David J., *International Law Frameworks,* West Publishing Company (2001).

Berman, Harold J., Faith and Order: The Reconciliation of Law and Religion (1993).

Beier, Friedrich-Karl & Schricker, Gerhard, *From GATT to TRIPs: the Agreement on Trade-Related Aspects of Intellectual Property Rights*, New York, VCH (1996).

Harold J. Berman, *Faith and Order: The Reconciliation of Law and Religion* (1993).

Bently, L. and Sherman, B., *Intellectual Property Law* OUP (2001).

Bently, Lionel & Maniatis, Spyros, *Intellectual Property and Ethics*, London, Sweet & Maxwell (1998).

Blakeney, Michael, *Trade Related Aspects of Intellectual Property Rights: A Concise Guide to the TRIPs Agreement*, London: Sweet & Maxwell (1997).

Bodde, Derk, and Morris, Clarence, *Law in Imperial China*, Harvard University Press (1967).

Brahm, Laurence J., *Intellectual Property Law in the People's Republic of China: A Specially Commissioned Report*, Hong Kong, Longman (1988).

Brazell, Lorna, *Intellectual Property Protection and Enforcement*, London, Thorogood (1998).

Buchanan, Allen and Moore, Margaret (eds), *States, Nations, and Borders: The Ethics of Making Boundaries* (2003).

Chen, Yongming, *Confucianism and China's Religious Tradition, Religious,* Culture Press (2003).

Clark, Donald N., *China: A Historical and Cultural Dictionary* (Michael Dillon ed., 1998), Culture and Customs of Korea (2000).

Coady, C. A. J., *Distributive Justice, A Companion to Contemporary Political Philosophy*, Blackwell Publishing (1995).

Cohen, Mark A., Bang, A. Elizabeth & Mitchell, Stephanie J., *Chinese intellectual property*: law and practice, London, Kluwer Law International (1999).

Confucius, *The Analects*, Raymond Dawson trans. (1993).

Connor, Mary E., The Koreas: *A Global Studies Handbook* (2002).

Cornish, W. R., *Intellectual Property: Patents, Copyright, Trade Marks and Allied Rights*. London, Sweet and Maxwell (1999).

Correa, Carlos M., *Intellectual Property Right, the WTO and Developing Countries-The TRIPs Agreement and Policy Options*, Zed Books Ltd (2000).

Correa, Carlos M. / Yusuf, Abdulqawi A, *Intellectual Property and International Trade: The TRIPs Agreement*, Kluwer Law International (1998).

Cottler, F. Abbott and Gurry, Francis, *The International Intellectual Property System*, The Hague: part 1, Kluwer (1999).

Craid, Paul, and Grainne De Burca, *EU Law, Text, Cases, and Materials*, Oxford University Press (2003).

De Mesquita, Bruce Bueno (ed), *Principles of International Politics: People's Power, Preferences, and Perceptions* (2003).

Dittmer, Lowell, *China under Reform*, (Westview 1994).

Doi, Teruo, *Intellectual Property Protection and Management: Law and Practice in Japan*, Tokyo, Institute of Comparative Law, Waseda University (1992).

Dolan, Ronald E. and Robert L. Worden (eds), *Japan: A Country Study* (1992).

Drahos, Peter, *A Philosophy of Intellectual Property,* Dartmouth (1996).

Dutfield, Graham, *Intellectual Property, Biogenetic Resources and Traditional Knowledge*, Earthscan Publications (2004).

Endeshaw, Assafa, Nanyang Business School/Nanyang Technological University Singapore, *Intellectual Property Policy for Non-Industrial Countries*, Dartmouth (1996).

Foster, N., *Transmigration and Transferability of Commercial Law in a Globalized World*, in Andrew Harding & Esin Orucu (eds.), *Comparative Law in the 21st Century*, Kluwer Law International (2002).

Friedman, Lawrence M., *Legal Culture and the Legal Profession* (1996).

Ganea Peter, *et al*, Intellectual Property Law in China (Kluwer Law International, 2005).

Gervais, Daniel J., *The TRIPS Agreement: Drafting History and Analysis* (London: Sweet & Maxwell, 2003).

Granstrand, Ove, *The Economics and Management of Intellectual Property: towards Intellectual Capitalism*, Cheltenham, Edward Elgar (1999).

Grant, Richard L., *The European Union and China: A European Strategy for the Twenty-first Century*, London: The Royal Institute of International Affairs, Asia-Pacific Programme (1995).

Gutterman, Alan S, and Bentley J Anderson, *Intellectual Property in Global Markets: A Guide for Foreign Lawyers and Managers*, Kluwer Law International (1997).

Gutterman, Alan S., *Intellectual Property Laws of East Asia*, Hong Kong, London, Sweet & Maxwell (1997).

Harding, Harry, "Political Reform" in Mark Borthwick (ed.), *Pacific Century – the Emergence of Modern Pacific Asia*, Westview Press (1992).

Health, Christopher (edited), *Intellectual Property in Asia Max Planck Series on Asian Intellectual Property Law*, Kluwer Law International (2003).

Hudec, Robert E., *Enforcing Intellectual Property Law: The Evolution of the Modern GATT Legal System* (1993).

Imparato, Nicholas, *Capital for Our Time: The Economic, Legal, and Management Challenges of intellectual Capital*, Stanford, California, Hoover Institution Press (1999).

Inshinomori, Shotaro, *Japan Inc.: An Introduction to Japanese Economics* (Betsey Scheiner trans.) (1988).

Jackson, John H., *the World Trading System: Law and Policy of International Economic Relations* (Second ed. 1989).

Kennedy, Daniel L. M. and Southwick, James D., *The Political Economy of International Trade Law*, Essays in Honour of Robert E. Hudec., Cambridge University Press (2002).

Kim, Choong Soon, *The Culture of Korean Industry: An Ethnography of Poongsan Corporation*, Tucson (Arizona) and London: University of Arizona Press (1992).

Kim, Hyung, *Fundamental Legal Concepts of China and the West: A Comparative Study* (1981).

Kong, Xiangjun, *WTO Zhishi Chuanquan Xieding jiqi Guonei Shiyong [WTO TRIPs Agreement and its Domestic Application in China]*, Law Press (2002).

Leith, Philip, *Harmonisation of Intellectual Property in Europe: a Case Study of Patent Procedure*, London, Sweet & Maxwell (1998).

Maskus, Keith E., *Intellectual Property Rights in the Global Economy*, Institute for International Economics (2000).

May, Christopher, *A Global Political Economy of Intellectual Property Rights*: the New Enclosures? London, Routledge (2000).

McCormack Gavan and Yoshio Sugimoto (eds), *The Japanese Trajectory: Modernization and Beyond*, Cambridge University Press (1988).

Mertha, Andrew C., *The Politics of Piracy, Intellectual Property in Contemporary China* (2005).

Morishima, Michio, *Why Has Japan "Succeeded"*? Cambridge University Press (1982).

Narnard, Catherine, *The Substantive Law of the EU: The Fourth Freedoms*, Oxford University Press (2004).

Nolff, Markus, *TRIPS, PCT, and Global Patent Procurement*, London, Kluwer Law International (2000).

Oda, Hiroshi, *Japanese Law*, Oxford University Press (2000).

Palmer, Vernon Valentine (ed.), *Louisiana: Microcosm of a Mixed Jurisdiction*, Carolina Academic Press (1999).

Panitchpakd, Supachai & Clifford Mark L., *China and the WTO: Changing China, Changing World Trade*, John Wiley & Sons (2002).

Pendleton, Michael D., *Intellectual Property Law in the People's Republic of China: A Guide to Patents, Trademarks and Technology Transfer*, Singapore, Butterworths (1986).

Porter, Douglas R., *et al*, *The Practice of Sustainable Development*, Urban Land Institute (2000).

Potter, Pitman R., *Foreign Business Law in the PRC: Past Progress and Future Challenges* (1995).

Reischauer, Edwin O., *Japan: The Story of A Nation* (4th ed. 1989).

Reischauer, Edwin O. and Marius B. Jansen, *Japanese Today: Change and Continuity*, Harvard University Press, (1995).

Riley, Mary, L., *Protecting Intellectual Property Rights in China*, Hong Kong, Sweet & Maxwell Asia (1997).

RoutledgeCurzon Encyclopedia of Confucianism, Xinzhong Yao ed., (2003).

R.J. Ruffin and P. R. Gregory, *Principles of Macroeconomics*, New York, Addison Wesley (2001).

Simensky, Melvin & Bryer, Lanning G., *The New Role of Intellectual Property in Commercial Transactions: Recent Tends in the Valuation, Exploitation and Protection of Intellectual Property*, John Wiley & Sons, New York (1994).

Slote, Walter H., and De Vos, George A., *Confucianism and the Family in an Interdisciplinary, Comparative Context*, Albany: State University of New York Press (1998).

South Centre, *The TRIPs Agreement: A Guide for the South,* South Centre, Geneva (1997).

Stewart, Terence P., *The GATT Uruguay Round: A Negotiating History (1986-1992)* (1993).

Sullivan, Patrick H., Value-driven, *Intellectual Capital: How to Convert Intangible Corporate Assets into Market Value*, New York & Chichester, Wiley (2000).

Sweet, Alec Stone, *The Judicial Construction of Europe*, Oxford University Press (2004).

Tamanaha, Brian Z., *A General Jurisprudence of Law and Society*, Oxford University Press (2005).

Twitchett, Denis and John K. Fairbank (eds.), *The Cambridge History of China*, Vol.1-15 (1991).

Vandoren, Paul, *Should Intellectual Property Feature in the New Round? Intellectual Property and the WTO: the EU Perspective* released from Financial Times Conferences, 30 September, London.

Vaughan, David (ed.), *Law of the European Comunities* (Butterworths, 1986).

Wadlow, Christopher, *Enforcement of intellectual property in European and international law: the new private international law of intellectual property in the United Kingdom and the European Community*, London, Sweet & Maxwell (1998).

Warshofsky, Fred, *The Patent Wars: the Battle to Own the World's Technology*, New York: John Wiley and Sons (1994).

Watson, Alan, *Legal Transplants: An Approach to Comparative Law* (1993).

Weatherley, Robert, *The Discourse of Human Rights in China: Historical and Ideological Perspectives*. St. Martin's Press (1999).

Weidenbaum, M. and Hughes, S., The Bamboo Network: How Expatriate Chinese Entrepreneurs Are Creating a New Economic Superpower in Asia, New York: The Free Press (1996).

Weiler, J., *The EU, the WTO and NAFTA: Towards a Common Law of International Trade* (2000).

Wong, John, *et al*, *Sino-US Trade Accord and China's Accession to the World Trade Organization* (2000).

Xue, Hong & Zheng, Chengsi, *Chinese Intellectual Property Law in the 21st Century*, Hong Kong: Sweet and Maxwell Asia (2002).

Yu, Yingshi, *Zhongguo Chuantong Sixiang de Xiandai Quanshi [The Modern Interpretation of Chinese Traditional Thought]* (1987).

Zhang, C., *Intellectual property Enforcement in China: Leading Cases and Commentary*, Hong Kong, London, Sweet & Maxwell 1997.

Zhang, Naigen *Guoji Maoyi zhongde Zhishi Chanquan [Intellectual Property Laws in International Trade]*, Fudan University Press (1999).

Journals and Periodicals

Abbott, Frederick M., "The Doha Declaration on the TRIPs Agreement and Public Health: Lighting a Dark Corner at WTO," 5 *Journal of International Economic Law*, Issue 2 (2002).

Adcock, Alan, "Opportunity Knocks for IP Owners in China," *Online Articles and Papers* (February 1, 2004).

Allison, John R. & Lianlian Lin, "The Evolution of Chinese Attitudes toward Property Rights in Invention and Discovery," *University of Pennsylvania Journal of International economic Law* (1999).

Arnold, Walter, "Science and Technology Development in Taiwan and South Korea," 28 *Asian Survey*, No. 4 (1988).

Bejesky, Robert, "Investing in the Dragon: Managing the Patent Versus Trade Secret Protection Decision for the Multinational Corporation in China," 11 *Tulsa Journal of Comparative and International Law* (2004).

Berkowitz, Daniel, *et al*, "The Transplant Effect," 51 *American Journal of Comparative Law* (2003).

Bird, Robert C., "Defending Intellectual Property Rights in the BRIC Economies," 43 *American Business Law Journal* (2006).

Birden, Paul B. Jr., "Trademark Protection in China: Trends and Directions," *Loyola of Los Angeles International & Comparative Law Journal* (1996).

Birkinshaw, Patrick, "Reform of Information and Openness: Fundamental Huam Rights?" 58 *Administrative Law Review* (2006).

Braga, Primo and Fink, "Carsten, Intellectual Property Rights and Economic Development," *World Bank Discussion Paper*, No. 412 (2000).

Branstetter, Lee G. *et al*, "Do Stronger Intellectual Property Rights Increase International Technology Transfer?" Empirical Evidence from U.S. Firm-Level Panel Data, *NBER Working Paper*, July 2005.

Chen, Alexander, "Climbing the Great Wall: A Guide to Intellectual Property Enforcement in the People's Republic of China," 25 *AIPLA Quarterly Journal* (1997).

Cheng, J., "China's Copyright System: Rising to the Spirit of TRIPs Requires an Internal Focus and WTO Membership," 21 *Fordham International Law Journal* (1998).

Chiappetta, Vincent, "The Desirability of Agreeing to Disagree: The WTO, TRIPs, International IPR Exhaustion and a Few Other Things," 21 *Michigan Journal of International Law* (2000).

Chin, Judith and Grossman, Gene, 1988, "Intellectual Property Rights and North-South Trade," *NBER Working Paper*, No.2769 (1998).

Chow, Daniel C.K., "Enforcement Against Counterfeiting in the People's Republic of China," *Northwest Journal of International Law and Business* (2000).

Ciraco, Danny, "Forget the Mechanics and Bring in the Gardeners: An Exploration of Mediation in Intellectual Property Disputes," 9 *U. Baltimore Intellectual Property Law Journal* (2000).

Clarke, Donald, "Private Enforcement of Intellectual Property Rights in China," 10 *NBR Analysis*, No. 2 (1999).

Clark, Douglas, "IP Rights Will Improve in China - Eventually," *the China Business Review* (May-June 2000).

Clement, Douglas, "Creation Myths: Does Innovation Require Intellectual Property Rights?" *Reason Online*, March 2003.

Corbett, Ronald J.C., "Protecting and Enforcing Intellectual Property Rights in developing Countries, 35 *International Lawyer* (2001).

Corne, Peter Howard, "Creation and Application of Law in the PRC," 50 *American Journal of Comparative Law* (2002).

Correa, Carlos M., "Public Health and Patent Legislation in Developing Countries," 3 *Tulane Journal of Technology & Intellectual Property* (2001).

Correa, Carlos M., "Recent International Developments in the Area of Intellectual Property Rights", *ICTSD-UNCTAD Dialogue*, 2nd Bellagio Series on Development and Intellectual Property (2003).

Cychosz, Allison, "The Effectiveness of International Enforcement of Intellectual Property Rights," 37 *John Marshall Law Review* (2004).

Deardorff, A.V., "Welfare Effects of Global Patent Protection," 59 *Economica* (1992).

Demiray, A. David, "Intellectual Property and the External Power of the European Community: The New Extension," 16 *Michigan Journal of International Law* (1995).

Diwan, Ishac and Rodrik, Dani, "Patents, Appropriate Technology, and North-South Trade," 30 *Journal of International Economics* (1991).

Duan, Ruichun, "China's Intellectual Property Rights Protection Towards the 21st Century," 9 *Duke Journal of Comparative & International Law* (1999).

Duncan, Christopher, "Out of Conformity: China's Capacity to Implement World Trade Organization Dispute Settlement Body Decisions after Accession," 18 *American University International Law Review* (2002).

Engle, Eric Allen, "When is Fair Use Fair?: A Comparison of E.U. and U.S. Intellectual Property Law", 15 *Transnational Lawyer* (2002).

Eglin, Michael, "*China's Entry into the WTO with a Little Help from the EU,*" *International Affairs* 73:3 (1997).

Endeshaw, Assafa, "The Paradox of Intellectual Property Lawmaking in the New Millennium: Universal Templates as Terms of Surrender for Non-industrial Nations; Piracy as an Offshoot," 10 *Cardozo Journal of International and Comparative Law* (2002).

Ewald, William, "Comparative Jurisprudence (II): The Logic of Legal Transplants," 43 *American Journal of Comparative Law.* (1995).

Feng, Zhenyu, "the Development and Innovation of Intellectual Property under the WTO," 29 *Yuedan Law Journal* (1997).

Forney, Matt., "Now We Get it: Foreigners Aren't the Only Ones Railing about Copyright Theft in China: A Growing Class of Creative Chinese is Singing the Same Tune," *Far-Eastern Economic Review* (1996).

Foster, Nicholas H. D., "Company Law Theory in Comparative Perspective: England and France," 48 *American Journal of Comparative Law* (2000).

Fowler, Peter, "Intellectual Property and the Global Marketplace: A Panel Discussion," *USIA Electronic Journals*, Vol. 3, No. 3 (1998).

Francis, Cardinal George, "Law and Culture," 1 *Ave Maria Law Review* 6 (2003).

Friedman, Lawrence M. "On the Emerging Sociology of Transnational Law," 32 *Stanford Journal of International Law* (1996).

Fung, Jill Chiang, "Can Mickey Mouse Prevail in the Court of the Monkey King? Enforcing Foreign Intellectual Property Rights in China," 18 *Loyola of Los Angeles International and Comparative Law Journal* (1996).

Gahrton, Per, "China in the WTO - in Whose Interests?" European Parliament, Brussels, Belgium, Released from a workshop of EU China Programme in Antwerp (May 2000).

Gaisford, James and Richardson, R. Stephen, "The Trips Disagreement: Should GATT Traditions Have Been Abandoned," 1 *Estey Centre Journal of International Law and Trade Policy* (2000).

Gallini, Nancy and Scotchmer, Suzanne, "Intellectual Property: When Is It the Best Incentive System?" *UC Berkeley Department of Economics*, Working Paper No. E01-303 (August 2001).

Grevi, Giovanni, "the Europe We Need," Working Paper Time for a Government of the Union (April 2003).

Grossman, Gene, and Helpman, Elhanan, "Endogenous Innovation in the Theory of Growth," 8 *The Journal of Economic Perspectives*, No. 1 (1994).

Grossman, Gene and Lai, Edwin, "International Protection of Intellectual Property," *NBER Working Papers* 8704 (2002).

Guo, Youqun, "Guanyu Tigao Woguo Xiaofeilu de Sikao [Reflections on Fuelling Consuming Standard in China]," 10 *Jingji Wenti [Economic Problems]* (2004).

Hahm, Chaihark, "Law, Culture, and the Politics of Confucianism," 16 *Columbia Journal of Asian Law* (2003).

Halverson, Karen, "China's WTO Accession: Economic, Legal, and Political Implications," 27 *BC Int'l & Comp. L. Rev.* (2004).

Hamada, Koichi, "Protection of Intellectual Property Rights in Japan," Working Paper, Council of Foreign Relations (April 1996).

Hamilton, Marci, "The TRIPs Agreement: Imperialistic, Outdated, and Overprotective," 29 *Vanderbilt Journal of Transnational Law* (1996).

Harris, Donald P., "TRIPs Rebound: An Historical Analysis of How the TRIPs Agreement Can Ricochet Back Against the United States," *Northwestern Journal of International Law and Business* (2004).

Hays, Thomas, "Paranova v. Merck and Co-branding of Pharmaceuticals in the European Economic Area," *The Trademark Reporter* (July-August, 2004).

Heath, Christopher, "Intellectual Property Rights in Asia - Projects, Programmes and Developments," Online Publication of Max Planck Institute for Intellectual Property, Competition and Tax Law (2002).

Helfer, Laurence R., "Regime Shifting: The TRIPs Agreement and New Dynamic of International Intellectual property Lawmaking," 29 *Yale Journal of International Law* (2004).

Helpman, Elhanan, "Innovation, Imitation, and Intellectual Property Rights," 61 *Econometrica*, No.6 (1993).

Hernandez-Truyol, Berta Esperanza, "Glocalizing Law and Culture: Towards a Cross-Constitutive Paradigm," 67 *Albany Law Review* 618, 623 (2003)

Hom, Sharon, "China and the WTO: Year One" 1 *China Rights Forum* (2003).

Huo, Zhengde, "On China-EU Strategic Relationship," 2 *International Studies*, China Institute of International Studies (2005).

Ishinomori, Shotaro, "Japan Inc.: An Introduction to Japanese Economics," Translated by Betsey Scheiner, 2 vols. *University of California Press* (1988).

Jackson, John H., "The WTO Dispute Settlement Understanding - Misunderstandings on the Nature of Legal Obligation," *American Journal of International Law* (1997).

Jackson, John H., & Feinerman, James V., "China's WTO Accession Survey of Materials," 4 (2) *Journal of International Economic Law* (2001).

Jamar, Steven D., "A Lawyering Approach to Law and Development," 27 *North Carolina Journal of International Law and Commercial Regulation* (2001).

Jiang, Peng, "Fighting the AIDS Epidemic: China's Options under the WTO TRIPS Agreement", 13 *Albany Law Journal of Science & Technology* (2002).

Kim, Young-Gwan, "The Confucian-Christian Context in Korean Christianity," 13 *B.C. Asian Review* (2002).

Kirchanski, Stefan, "Protection of US Patent Rights in Developing Countries: US Efforts To Enforce Pharmaceutical Patents in Thailand," 16 *Loyola of Los Angeles International and Comparative Law Review* (1994).

Kroszner, Randall, "Economic Organization and Competition Policy," 19 *Yale Journal on Regulation* (2002).

La Croix, Sumner J., & Konan, Denise Eby, "Intellectual Property Rights in China: The Changing Political Economy of Chinese-American Interests," 25 *World Economy* (2002).

Lai, Edwin and Qiu, Larry, "the North's Intellectual Property Rights Standard for the South?" 59 *Journal of International Economics* (2003).

Laroche, Lionel, "The Cultural Differences between the European Union and North America and their Impact on Transatlantic Business," *Paper of ITAP International* (1999).

Lembcke, Oliver, "China's Economic Integration in the WTO: A Test for the Political Integration of the European Union?" Harvard China Review 4th Annual Conference (2001).

Lerner, Josh, "Patent Protection and Innovation Over 150 Years," *NBER Working Papers* 8977 (2002).

Liang, Zhicheng, "Financial Development, Growth, and Regional Disparity in Post-Reform China," *United Nation University Research Paper* No. 2006/90 (August 2006).

Li, Yahong, "The Wolf Has Come: Are China's Intellectual Property Industries Prepared for the WTO?" 20 *UCLA Pacific Basin Law Journal* (2002).

Li, Yiqiang, "Evaluation of the Sino-American Intellectual Property Agreements: A Judicial Approach to Solving the Local Protectionism Problem," 10 *The Columbia Journal of Asian Law*, No 2 (1996).

Lin, Maria C.H., "China after the WTO: What You Need to Know Now, Practicing Law Institute," *Commercial Law and Practice Course Handbook Series* (2001).

Lin, Yifu, Hu, Shudong, "Jiaru Shijie Maoyi Zuzhi: Tiaozhan he Jiyu [Access to the WTO: Challenges and Opportunities]," *China Centre for Economic Research*, Working Paper Series, March 2000.

Liu, Mengxi, "Lun Chuantong Wenhua de Liushi yu Chongjian [the Erosion and Reconstruction of the Traditional Culture]," *Contemporary Philosophy* (2004).

Liu, Weihua, "Confucianism: Traditional Culture and Contemporary Civilization," 3 *Confucian Research* (1998).

Lubman, Stanley, "Bird in a Cage: Chinese Law Reform after Twenty Years," 20 *Northwestern Journal of International Law and Business* (2000).

Masashi, Kurose, "Law Strengthened to Fight Flow of Counterfeit Goods," *Managing Intellectual Property Issues, SNIPER* (May 2004).

Maskus, Keith, "Intellectual Property Rights in the Global Economy" (Institute for International Economics (2000).

Mattei, Ugo, "Efficiency in Legal Transplants: An Essay in Comparative Law and Economics," 14 *International Review of Law and Economics* (1994).

McCalman, Phillip, "Reaping What You Sow: An Empirical Analysis of International Patent Harmonization," 55 *Journal of International Economics* (2001).

Meléndez-Ortiz, Ricardo and Dehlavi, Ali, "Sustainable Development and Environmental Policy Objectives: A Case for Updating Special and Differential Treatment in the WTO," *ICTSD Publication* (1998).

Mensik, Stan, *et al*, "Trends and Transitions in Japanese and Korean Approaches," 7th International Conference on Global Business and Economic Development, Bangkok, Thailand (2003).

Miller, Jonathan M., "A Typology of Legal Transplants: Using Sociology, Legal History and Argentine Examples to Explain the Transplant Process," 51 *American Journal of Comparative Law* (2003).

Mills, Jennifer, "Comment, Alternative Dispute Resolution in International Intellectual Property Disputes," 11 *Ohio State Journal on Dispute Resolution* (1996).

Monten, Lina M., "The Inconsistency between Section 301 and TRIPs: Counterproductive with Respect to the Future of International Protection of Intellectual Property Rights?" 9 *Marquette Intellectual Property Law Review* (2005).

Oddi, A. Samuel, "TRIPs - Natural Rights and a 'Polite Form of Economic Imperialism'", 29 *Vanderbilt Journal of Transnational Law* (1996).

Oh, Kang-nam, "The Confucian-Christian Encounter in Korea," *Journal of the American Academy of Religion* (1993).

Okedji, Ruth, "Towards an International Fair Use Doctrine," 39 *Columbia Journal of Transnational Law* (1997).

Olivier, Jacques and Goh, Aiting, "Free Trade and Protection of Intellectual Property Rights: Can We Have One without the Other?" *HEC Working Paper* (2001).

Paliwala, Abdul, "Digital Divide Globalisation and Legal Regulation," 6 *UTS Law Review* (2004).

Palmer, Scott J., "An Identity Crisis: Regime Legitimacy and the Politics of Intellectual Property Rights in China," 8 *Indiana Journal of Global Legal Studies* (2001).

Pantages, Christian John, Avast Ye, "Hollywood! Digital Motion Picture Piracy Comes of Age," *Transnational Lawyer* (2001).

Pastor, Alfredo and David Gosset, "the EU-China Relationship: A Key to the 21st Century Order", *ARI* 142/2005.

Pauwelyn, Joost, "Enforcement and Countermeasures in the WTO: Rules Are Rules—Toward a More Collective Approach," 94 *American Journal of International Law* (2000).

Reichman, J. H., "The TRIPs Agreement Comes of Age: Conflict or Cooperation with the Developing Countries?" 32 *Case Western Reserve Journal of International Law* (2000).

Reichman, J.H., & Lange, David, "Bargaining Around the TRIPs Agreement: The Case for Ongoing Public-Private Initiatives to Facilitate Worldwide Intellectual Property Transactions," 9 *Duke Journal of Comparative & International Law* (1998).

Rein, Judy, "International Governance through Trade Agreements: Patent Protection for Essential Medicines," 21 *Northwest Journal of International & Business* (2001).

Richardson, Stephen, and Gaisford, James, "North-South Disputes over the Protection of Intellectual Property," 29 *Canadian Journal of Economics* (Special Issue, April 1996).

Roberts, Lawrence D., "Beyond Notions of Diplomacy and Legalism: Building a Just Mechanism for WTO Dispute Resolution," 40 *American Business Law Journal* (2003).

Rose, Gideon, "Neoclassical Realism and Theories of Foreign Policy," 51 (1) *World Politics* (1998).

Rosen, Jeremy Brooks, "China, Emerging Economies, and the World Trade Order," 46 *Duke Law Journal* (1997).

Schlesinger, Michael N., "A Sleeping Giant Awakens: The Development of Intellectual Property Law in China," 9 *Journal of Chinese Law,* the Centre for Chinese Legal Studies (1995).

Sell, Susan K., "Intellectual Property Protection and Antitrust in the Developing World: Crisis, Coercion, and Choice," 49 (2) *International Organization* (1995).

Shi, Wei, "Cultural Perplexity in Intellectual Property: Is Stealing a Book an Elegant Offense?" 32(1) *North Carolina Journal of International and Commercial Regulation* (2006).

Shi, Wei, "The Impact of TRIPs on the Protection of Intellectual Property Rights in China," *Chinese Yearbook of Private International Law and Comparative Law* (1998).

Smith, Gary W., "Intellectual Property Rights, Developing Countries, and Trips: An Overview of Issues for Consideration during the Millennium Round of Multilateral Trade Negotiations", 2 (6) *The Journal of World Intellectual Property* 969-975 (1999).

Steinberg, William, "Monitor With No Teeth, An Analysis of the WTO China Trade Review Mechanism," 6 *U.C. Davis Business Law Journal* (2005).

Subedi, Surya P., "The Road from Doha: The issues for the development of the WTO and the Future of International Trade," *British Institute of International and Comparative Law* (2003).

Taylor, Ramona L, "Tearing Down the Great Wall: China's Road to WTO Accession," 41 *The Journal of Law and Technology* (2001).

Templeman, Lord Sydney, "Intellectual Property," 1(4) *Journal of International Economic Law* (1998).

Thurston, Anne, "Muddling toward Democracy: Political Change in Grassroots China," *United States Institute of Peace.*

Ullrich, Hanns, "Expansionist of Intellectual Property Protection and Reductionist Competition Rules, A TRIPs Perspective," *EUI Working Paper*, Law No. 2004/3.

Vaughan, Richard E., "Defining Terms in the Intellectual Property Protection Debate: Are the North and South Arguing Past Each Other When we say 'Property'? A Lockean, Confucian, and Islamic Comparison," 2 *ILSA Journal of Intentional & Comparative Law* (1996).

Vaver, David, "The Future of Intellectual Property Law: Japanese and European Perspectives Compared," Electronic Journal of Intellectual Property Rights, Working Papers of Oxford IP Research Centre, WP 09/99.

Watson, Alan, "Comparative Law and Legal Change," 37 *Cambridge Law Journal* (1978).

Wijk, Van and Junne, G., "Intellectual Property Protection of Advanced Technology-Changes in the Global Technology System: Implications and Options for Developing Countries," United Nations University, Institute for New Technologies, Maastricht, Working Paper No.10 (1993).

Willard, Geoffrey T., "An Examination of China's Emerging Intellectual Property Regime: Historical Underpinnings, the Current System and Prospects for the Future," 6 *Indiana International and Comparative Law Review* (1996).

Whyte, Martin King, "Chinese Popular Views about Inequality, in "Credibility Gap": Public Opinion and Instability in China," *Asian Program Special Report*, August (2002).

Wiese, Leopold von, "What Is European Culture?" 11 (1) *The British Journal of Sociology*, (March 1960)

Wong, Cindy Wai Chi, "Parallel Importation of Trademarked Goods in Hong Kong and China," 34 *Hong Kong Law Journal* (2004).

Wooldridge, Frank, "Affordable Medicines - TRIPs and United States Policies," 4(1) *Intellectual Property Quarterly* (2000).

Xu, Xianglin, "Yi Zhengzhi Wending Wei Jichu de Zhongguo Jianjin Gaige [China's Political Reform is Preoccupied by Incrementalism]," 5 *Strategy and Management* (2000).

Yang, Guifang and Maskus, Keith, "Intellectual Property Rights, Silencing, and Innovation in an Endogenous Product Cycle Model", 53(1) *Journal of International Economics, November* (2000).

Yang, Key P., and Henderson, Gregory, "An Outline History of Korean Confucianism: Part I: The Early Period and Yi Factionalism," 18 *The Journal of Asian Studies*, No. 1 (1958).

Yeh, Michael, "Up Against a Great Wall: The Fight against Intellectual Property Piracy in China," 5 *Minnesota Journal of Global Trade* (1996).

Yonehara, Brent T., "Enter the Dragon: China's WTO Accession, Film Piracy and Prospects for Enforcement of Copyright Laws," 22 *DePaul-LCA Journal of Art and Entertainment Law* (2002).

Yu Peter K., "Piracy, Prejudice, and Perspectives: An Attempt to Use Shake-speare to Reconfigure the U.S.-China Intellectual Property Debate," 19 *Boston University International Law Journal* (2001).

Yu, Peter K., "The Copyright Divide," *25 Cardozo Law Review* (2003).

Yu, Peter K., "Toward a Nonzero-sum Approach to Resolving Global Intellec-tual Property Disputes: What We Can Learn from Mediators, Business Strategists, and International Relations Theorists," 70 *University of Cincin-nati Law Review* (2001-2002).

Yuan, Xiaodong, "Research on Trade Mark Parallel Imports in China," 25 (5) European Intellectual Property Review (2003).

Zhang, Hui, "Comparative Study on Parallel Imports in Trade Marks", *EU-China Legal and Judicial Cooperation Programme* (October 2002).

Zhang, Wei-Wei, "China's Political Transition: Trends and Prospects," 7 *EurAsia Bulletin*, Publication of European Institute for Asian Studies (2003).

Zheng, Yongnian, "Political Incrementalism: Political Lessons from China's 20 Years of Reform," *Third World Quarterly* (1999).

Official Documents

Agreement on Trade and Economic Cooperation between the European Eco-nomic Community and the People's Republic of China - 1985

A Long Term Policy for China-Europe Relations, Communication of the Commission, COM (1995)/279/FINAL

A Maturing Partnership - Shared Interests and Challenges in EU-China Rela-tions (Updating the European Commission's Communications on EU-China Relations of 1998 and 2001), Commission Policy Paper for Transmission to the Council and the European Parliament, Commission of the European Communities, Brussels, 10/09/03 COM(2003) 533 fin

A Secure Europe in a Better World, European Security Strategy, Brussels, De-cember 12, 2003

Bilateral Agreement on China's Entry into the WTO between China and the United States, November 17, 2000

Bilateral Trade Relations/China

Building a Comprehensive Partnership with China, Brussels, 1998, COM (1998) 181

China in the WTO – Year 3, A Research Report, Prepared for the U.S.-China Economic and Security Review Commission, January 21, 2005

China's EU Policy Paper, Ministry of Foreign Affairs of People's Republic of China October 2003

China's WTO Implementation: An Assessment of China's Fourth Year WTO membership, Written Testimony of US-China Business Council, September 14, 2005

China's WTO Implementation: A Three-Year Assessment, U.S. Chamber of Commerce, September, 2004

Commission on Intellectual Property Rights, Integrating Intellectual Property Rights and Development Policy, UK (2002)

Commission Policy Paper for Transmission to the Council and the European Parliament, A maturing partnership - shared interests and challenges in EU-China relations (Updating the European Commission's Communications on EU-China relations of 1998 and 2001), Commissions of the European Communities, Brussels, 10/09/03 COM (2003) 533 fin

Declaration on the TRIPs Agreement and Public Health, adopted in Doha on November 14, 2001

EU Strategy towards China: Implementation of the 1998 Communication and Future Steps for a More Effective EU Policy', Commission of the European Union, Brussels, 15.5.2001, COM (2001) 265 final

Europe and Asia: A Strategic Framework for Enhanced Partnerships, Commission of the European Union, Brussels, Brussels, 4.9.2001, COM(2001) 469 final

European Business in China Position Paper 2004/2005, European Union Chamber of Commerce in China

European Commission and Engineering Industry Focus on Counterfeiting, March 27, 2001

Follow-up the Green Paper on Counterfeiting and Piracy in the Single Market, COM (2000) 789 final of 30 November 2000

Freedom of Religious Belief in China (October 1997), White Papers of Chinese Government, Information Office of the State Council of the People's Republic of China, Beijing, October, 1997

Global Economic Prospects and the Developing Countries 2002, World Bank, 2001-2004

Green Paper on Combating Counterfeiting and Piracy in the Single Market, Presented by European Commission, 1998

Integrating China Further in the World Economy, Commission of the European Communities: Building a Comprehensive Partnership with China, Brussels, 25.3.1998, COM (1998)/181/final

Integrating Intellectual Property Rights and Development Policy, Report of the Commission on Intellectual Property Rights (UK) September 2002

Intellectual property: Commission Welcomes European Parliament Support against Counterfeiting and Piracy, Brussels, IP/04/316, March 9, 2004

Intellectual Property Policy Outline, Strategic Council on Intellectual Property (Japan), July 3, 2002

Intellectual Property Protection in China, Chinese Government's White Paper on Intellectual Property Protection, Information Office of the State Council of the People's Republic of China, June 2004

Intergovernmental Committee on Intellectual Property and Genetic Resources, Traditional Knowledge and Folklore, Second Session, Geneva, December 10-14, 2001

International Intellectual Property Alliance, 2000 Special 301 Report, People's Republic of China

Joint Statement of the 7th China-EU Summit, 8th December 2004, Hague, Netherlands

Joint Statement of the 8th China-EU Summit, 5 September 2005, Beijing, China

Joint Statement of the 9th China-EU Summit, 9 September 2006, Helsinki, Finland

Joint Statement of the 10th China-EU Summit, Beijing," 28 November, 2007, Beijing, China

Making Global Trade Work for People, UN Development Programme (2003)

Memorandum of Understanding on the Protection of Intellectual Property (MOU), US and China, 2002/2005

Memorandum to the Representatives of Community Trade Marks Registered with the Office on the Possibility of Defending the Rights of the Proprietors of Community Trade Marks, OHIM

Outcome of the Third Meeting of the EU-China IP Dialogue, Brussels, 15-16 March 2007

Overview of China's Economic Reforms and WTO Negotiations, Delegation of the European Commission to China

Report of the Working Party on the Accession of China, WTO Ministerial Conference, Doha

Status Regarding China's Enforcement of IPR, China MOFCOM, April 12, 2005

Study of the Impact of Movie Piracy on China's Economy, Chinese Academy of Social Sciences Report, June 2006

Trade Policy Agenda and 2001 Annual Report of the President of the United States on the Trade Agreements Programme, 2002

Trade Policy Reviews - Ensuring Transparency, World Trade Organisation

Transitional Review Mechanism of China, Communication from the European Communities and their member States, WTO Council for Trade-Related Aspects of Intellectual Property Rights, IP/C/W371, August 29, 2002

UNCTAD World Investment Report 2004

WIPO Intellectual Property Handbook: Policy, Law and Use

Press Articles

"A Making of a China-EU World," David Gosset, *Asia Times*, July 20, 2005.

"A Symphony of Civilizations," Gosset, David, *Asia Times*, August 12, 2006.

"Balanced Progress Planned for Country," Zhao Huanxin and Fu Jing, *China Daily*, 8 March, 2004.

"Beijing's Balancing Act on Reform," Anthony Saich, *the Financial Times*, November 4, 2002.

"Big Events in EU-China Relations," *China Info Network*, April 29, 2004.

"China EU WTO Deal: A Double-Edged Sword For Chinese Firms," *Agence France Presse*, May 19, 2000.

"China Faces Uphill Battle against Counterfeits," *People's Daily*, July 23, 2003.

"China Gets Ready for National IP Strategy", Peter Ollier, *Managing Intellectual Property*, January 14, 2008.

"China Losing TCM Intellectual Property," *China News Network*, December 13, 2005.

"China Piracy Costs Film Industry $2.7 Billion in 2005," *Reuters*, June 19, 2006.

"China Pledges Increased Protection for Intellectual Property," *People's Daily*, April 27, 2002

"China Resolved to Protect IPR," *Xinhua News Agency*, January 13, 2005.

"China's Action Plan on IPR Protection 2006," *People's Daily*, April 30, 2006.

"China's Fading Free-Trade Fervour," *Business Week*, Mark L. Clifford, June 5, 2002.

"China's Patent Cooperation with WIPO to Improve," *China Daily*, May 22, 2002.

"China's Pirate Industry Thriving," Robert Marquand, *The Christian Science Monitor*, January 9, 2002.

"Chinese Government Backs down on Google," Jason Deans, *Guardian*, Friday September 13, 2002.

"Crackdown Stepped up against Counterfeit Merchandise," *China Daily*, page 5, December 6, 2004.

"EU-China Trade to Benefit Both," *China Daily*, Wei Wang, October 9, 2004.

"Europe's "DMCA on Steroids" Gets Go-Ahead," *ZDNet UK*, November 27, 2003.

"European Chamber Business Confidence Survey: Paints A Rosy Picture," Lin Guan, *China Daily*, December 22, 2007.

"European Companies in China Generally Optimistic", *China CSR*, November 23, 2007.

"In Candor from China, Efforts to Ease Anxiety," Joseph Kahn, *The New York Times*, April 17, 2006.

"It's True. Asians Can't Think," Shaw, Sin-ming, *Time International*, May 31, 1999.

"Lun WTO yu Woguo Fada Diqu Fazhi Jianshe [the WTO and the Legal Construction in the Less-developed Regions]," Sibao Shen & Yongmin Cai, *Legal Daily*, September 5, 2006.

"Major Breakthrough Made in China's Entry Into WTO," *Peoples' Daily*, Wednesday, November 17, 1999.

"More Chinese Lawyers Assist Government Decisions," *China Daily*, April 11, 2001.

"Music Industry Attacks EU Copyright Proposal," Matthew Broersma, *ZDNet UK*, February 03, 2003.

"Nations Hail Sino-European Trade," *People's Daily*, December 15, 2004.

"Nuli Tigao Zhishi Chanquan de Sifa Baohu Shuiping [Improving the Judicial Protection for Intellectual Property Rights in China]," Jianming Cao, *Judicial Protection of IPR in China*, June 28, 2004.

"On Piracy, an Advocate for China's Progress," Chris Buckley, *International Herald Tribune*, Tuesday, October 4, 2005.

"Pushed on Patents, China Shoves Back," Chris Buckley, *International Herald Tribune*, January 14, 2005.

"Rising Tide of Counterfeit Goods Costs UK £10bn," Jamie Doward, *Sunday*, January 18, 2004.

"Shidai Huhuan Zhishi Chanquan: Fang Guojia Zhishi Chuanquan Ju Juzhang Tian Liqu [A New Era Calls for an Improved Intellectual Property: An Interview with Tian Lipu], Commissioner of the State Intellectual Property Office," Jianke Jiang, *People's Daily*, August 25, 2005.

"Sulian Jubian Gaosu Women Shenme [What the Collapse of the Soviet Union Tells Us]?" Mu Bai, *People's Daily*, November 3, 2004.

"Vice Premier on Intellectual Property Rights," *China Daily*, December 26, 2001.

"What's Wrong with Chinese Lawyers over the Past Five Years," *Chinese Lawyers Network*, June 14, 2006.

"WTO Access Urges Protection of Intellectual Property Rights," *China Daily*, December 28, 2001.

"WTO-Affiliated China Still Awash in Pirated Goods," Indira A.R. Lakshmanan, *Contra Costa Times*, May 31, 2002.

Index